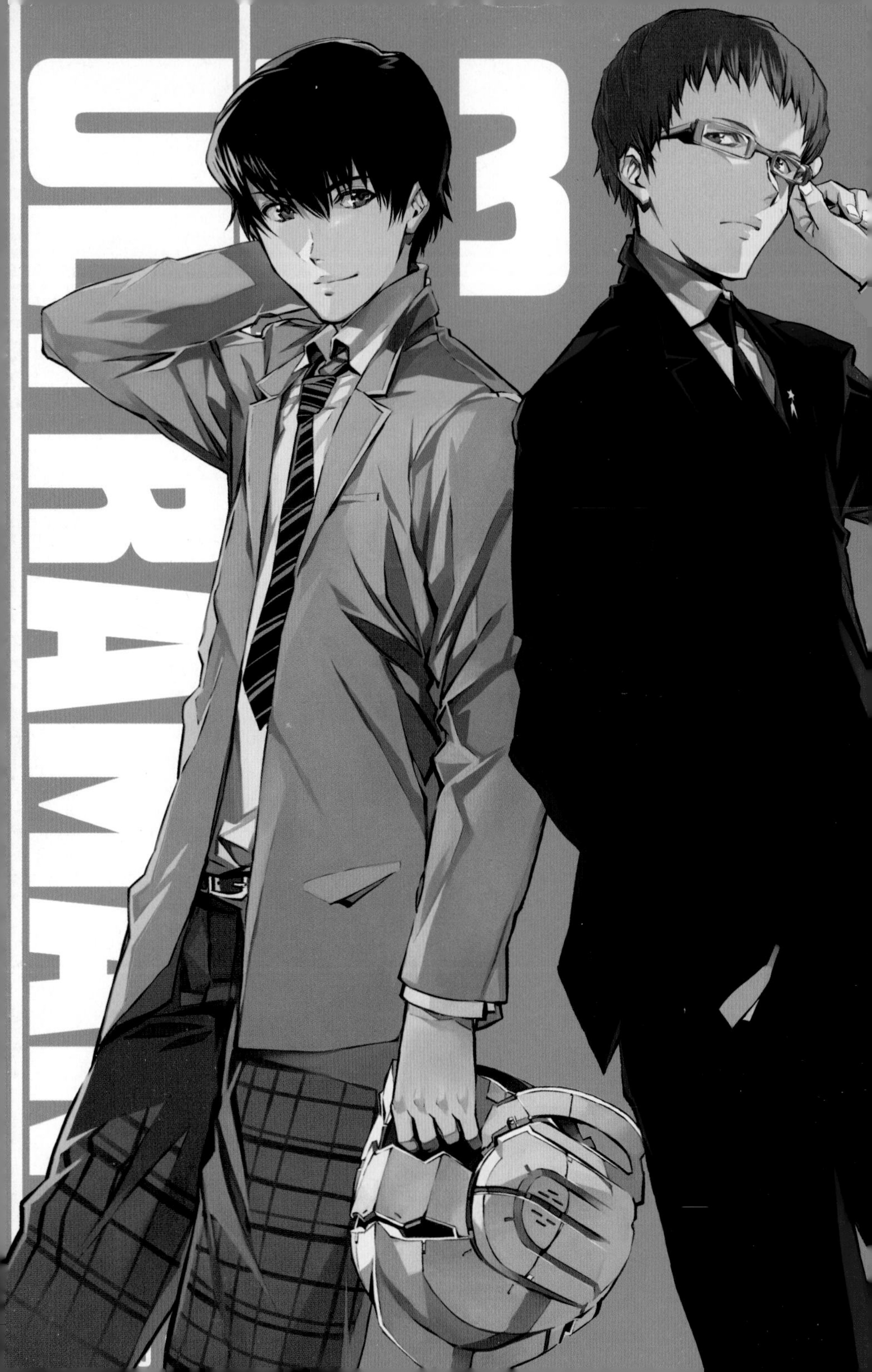
3

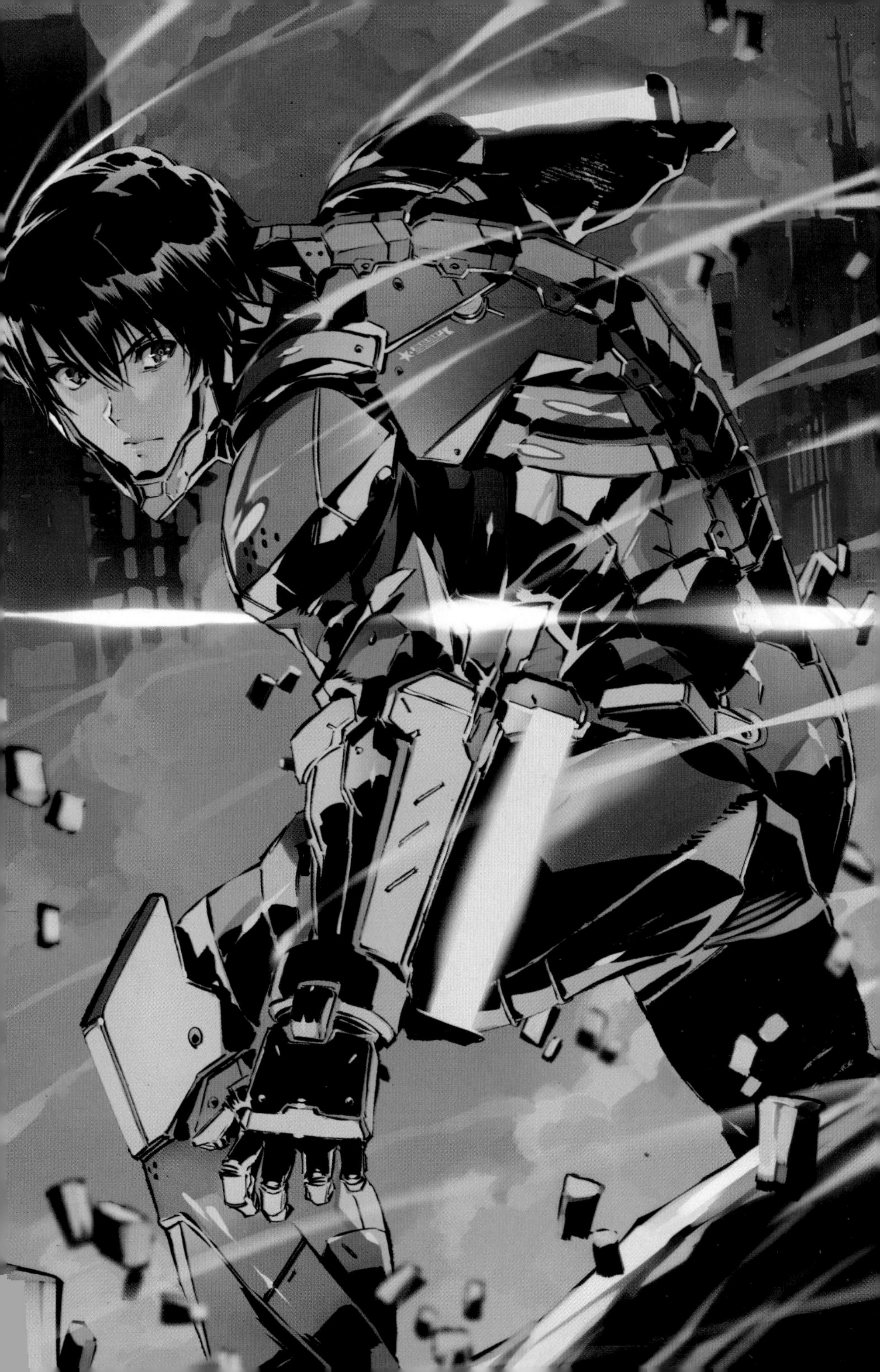

THIS IS THE BEGINNING OF A NEW AGE.

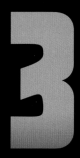

CONTENTS

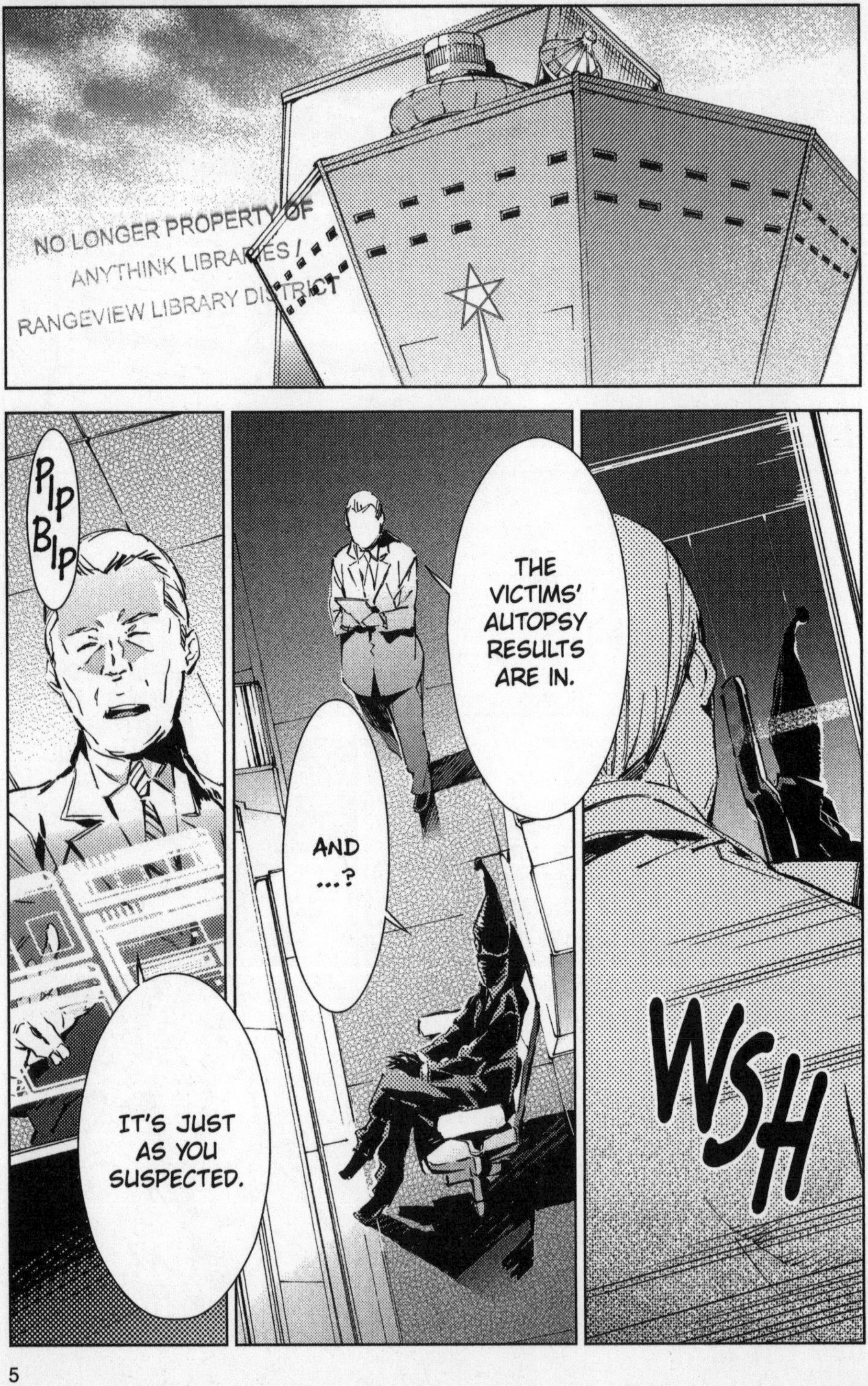
WSH
THE VICTIMS' AUTOPSY RESULTS ARE IN.
AND ...?
PIP BIP
IT'S JUST AS YOU SUSPECTED.

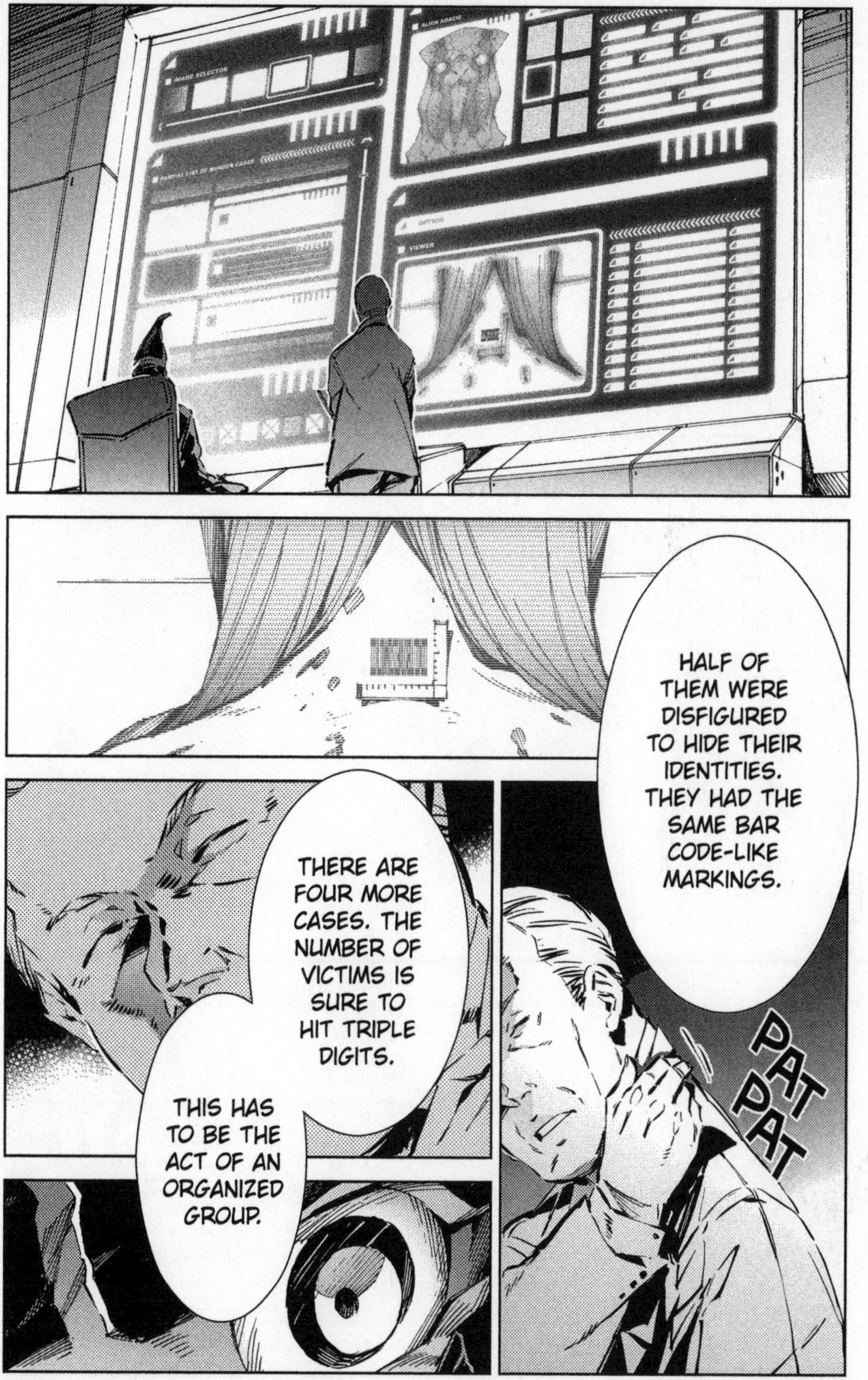
HALF OF THEM WERE DISFIGURED TO HIDE THEIR IDENTITIES. THEY HAD THE SAME BAR CODE-LIKE MARKINGS.
PAT PAT
THERE ARE FOUR MORE CASES. THE NUMBER OF VICTIMS IS SURE TO HIT TRIPLE DIGITS.
THIS HAS TO BE THE ACT OF AN ORGANIZED GROUP.

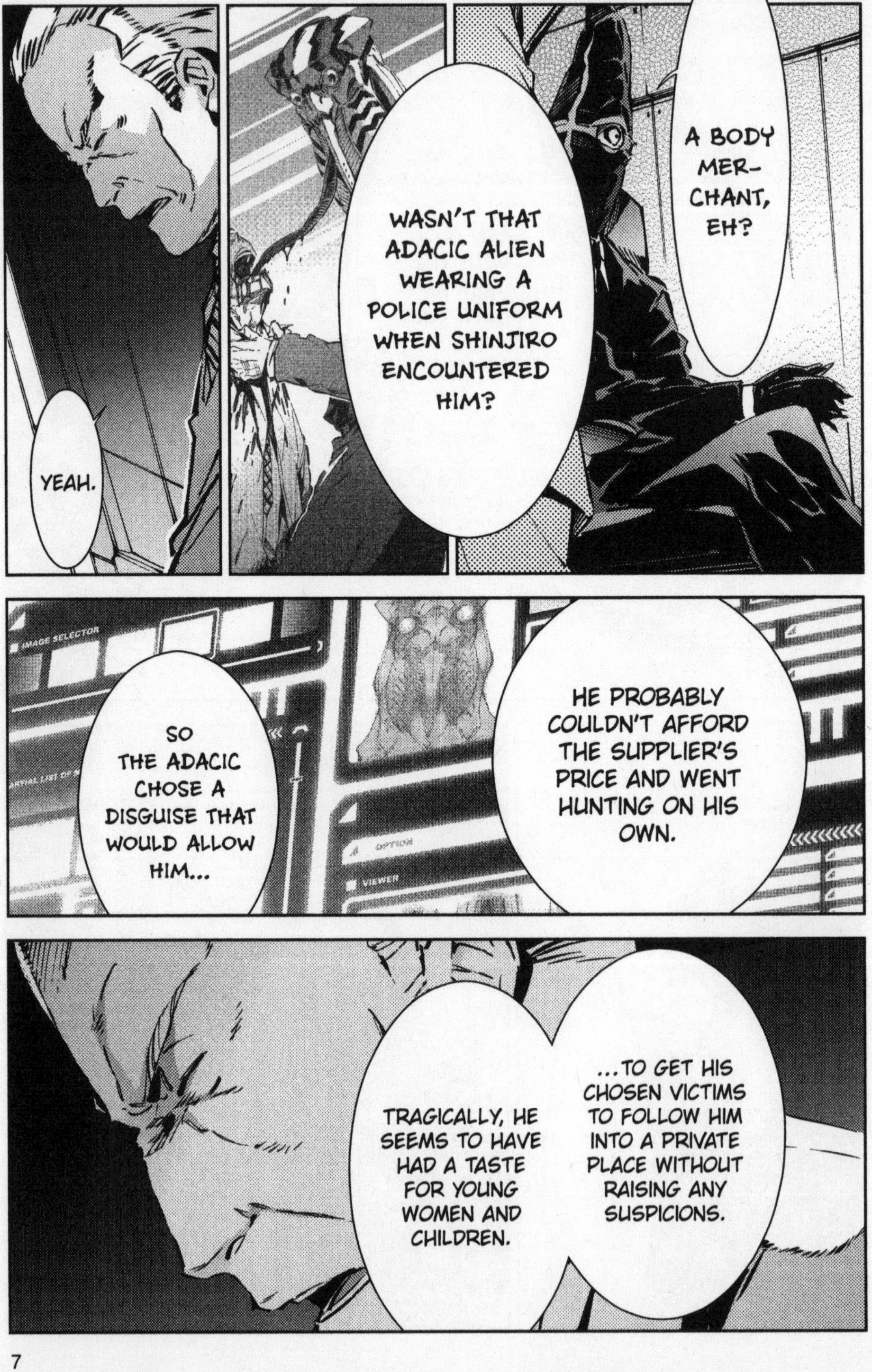

A BODY MER- CHANT, EH?
WASN'T THAT ADACIC ALIEN WEARING A POLICE UNIFORM WHEN SHINJIRO ENCOUNTERED HIM?
YEAH.
HE PROBABLY COULDN'T AFFORD THE SUPPLIER'S PRICE AND WENT HUNTING ON HIS OWN.
IMAGE SELECTOR
VIEWER
SO THE ADACIC CHOSE A DISGUISE THAT WOULD ALLOW HIM...
...TO GET HIS CHOSEN VICTIMS TO FOLLOW HIM INTO A PRIVATE PLACE WITHOUT RAISING ANY SUSPICIONS.
TRAGICALLY, HE SEEMS TO HAVE HAD A TASTE FOR YOUNG WOMEN AND CHILDREN.

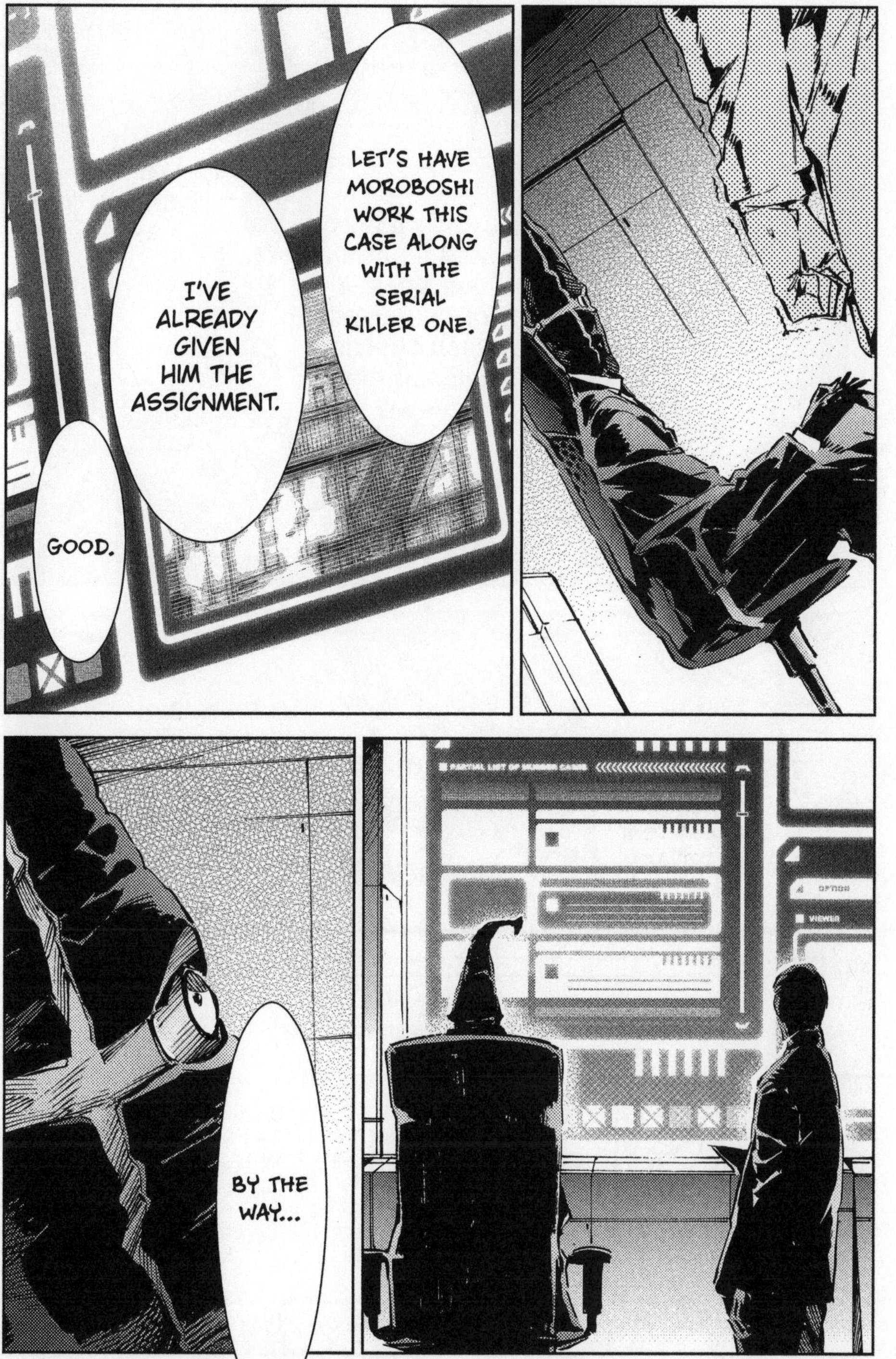
LET'S HAVE MOROBOSHI WORK THIS CASE ALONG WITH THE SERIAL KILLER ONE.
I'VE ALREADY GIVEN HIM THE ASSIGNMENT.
GOOD.
BY THE WAY...

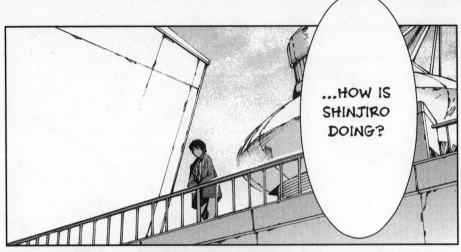

...HOW IS SHINJIRO DOING?

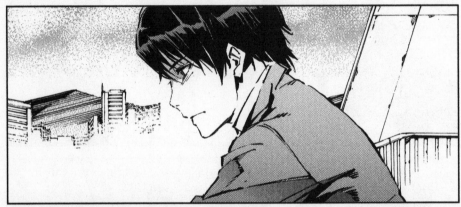

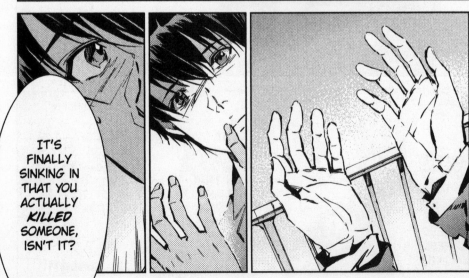

IT'S FINALLY SINKING IN THAT YOU ACTUALLY *KILLED* SOMEONE, ISN'T IT?

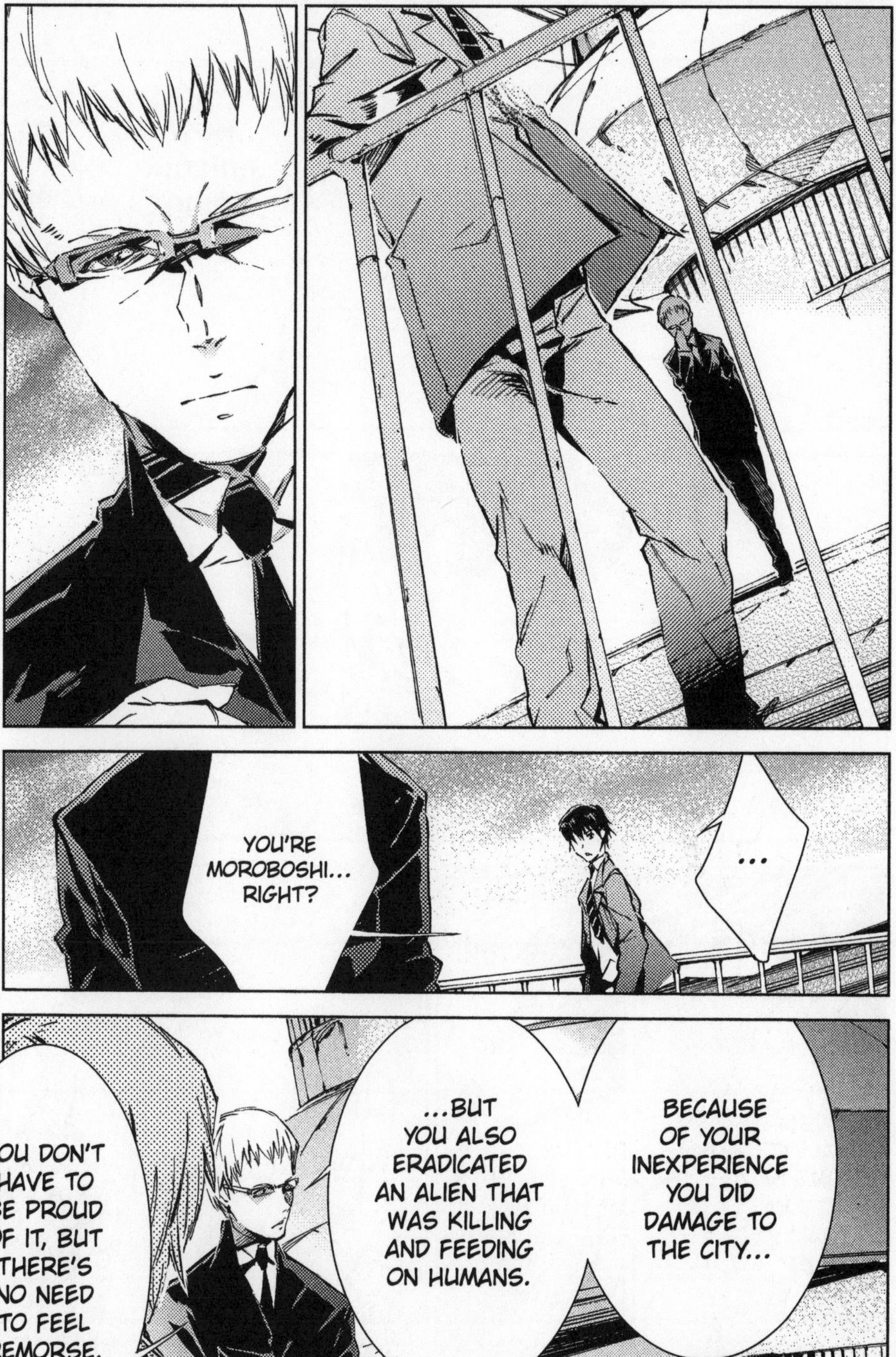
...
YOU'RE MOROBOSHI... RIGHT?
BECAUSE OF YOUR INEXPERIENCE YOU DID DAMAGE TO THE CITY...
...BUT YOU ALSO ERADICATED AN ALIEN THAT WAS KILLING AND FEEDING ON HUMANS.
YOU DON'T HAVE TO BE PROUD OF IT, BUT THERE'S NO NEED TO FEEL REMORSE.

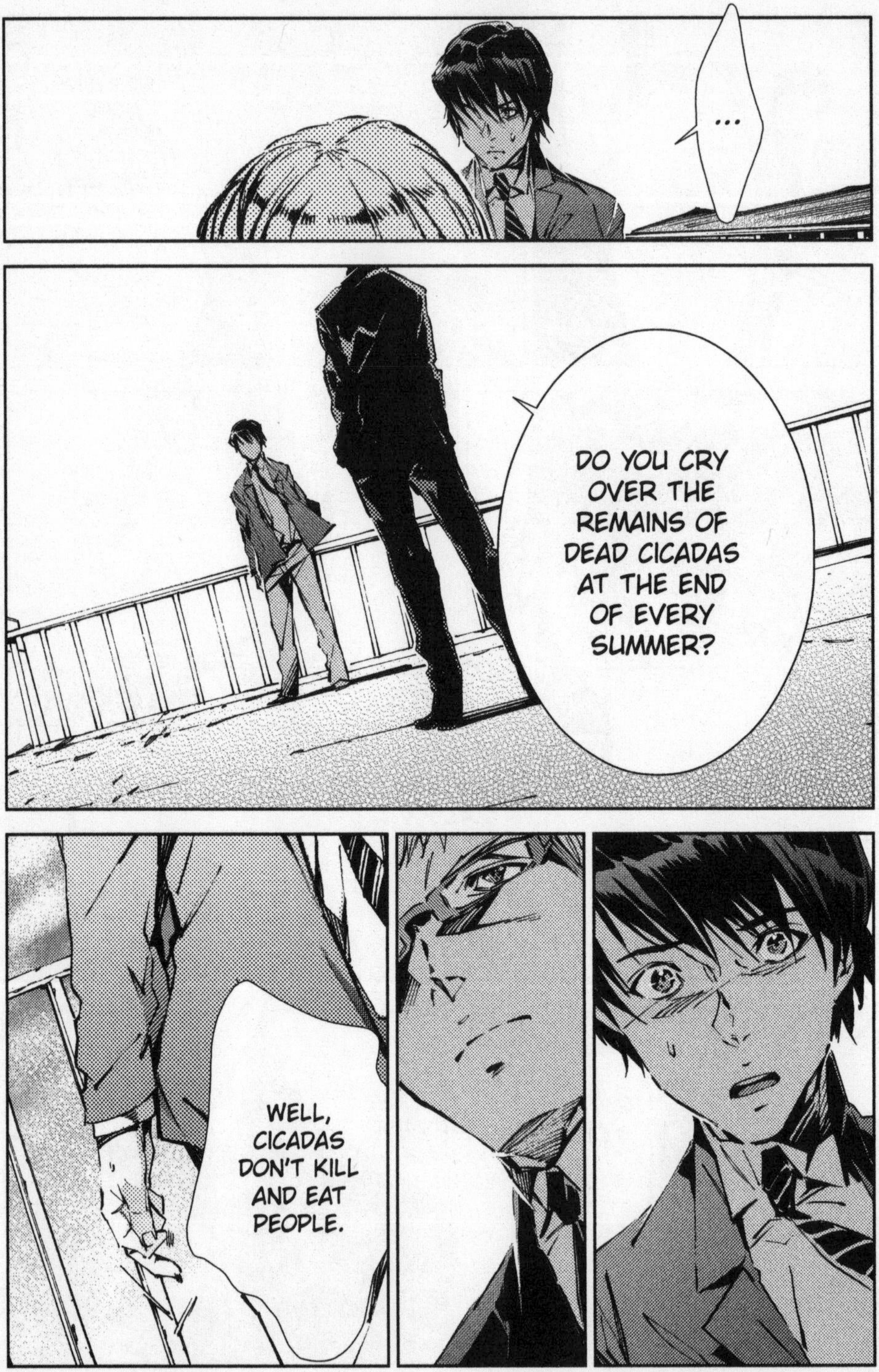
...
DO YOU CRY OVER THE REMAINS OF DEAD CICADAS AT THE END OF EVERY SUMMER?
WELL, CICADAS DON'T KILL AND EAT PEOPLE.

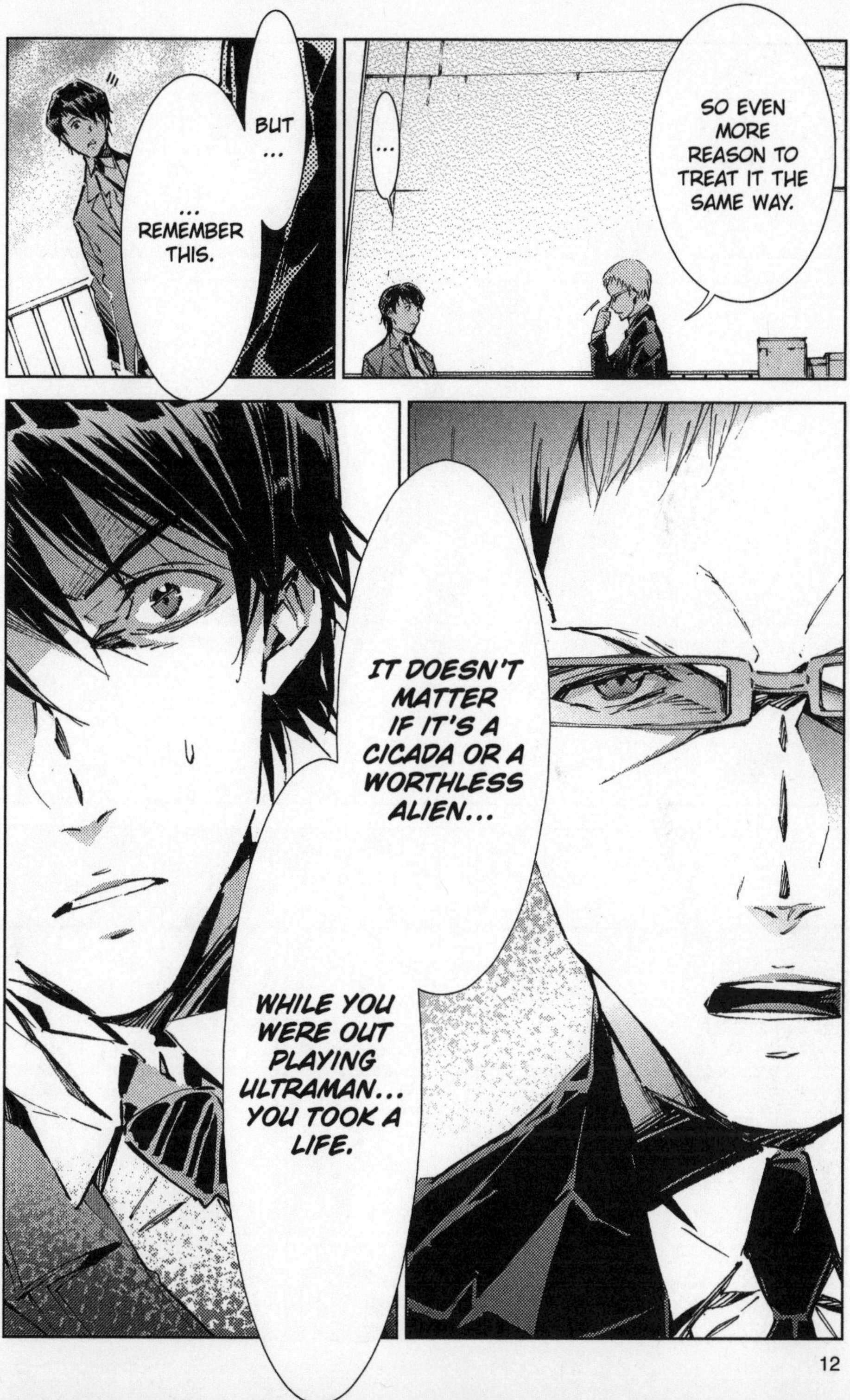
SO EVEN MORE REASON TO TREAT IT THE SAME WAY.
...
BUT ...
... REMEMBER THIS.
IT DOESN'T MATTER IF IT'S A CICADA OR A WORTHLESS ALIEN...
WHILE YOU WERE OUT PLAYING ULTRAMAN... YOU TOOK A LIFE.

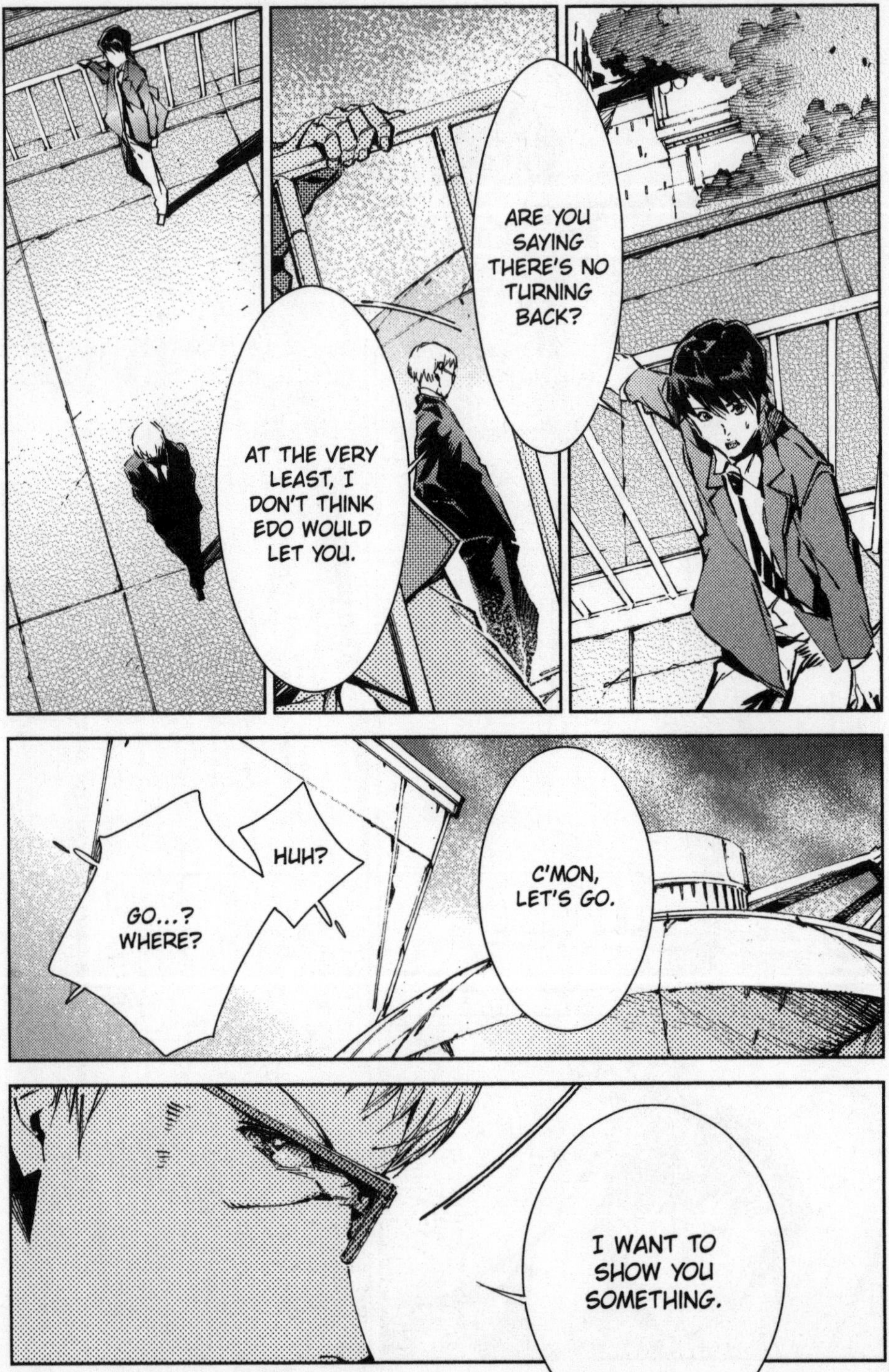
ARE YOU SAYING THERE'S NO TURNING BACK?
AT THE VERY LEAST, I DON'T THINK EDO WOULD LET YOU.
C'MON, LET'S GO.
HUH?
GO...? WHERE?
I WANT TO SHOW YOU SOMETHING.

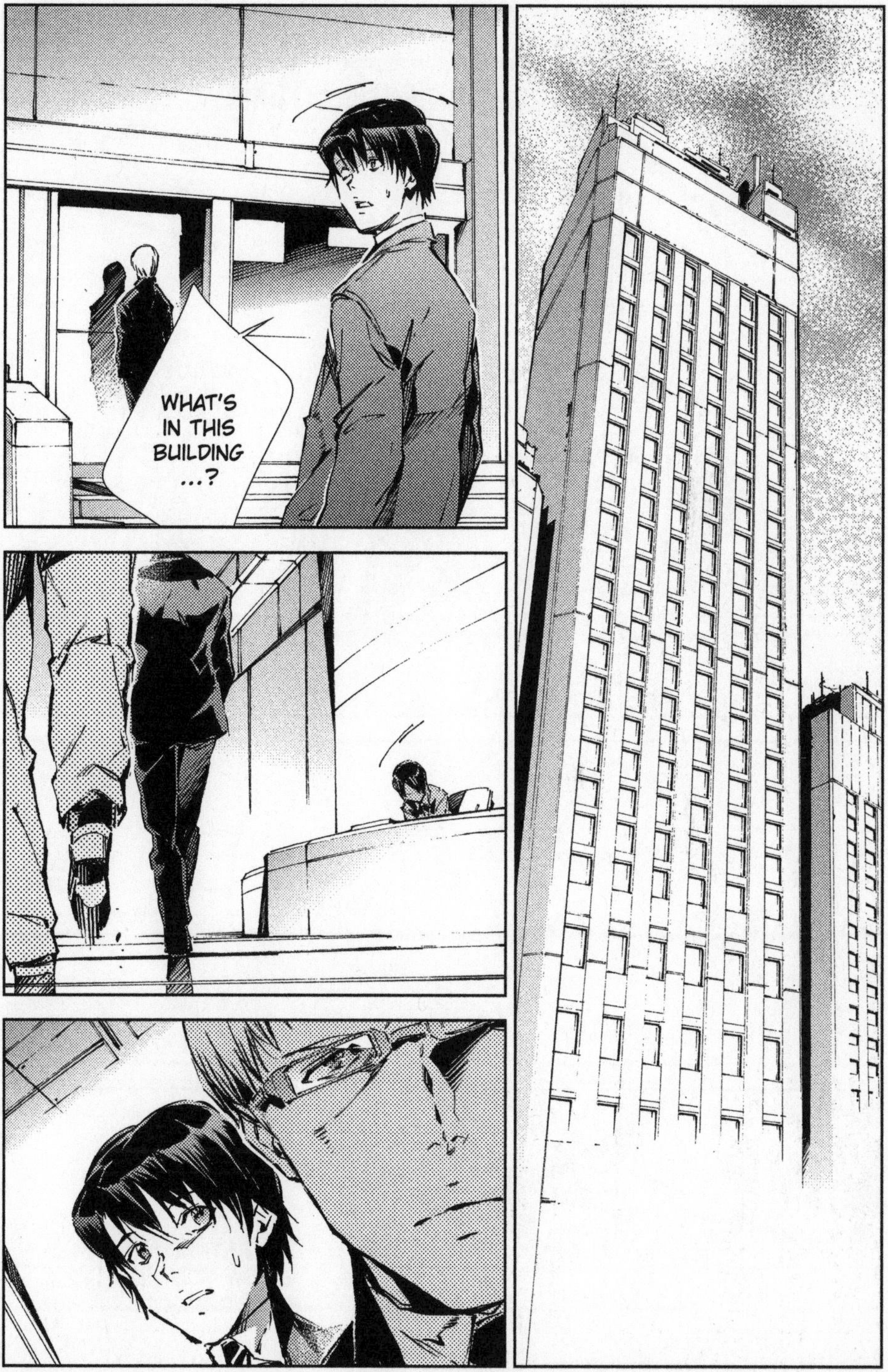
WHAT'S IN THIS BUILDING ...?

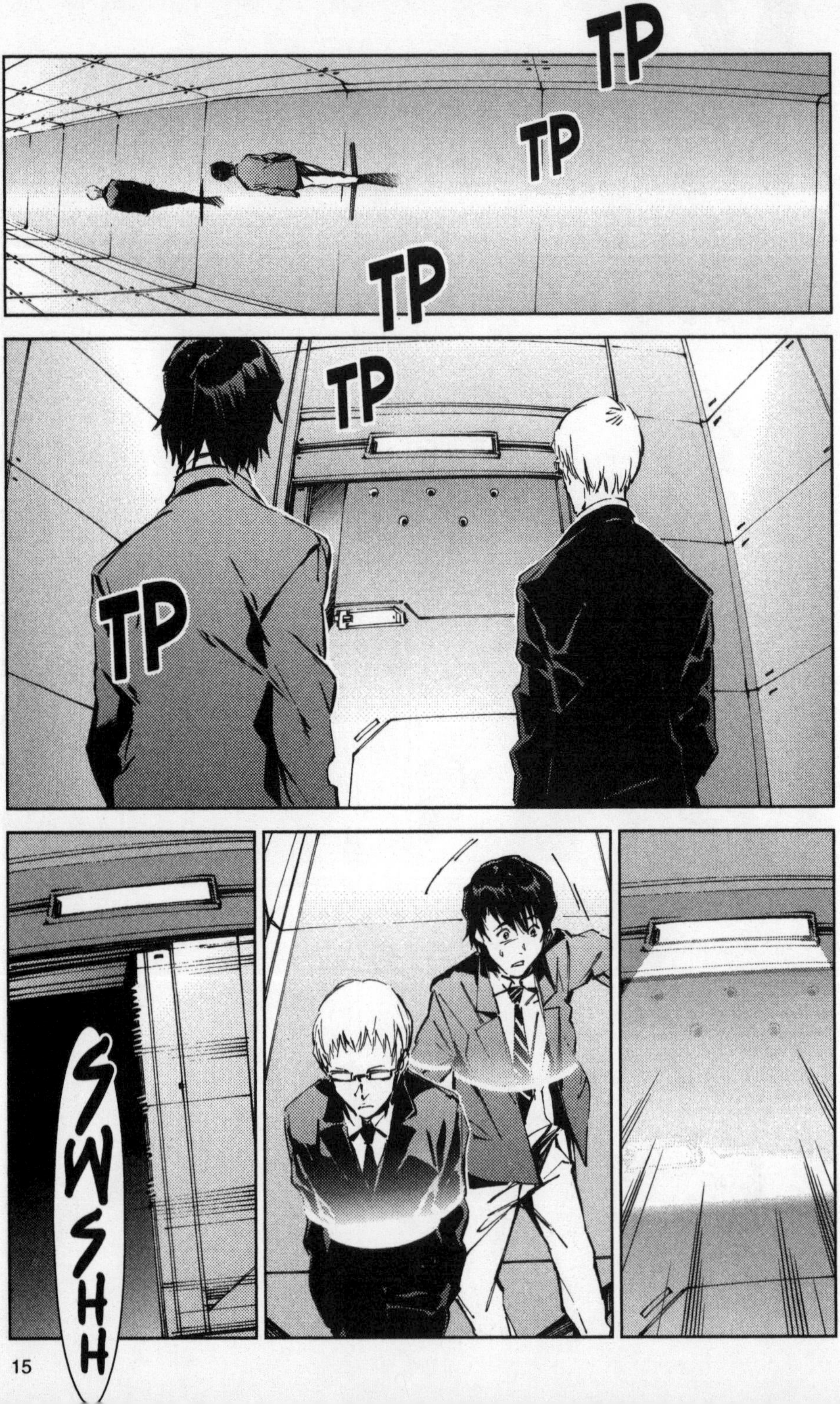
TP
TP
TP
TP
TP
SWSHH

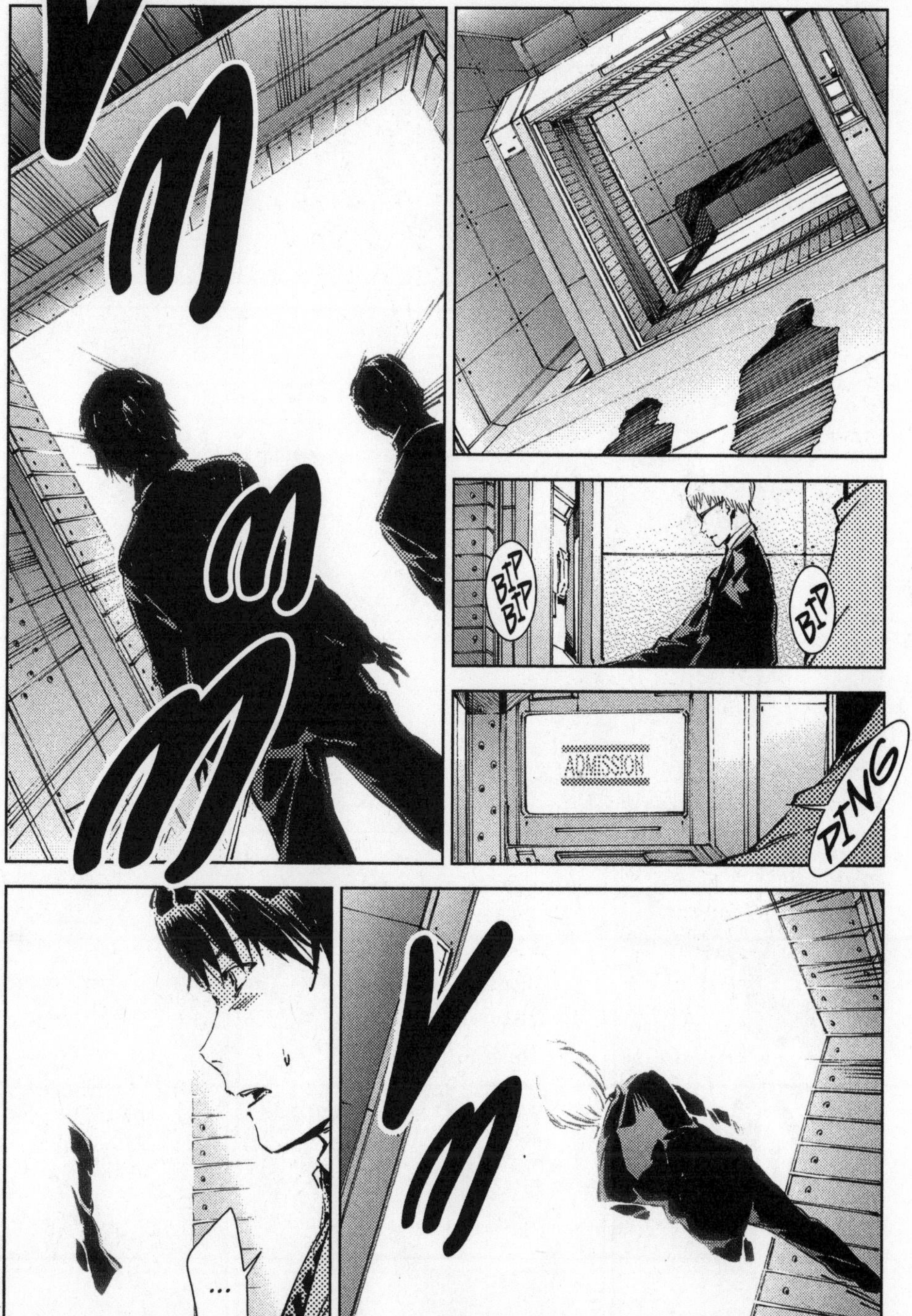
BIP BIP
BIP
ADMISSION
PING
...

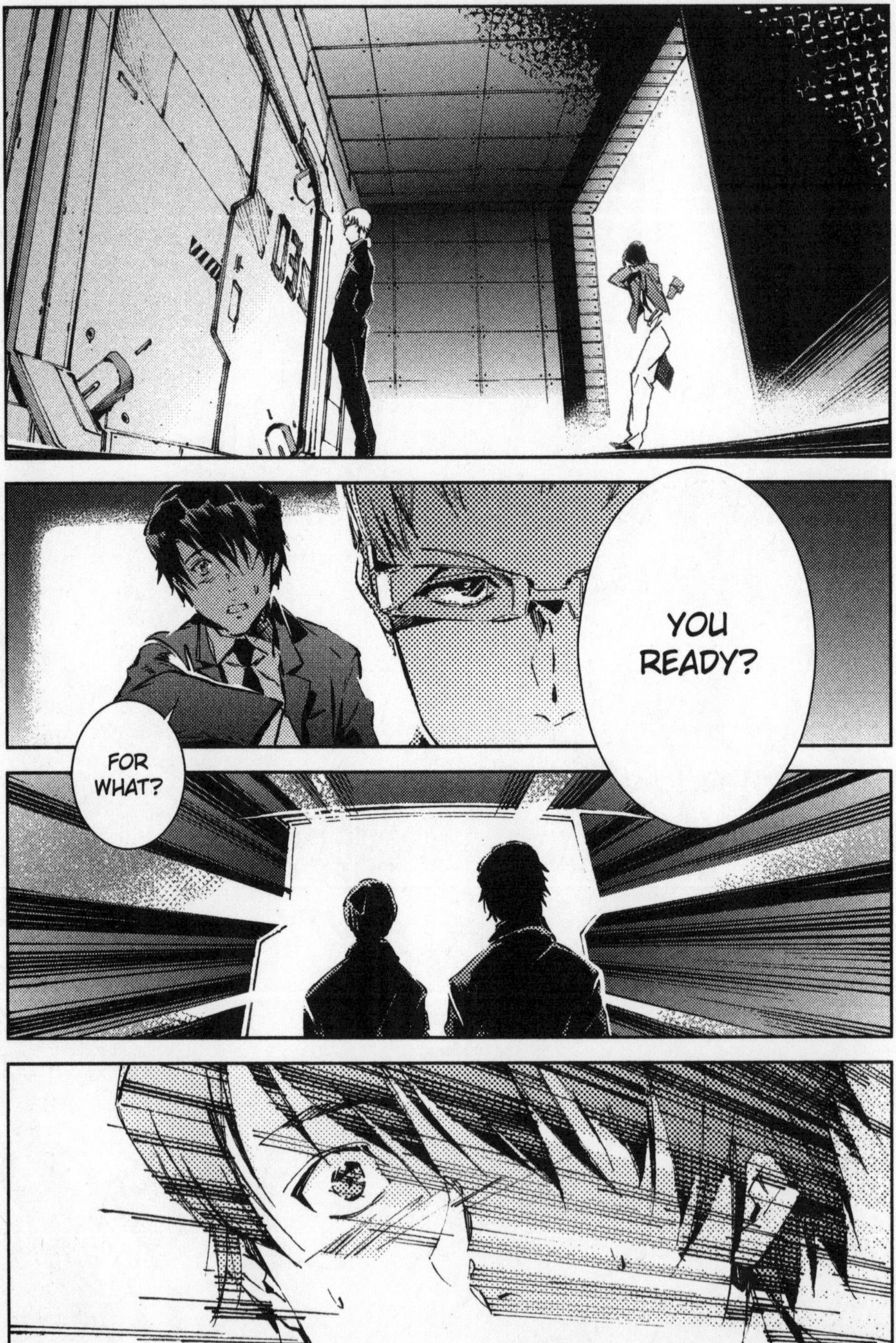
YOU READY?
FOR WHAT?

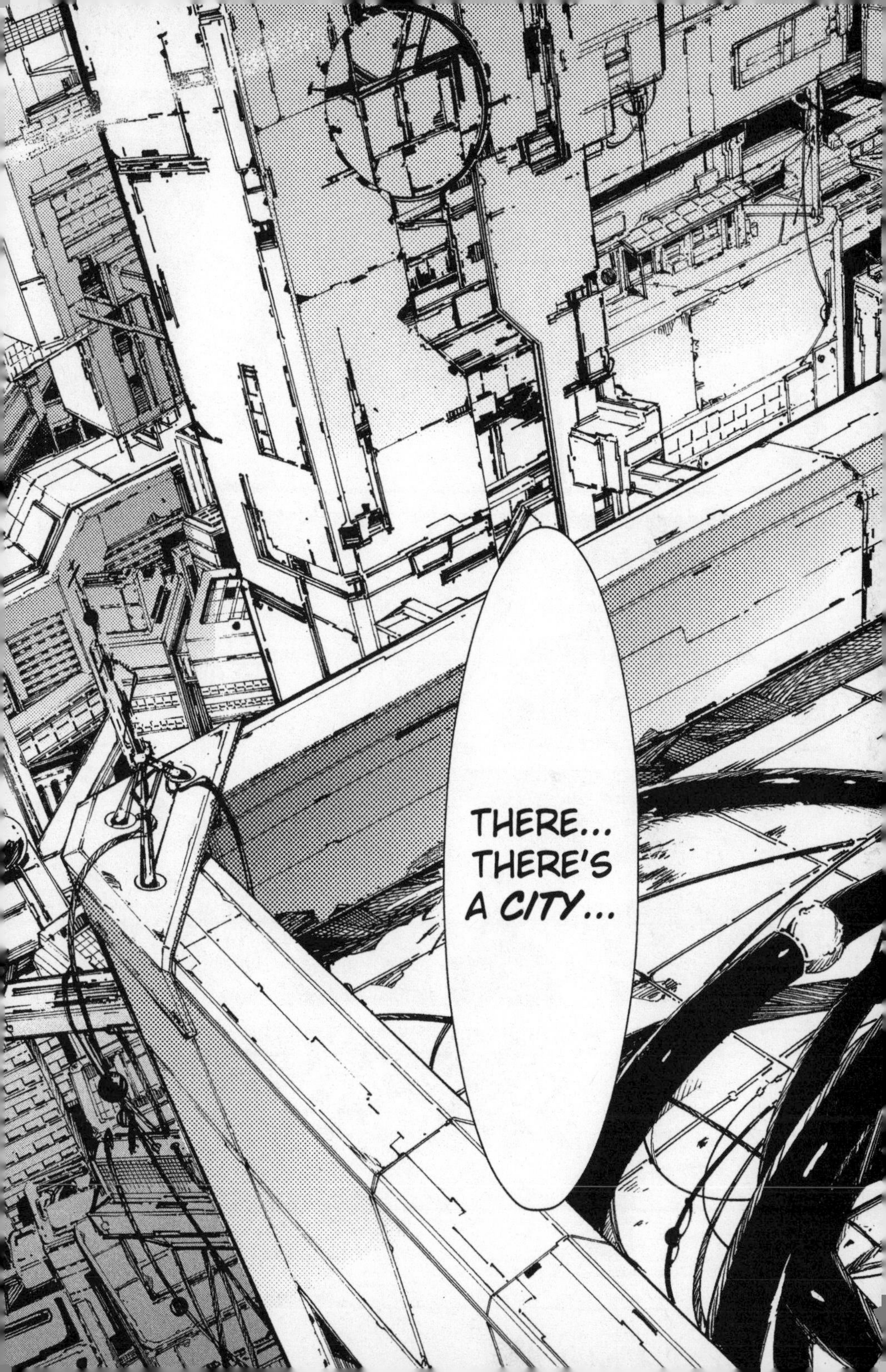
THERE... THERE'S A *CITY*...

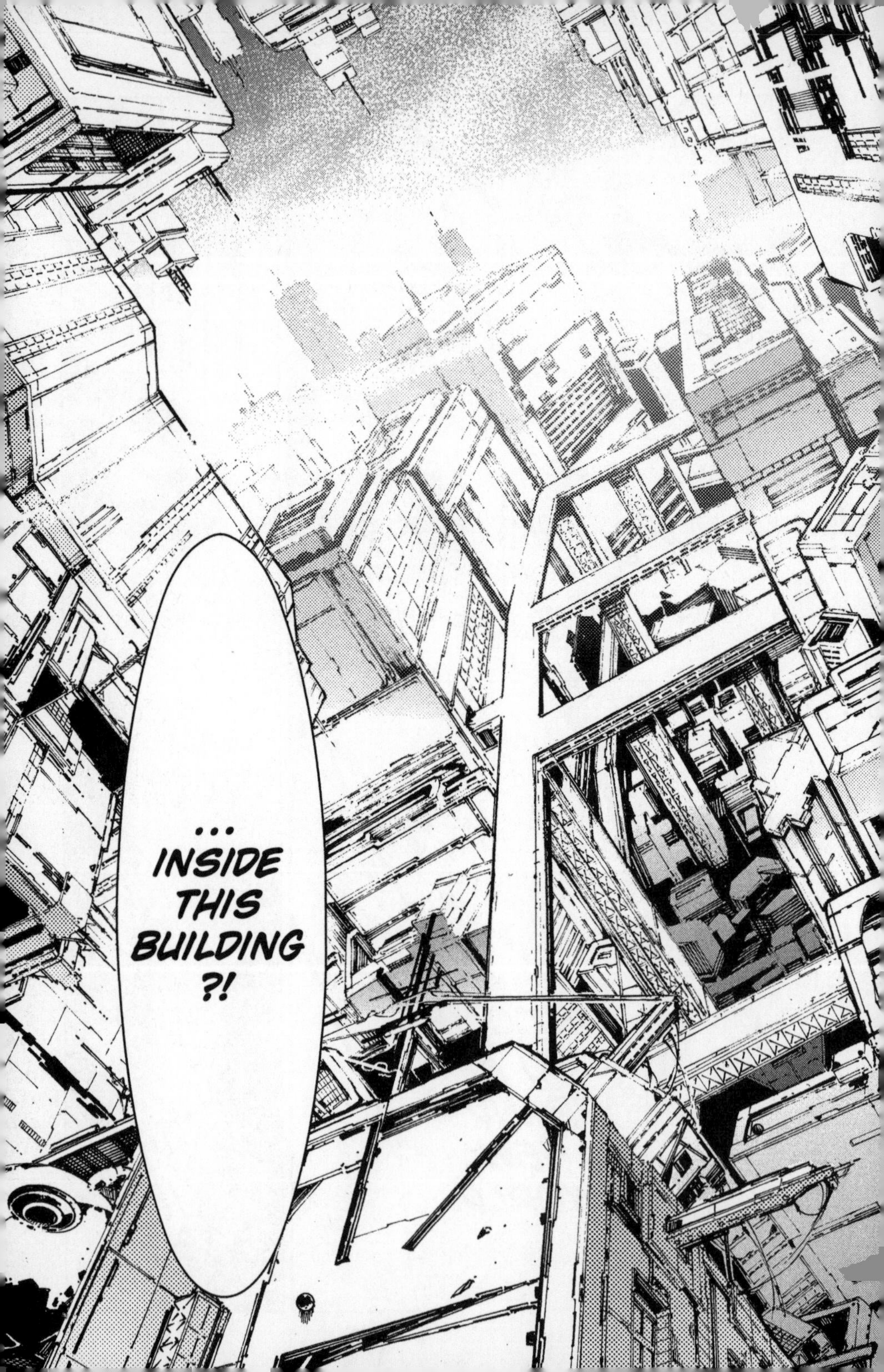
...INSIDE THIS BUILDING?!

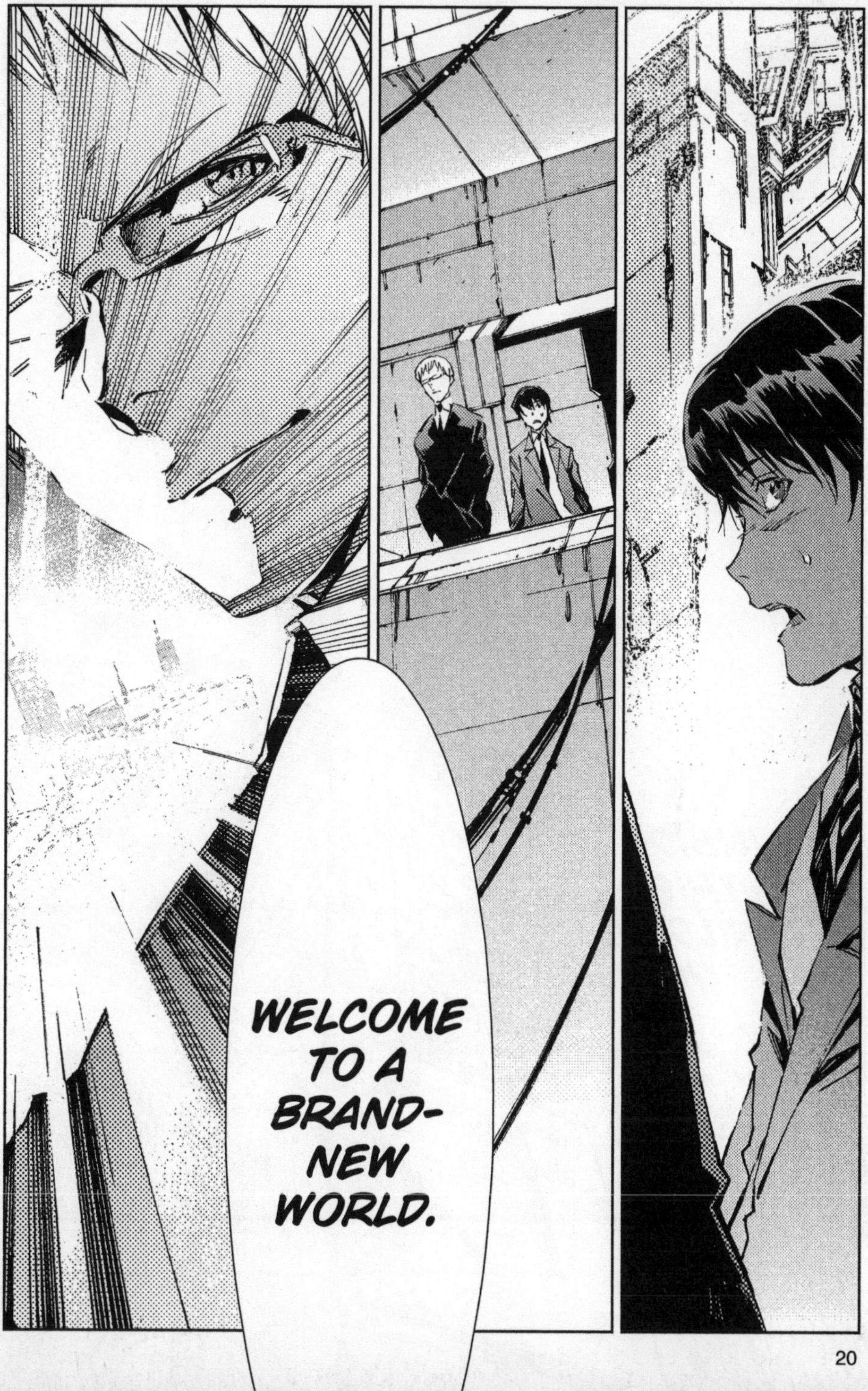
WELCOME TO A BRAND-NEW WORLD.

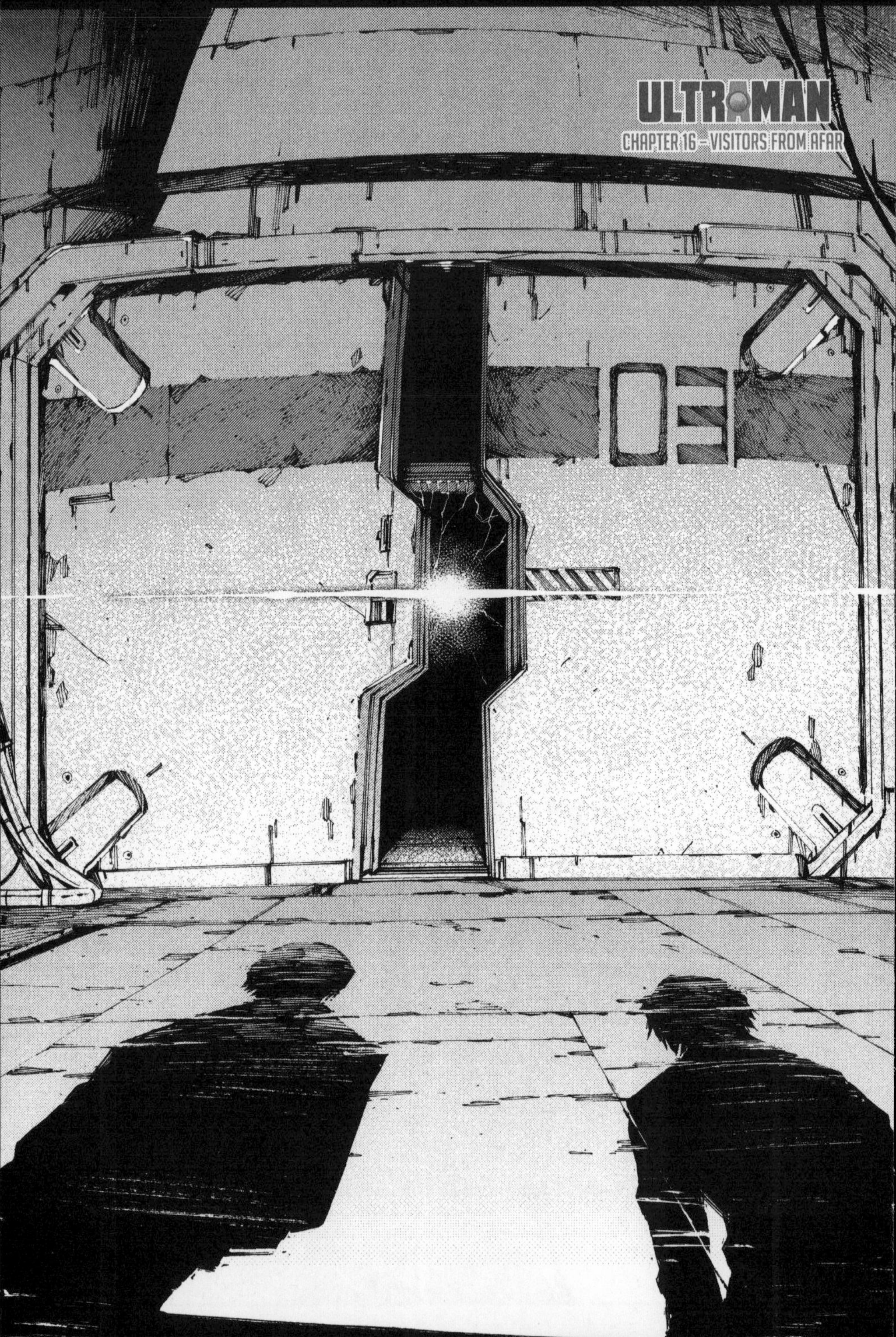
ULTRAMAN
CHAPTER 16 – VISITORS FROM AFAR

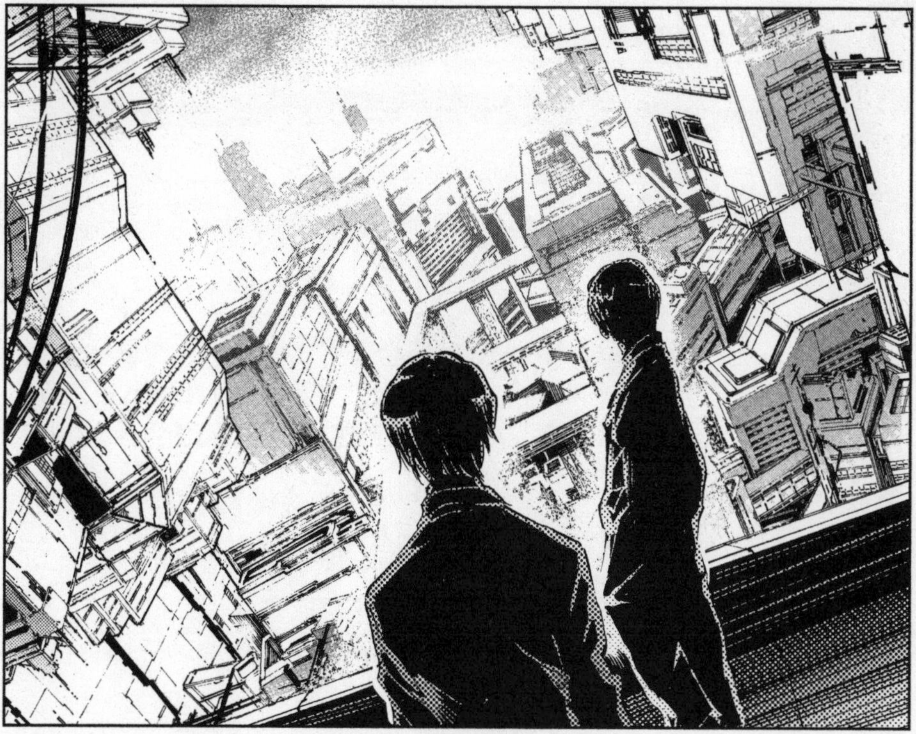

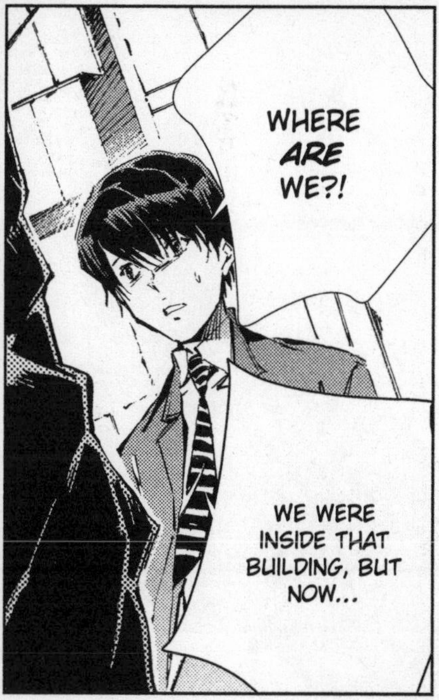
WHERE *ARE* WE?!
WE WERE INSIDE THAT BUILDING, BUT NOW...

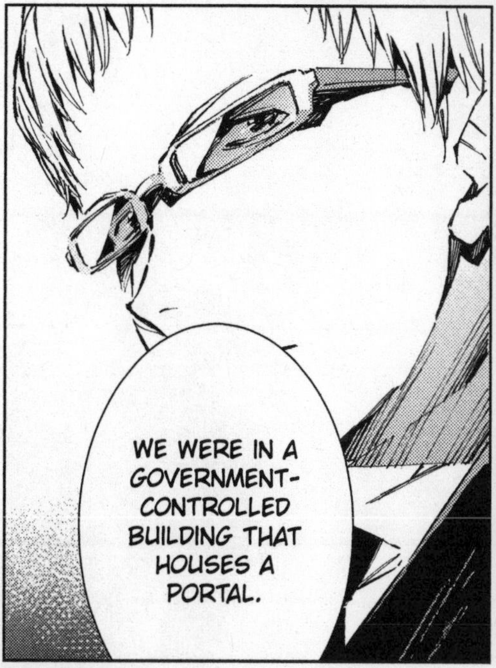
WE WERE IN A GOVERNMENT-CONTROLLED BUILDING THAT HOUSES A PORTAL.

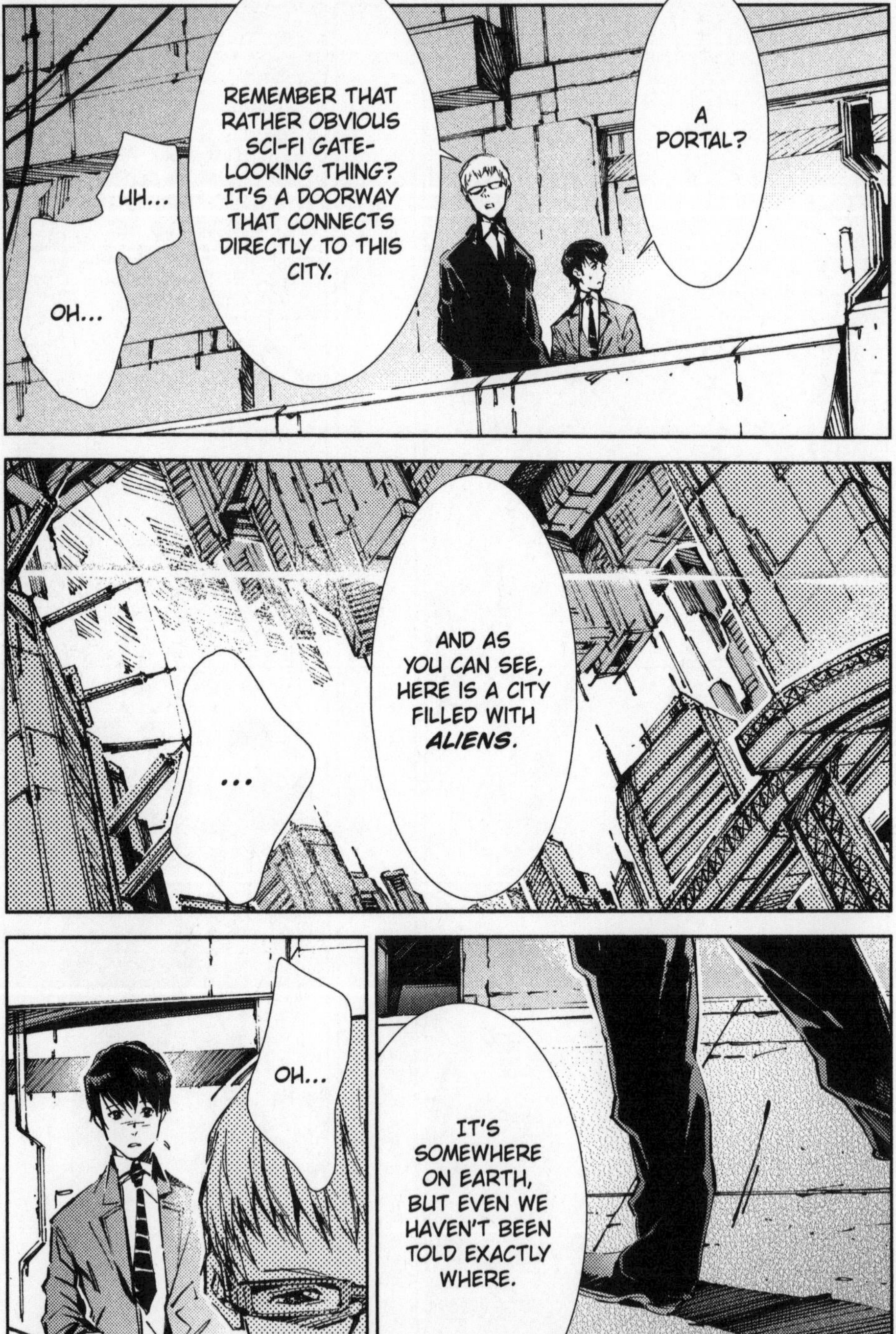
A PORTAL?
REMEMBER THAT RATHER OBVIOUS SCI-FI GATE-LOOKING THING? IT'S A DOORWAY THAT CONNECTS DIRECTLY TO THIS CITY.
UH...
OH...
AND AS YOU CAN SEE, HERE IS A CITY FILLED WITH *ALIENS.*
...
IT'S SOMEWHERE ON EARTH, BUT EVEN WE HAVEN'T BEEN TOLD EXACTLY WHERE.
OH...

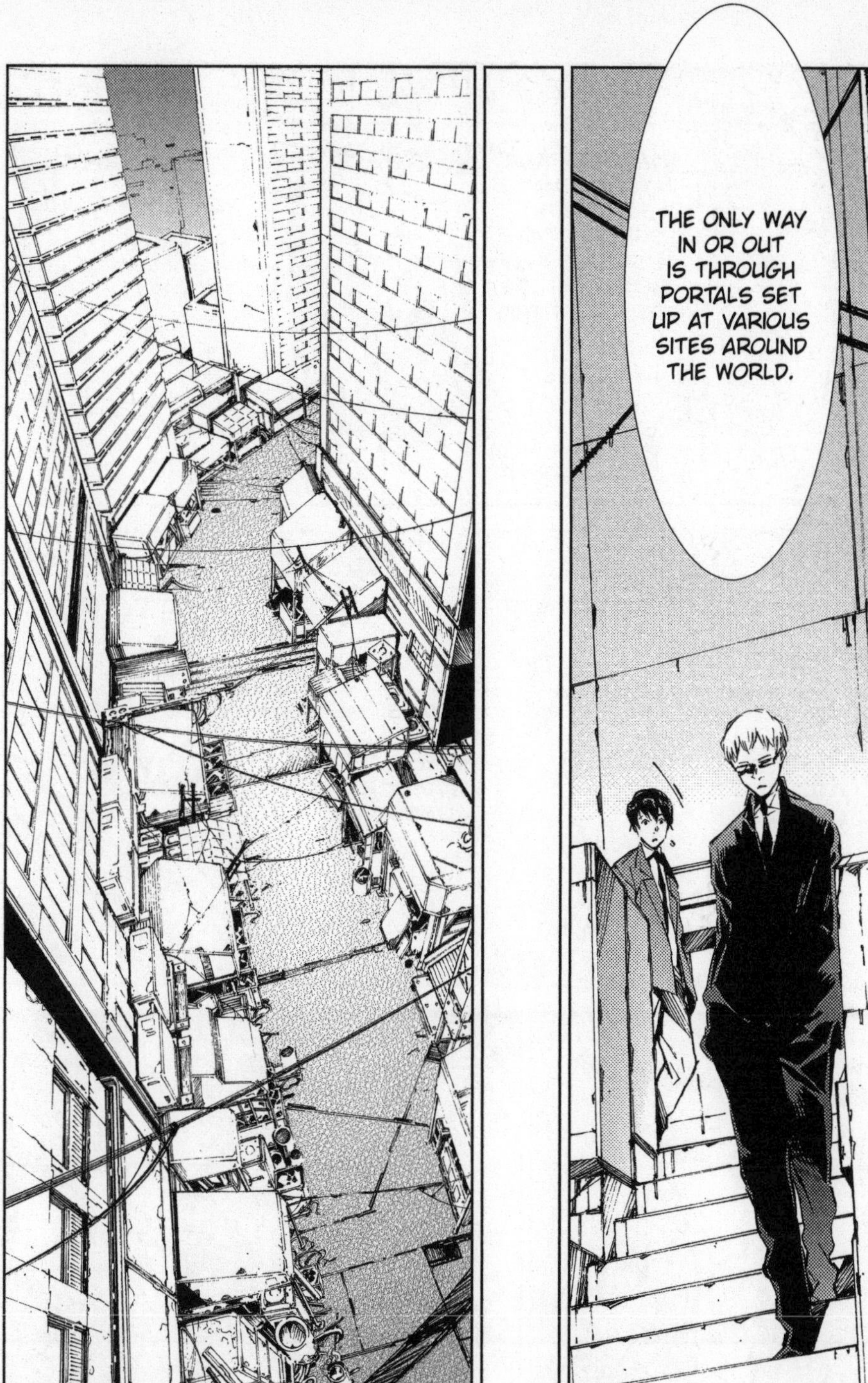
THE ONLY WAY IN OR OUT IS THROUGH PORTALS SET UP AT VARIOUS SITES AROUND THE WORLD.

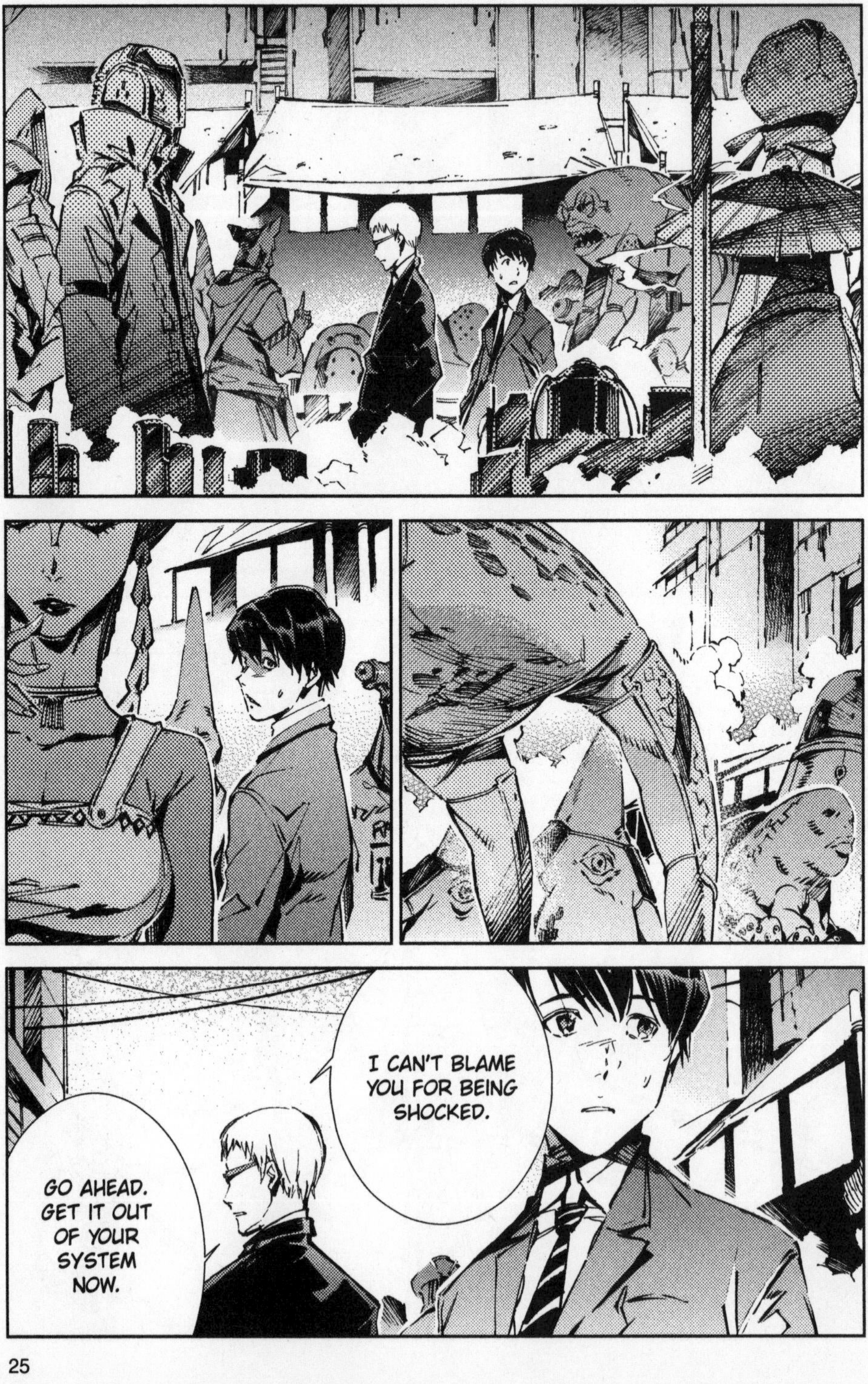
I CAN'T BLAME YOU FOR BEING SHOCKED.
GO AHEAD. GET IT OUT OF YOUR SYSTEM NOW.

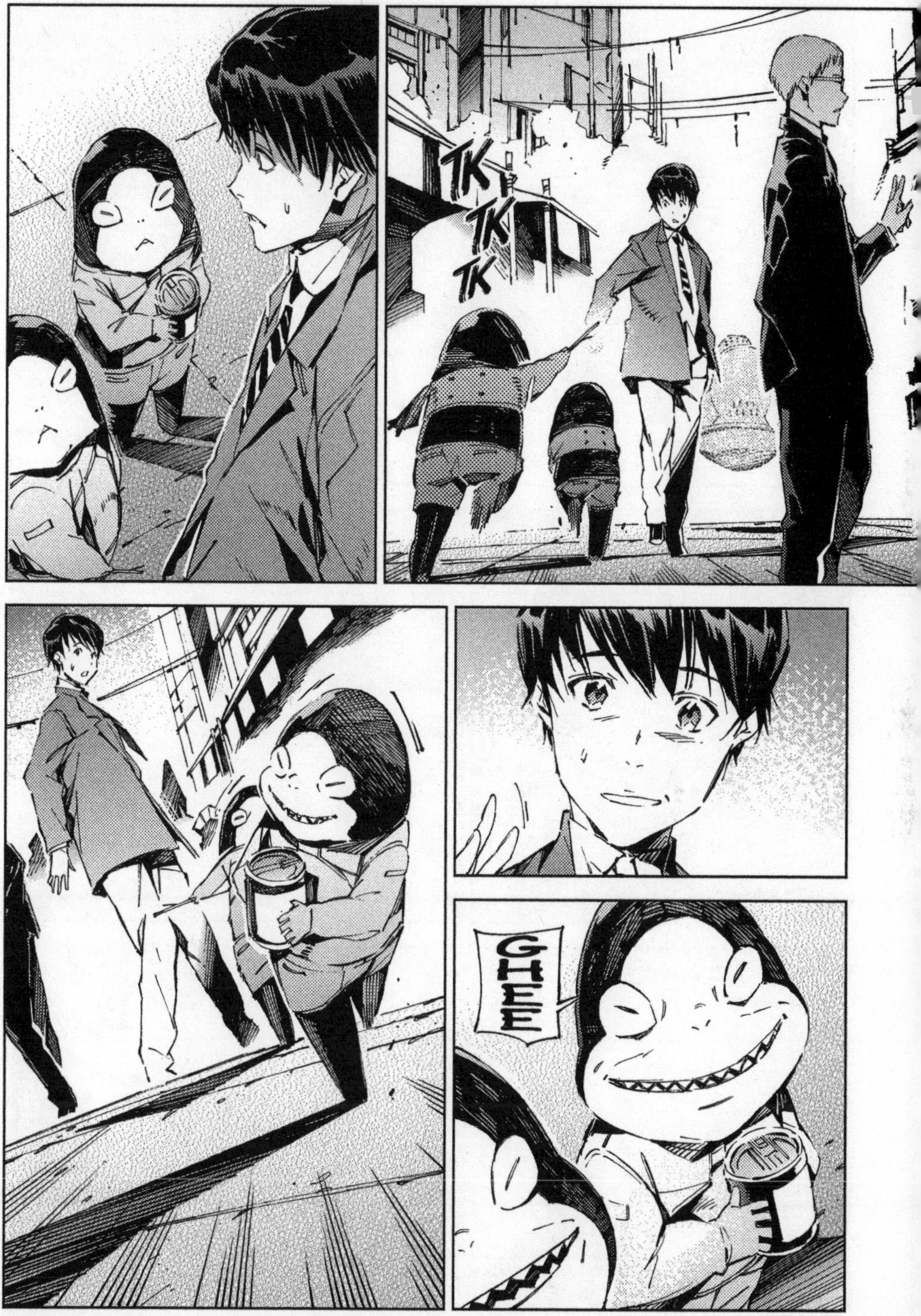
TK
TK
TK
GHEE

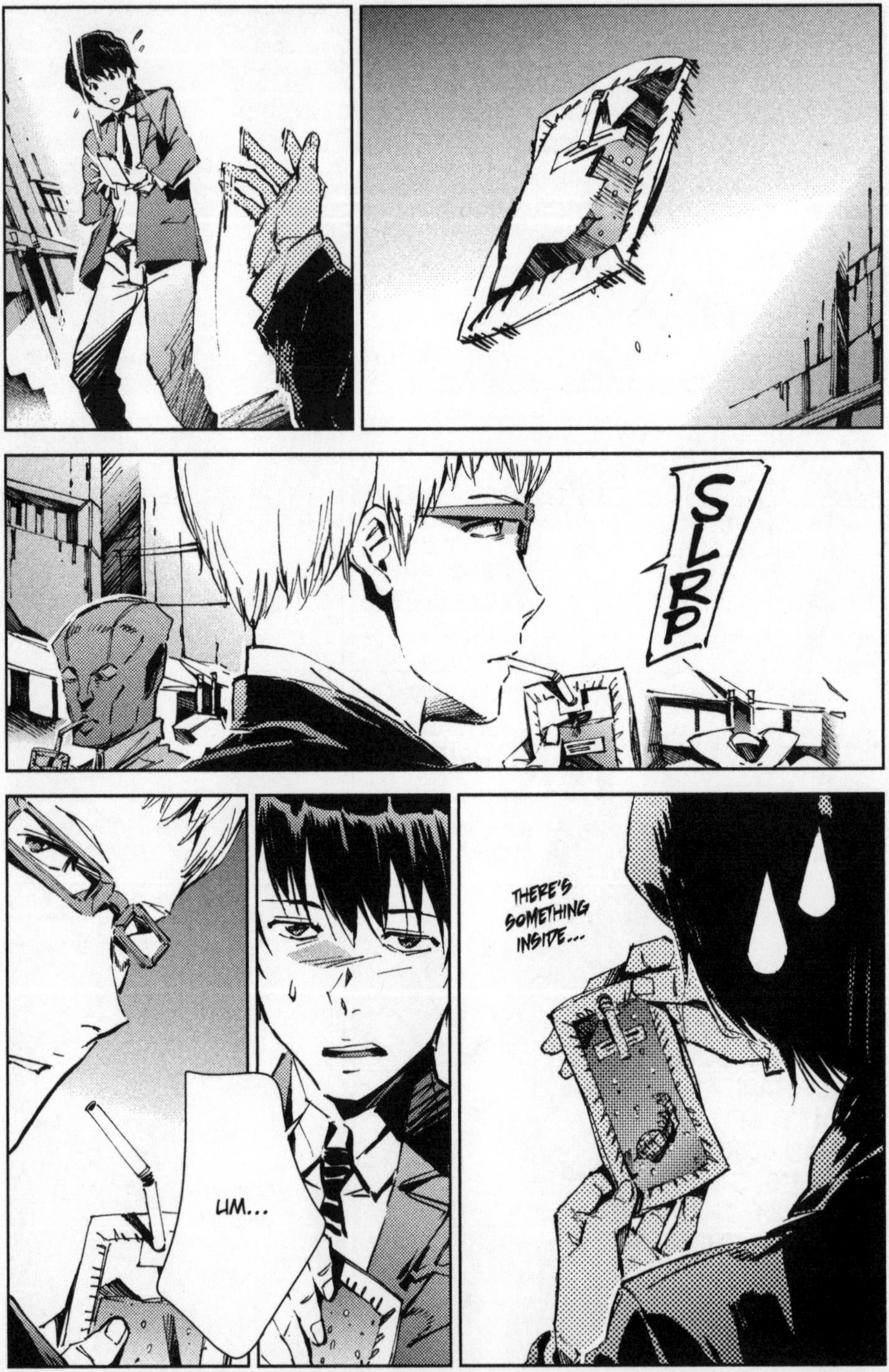
SLRP
THERE'S SOMETHING INSIDE...
UM...

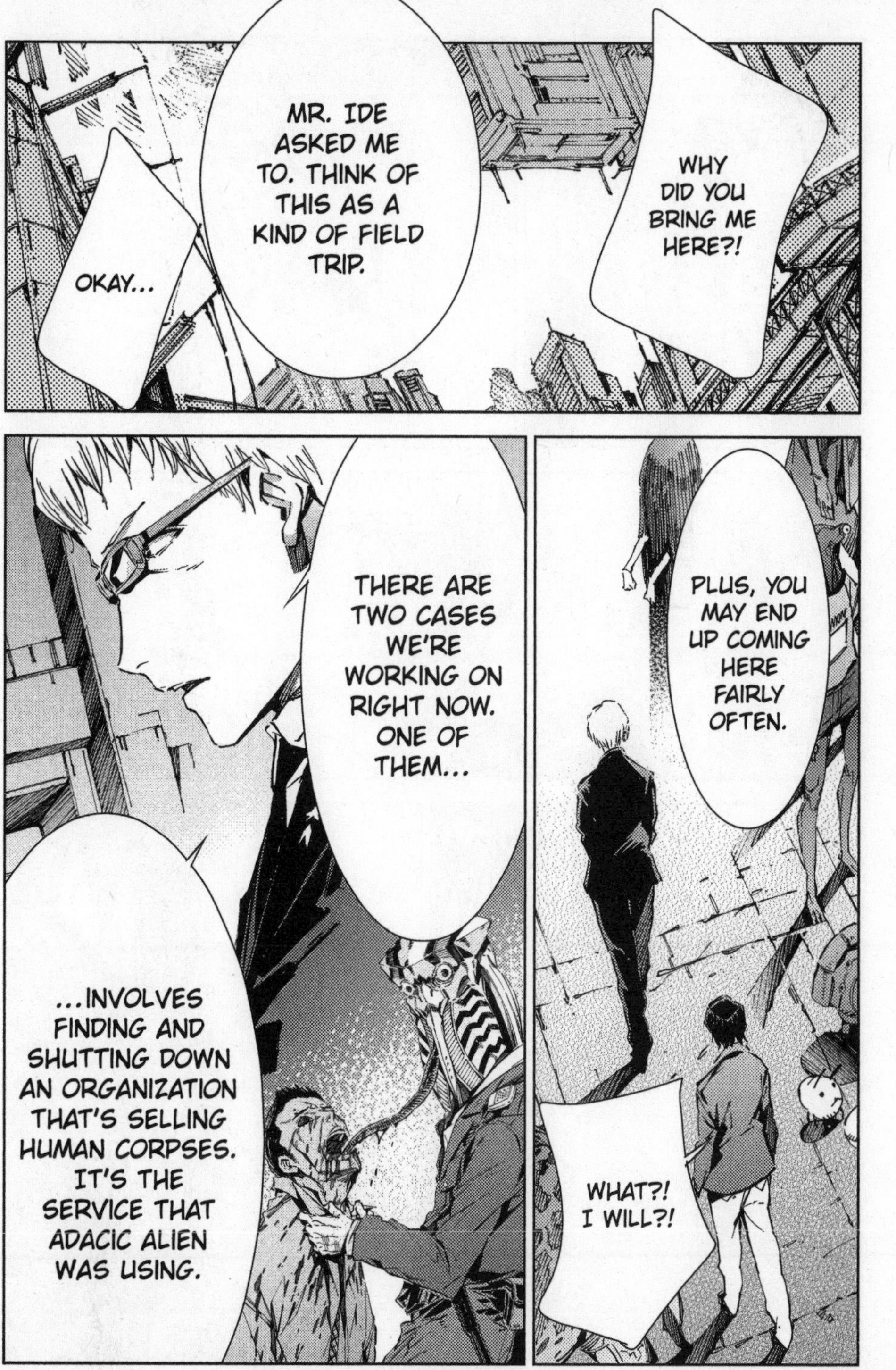
WHY DID YOU BRING ME HERE?!
MR. IDE ASKED ME TO. THINK OF THIS AS A KIND OF FIELD TRIP.
OKAY...
PLUS, YOU MAY END UP COMING HERE FAIRLY OFTEN.
WHAT?! I WILL?!
THERE ARE TWO CASES WE'RE WORKING ON RIGHT NOW. ONE OF THEM...
...INVOLVES FINDING AND SHUTTING DOWN AN ORGANIZATION THAT'S SELLING HUMAN CORPSES. IT'S THE SERVICE THAT ADACIC ALIEN WAS USING.

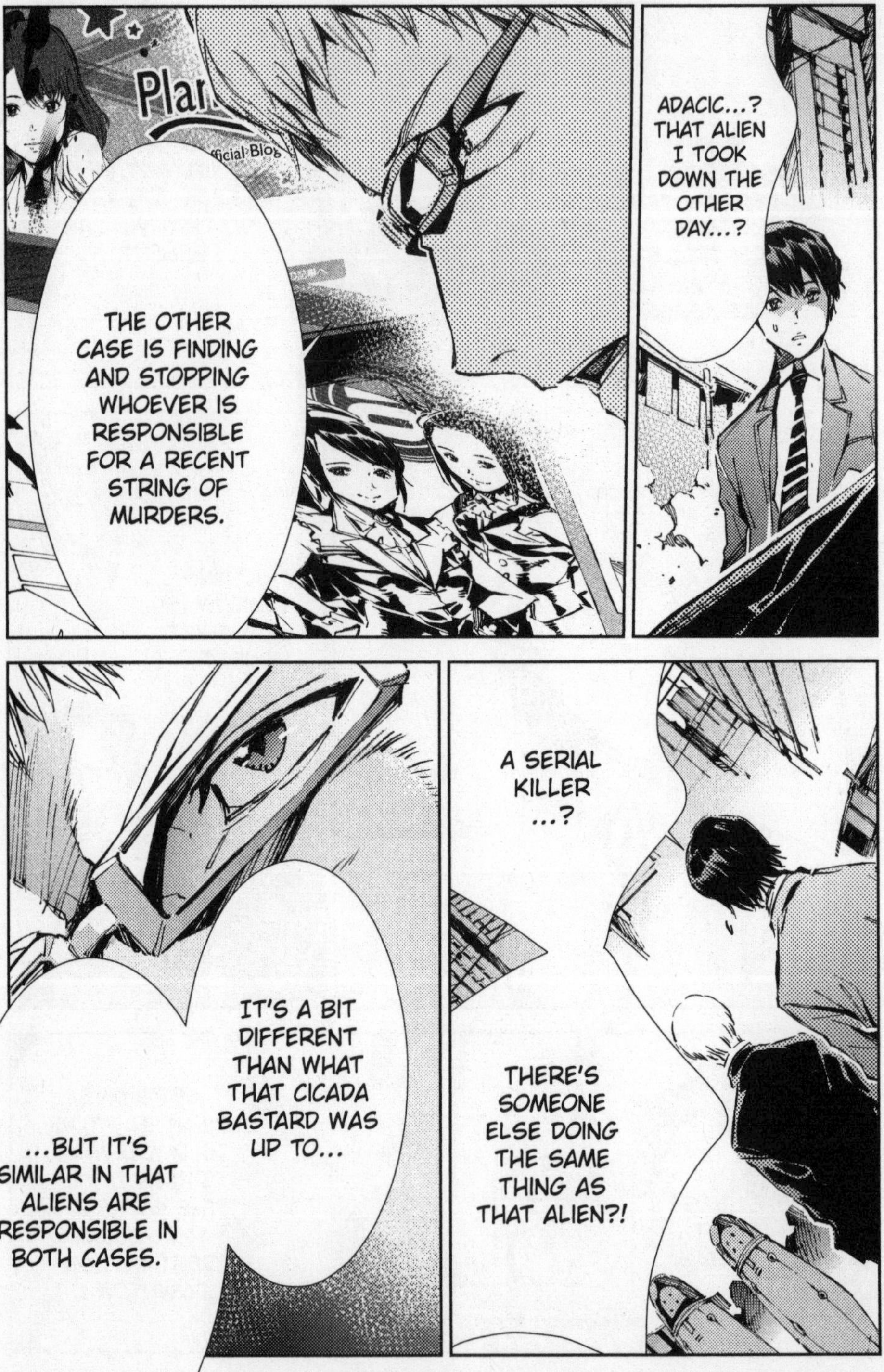
ADACIC...? THAT ALIEN I TOOK DOWN THE OTHER DAY...?
THE OTHER CASE IS FINDING AND STOPPING WHOEVER IS RESPONSIBLE FOR A RECENT STRING OF MURDERS.
A SERIAL KILLER ...?
THERE'S SOMEONE ELSE DOING THE SAME THING AS THAT ALIEN?!
IT'S A BIT DIFFERENT THAN WHAT THAT CICADA BASTARD WAS UP TO...
...BUT IT'S SIMILAR IN THAT ALIENS ARE RESPONSIBLE IN BOTH CASES.

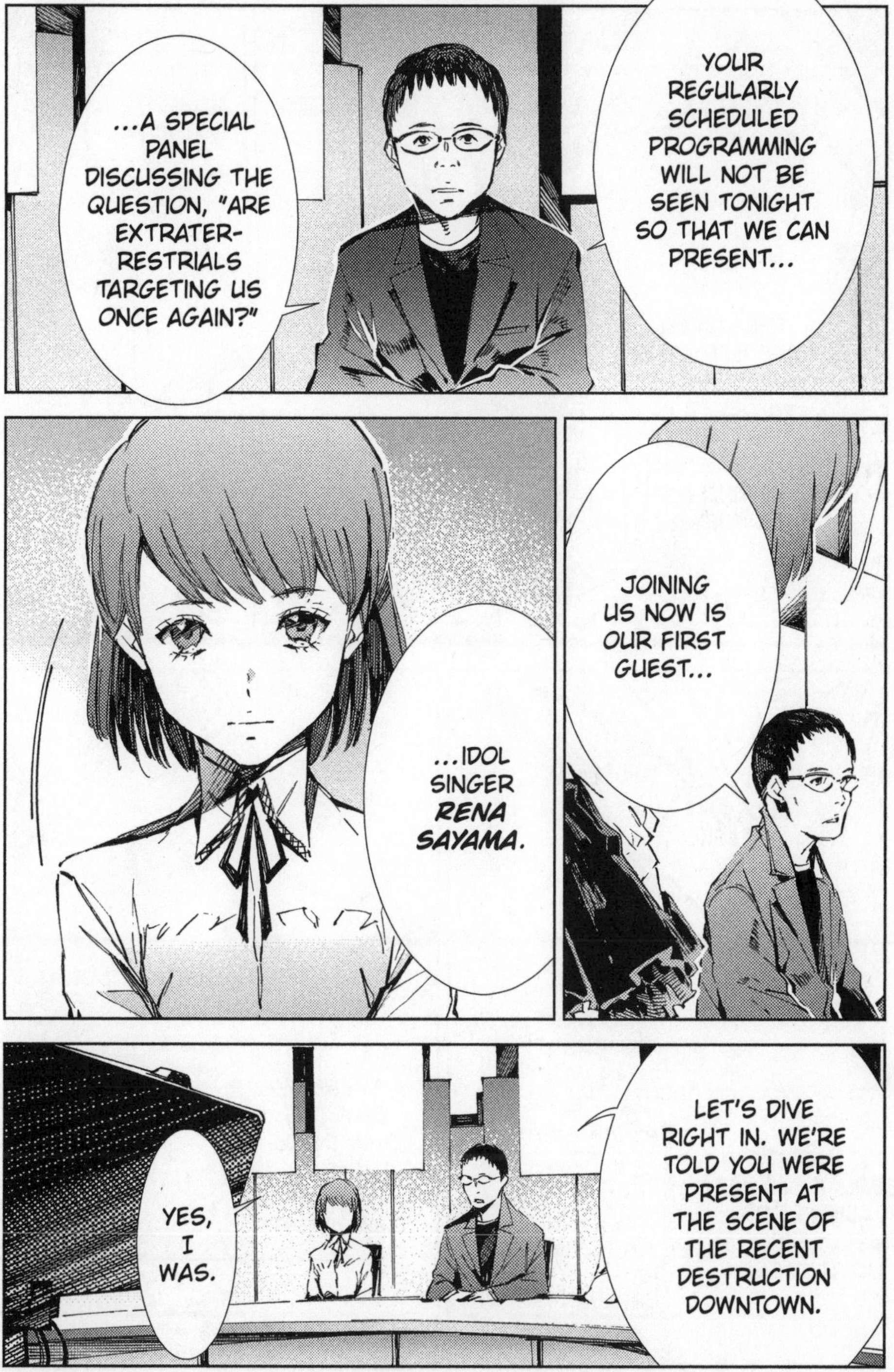
YOUR REGULARLY SCHEDULED PROGRAMMING WILL NOT BE SEEN TONIGHT SO THAT WE CAN PRESENT...
...A SPECIAL PANEL DISCUSSING THE QUESTION, "ARE EXTRATER-RESTRIALS TARGETING US ONCE AGAIN?"
JOINING US NOW IS OUR FIRST GUEST...
...IDOL SINGER *RENA SAYAMA*.
LET'S DIVE RIGHT IN. WE'RE TOLD YOU WERE PRESENT AT THE SCENE OF THE RECENT DESTRUCTION DOWNTOWN.
YES, I WAS.

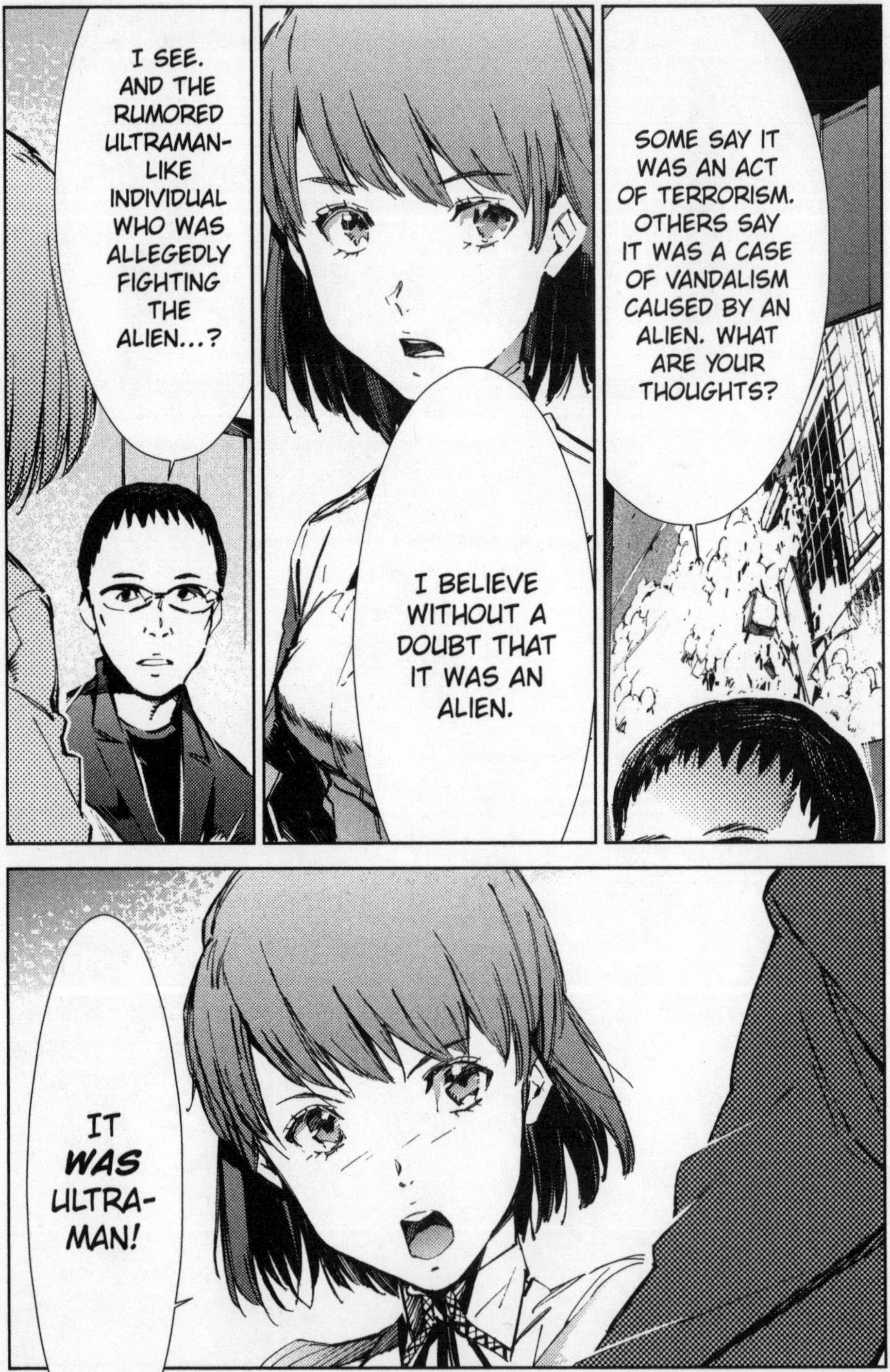
SOME SAY IT WAS AN ACT OF TERRORISM. OTHERS SAY IT WAS A CASE OF VANDALISM CAUSED BY AN ALIEN. WHAT ARE YOUR THOUGHTS?
I BELIEVE WITHOUT A DOUBT THAT IT WAS AN ALIEN.
I SEE. AND THE RUMORED ULTRAMAN-LIKE INDIVIDUAL WHO WAS ALLEGEDLY FIGHTING THE ALIEN...?
IT *WAS* ULTRA-MAN!

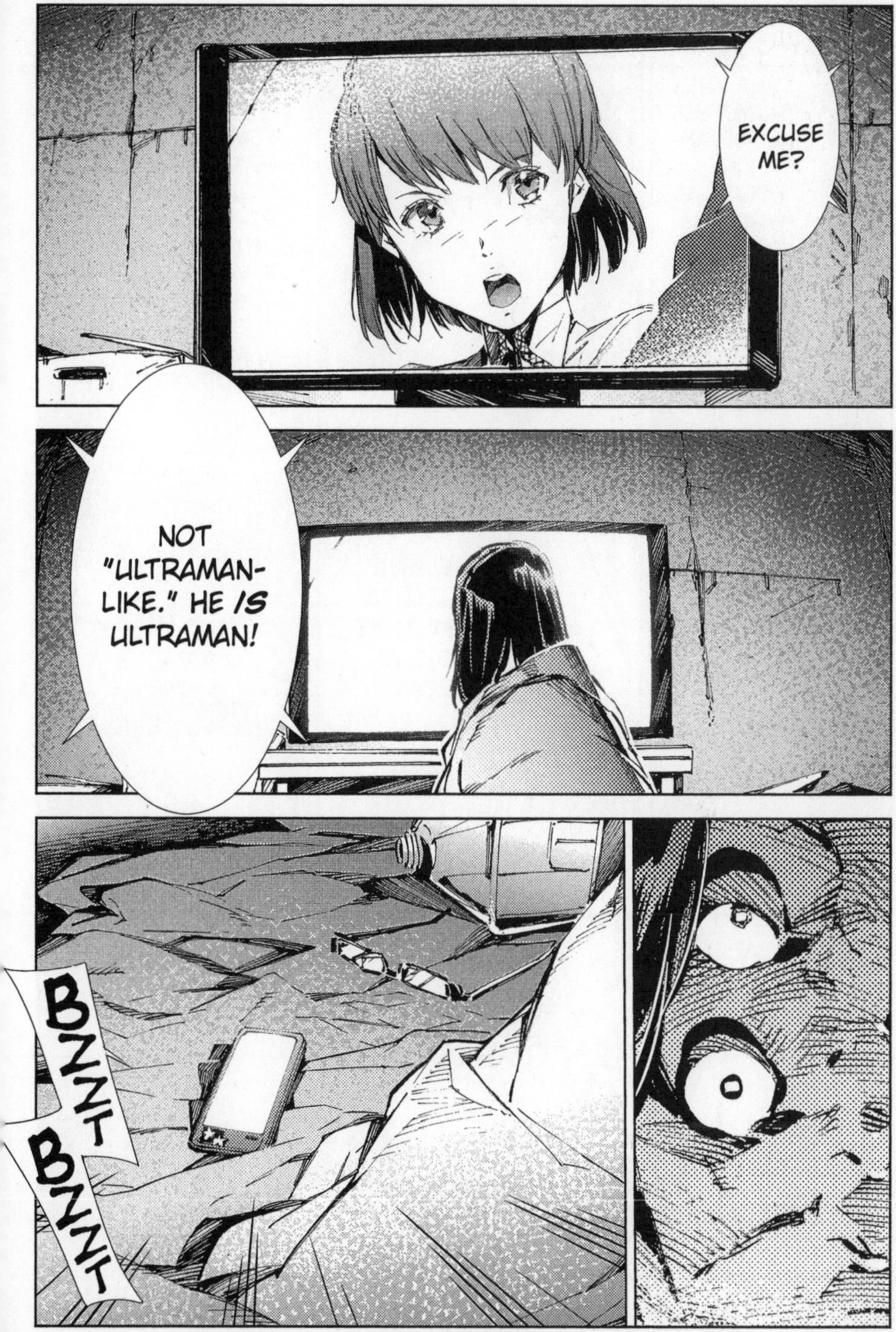
EXCUSE ME?
NOT "ULTRAMAN-LIKE." HE IS ULTRAMAN!
BZZZT BZZZT

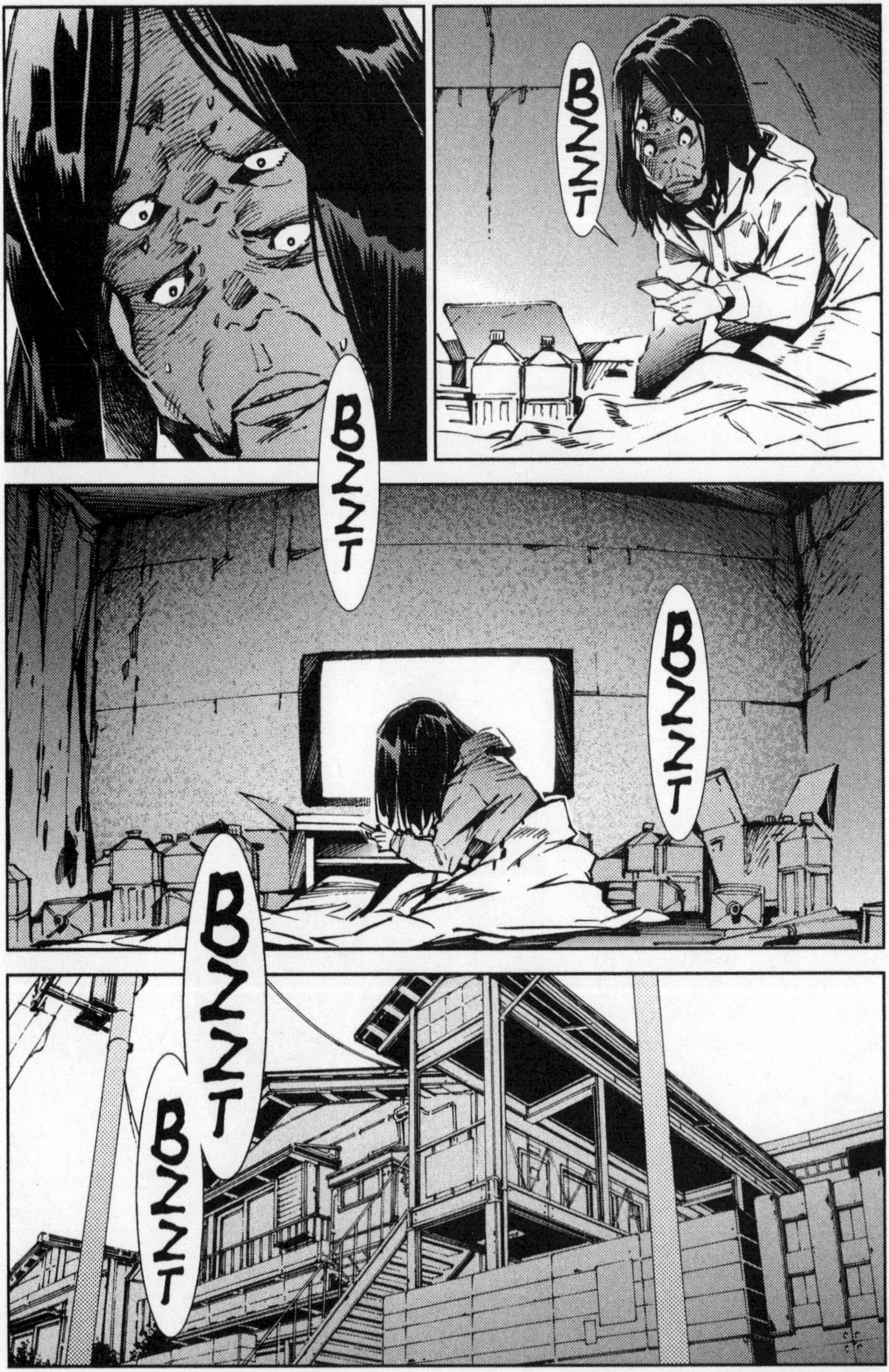
BZZZT
BZZZT
BZZZT
BZZZT
BZZZT

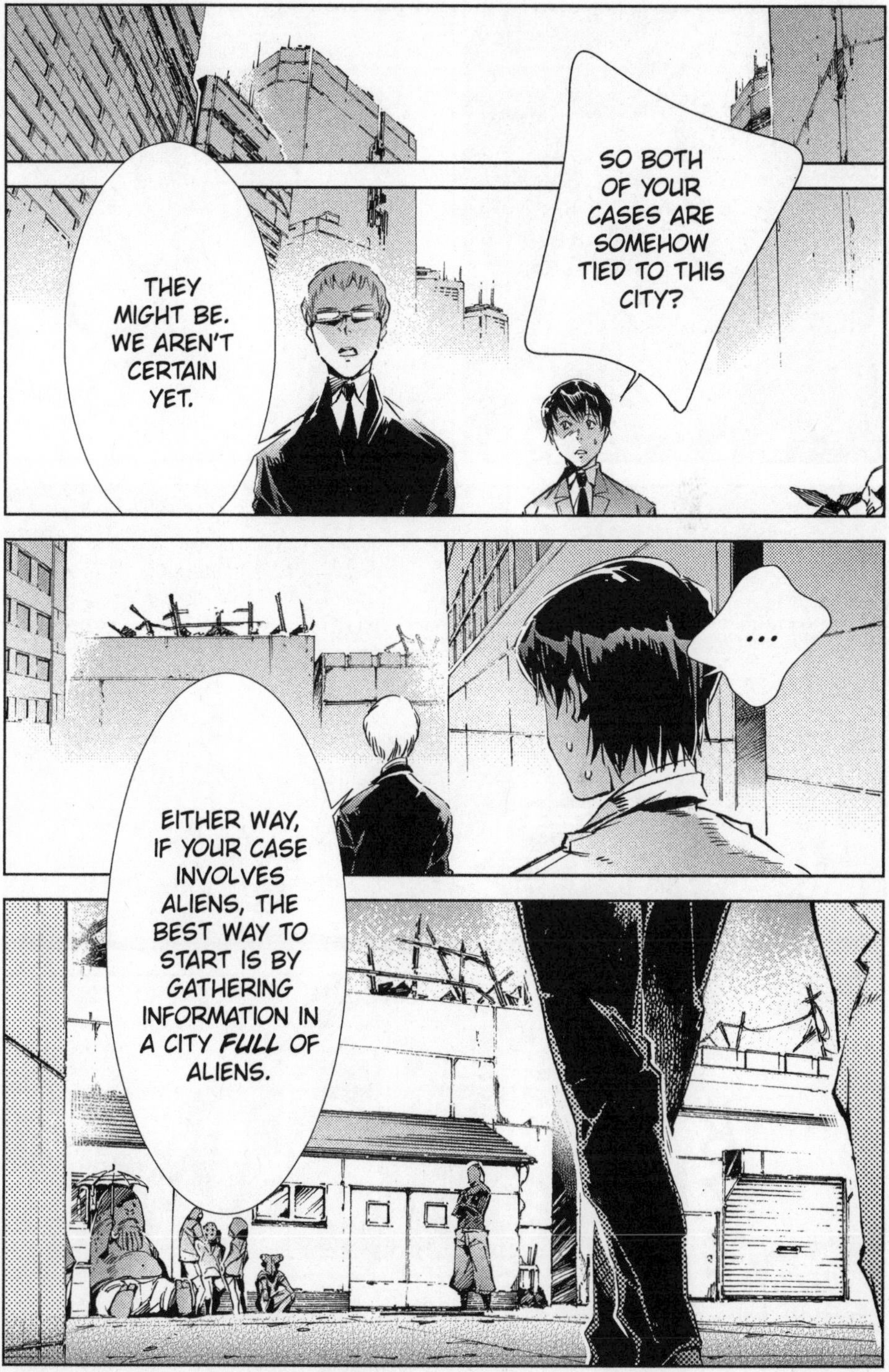
SO BOTH OF YOUR CASES ARE SOMEHOW TIED TO THIS CITY?
THEY MIGHT BE. WE AREN'T CERTAIN YET.
...
EITHER WAY, IF YOUR CASE INVOLVES ALIENS, THE BEST WAY TO START IS BY GATHERING INFORMATION IN A CITY *FULL* OF ALIENS.

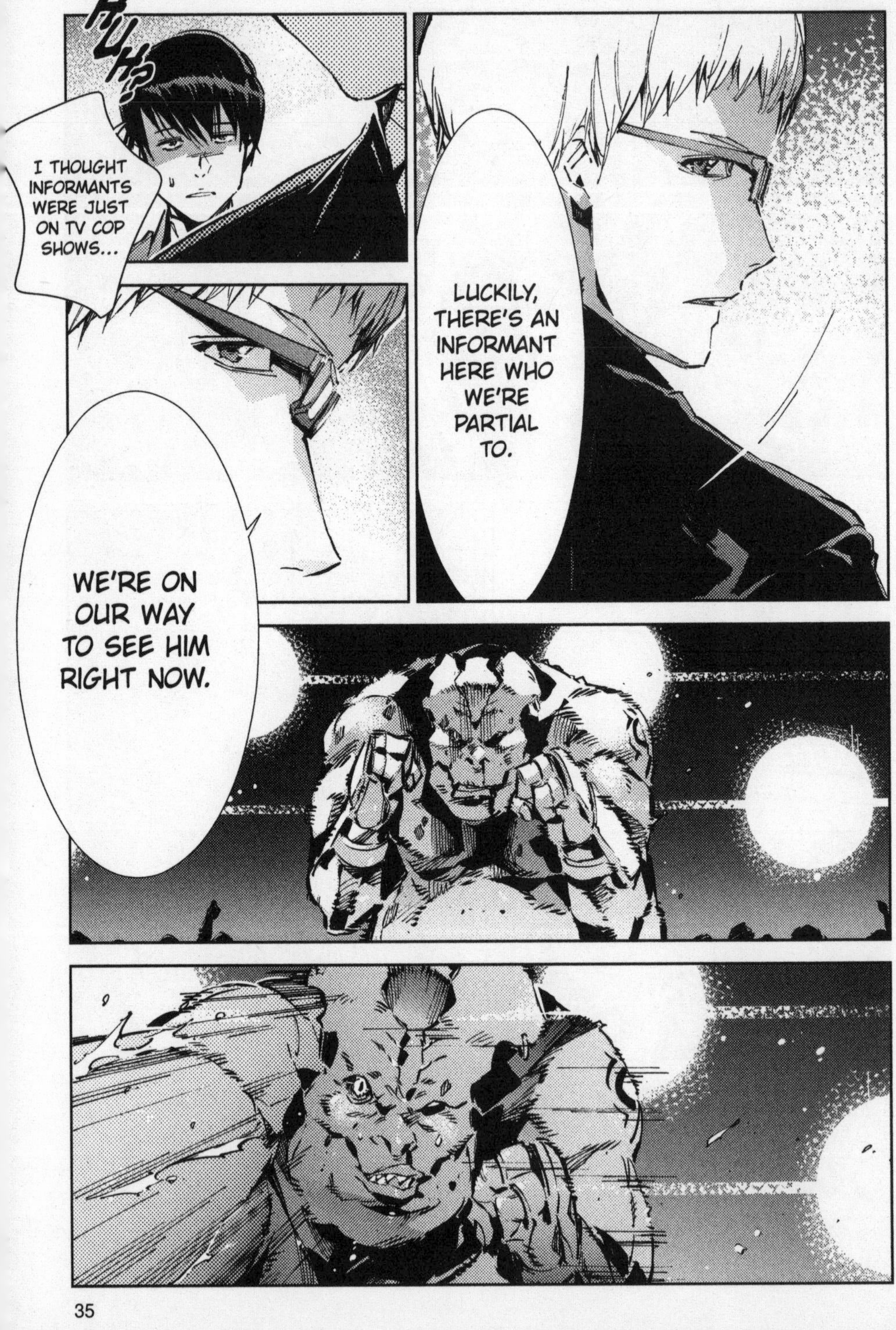
LUCKILY, THERE'S AN INFORMANT HERE WHO WE'RE PARTIAL TO.
HUH?
I THOUGHT INFORMANTS WERE JUST ON TV COP SHOWS...
WE'RE ON OUR WAY TO SEE HIM RIGHT NOW.

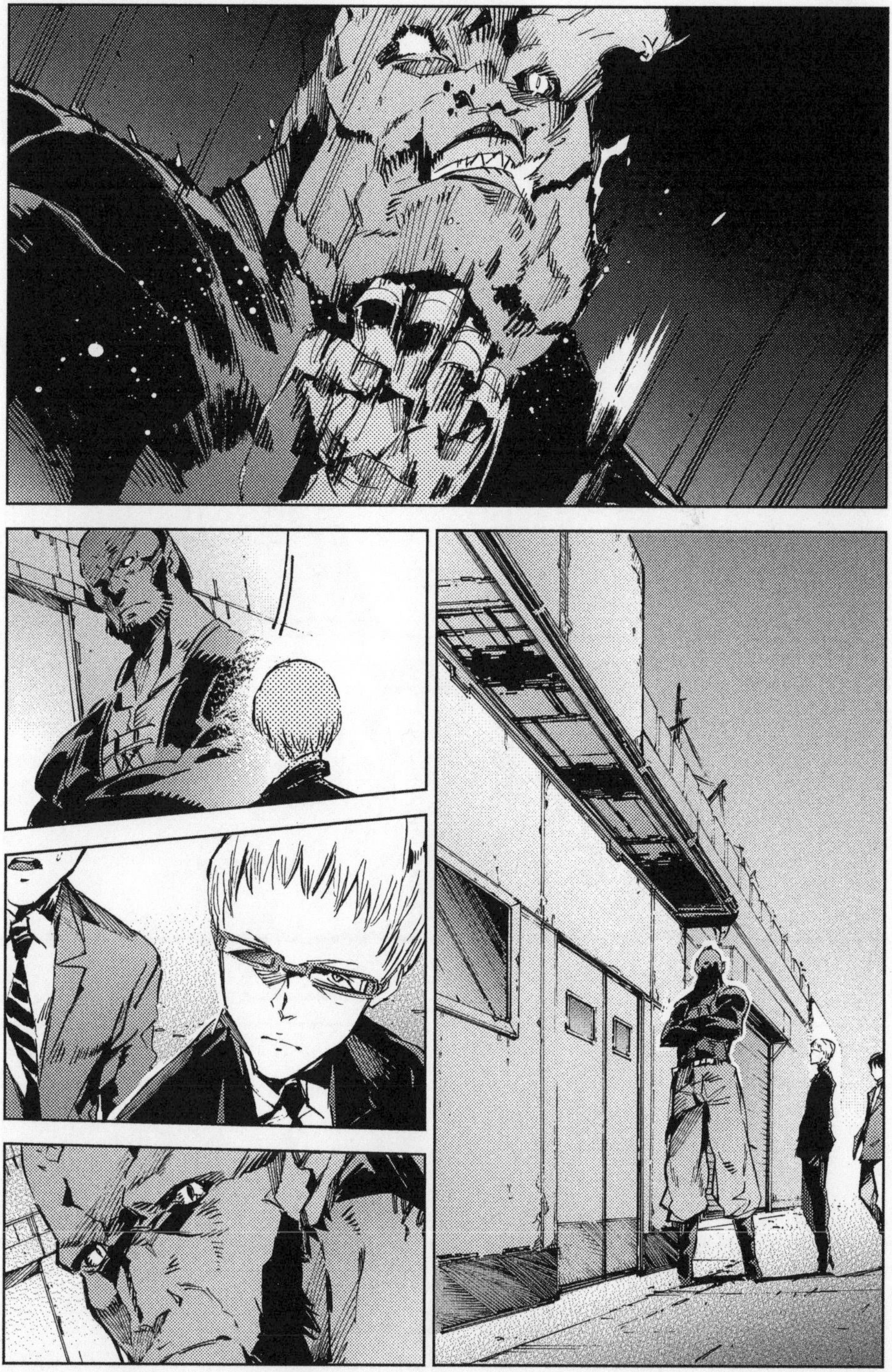

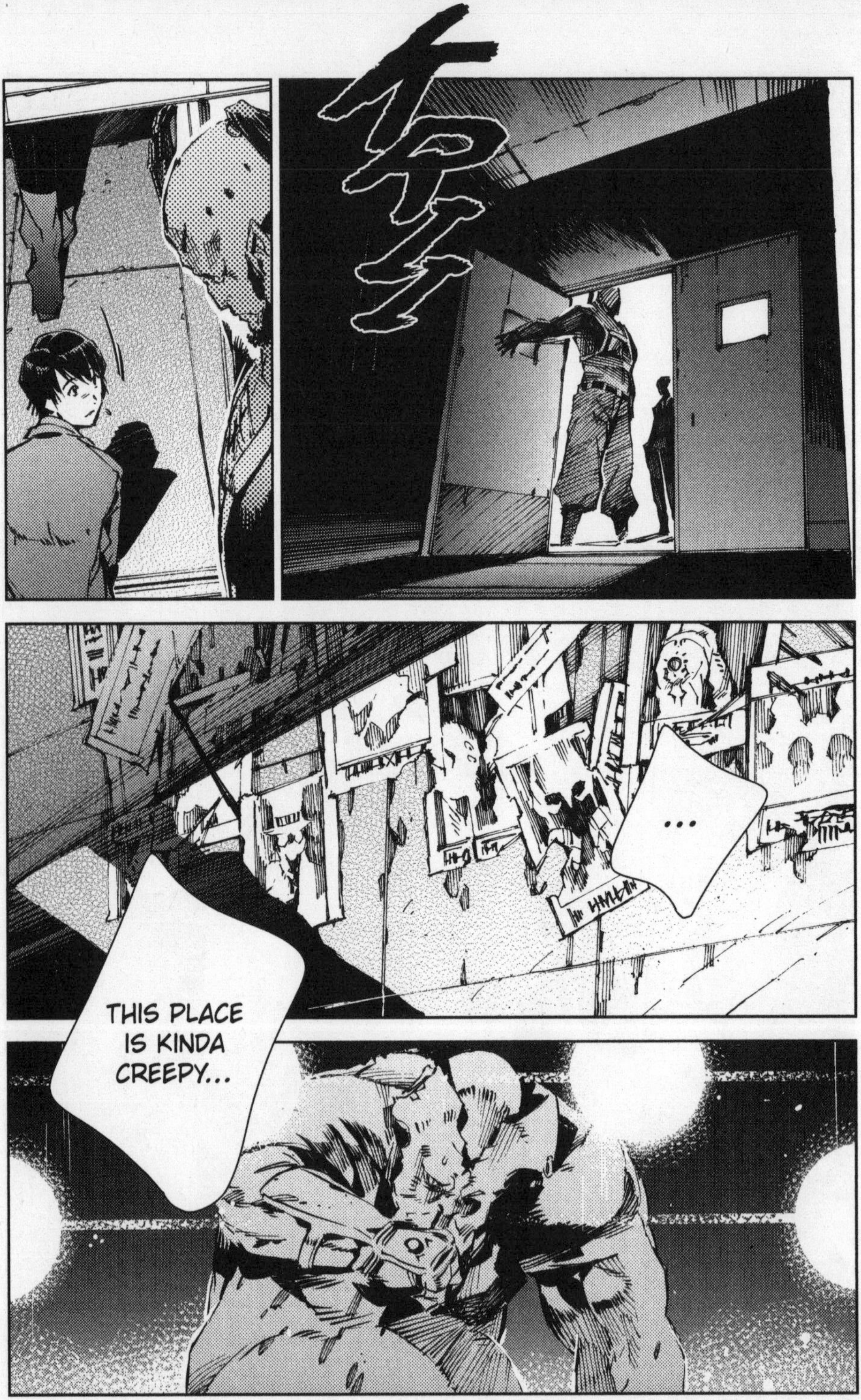
...
THIS PLACE IS KINDA CREEPY...

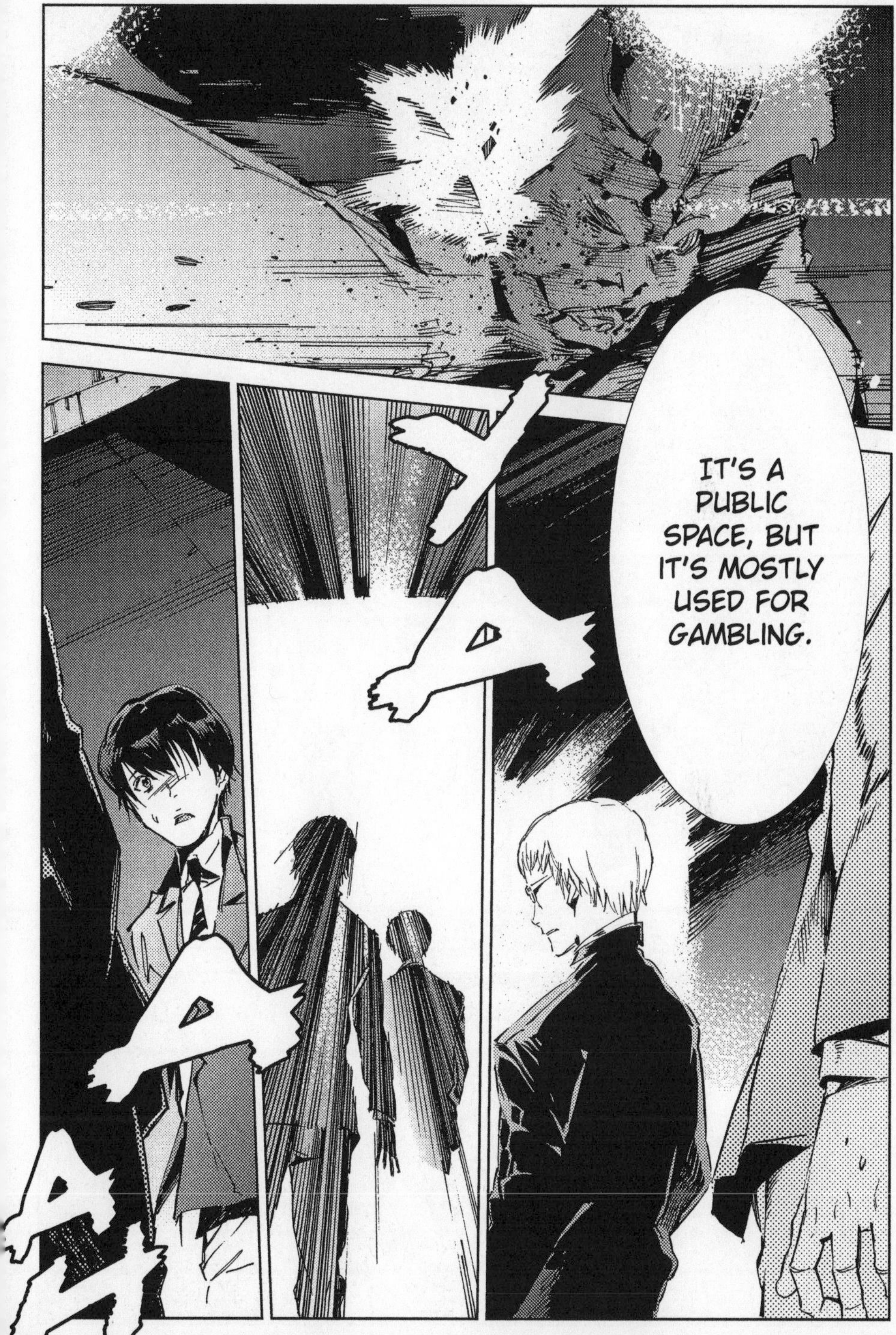
IT'S A PUBLIC SPACE, BUT IT'S MOSTLY USED FOR GAMBLING.

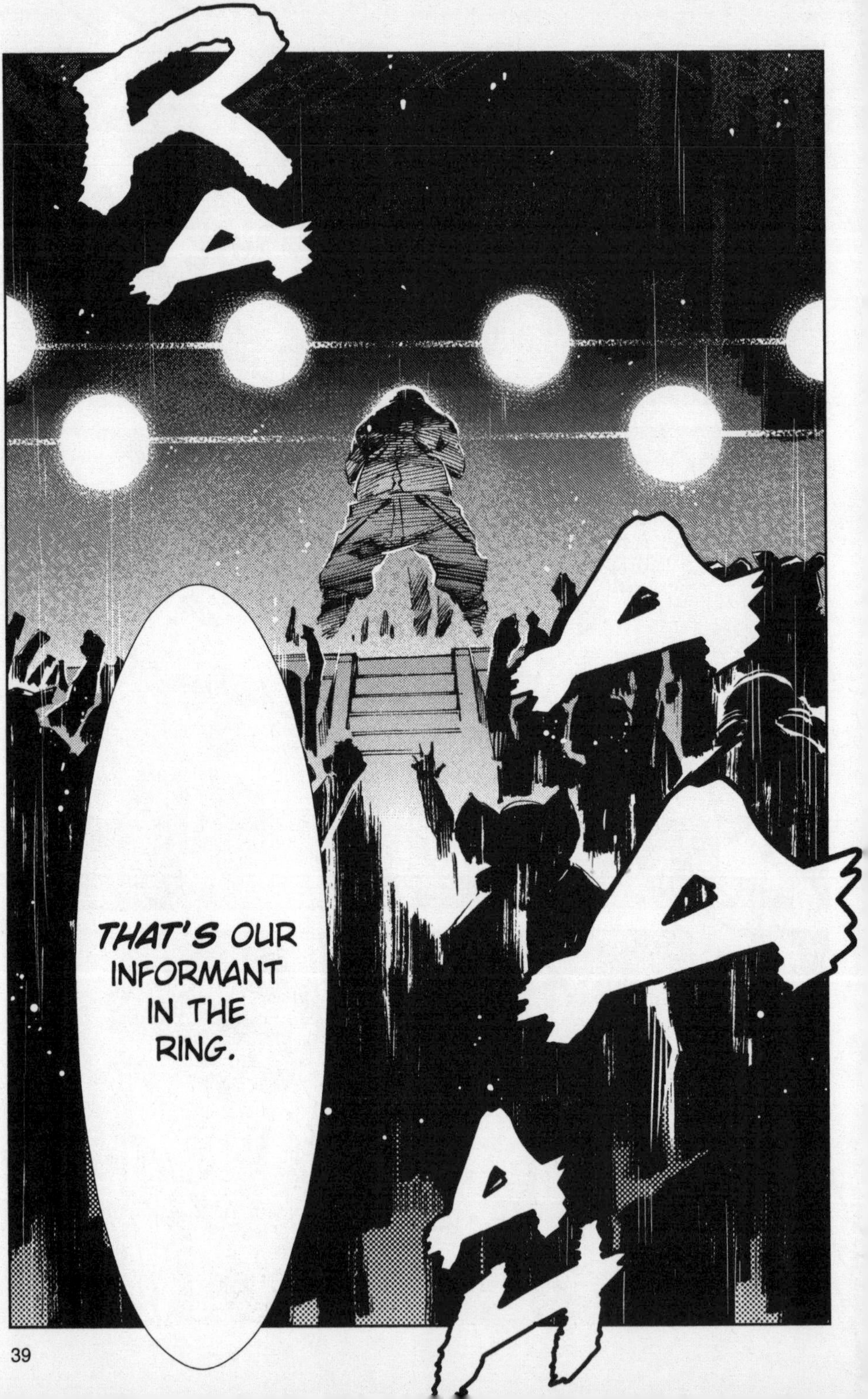
RAAAAA
THAT'S OUR INFORMANT IN THE RING.

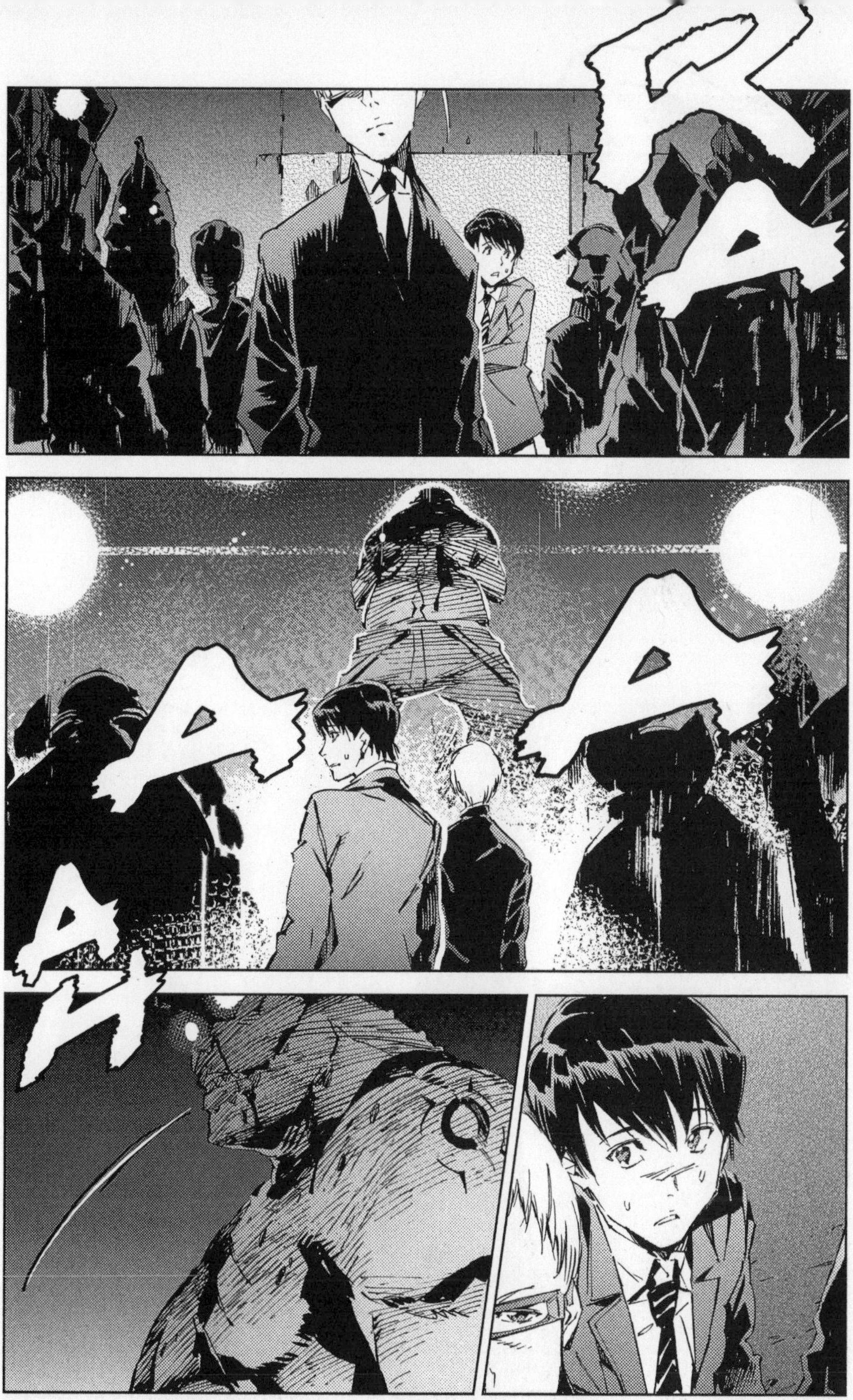

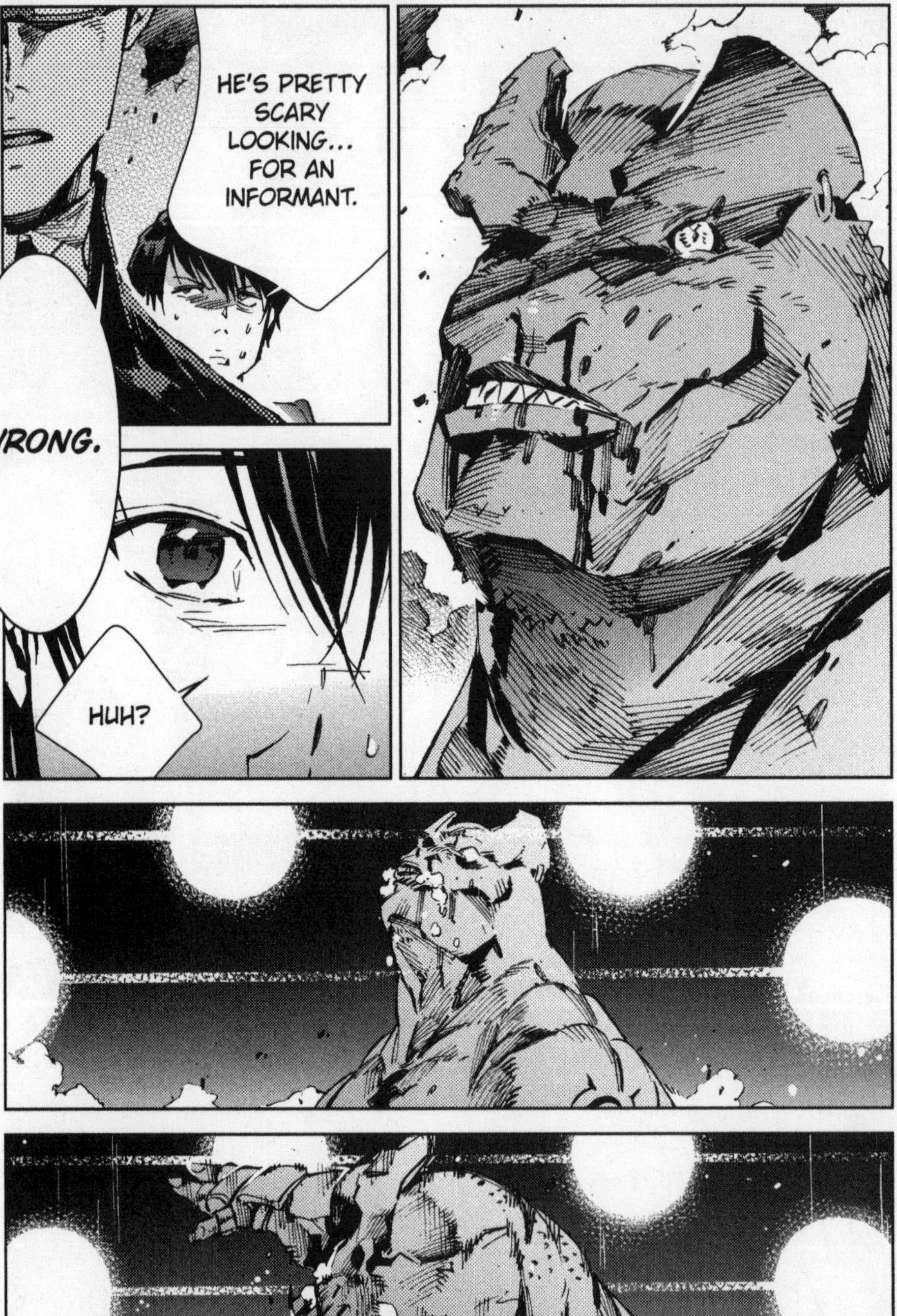
HE'S PRETTY SCARY LOOKING... FOR AN INFORMANT.
WRONG.
HUH?

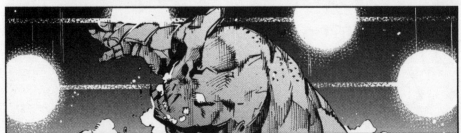

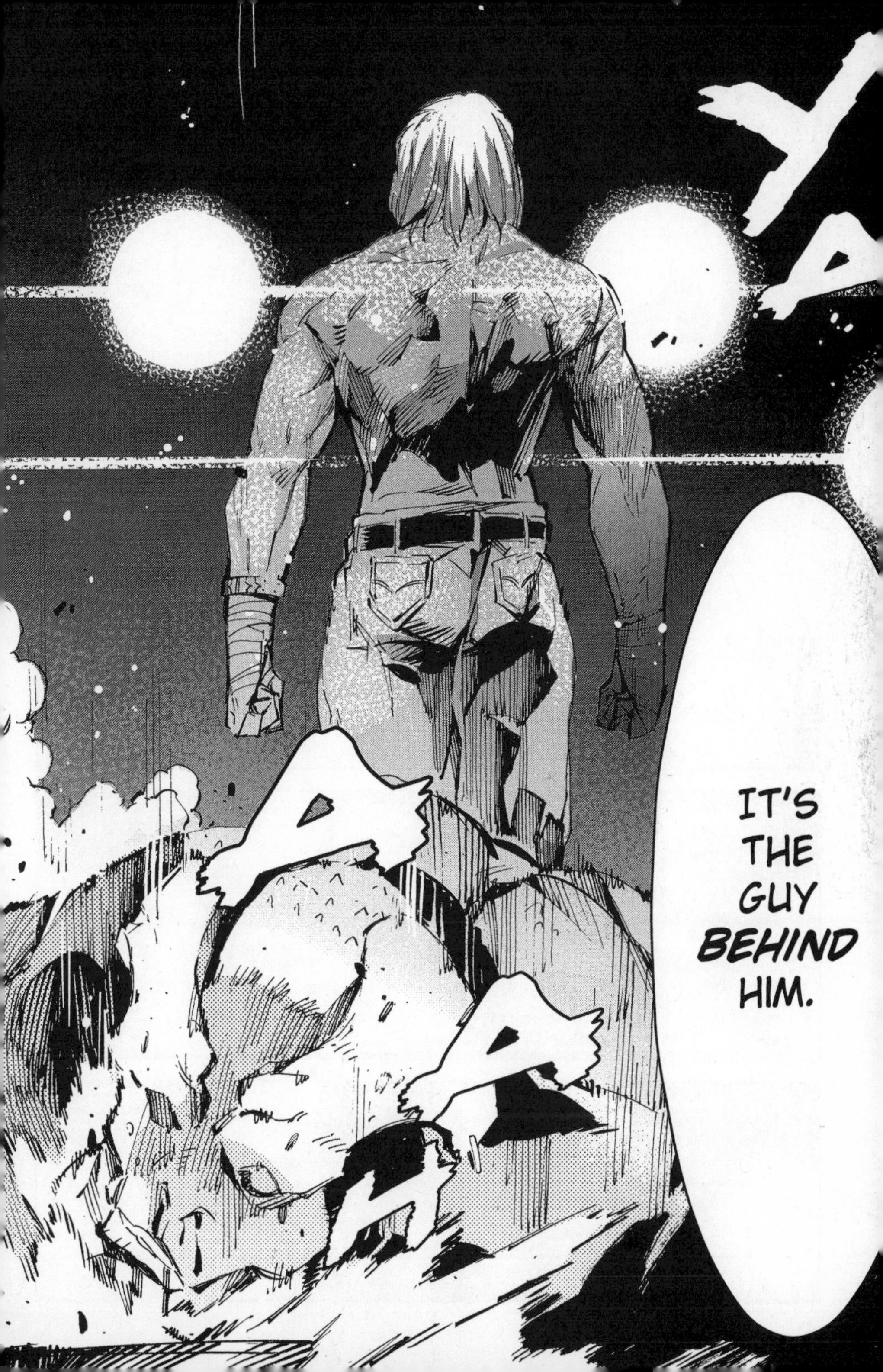
IT'S THE GUY *BEHIND* HIM.

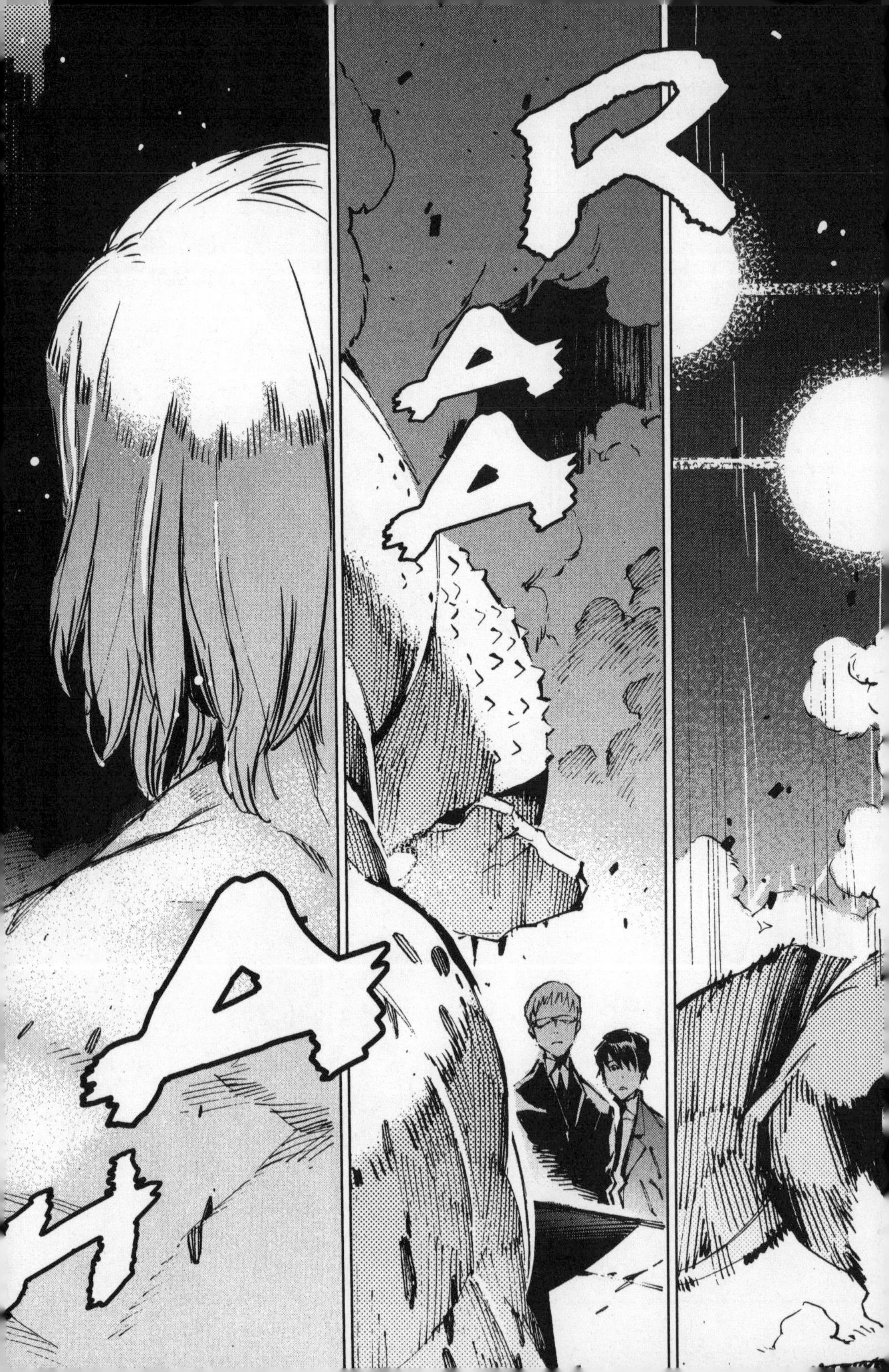

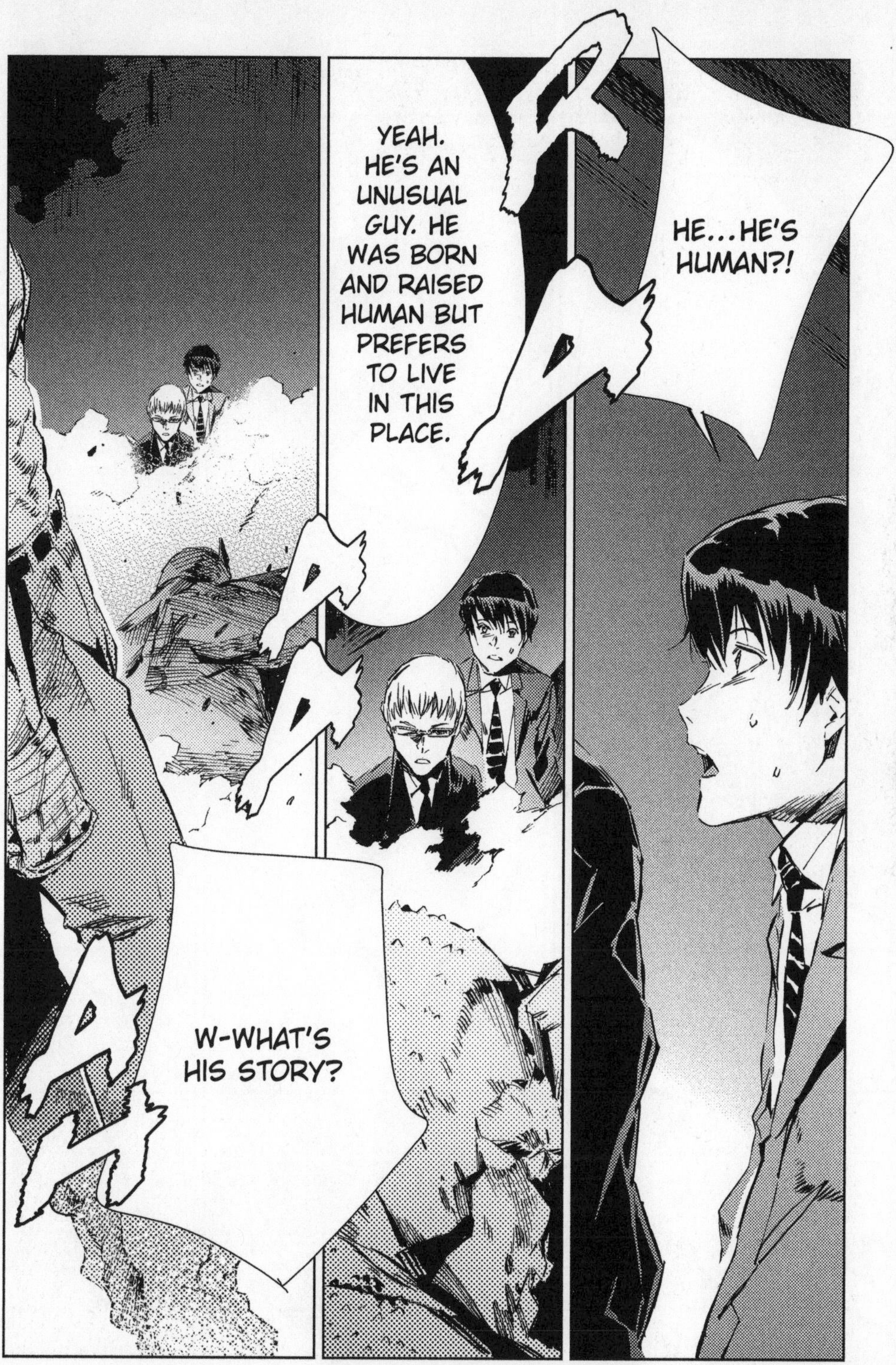
HE...HE'S HUMAN?!
YEAH. HE'S AN UNUSUAL GUY. HE WAS BORN AND RAISED HUMAN BUT PREFERS TO LIVE IN THIS PLACE.
W-WHAT'S HIS STORY?

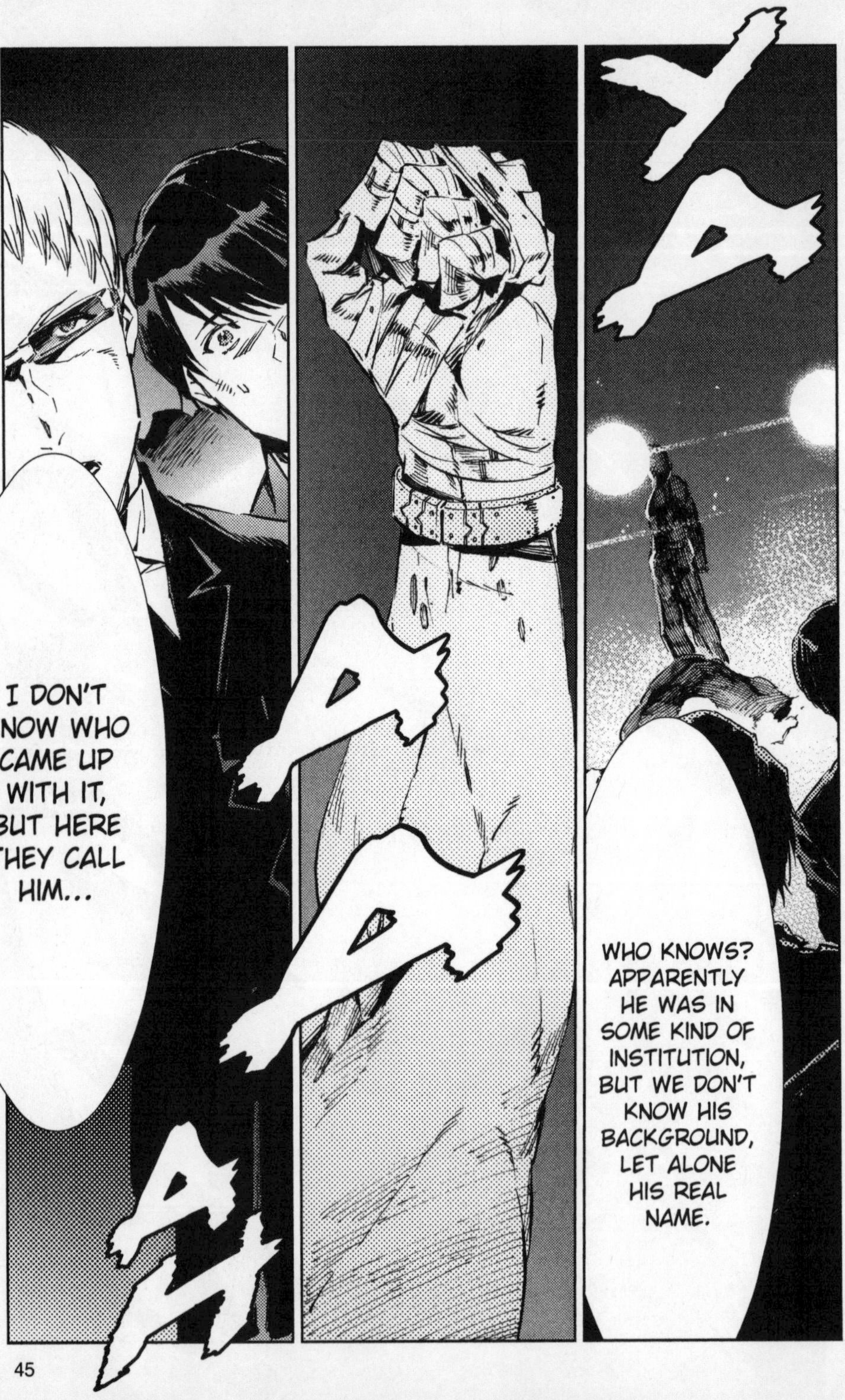
WHO KNOWS? APPARENTLY HE WAS IN SOME KIND OF INSTITUTION, BUT WE DON'T KNOW HIS BACKGROUND, LET ALONE HIS REAL NAME.
I DON'T KNOW WHO CAME UP WITH IT, BUT HERE THEY CALL HIM...

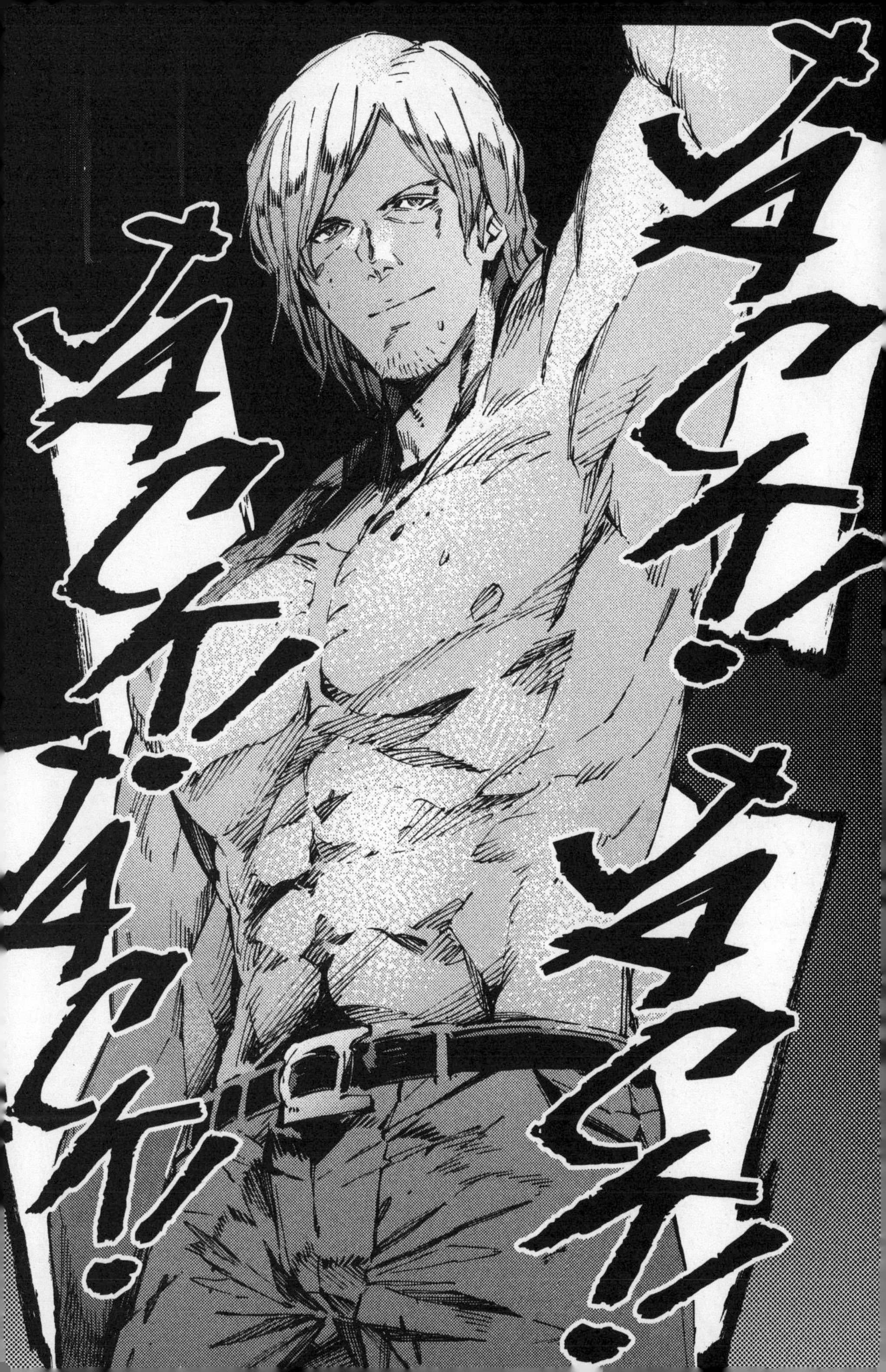
ジャクソン!ジャクソン!!
ジャクソン!ジャクソン!!

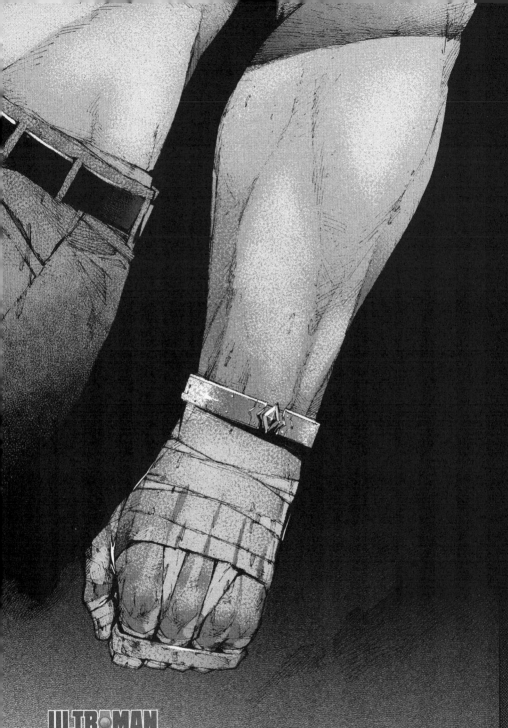

ULTRAMAN
CHAPTER 17 – TYRANT

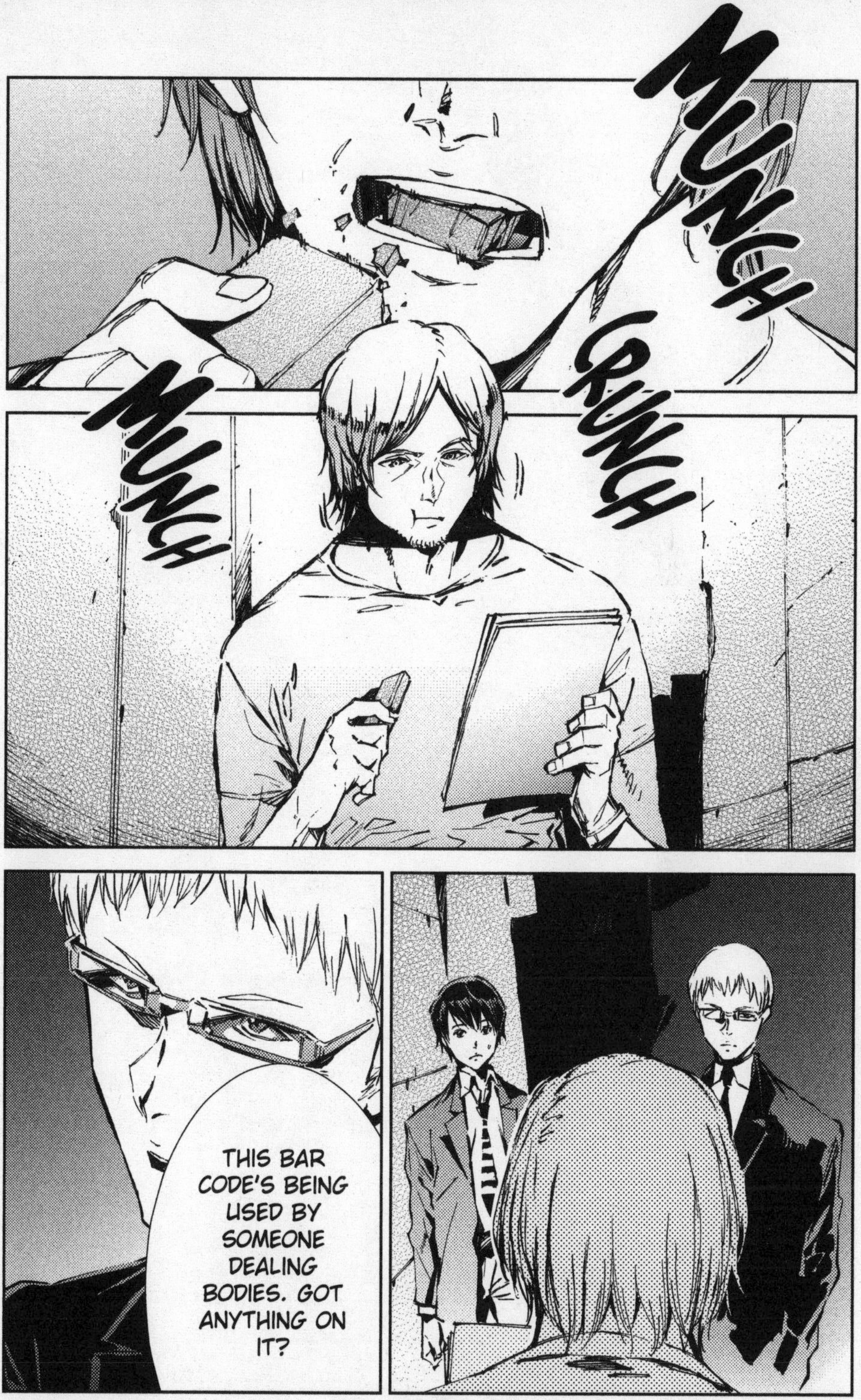
MUNCH
CRUNCH
MUNCH
THIS BAR CODE'S BEING USED BY SOMEONE DEALING BODIES. GOT ANYTHING ON IT?

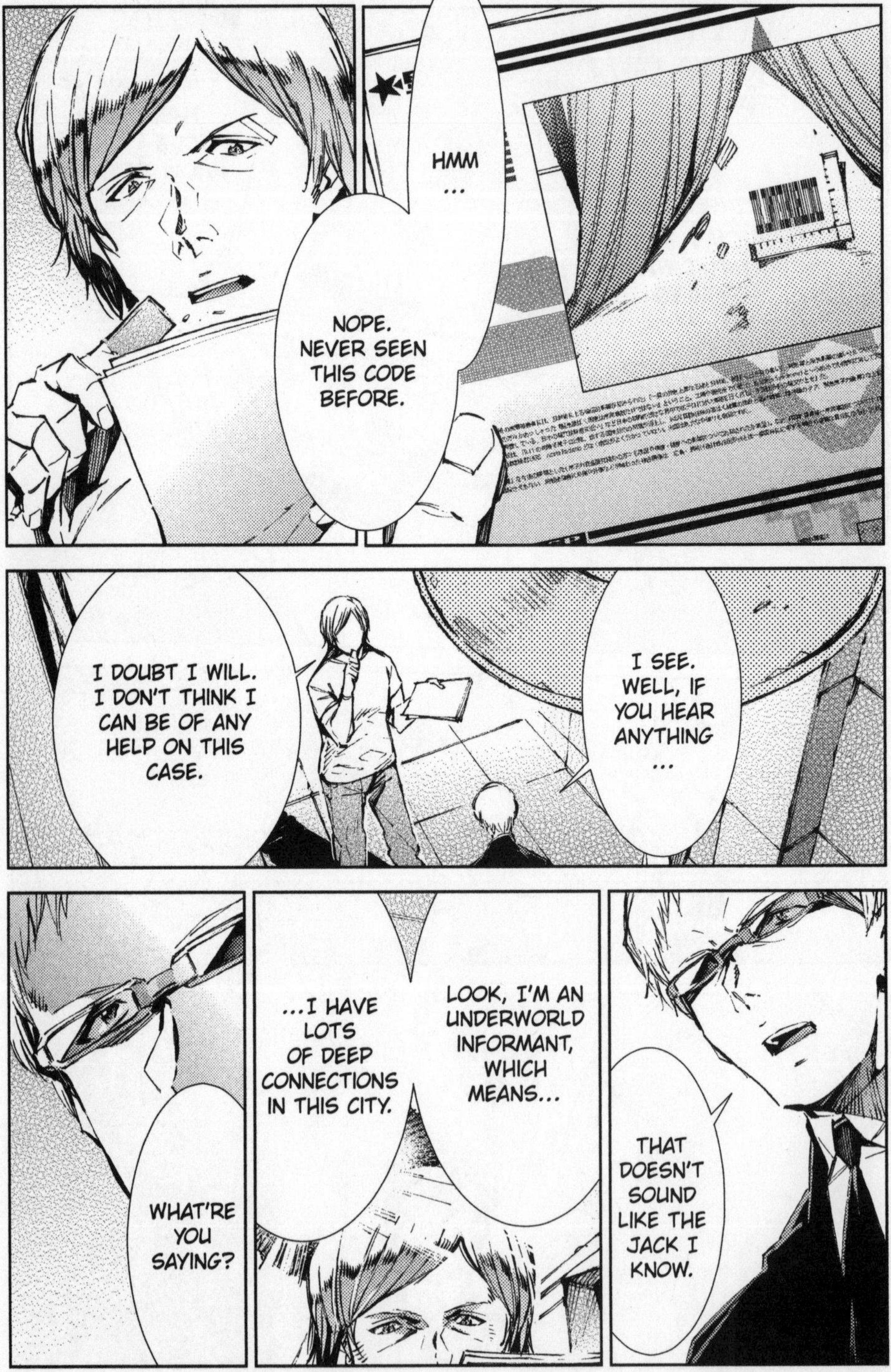
HMM ...
NOPE. NEVER SEEN THIS CODE BEFORE.
I SEE. WELL, IF YOU HEAR ANYTHING ...
I DOUBT I WILL. I DON'T THINK I CAN BE OF ANY HELP ON THIS CASE.
THAT DOESN'T SOUND LIKE THE JACK I KNOW.
LOOK, I'M AN UNDERWORLD INFORMANT, WHICH MEANS...
...I HAVE LOTS OF DEEP CONNECTIONS IN THIS CITY.
WHAT'RE YOU SAYING?

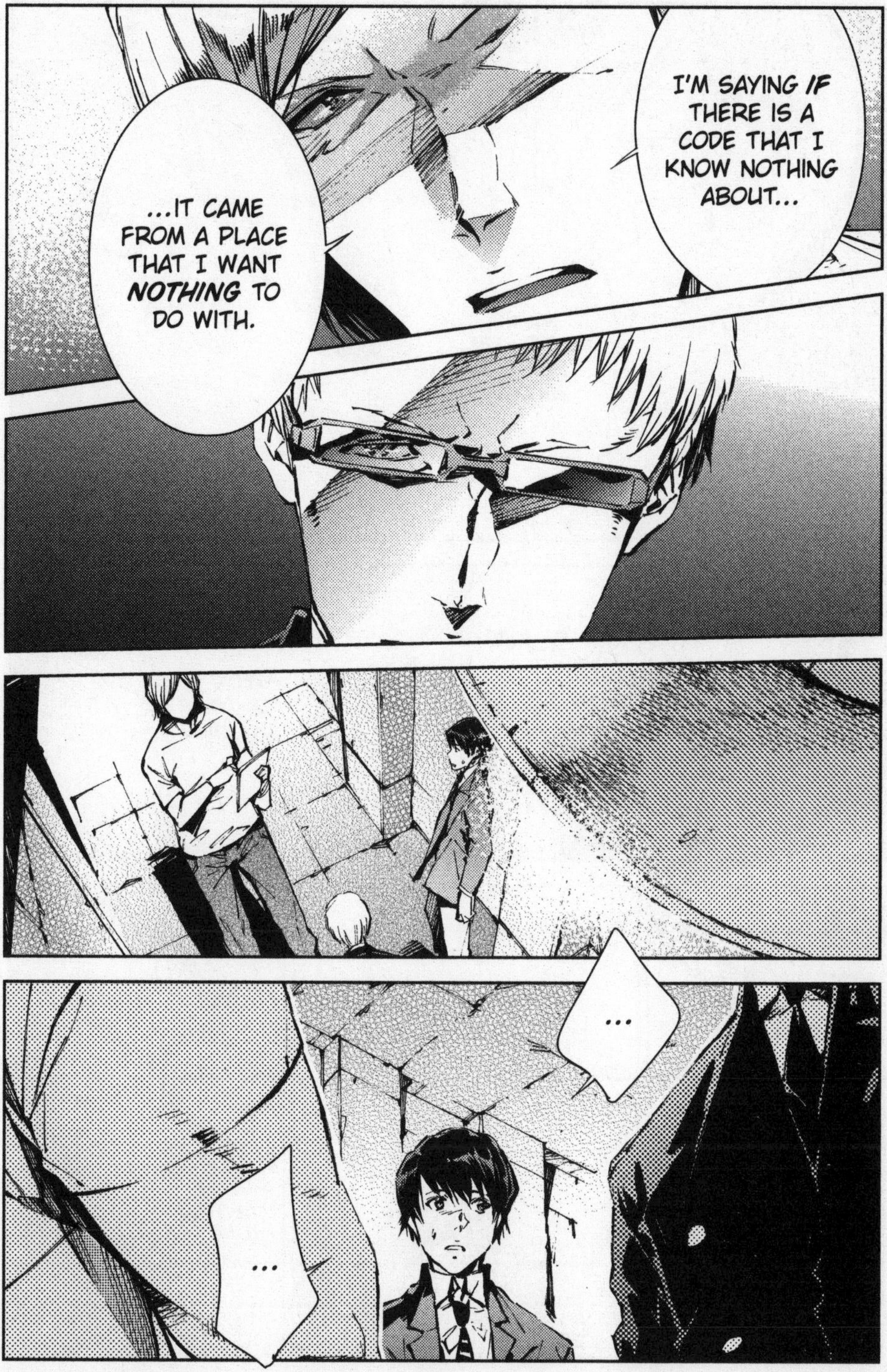
I'M SAYING *IF* THERE IS A CODE THAT I KNOW NOTHING ABOUT...
...IT CAME FROM A PLACE THAT I WANT ***NOTHING*** TO DO WITH.
...
...

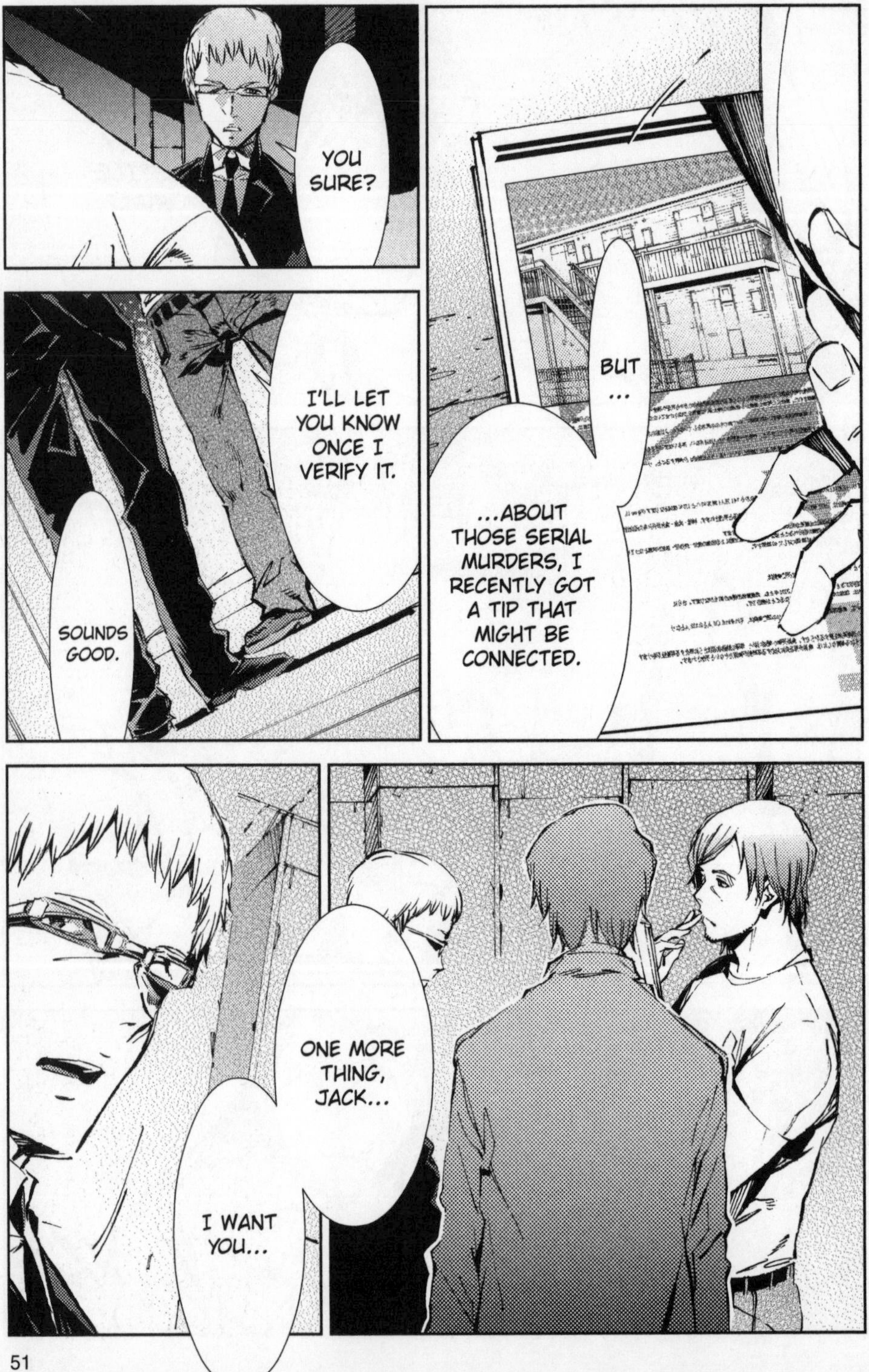
BUT ...
...ABOUT THOSE SERIAL MURDERS, I RECENTLY GOT A TIP THAT MIGHT BE CONNECTED.
YOU SURE?
I'LL LET YOU KNOW ONCE I VERIFY IT.
SOUNDS GOOD.
ONE MORE THING, JACK...
I WANT YOU...

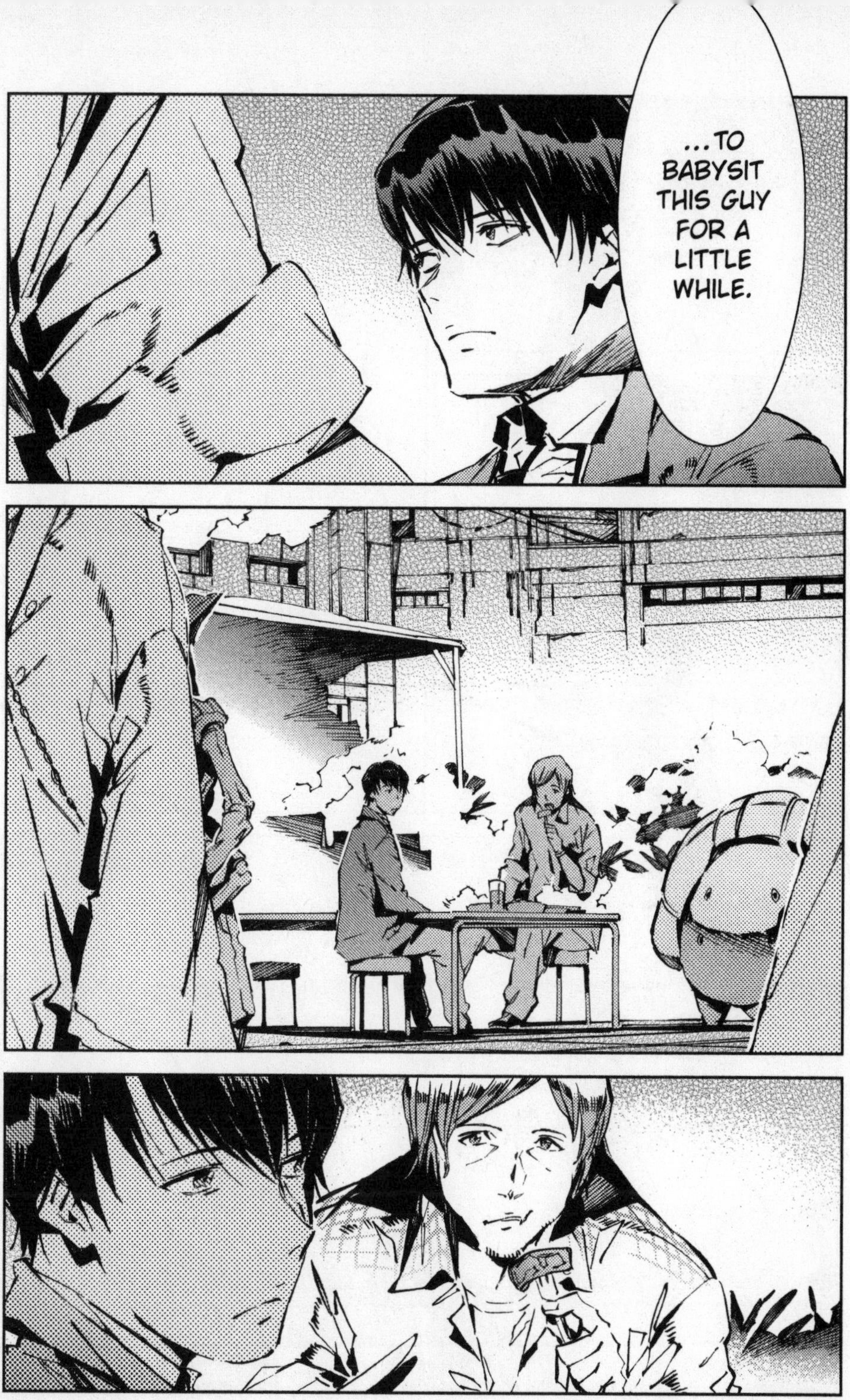
...TO BABYSIT THIS GUY FOR A LITTLE WHILE.

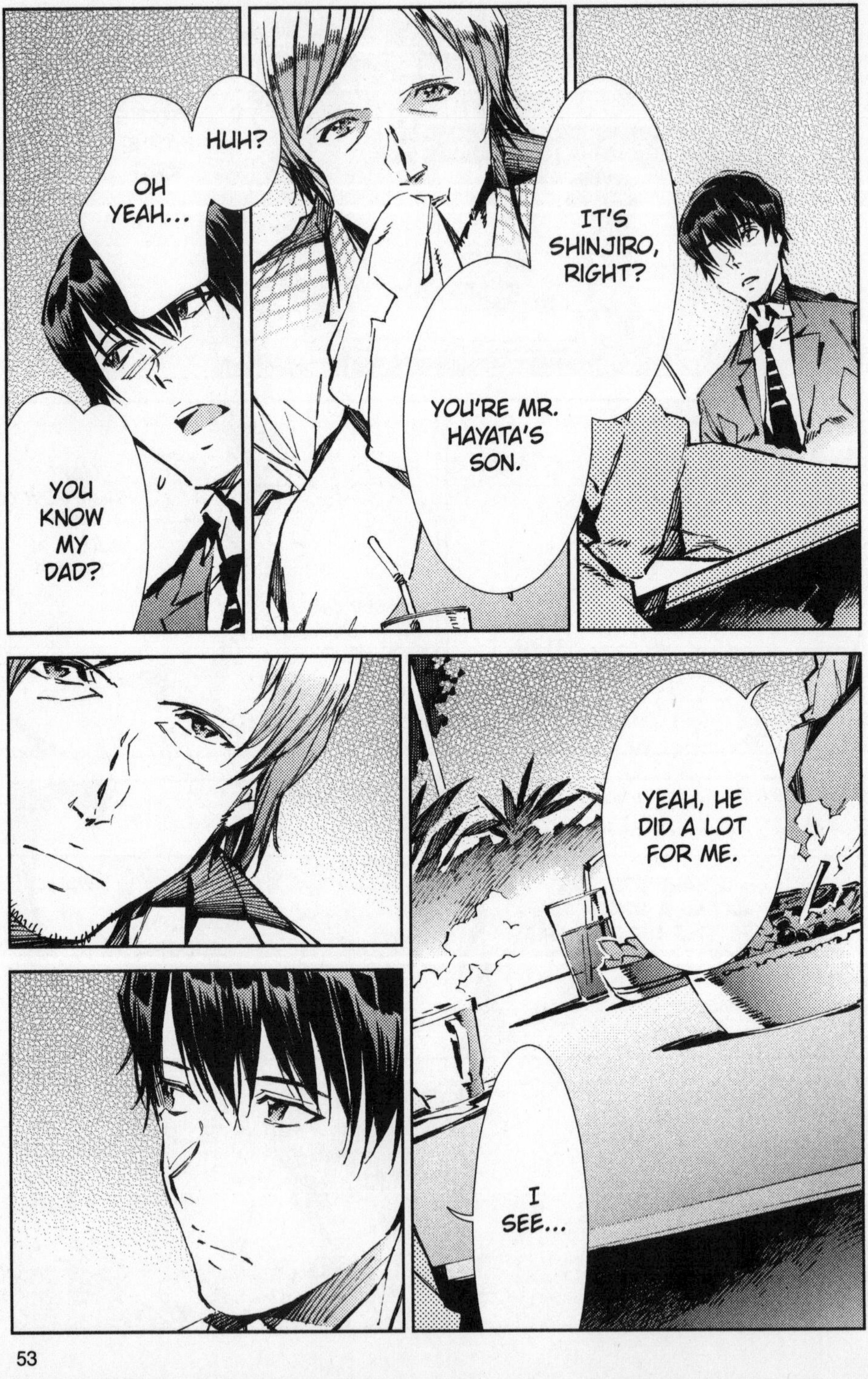
IT'S SHINJIRO, RIGHT?
YOU'RE MR. HAYATA'S SON.
HUH? OH YEAH...
YOU KNOW MY DAD?
YEAH, HE DID A LOT FOR ME.
I SEE...

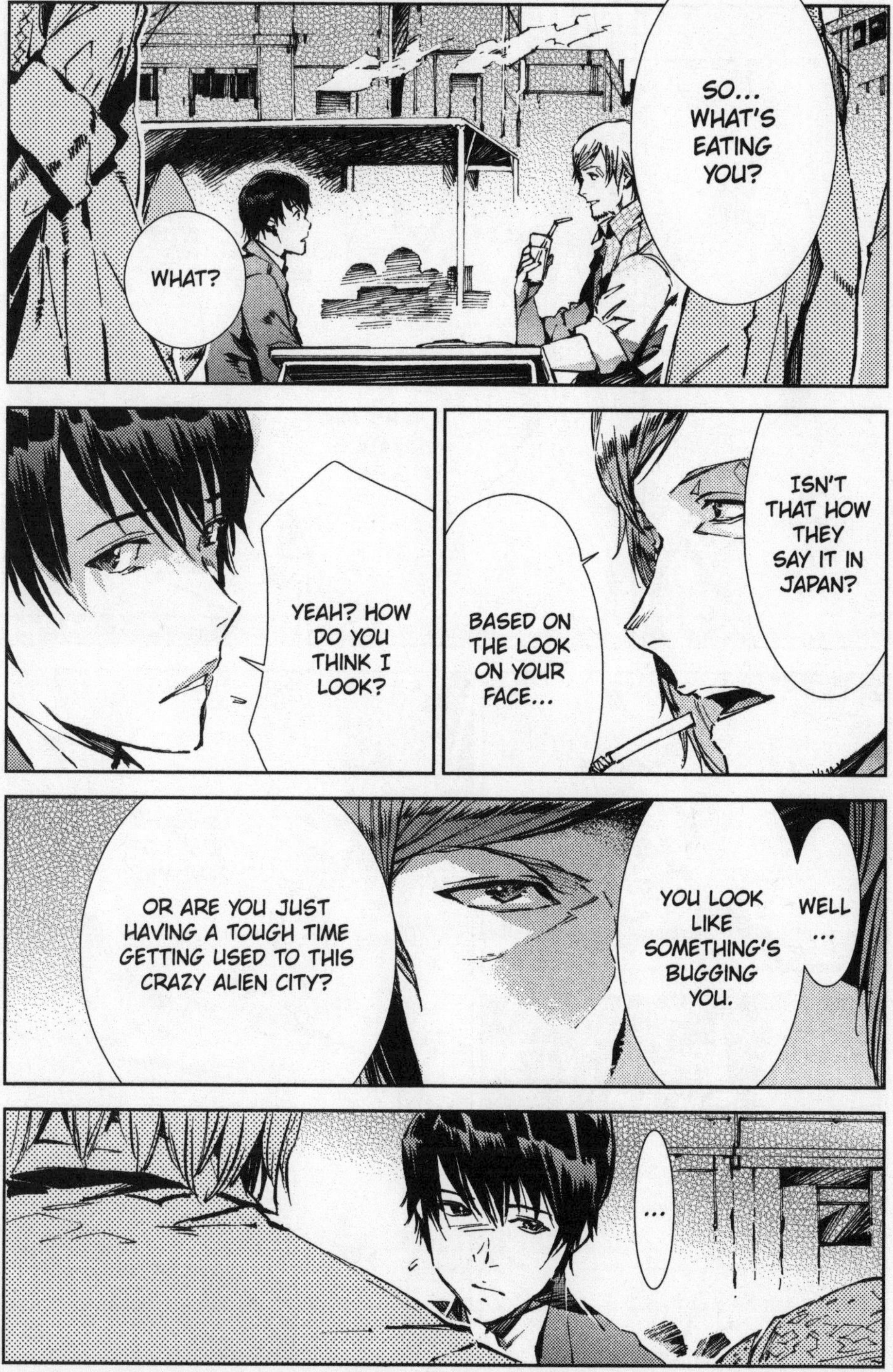
SO... WHAT'S EATING YOU?
WHAT?
ISN'T THAT HOW THEY SAY IT IN JAPAN?
BASED ON THE LOOK ON YOUR FACE...
YEAH? HOW DO YOU THINK I LOOK?
WELL...
YOU LOOK LIKE SOMETHING'S BUGGING YOU.
OR ARE YOU JUST HAVING A TOUGH TIME GETTING USED TO THIS CRAZY ALIEN CITY?
...

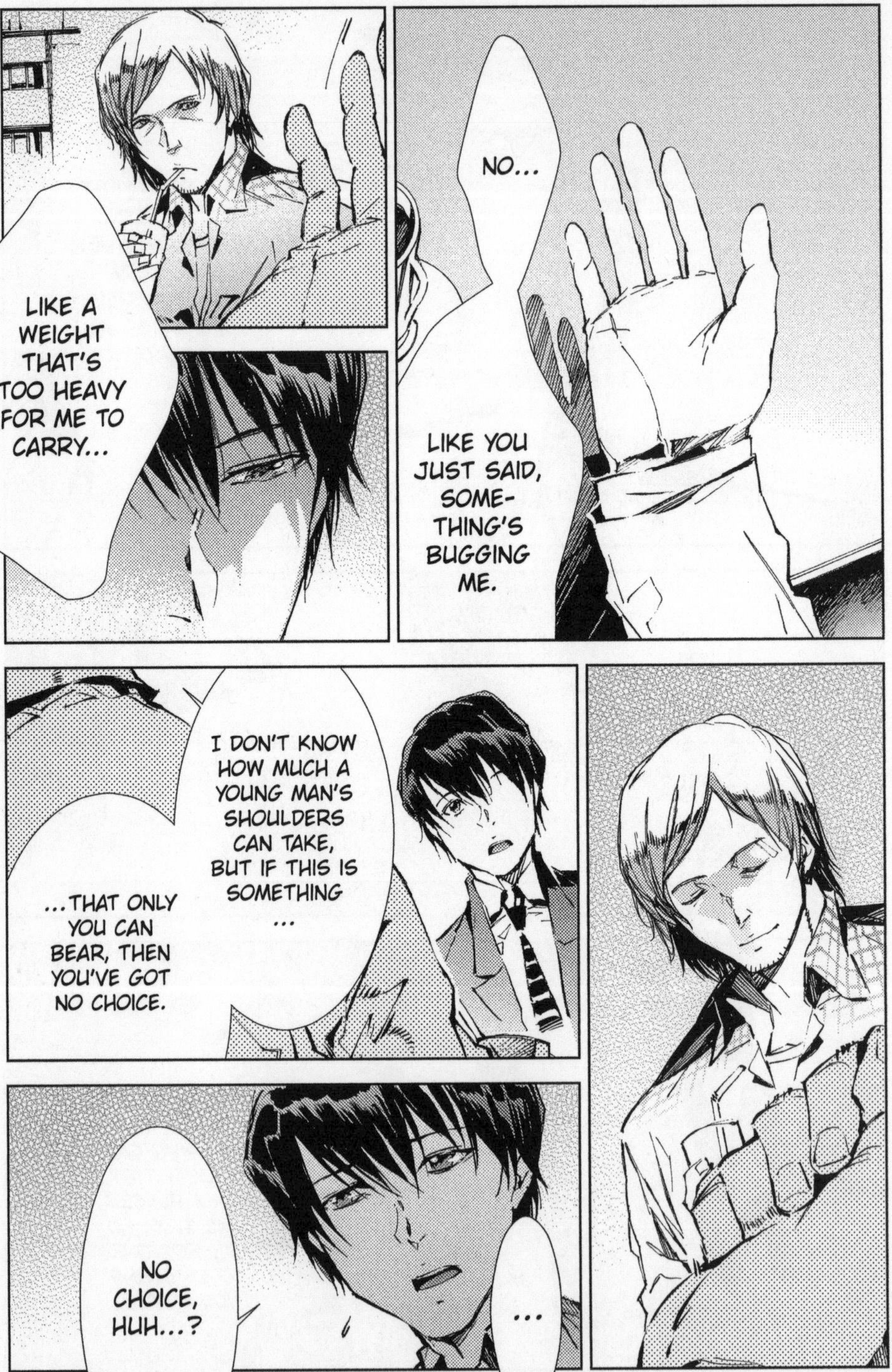
NO...
LIKE YOU JUST SAID, SOME-THING'S BUGGING ME.
LIKE A WEIGHT THAT'S TOO HEAVY FOR ME TO CARRY...
I DON'T KNOW HOW MUCH A YOUNG MAN'S SHOULDERS CAN TAKE, BUT IF THIS IS SOMETHING ...
...THAT ONLY YOU CAN BEAR, THEN YOU'VE GOT NO CHOICE.
...
NO CHOICE, HUH...?

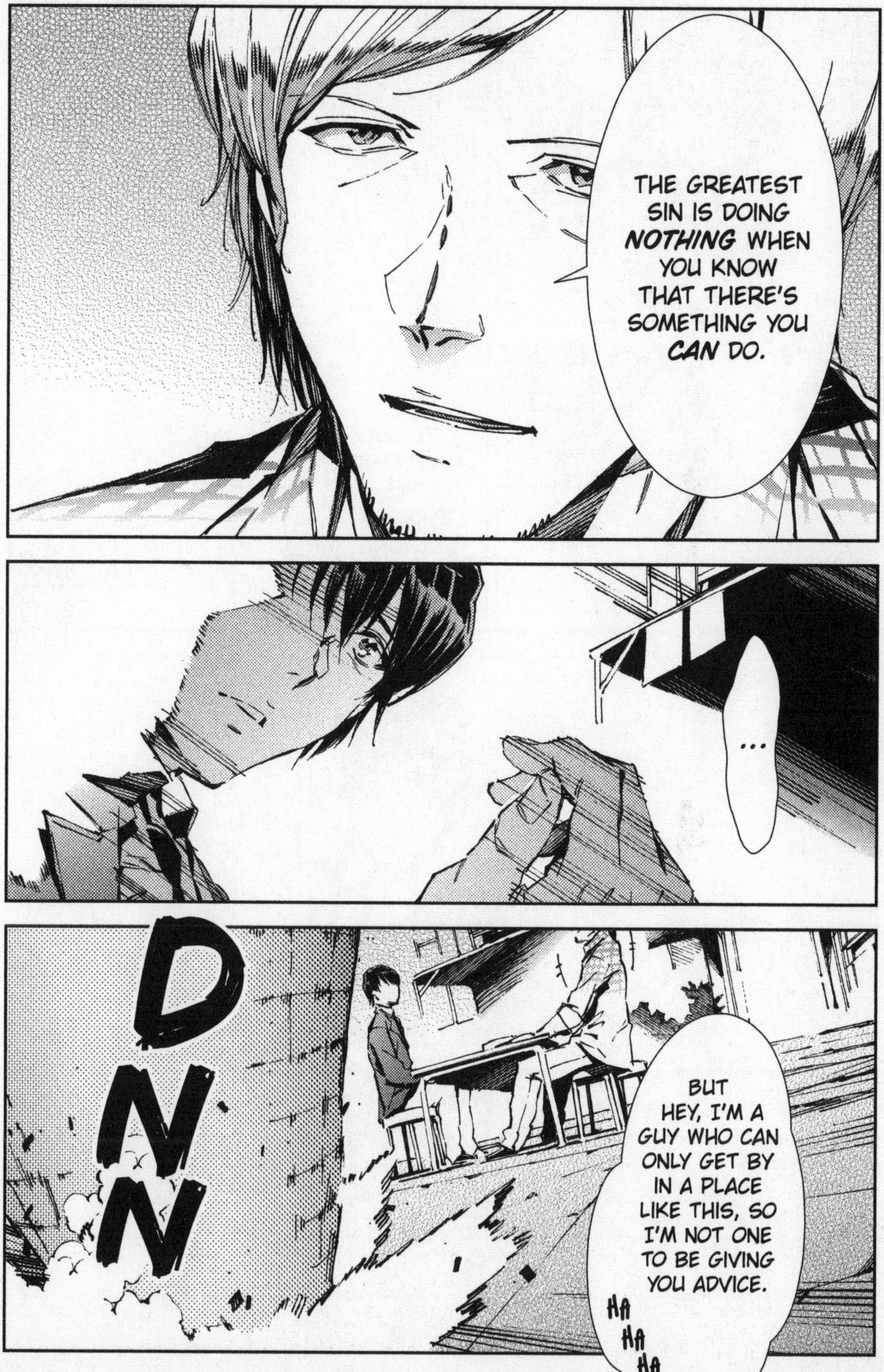
THE GREATEST SIN IS DOING NOTHING WHEN YOU KNOW THAT THERE'S SOMETHING YOU CAN DO.
...
DNN
BUT HEY, I'M A GUY WHO CAN ONLY GET BY IN A PLACE LIKE THIS, SO I'M NOT ONE TO BE GIVING YOU ADVICE.
HA HA HA HA HA

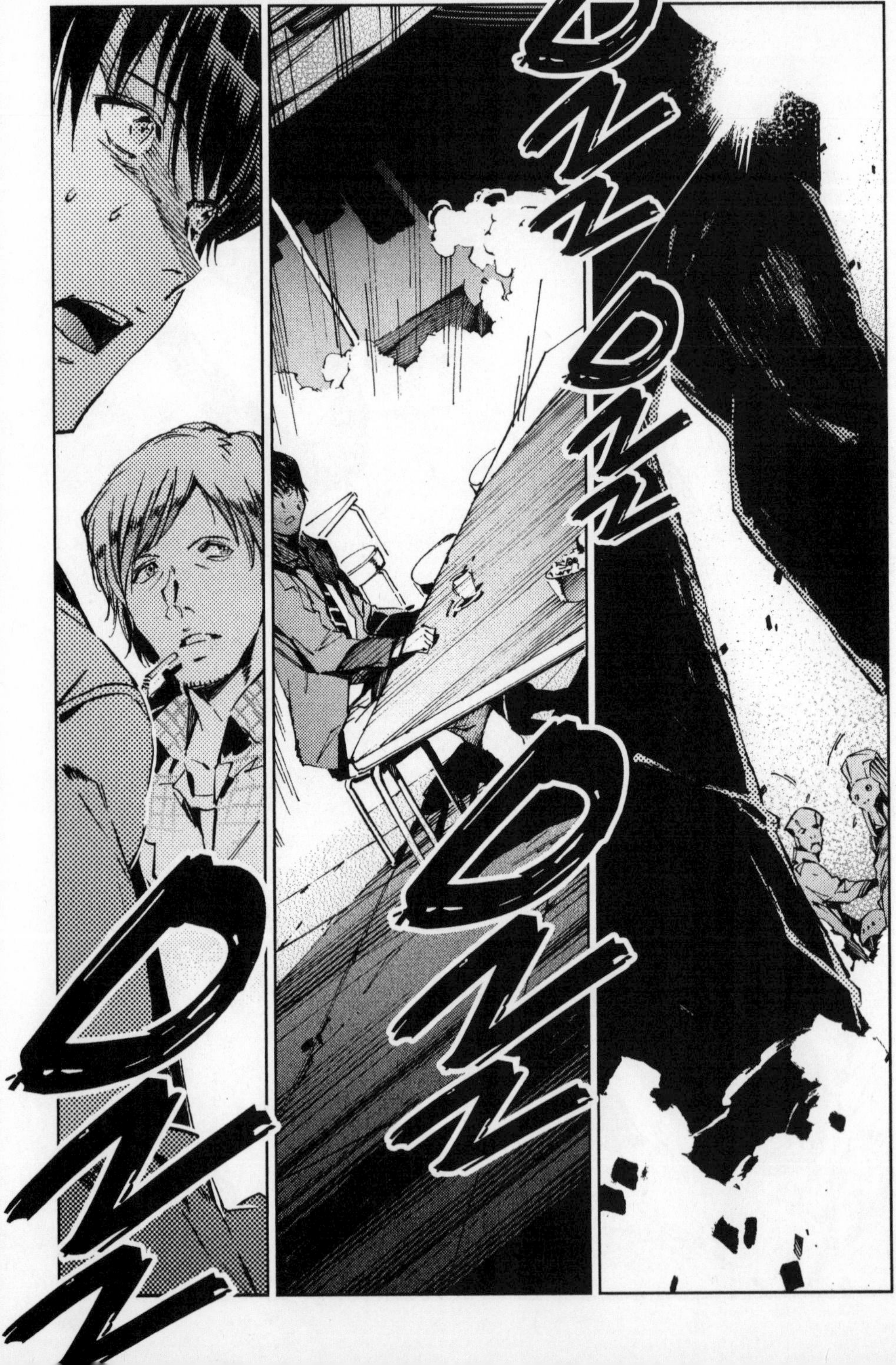
DNN
DNN
DNN
DNN

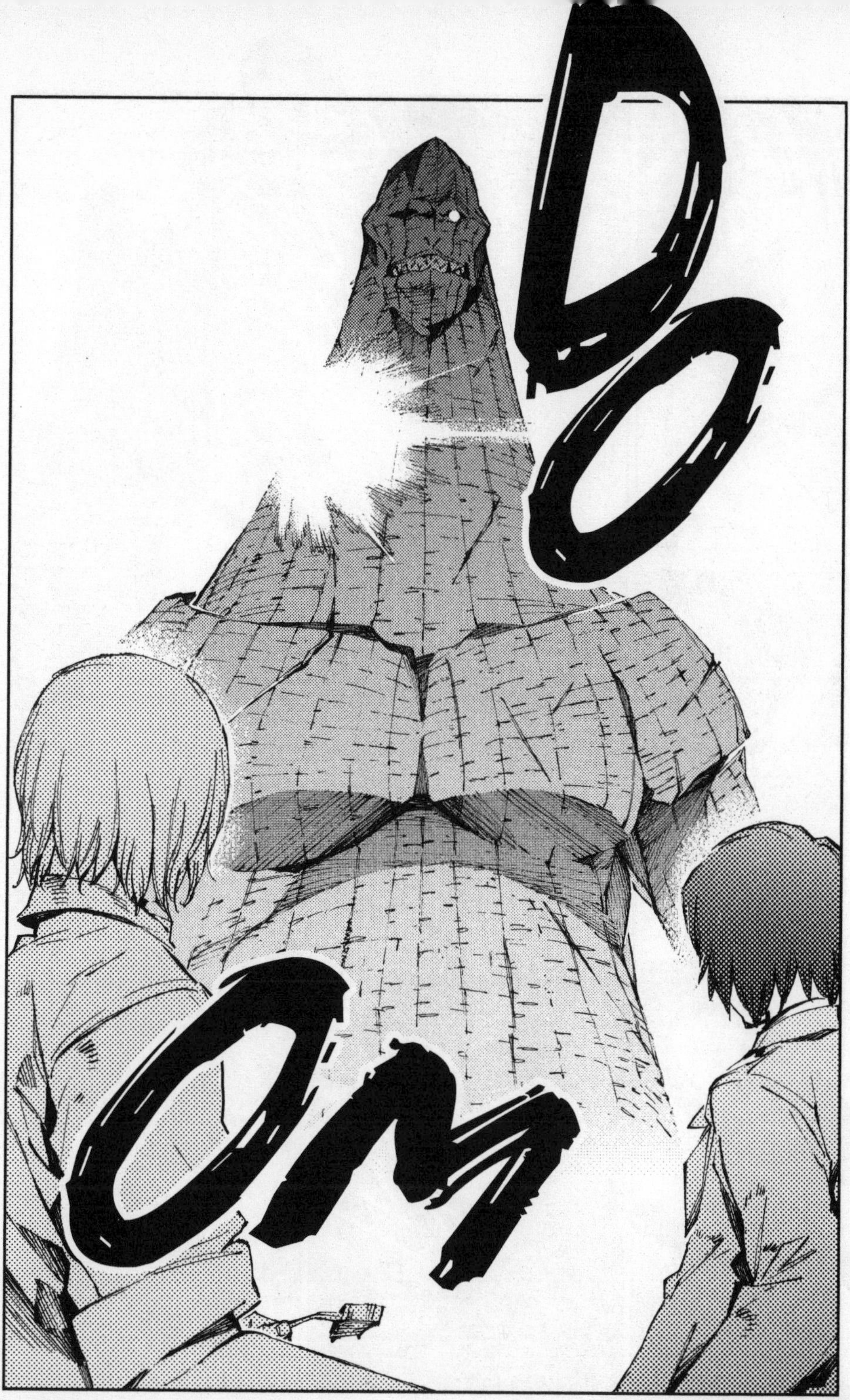
DOOM

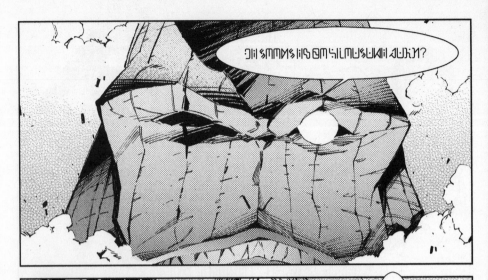

WELL, WELL ...

IF IT ISN'T RED, THE FORMER CHAMP!

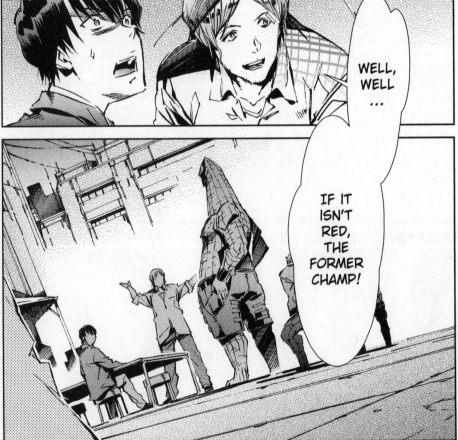

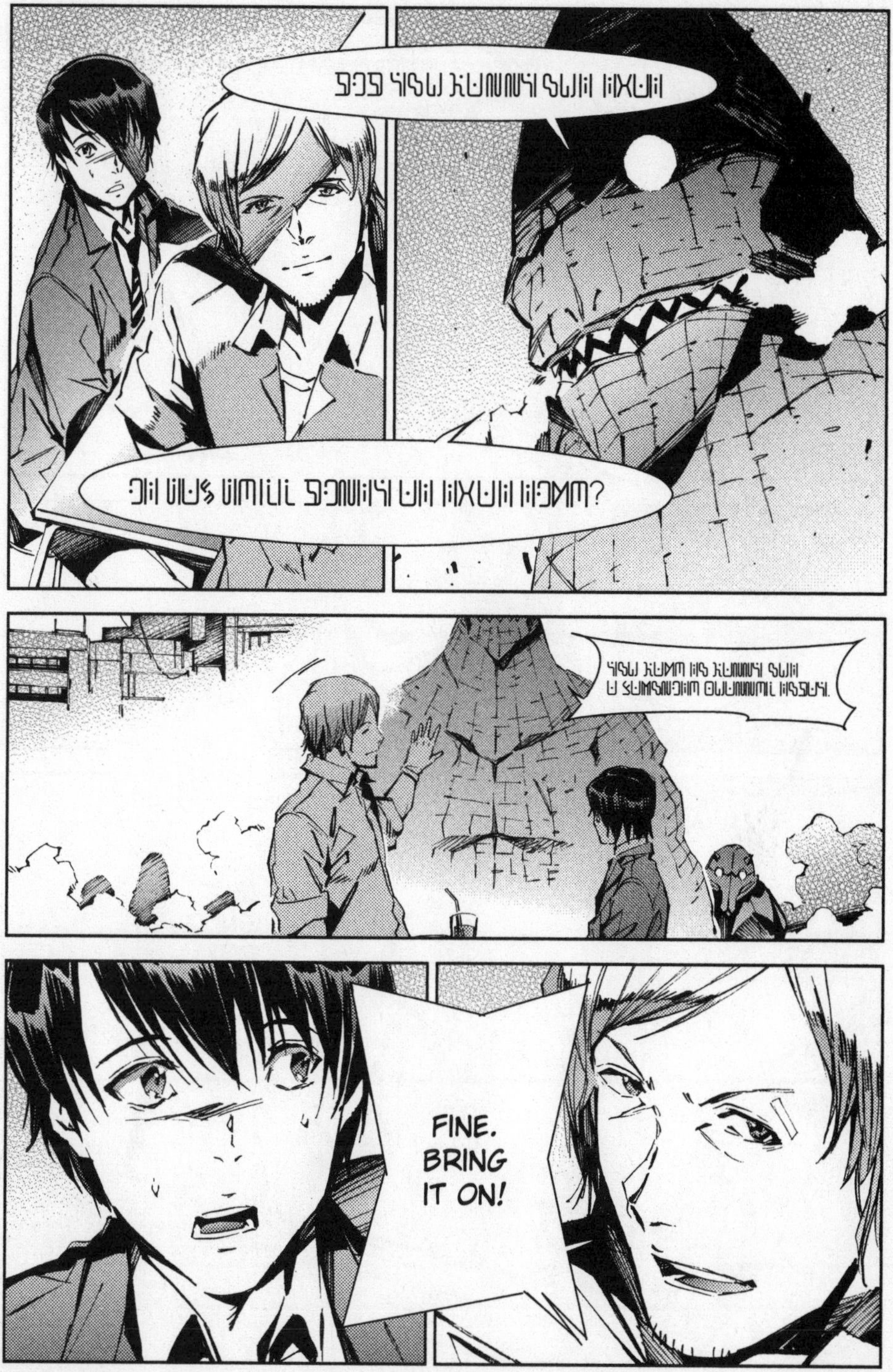
FINE. BRING IT ON!

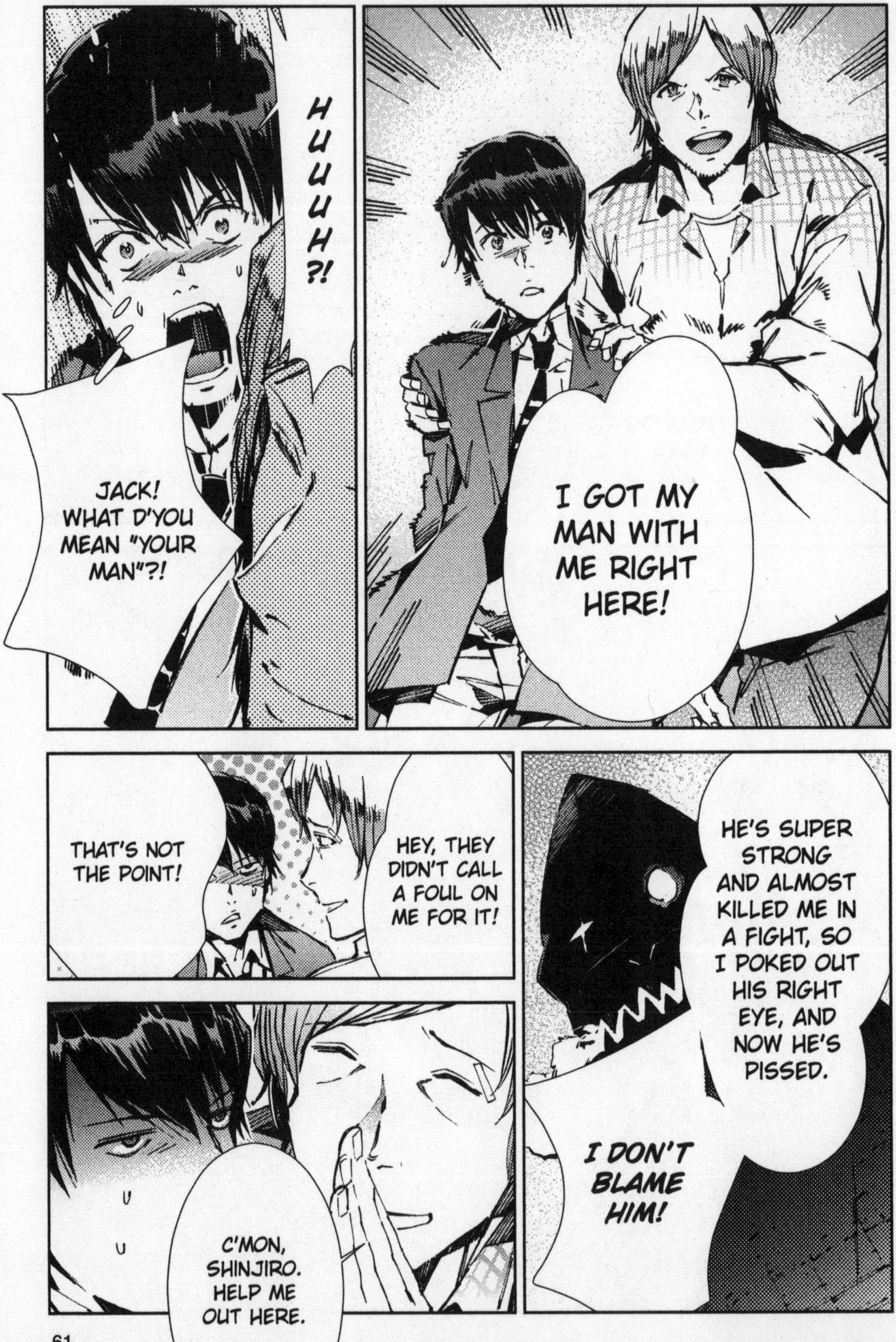
I GOT MY MAN WITH ME RIGHT HERE!
HUUUUH?!
JACK! WHAT D'YOU MEAN "YOUR MAN"?!
HE'S SUPER STRONG AND ALMOST KILLED ME IN A FIGHT, SO I POKED OUT HIS RIGHT EYE, AND NOW HE'S PISSED.
I DON'T BLAME HIM!
HEY, THEY DIDN'T CALL A FOUL ON ME FOR IT!
THAT'S NOT THE POINT!
C'MON, SHINJIRO. HELP ME OUT HERE.

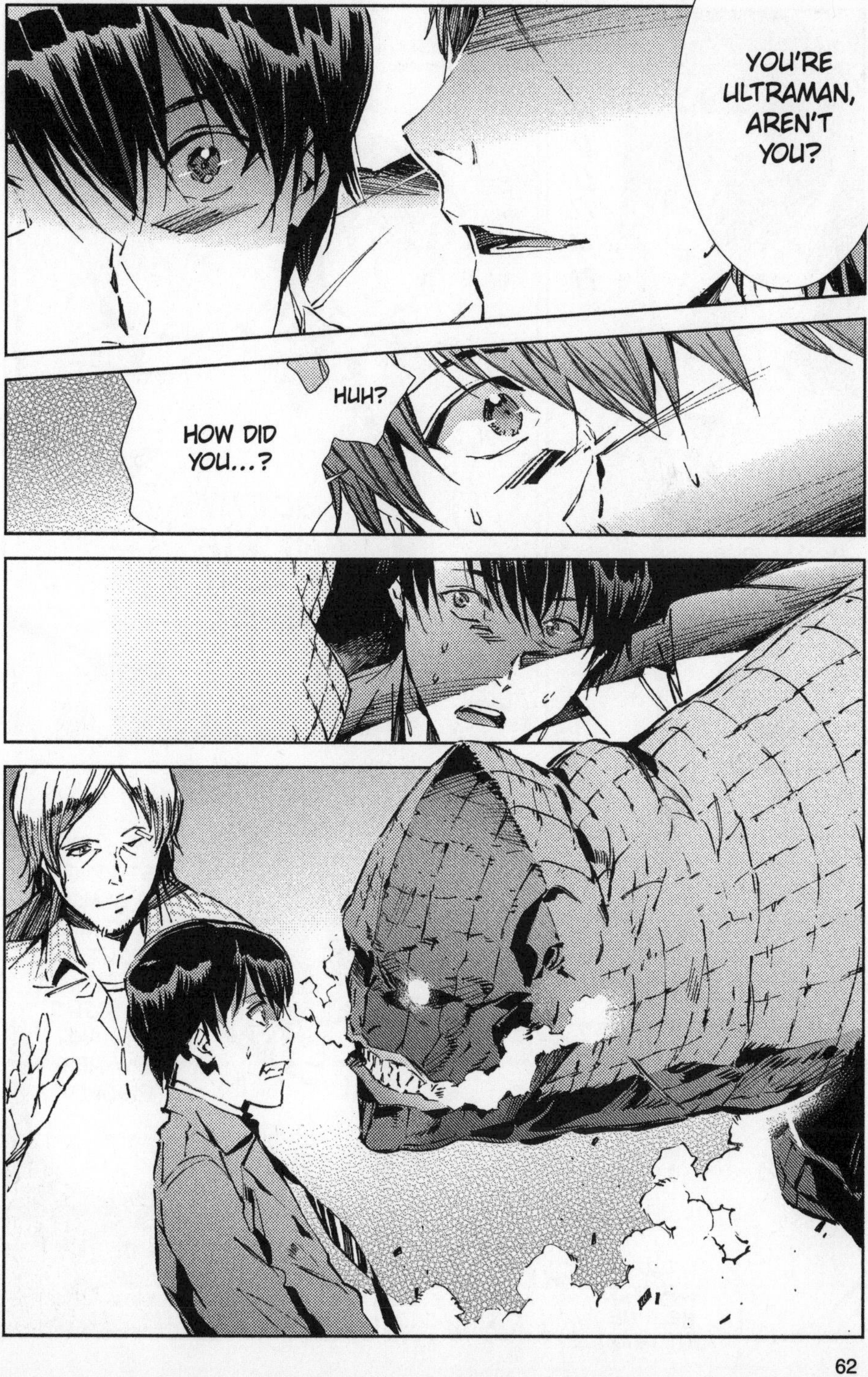
YOU'RE ULTRAMAN, AREN'T YOU?
HUH?
HOW DID YOU...?

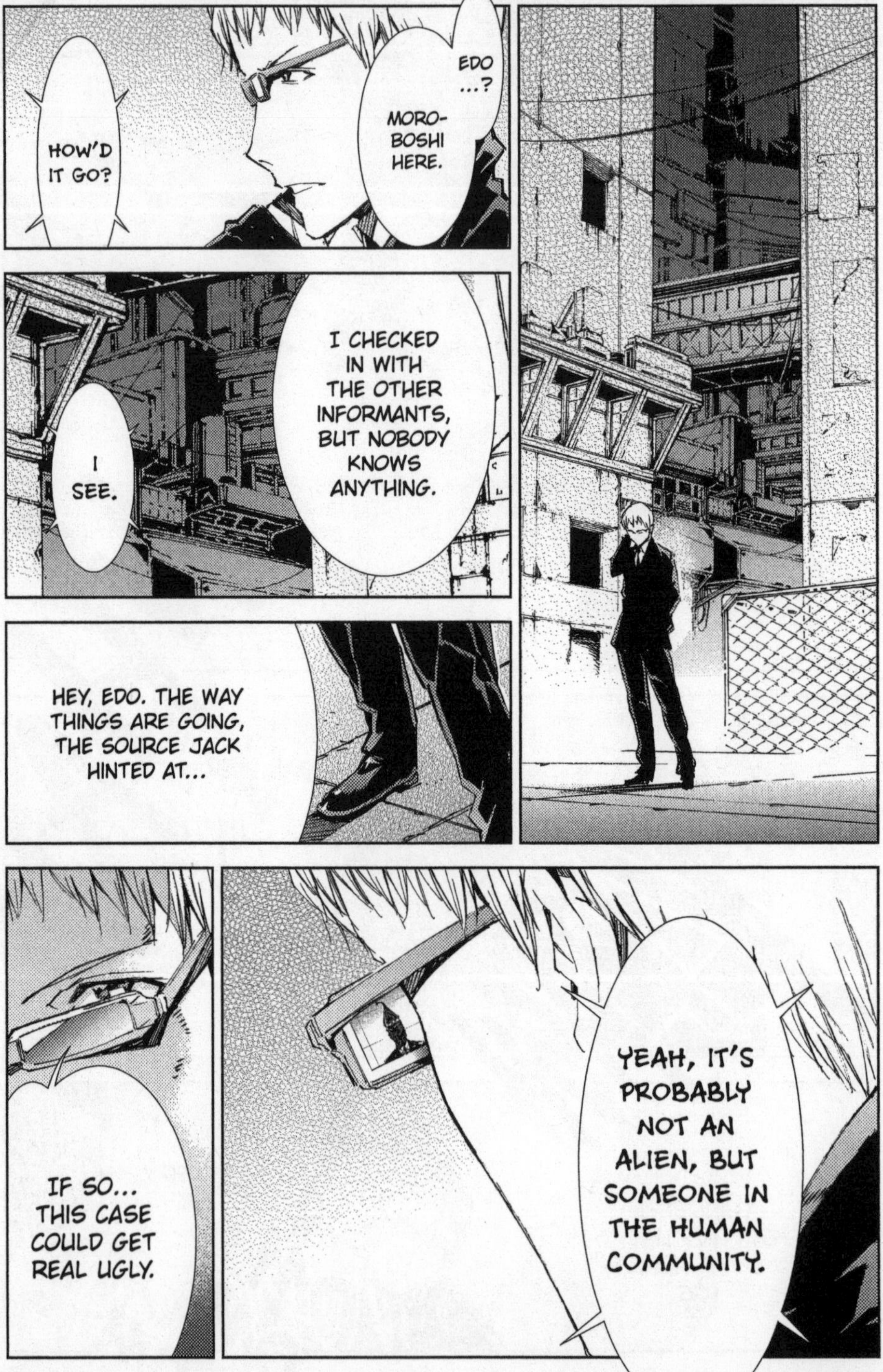
EDO ...? MORO-BOSHI HERE.
HOW'D IT GO?
I CHECKED IN WITH THE OTHER INFORMANTS, BUT NOBODY KNOWS ANYTHING.
I SEE.
HEY, EDO. THE WAY THINGS ARE GOING, THE SOURCE JACK HINTED AT...
YEAH, IT'S PROBABLY NOT AN ALIEN, BUT SOMEONE IN THE HUMAN COMMUNITY.
IF SO... THIS CASE COULD GET REAL UGLY.

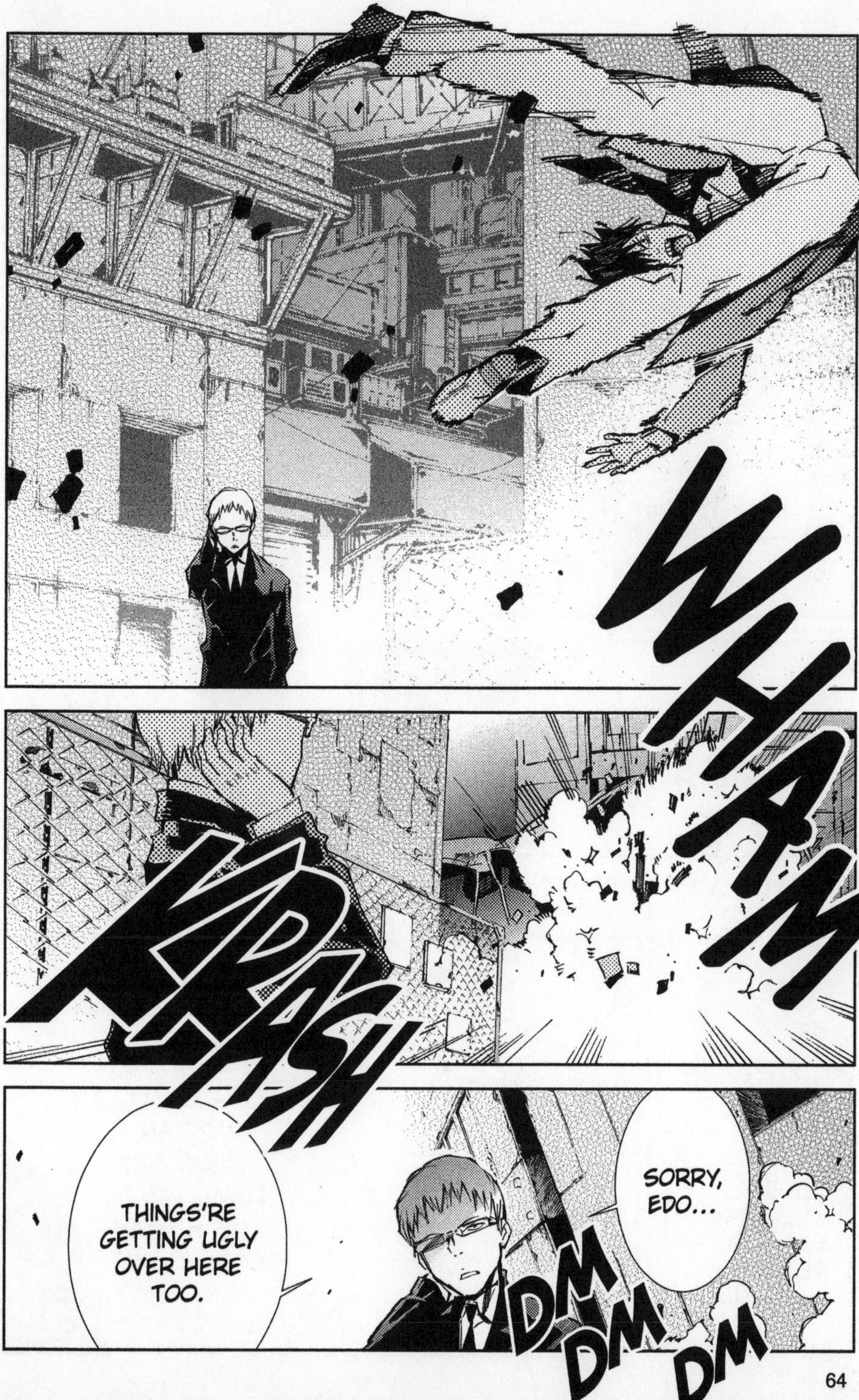
WHAM
KRASH
SORRY, EDO...
THINGS'RE GETTING UGLY OVER HERE TOO.
DM DM DM

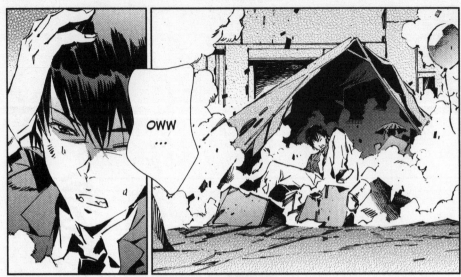

OWW
...

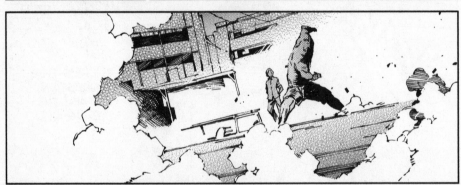

ⵏⵓⵥⴻⵥⵉⴽⴻ! ⴰⵓ ⵏⵓⵎⵘⵘⵙⵙⴽⴻⵎ
ⵍⵏⵙ ⴻⵢⵙⵉ ⵓⴰⴰⵍⵓⵅⵉ ⵓⵙ ···

ⵜⵍⵏⵓⵎ ⵇⵉⵙⵓⵍ ⵓⵓⵅⵙ?

HE
SURE IS
TOUGH.

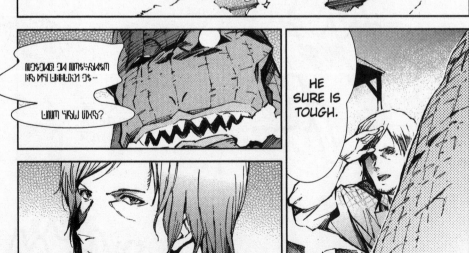

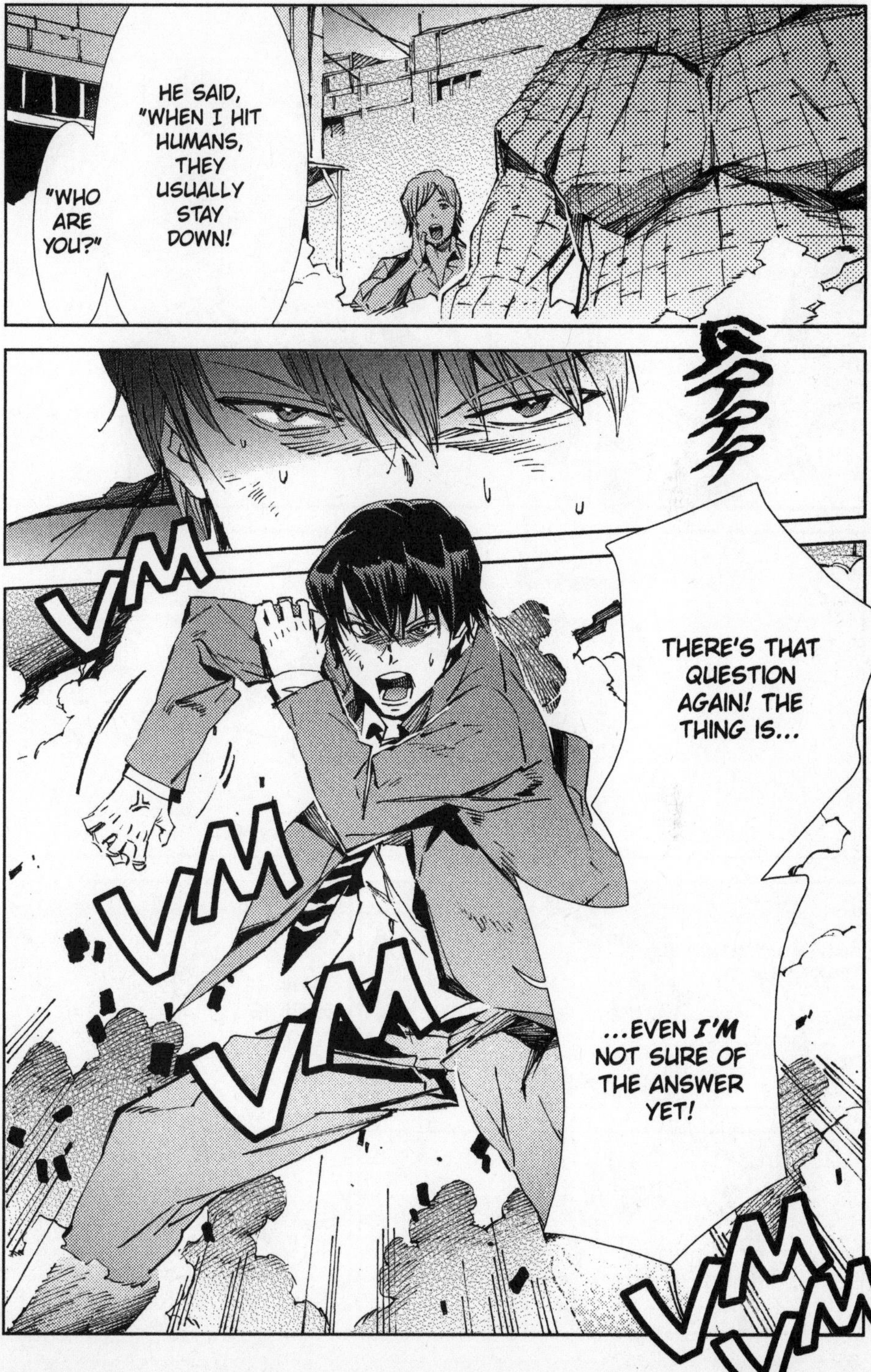
HE SAID, "WHEN I HIT HUMANS, THEY USUALLY STAY DOWN!
"WHO ARE YOU?"
THERE'S THAT QUESTION AGAIN! THE THING IS...
VM
VM
VM
...EVEN I'M NOT SURE OF THE ANSWER YET!
VM VM

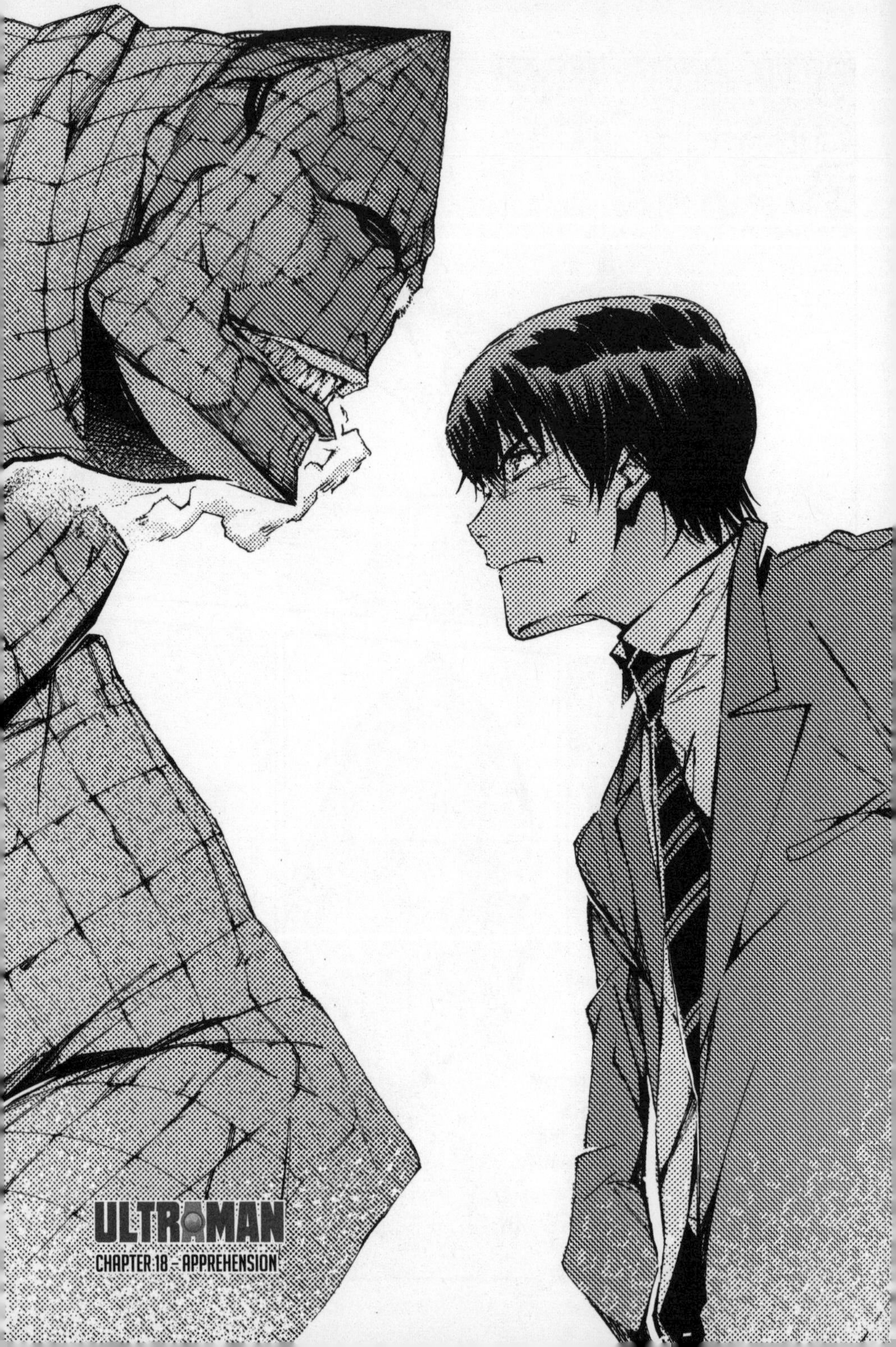
ULTRAMAN
CHAPTER 18 – APPREHENSION

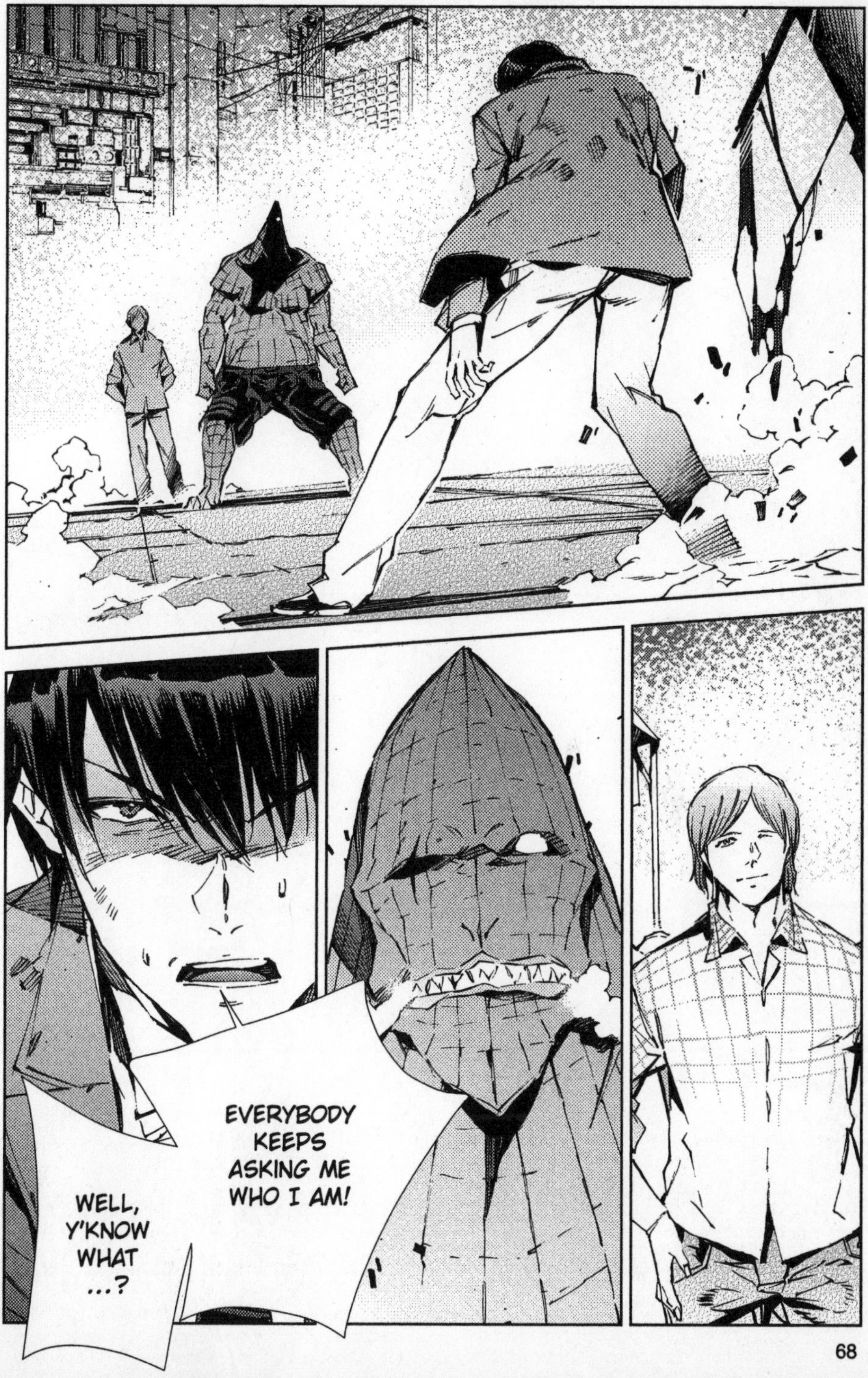
EVERYBODY KEEPS ASKING ME WHO I AM!
WELL, Y'KNOW WHAT ...?

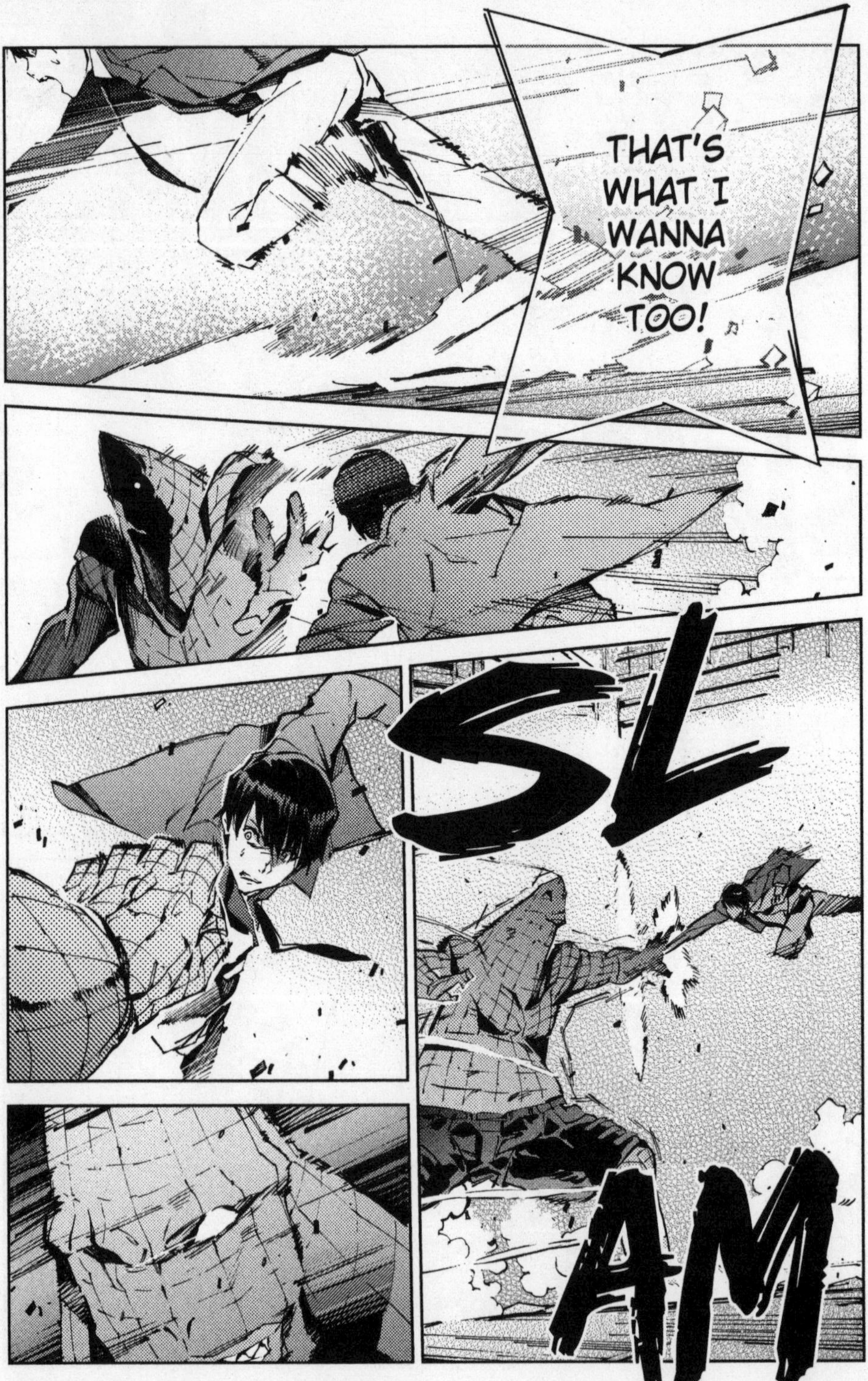
THAT'S WHAT I WANNA KNOW TOO!
SLAM

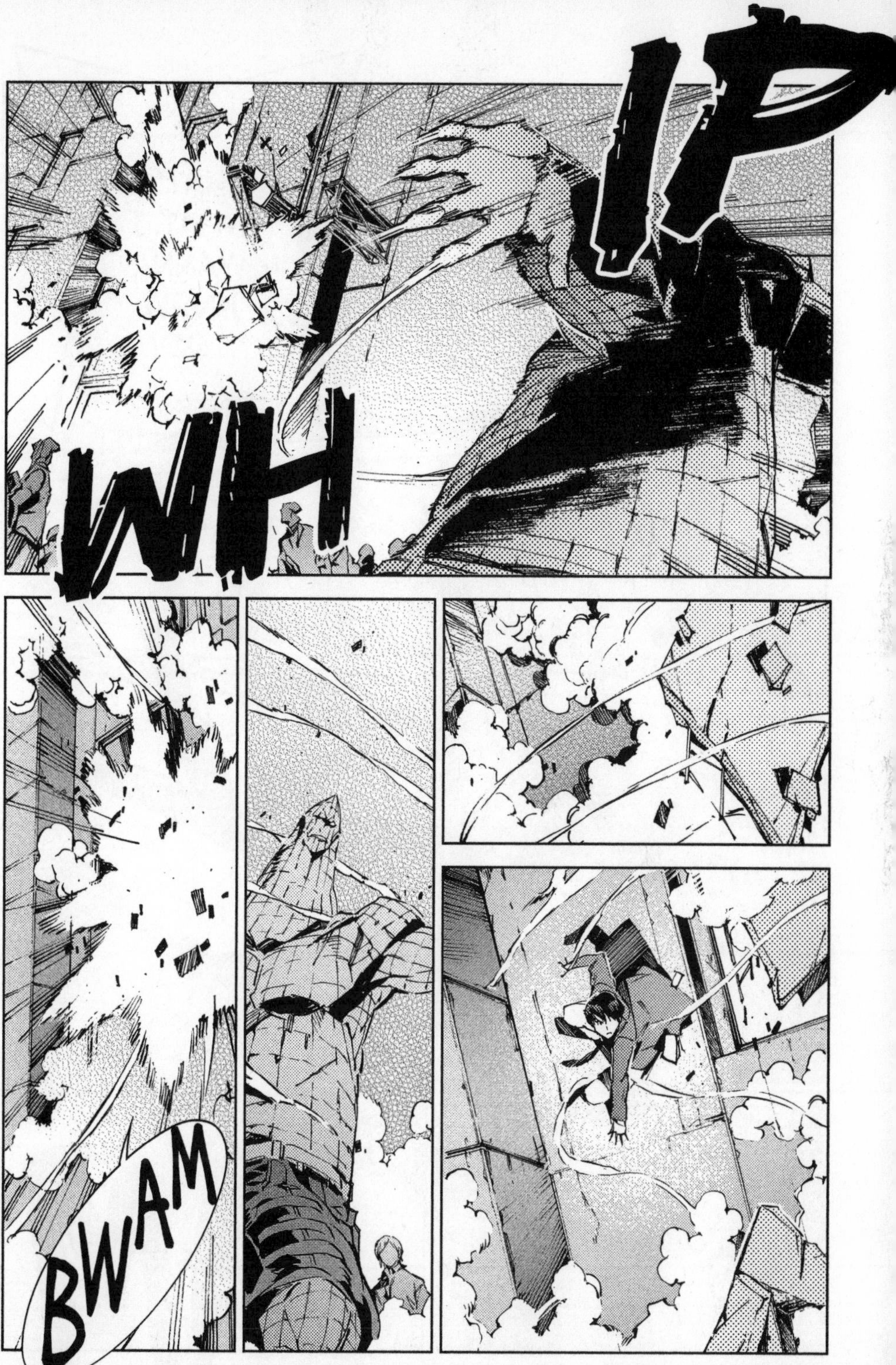
WHIP
BWAM

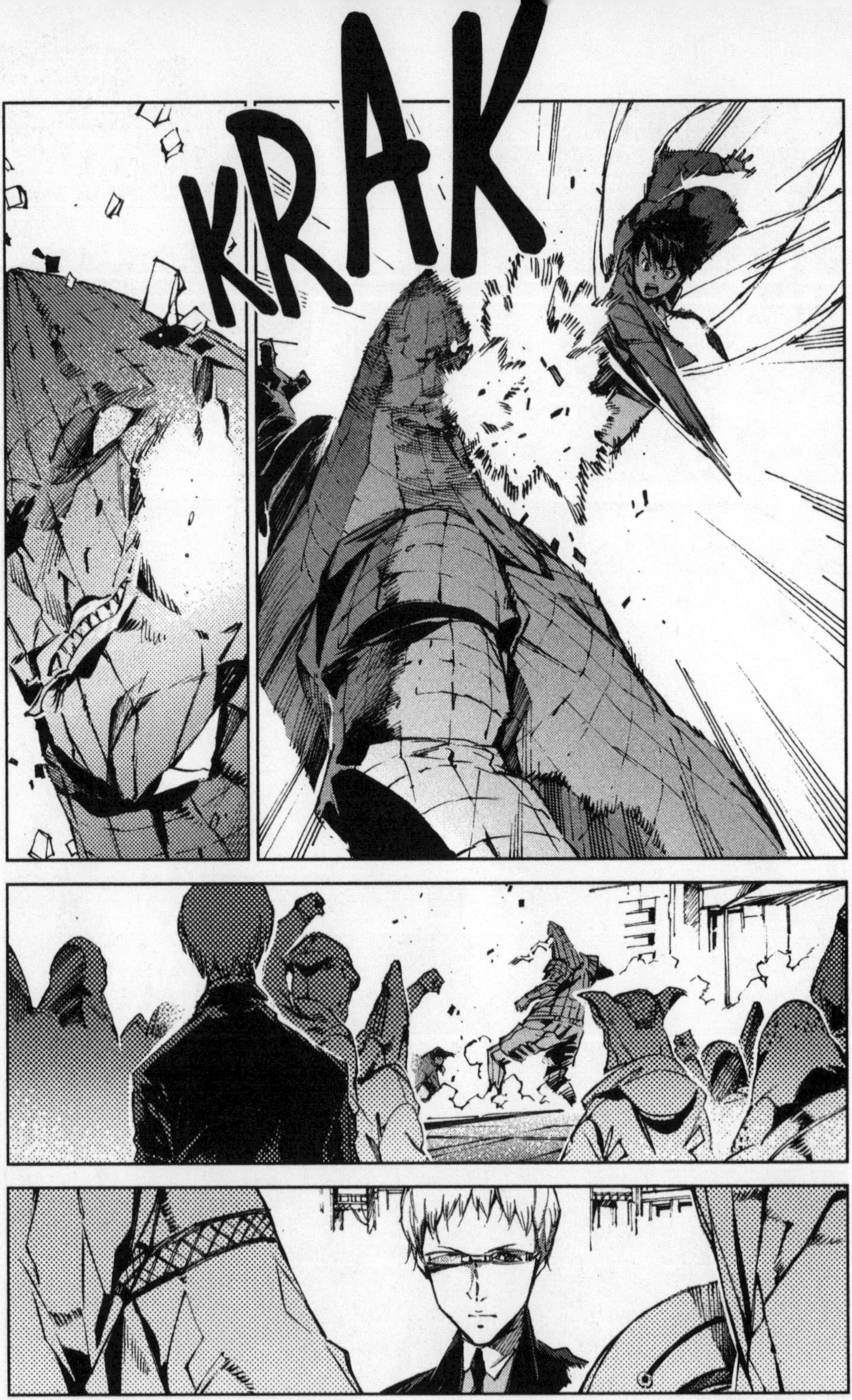
KRAK

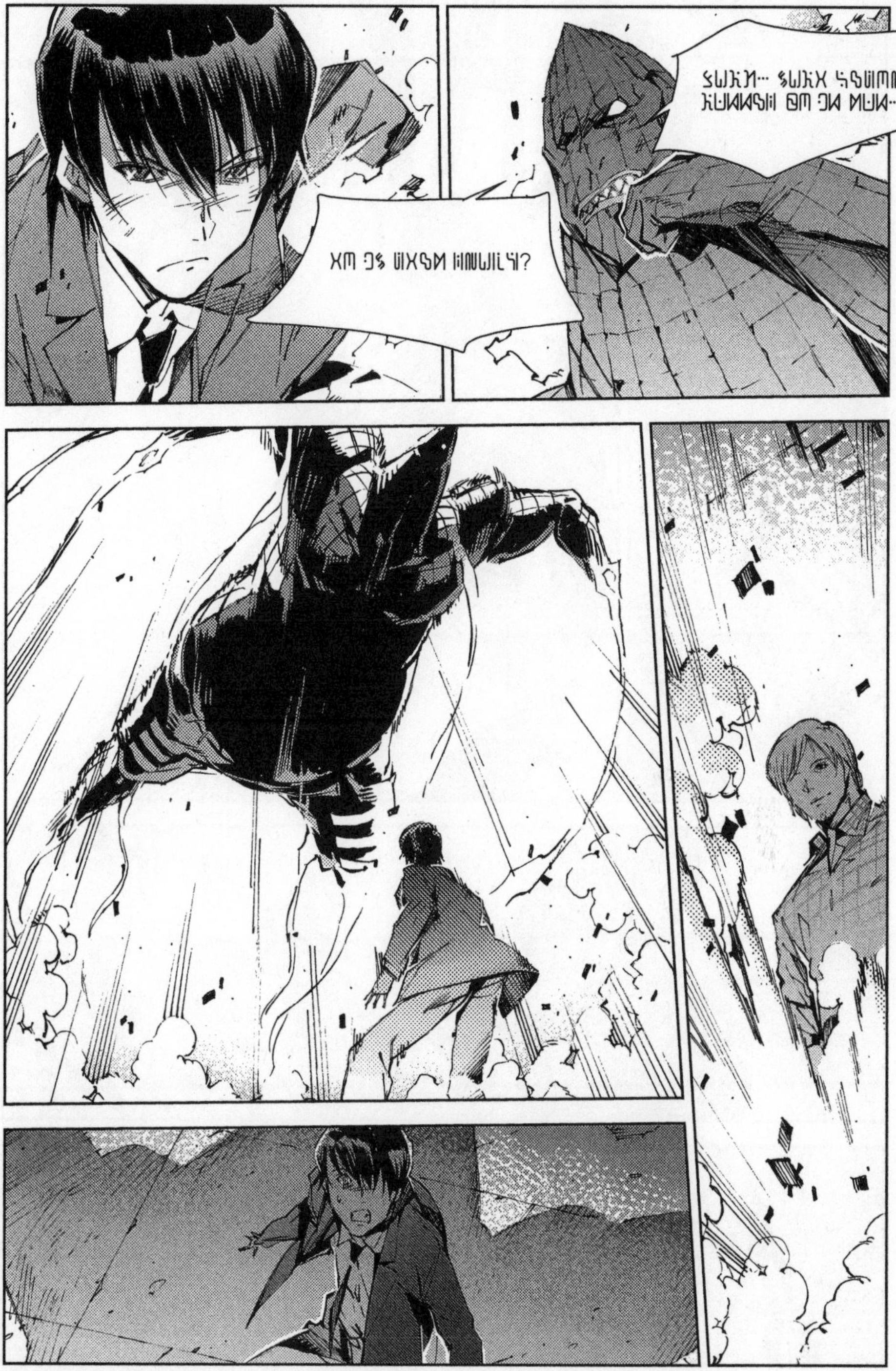

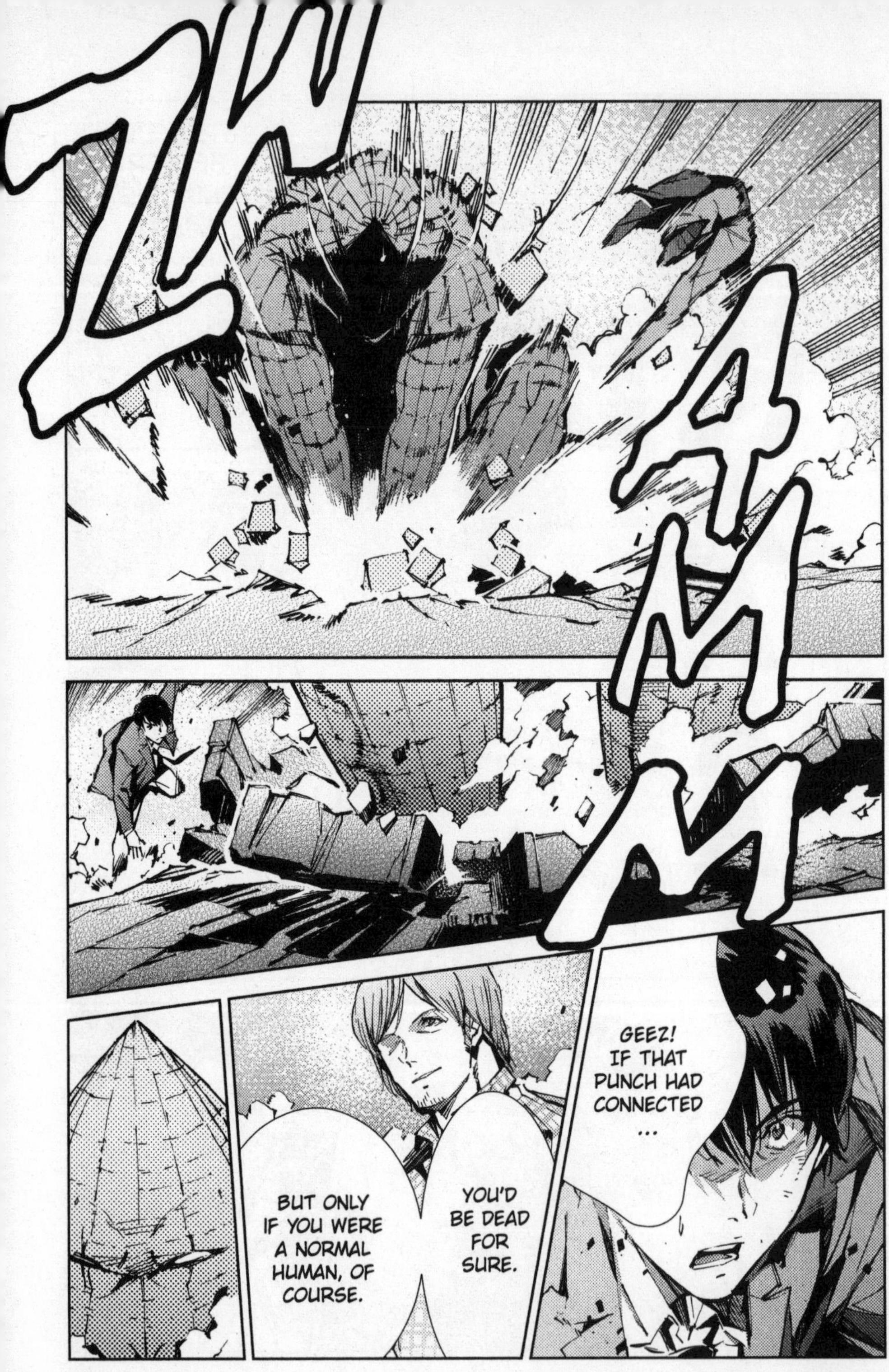
ZWAMM
GEEZ! IF THAT PUNCH HAD CONNECTED ...
YOU'D BE DEAD FOR SURE.
BUT ONLY IF YOU WERE A NORMAL HUMAN, OF COURSE.

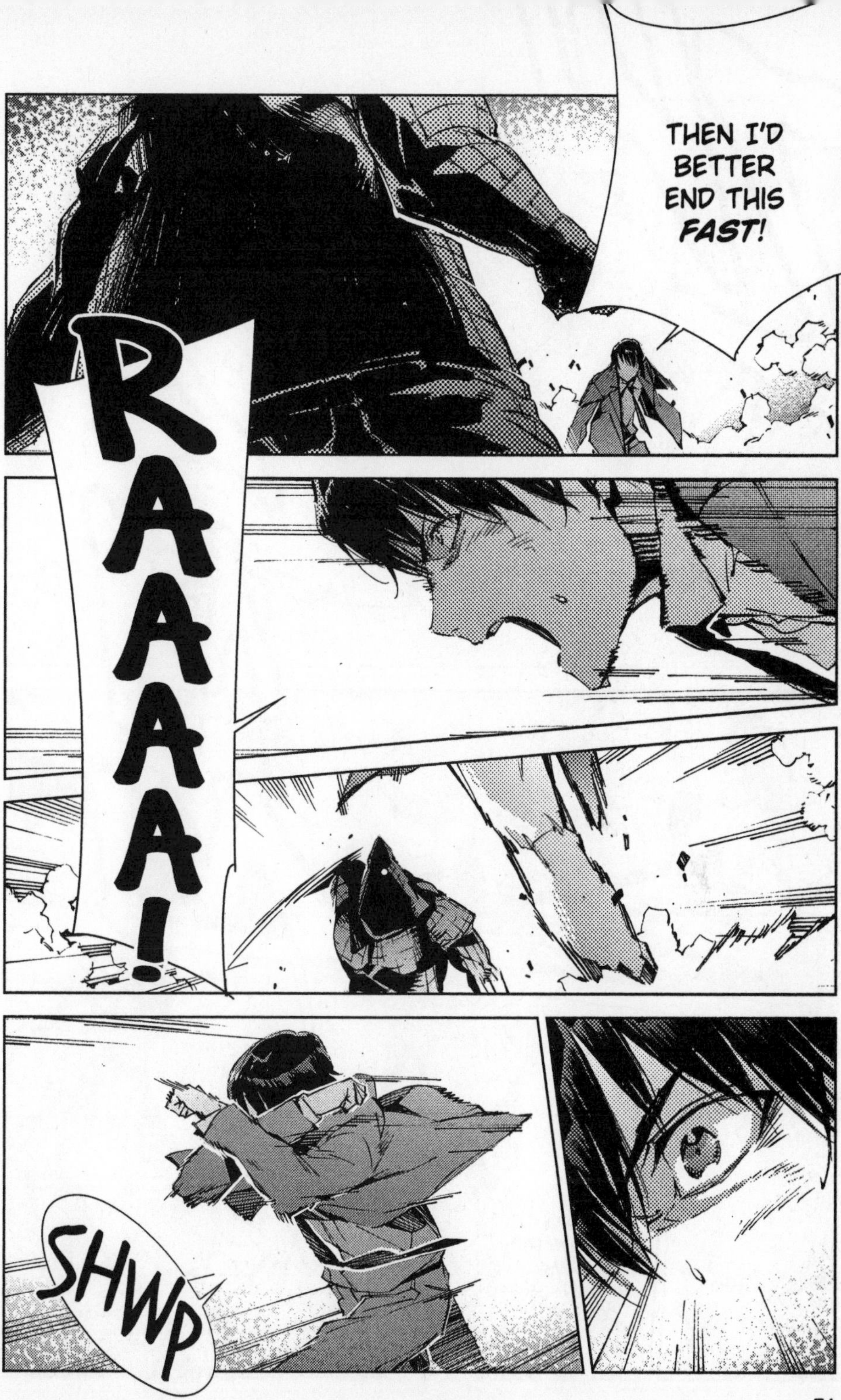
THEN I'D BETTER END THIS FAST!
RAAAAA!
SHWP

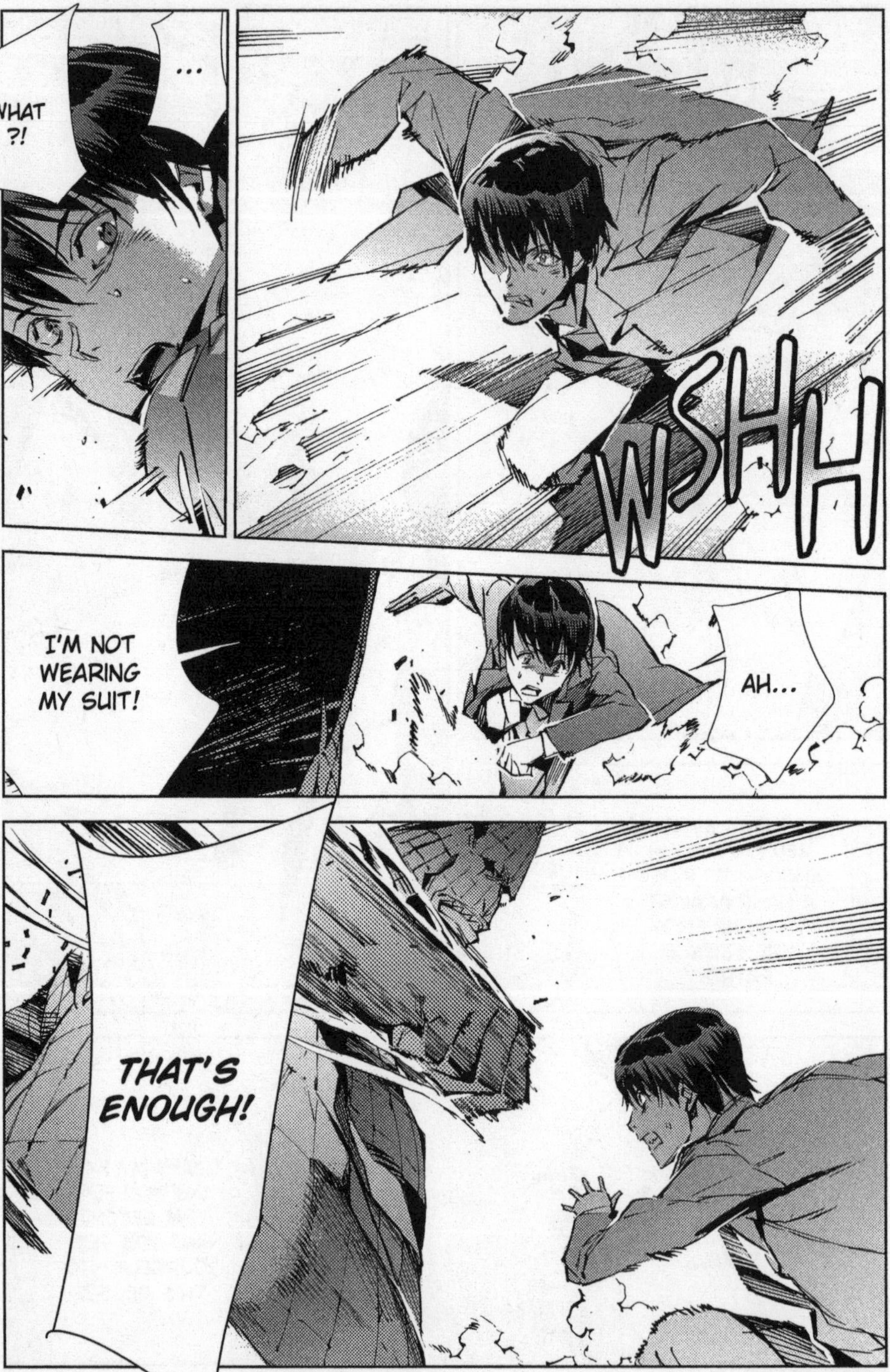
WSHH
...
WHAT ?!
AH...
I'M NOT WEARING MY SUIT!
THAT'S ENOUGH!

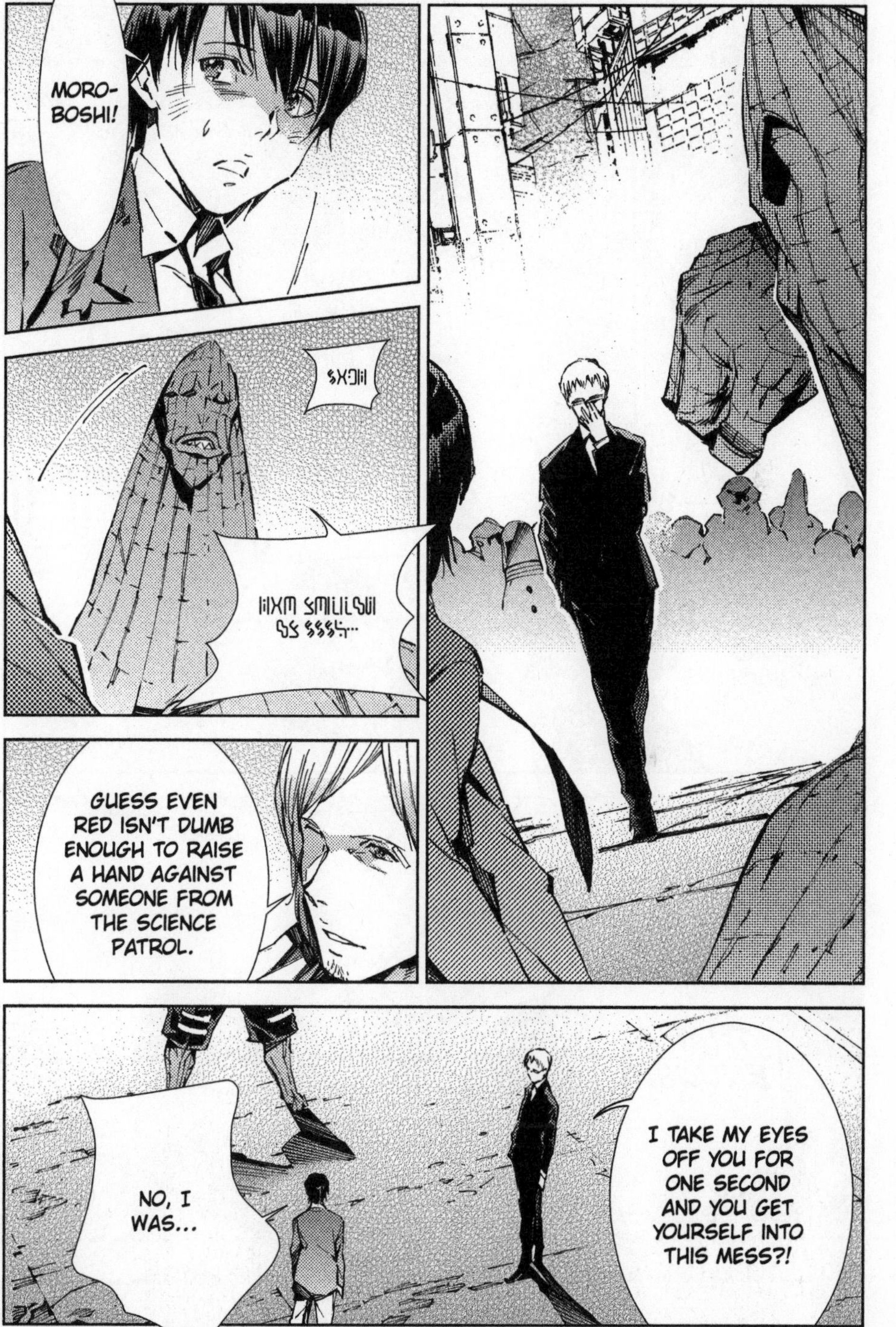
MORO-BOSHI!
GUESS EVEN RED ISN'T DUMB ENOUGH TO RAISE A HAND AGAINST SOMEONE FROM THE SCIENCE PATROL.
I TAKE MY EYES OFF YOU FOR ONE SECOND AND YOU GET YOURSELF INTO THIS MESS?!
NO, I WAS...

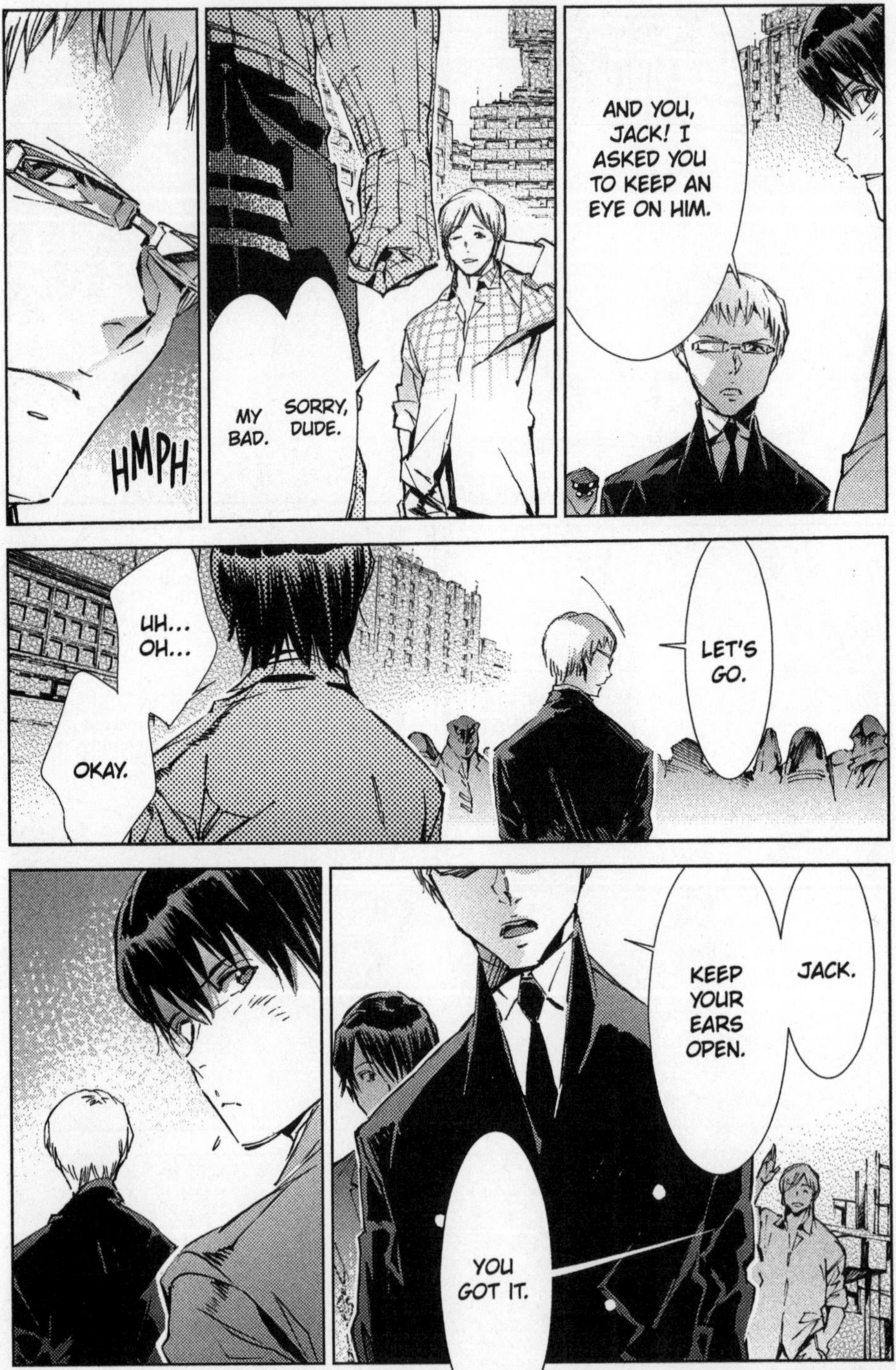
AND YOU, JACK! I ASKED YOU TO KEEP AN EYE ON HIM.
SORRY, DUDE.
MY BAD.
HMPH
LET'S GO.
UH... OH...
OKAY.
JACK.
KEEP YOUR EARS OPEN.
YOU GOT IT.

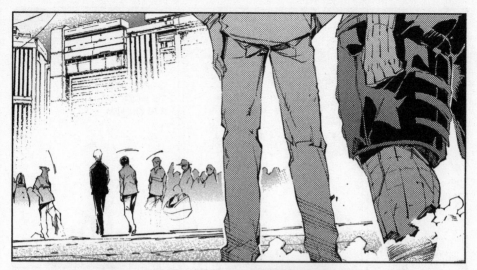

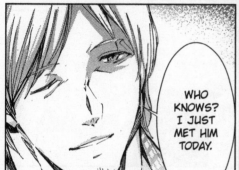

WHO KNOWS? I JUST MET HIM TODAY.

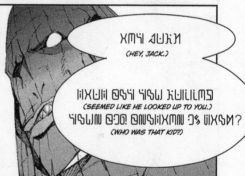

ᛋᛗᚴᛁ ᚨᚢᚴᛁ
(HEY, JACK.)

ᛁᛁᚷᚢᛁᛁ ᚦᚦᛋᚴᛁ ᚴᚦᛋᚢ ᚴᚢᛁᛁᛁᛚᛗᚷ
(SEEMED LIKE HE LOOKED UP TO YOU.)
ᚴᚷᚢᚢᛁ ᚦᛃᚦ. ᚦᚢᚷᛋᛁᛁᚡᛗᛁ ᛃᚴ ᛁᛁᚡᚷᛁ?
(WHO WAS THAT KID?)

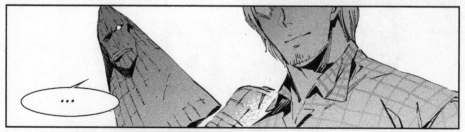

...

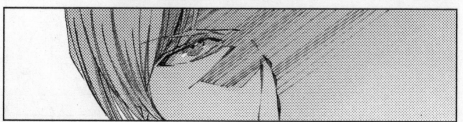

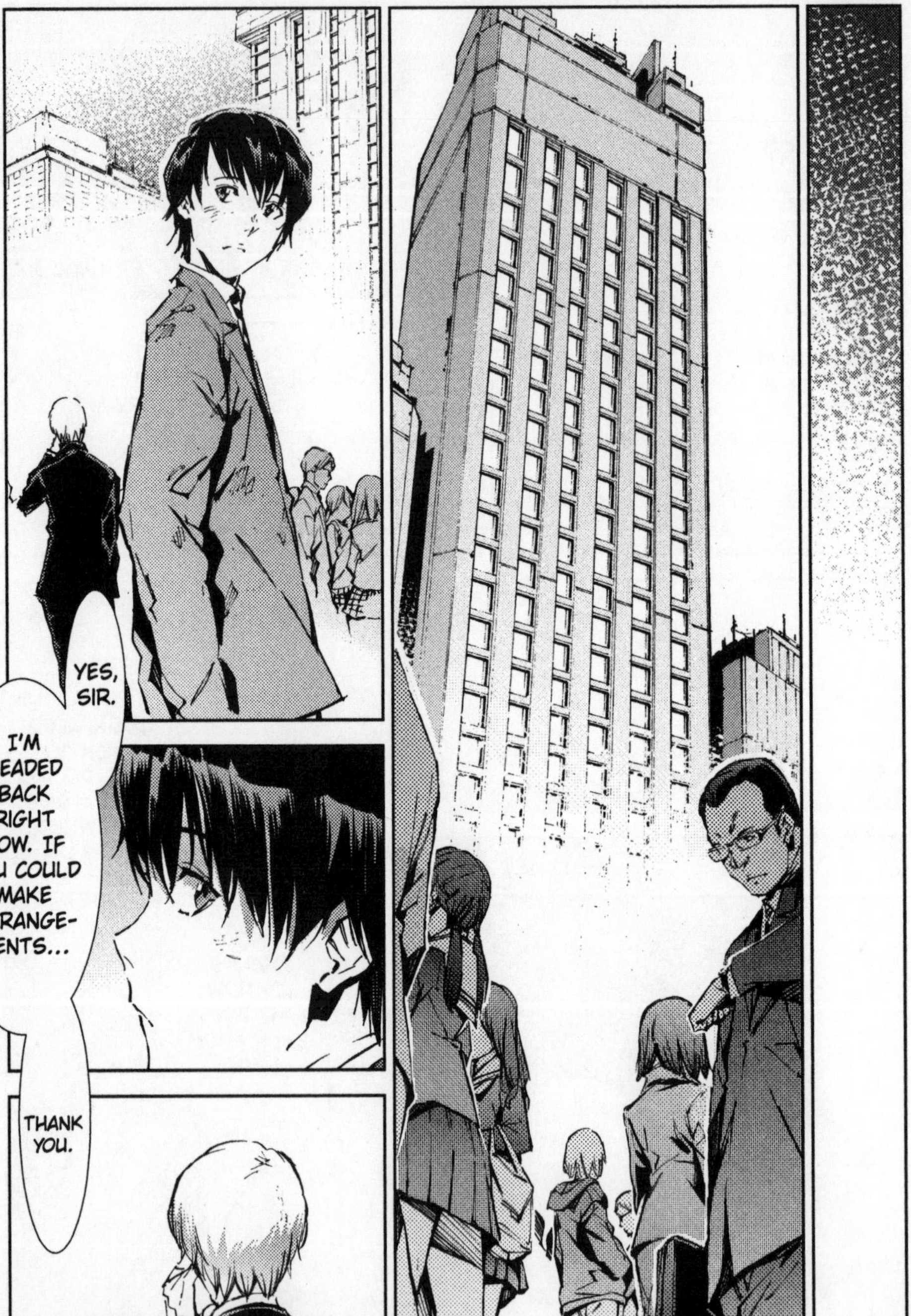
YES, SIR.
I'M HEADED BACK RIGHT NOW. IF YOU COULD MAKE ARRANGE-MENTS...
THANK YOU.

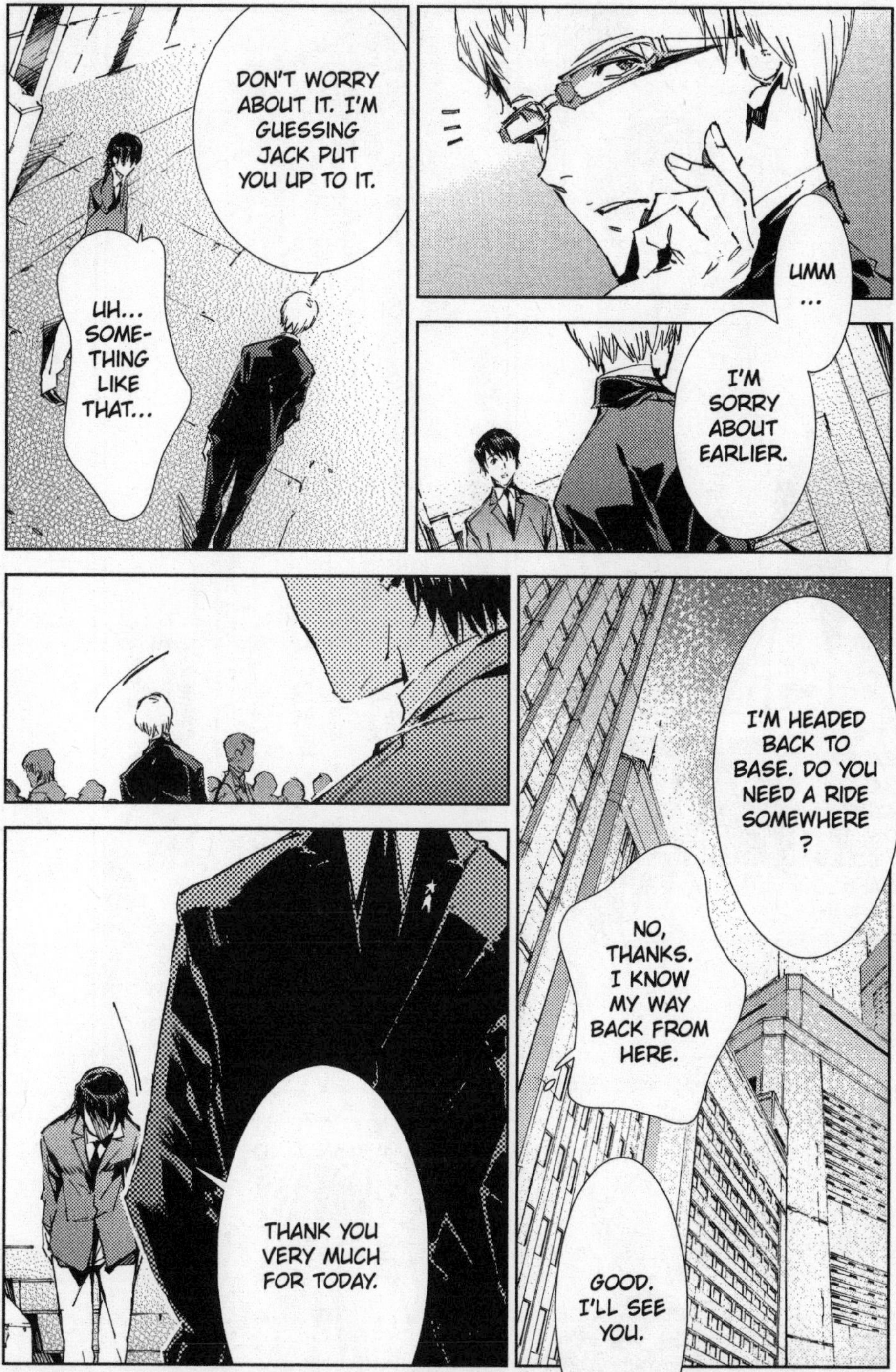
UMM ...
I'M SORRY ABOUT EARLIER.
DON'T WORRY ABOUT IT. I'M GUESSING JACK PUT YOU UP TO IT.
UH... SOME-THING LIKE THAT...
I'M HEADED BACK TO BASE. DO YOU NEED A RIDE SOMEWHERE ?
NO, THANKS. I KNOW MY WAY BACK FROM HERE.
GOOD. I'LL SEE YOU.
THANK YOU VERY MUCH FOR TODAY.

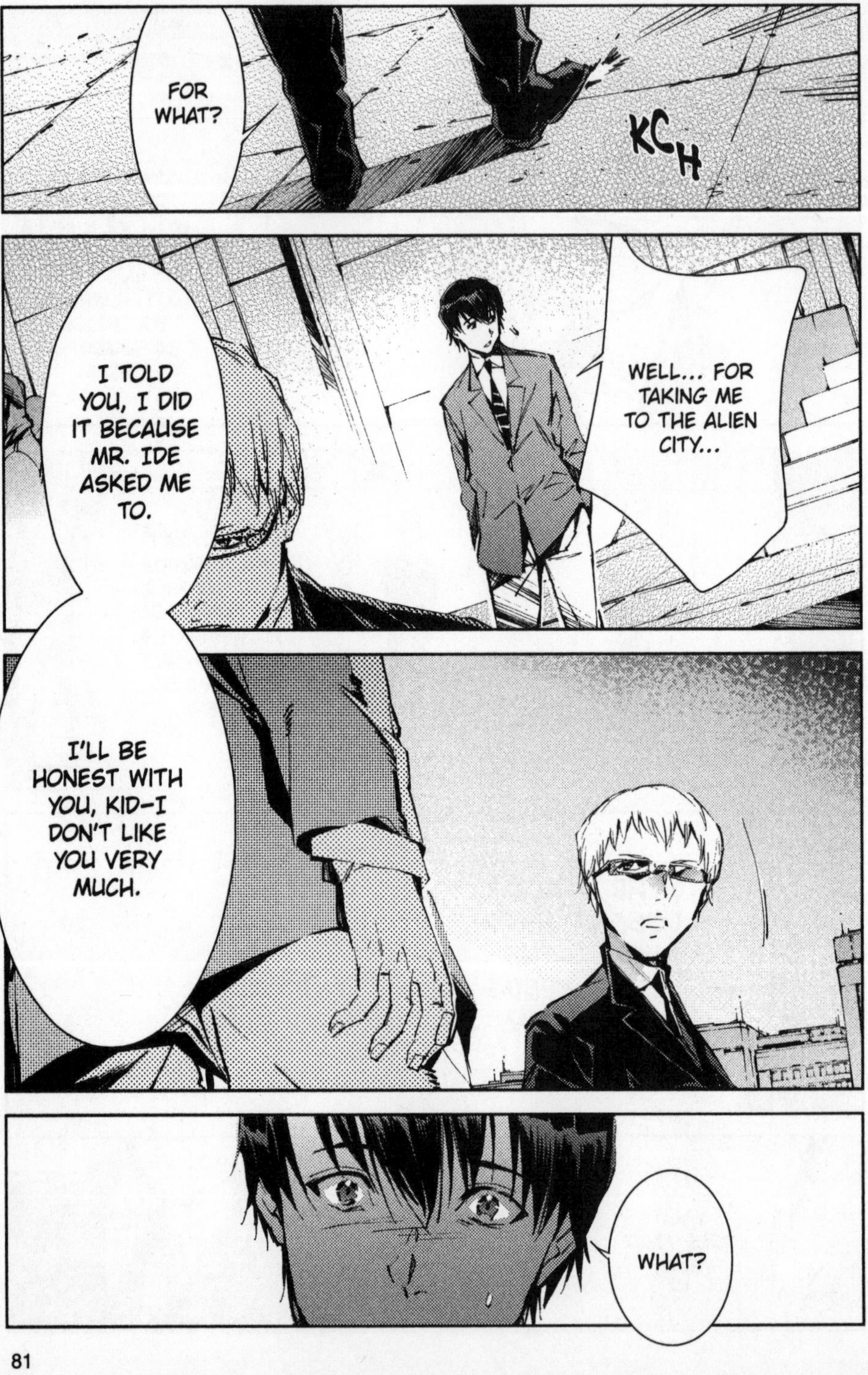
KCH
FOR WHAT?
WELL... FOR TAKING ME TO THE ALIEN CITY...
I TOLD YOU, I DID IT BECAUSE MR. IDE ASKED ME TO.
I'LL BE HONEST WITH YOU, KID–I DON'T LIKE YOU VERY MUCH.
WHAT?

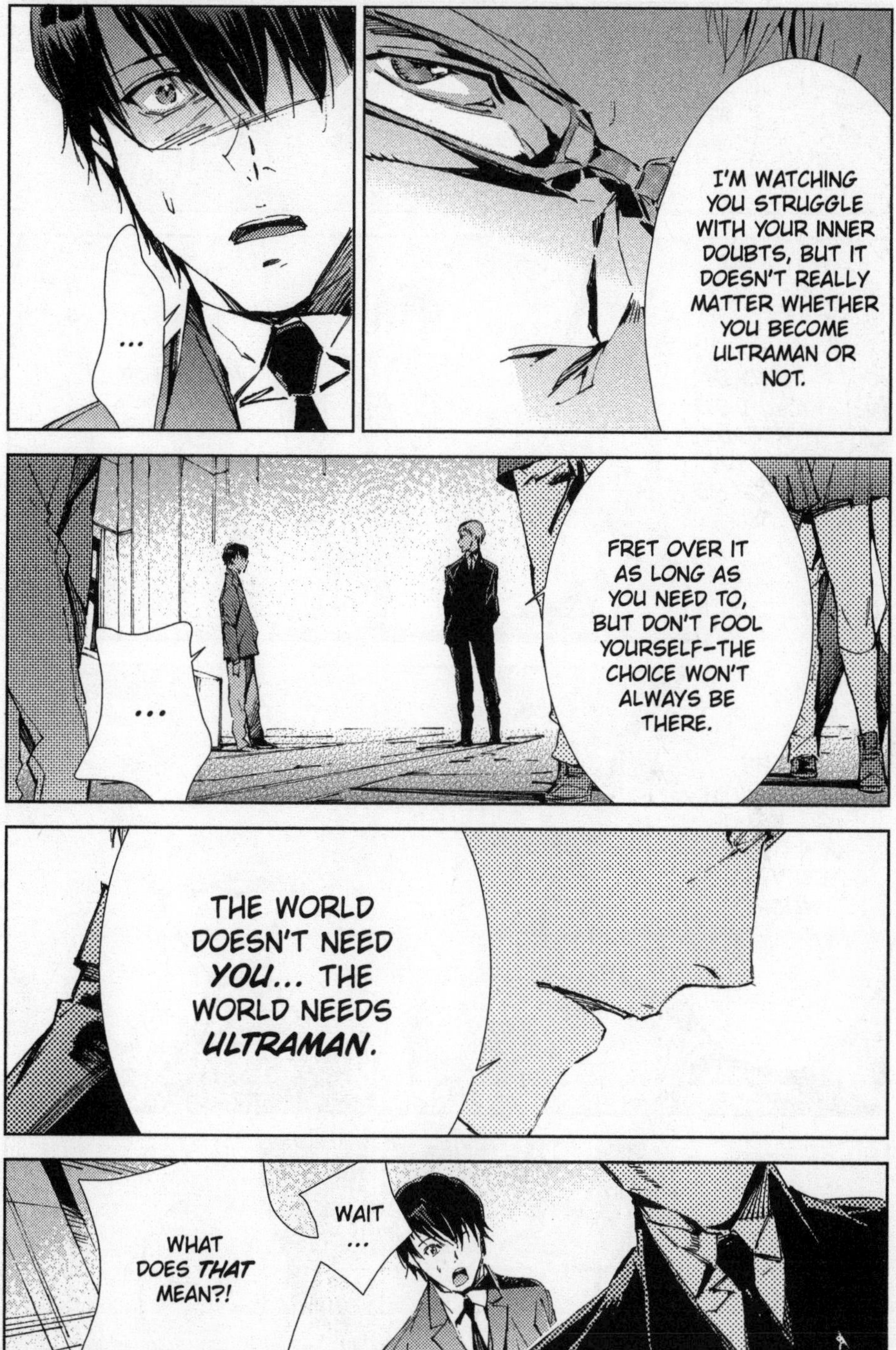
I'M WATCHING YOU STRUGGLE WITH YOUR INNER DOUBTS, BUT IT DOESN'T REALLY MATTER WHETHER YOU BECOME ULTRAMAN OR NOT.
...
FRET OVER IT AS LONG AS YOU NEED TO, BUT DON'T FOOL YOURSELF—THE CHOICE WON'T ALWAYS BE THERE.
...
THE WORLD DOESN'T NEED *YOU*... THE WORLD NEEDS ***ULTRAMAN***.
WAIT...
WHAT DOES *THAT* MEAN?!

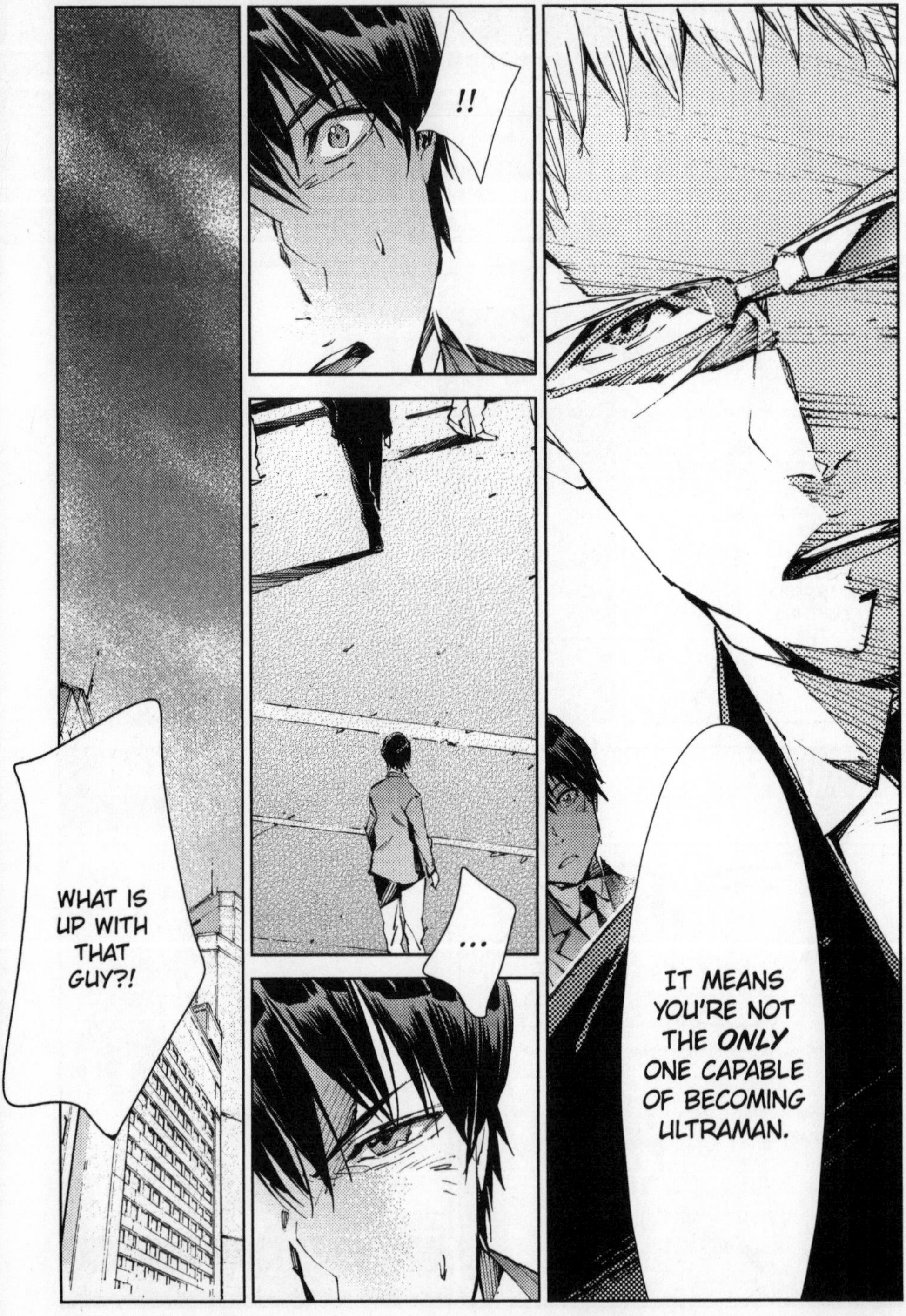
IT MEANS YOU'RE NOT THE *ONLY* ONE CAPABLE OF BECOMING ULTRAMAN.
!!
...
WHAT IS UP WITH THAT GUY?!

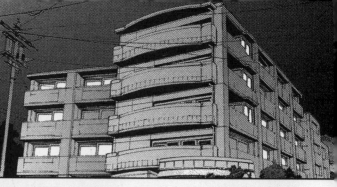

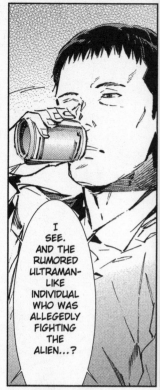

I. SEE. AND THE RUMORED ULTRAMAN-LIKE INDIVIDUAL WHO WAS ALLEGEDLY FIGHTING THE ALIEN...?

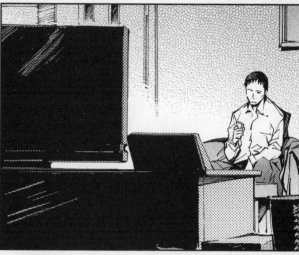

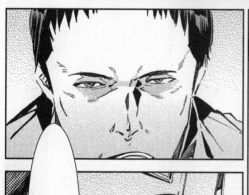

I'M HOME!

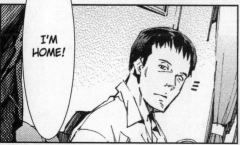

IT *WAS* ULTRA-MAN!

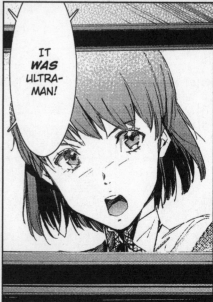

84

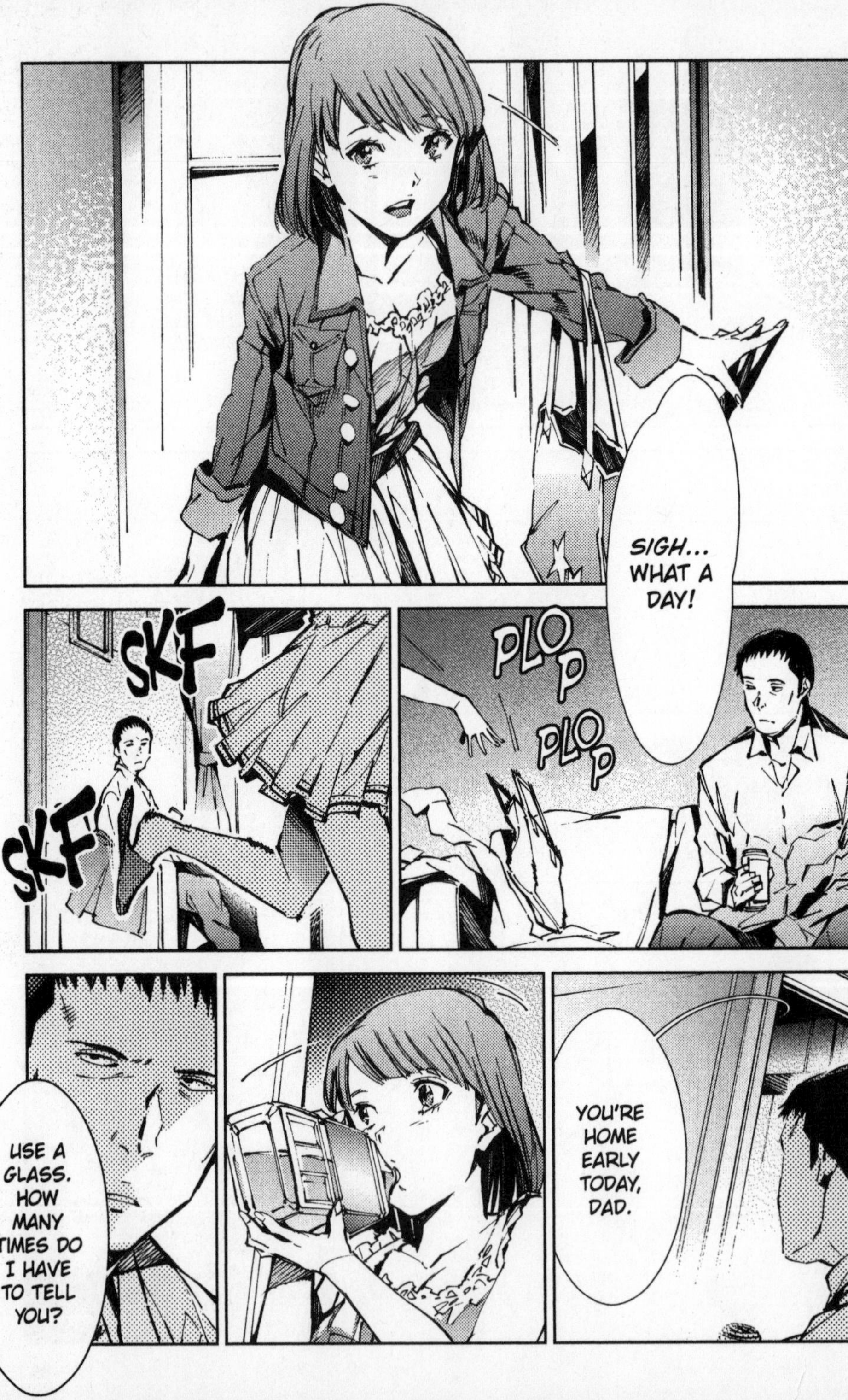
SIGH... WHAT A DAY!
PLOP
PLOP
SKF
SKF
YOU'RE HOME EARLY TODAY, DAD.
USE A GLASS. HOW MANY TIMES DO I HAVE TO TELL YOU?

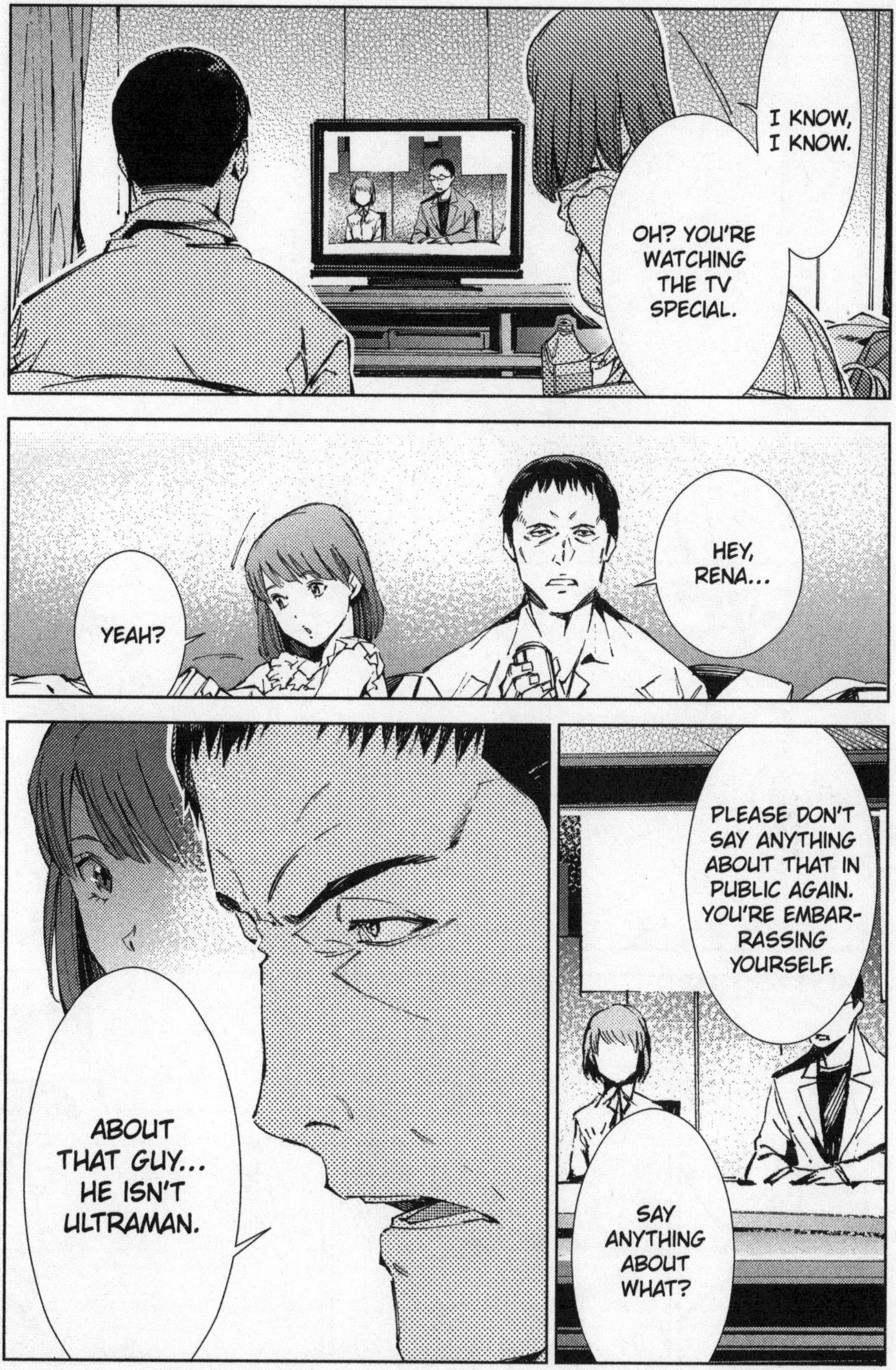
OH? YOU'RE WATCHING THE TV SPECIAL.
I KNOW, I KNOW.
HEY, RENA...
YEAH?
PLEASE DON'T SAY ANYTHING ABOUT THAT IN PUBLIC AGAIN. YOU'RE EMBARRASSING YOURSELF.
SAY ANYTHING ABOUT WHAT?
ABOUT THAT GUY... HE ISN'T ULTRAMAN.

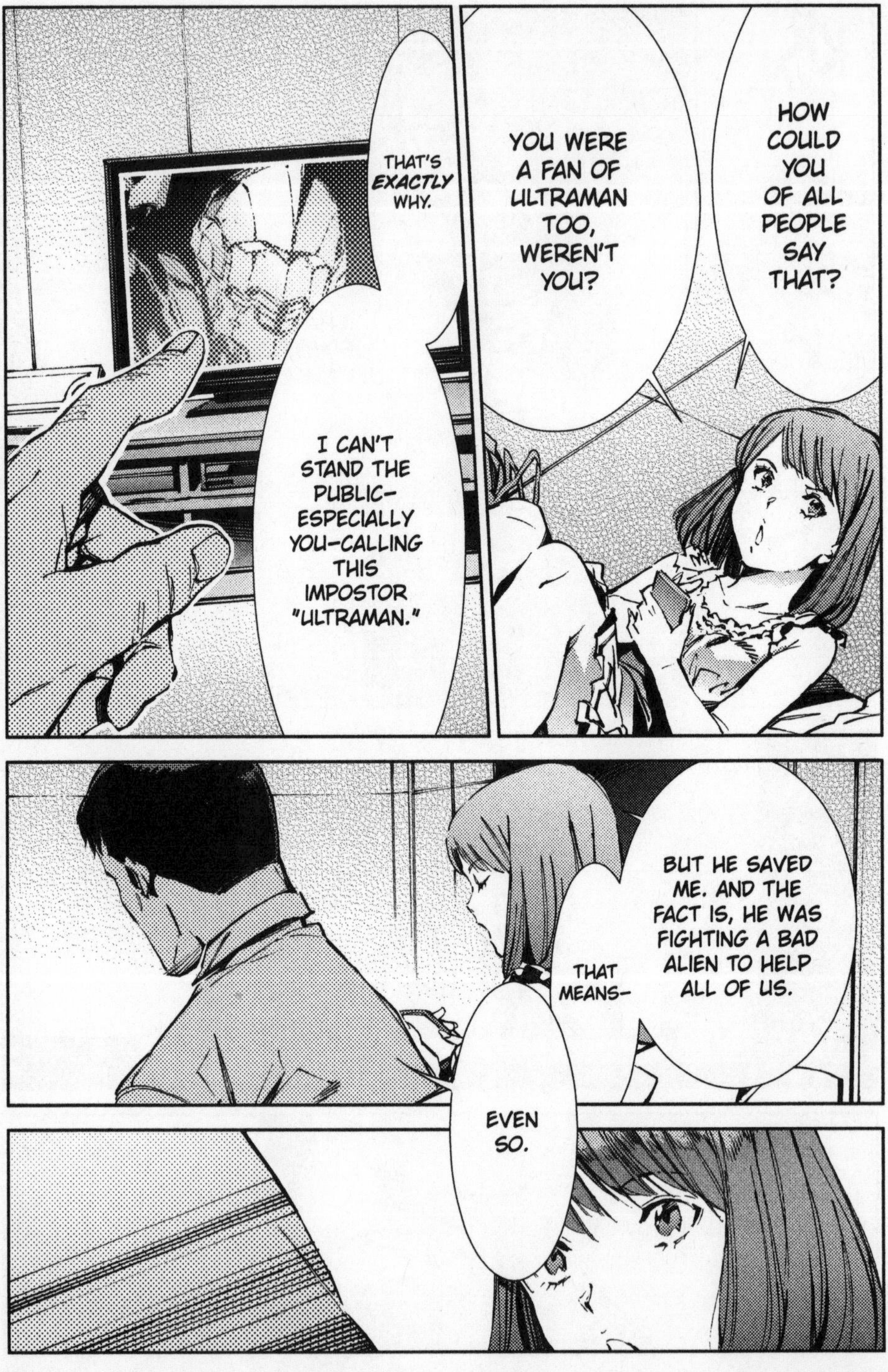
HOW COULD YOU OF ALL PEOPLE SAY THAT?
YOU WERE A FAN OF ULTRAMAN TOO, WEREN'T YOU?
THAT'S *EXACTLY* WHY.
I CAN'T STAND THE PUBLIC—ESPECIALLY YOU—CALLING THIS IMPOSTOR "ULTRAMAN."
BUT HE SAVED ME. AND THE FACT IS, HE WAS FIGHTING A BAD ALIEN TO HELP ALL OF US.
THAT MEANS—
EVEN SO.

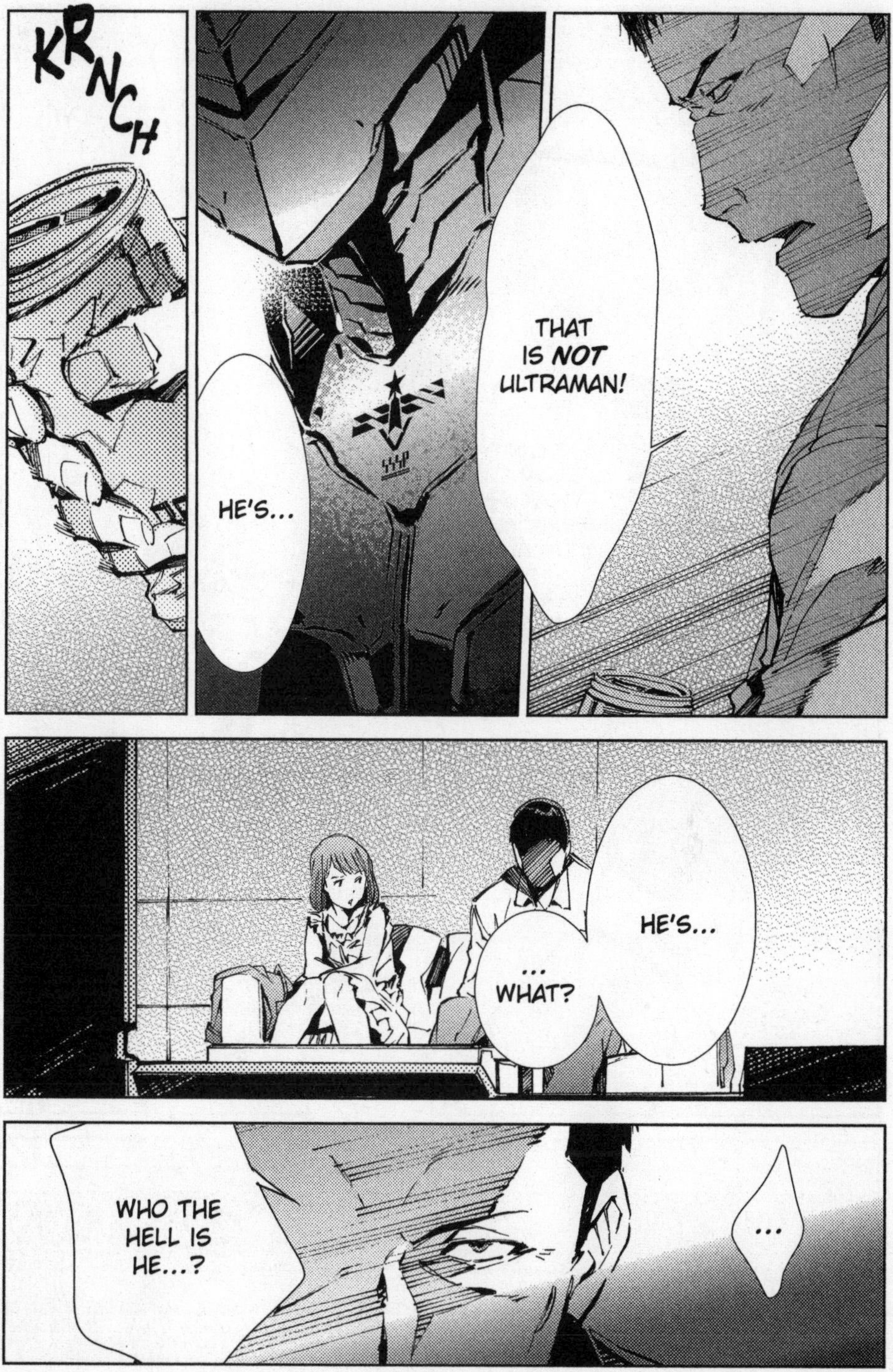
THAT IS NOT ULTRAMAN!
HE'S...
KRNCH
HE'S...
... WHAT?
...
WHO THE HELL IS HE...?

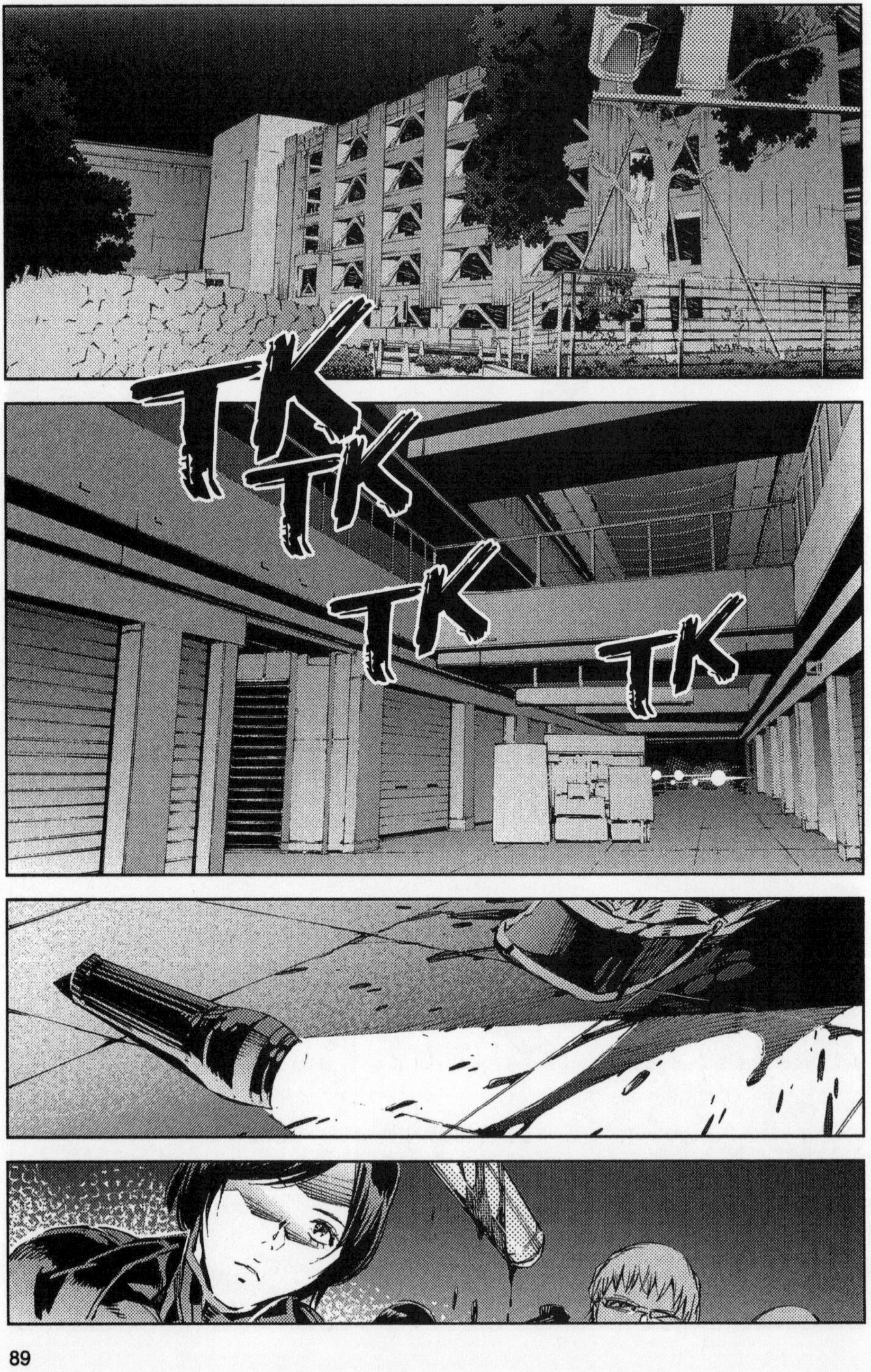
TK
TK
TK
TK

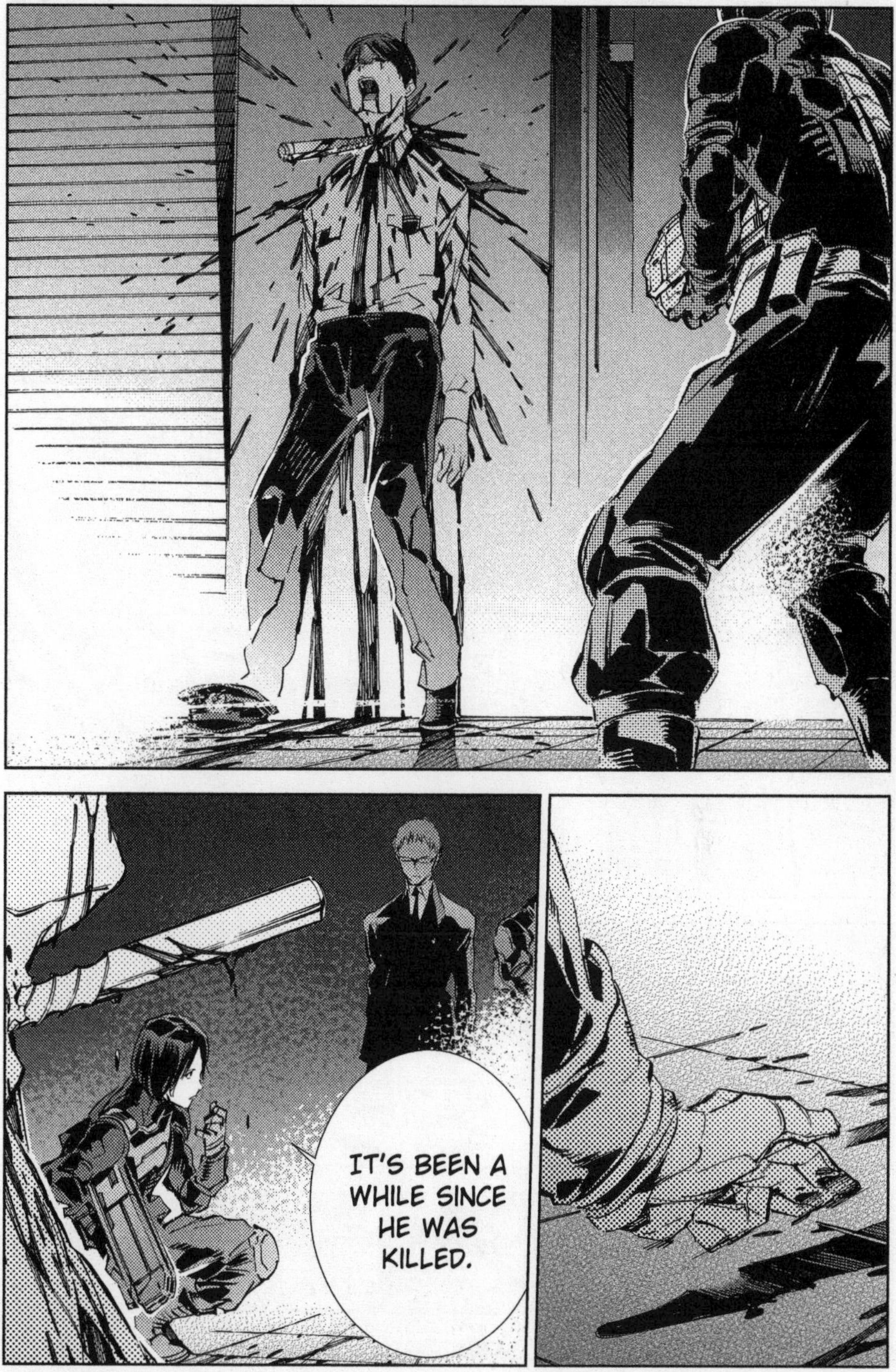
IT'S BEEN A WHILE SINCE HE WAS KILLED.

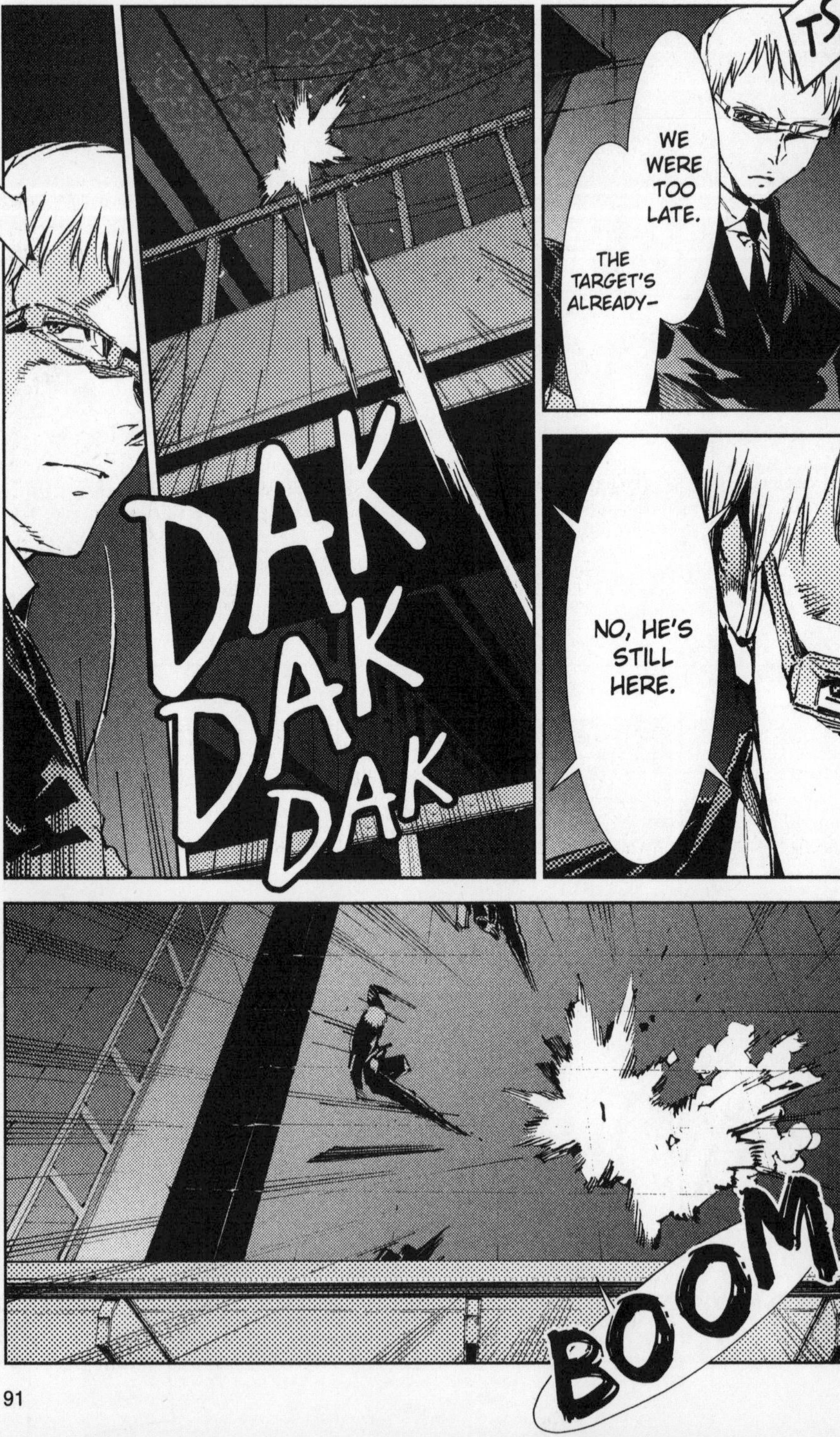
TSK
WE WERE TOO LATE.
THE TARGET'S ALREADY—
NO, HE'S STILL HERE.
DAK DAK DAK DAK
BOOM

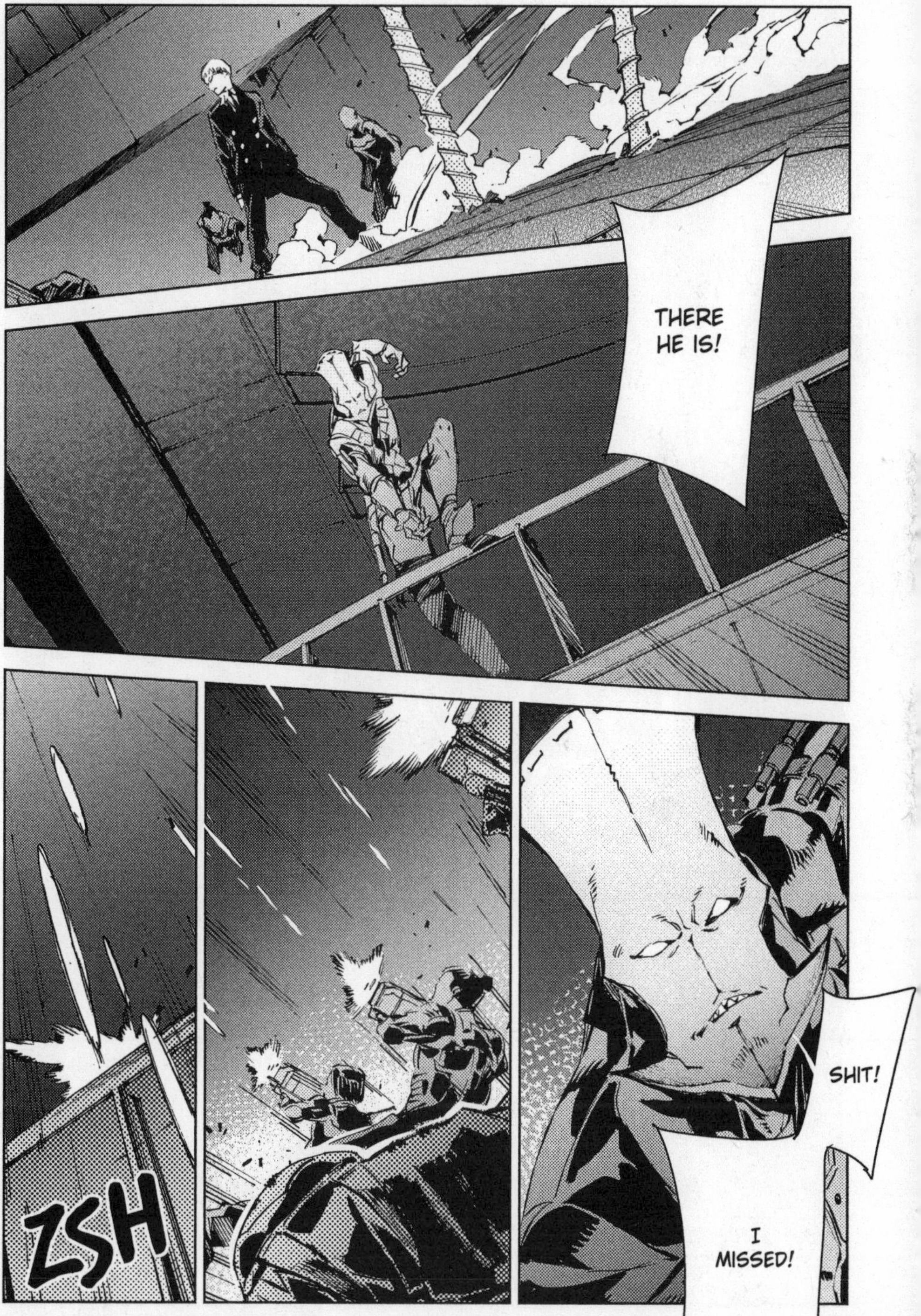
THERE HE IS!
ZSH
SHIT!
I MISSED!

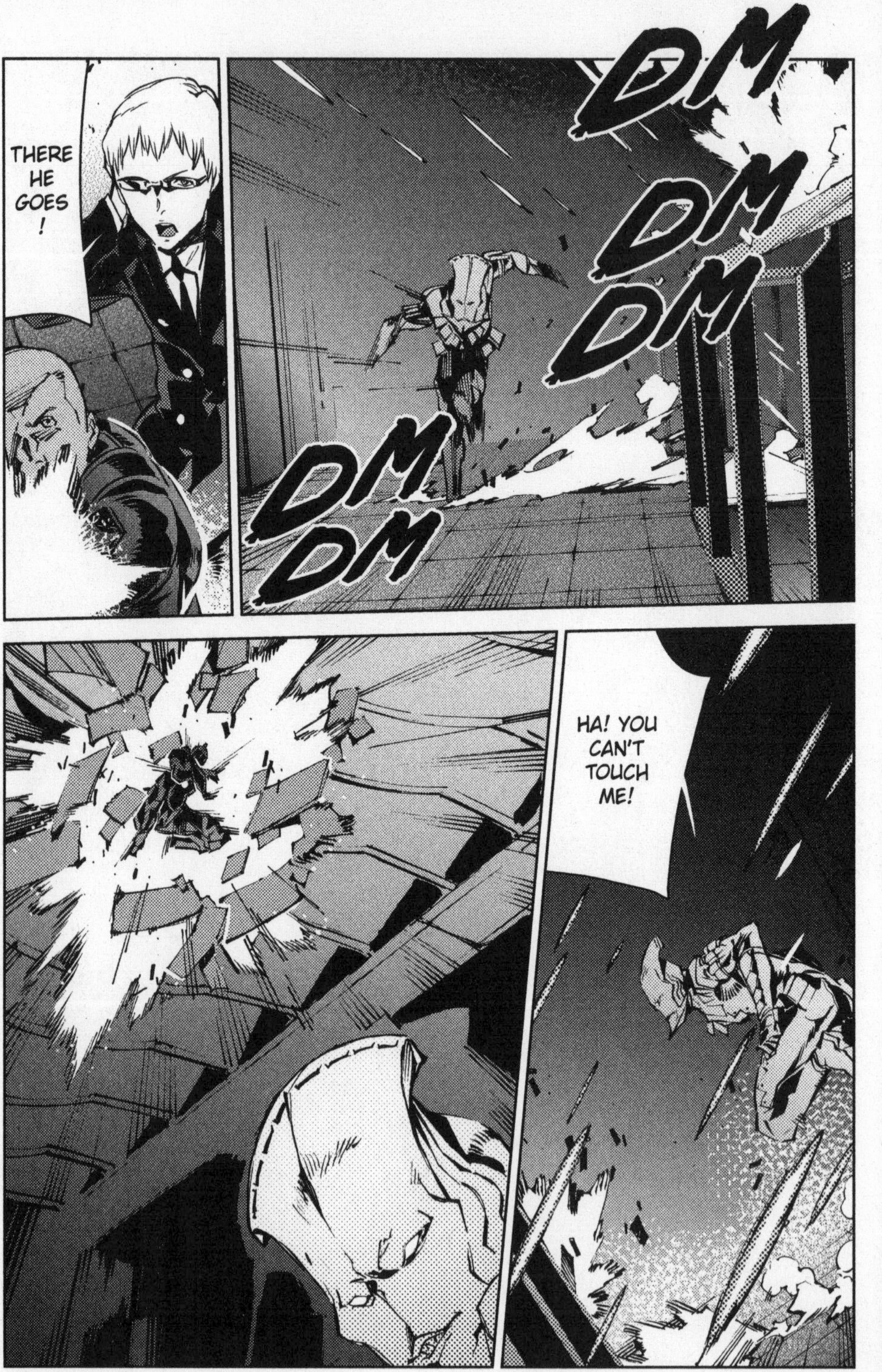
DM
DM
DM
DM
DM
THERE HE GOES!
HA! YOU CAN'T TOUCH ME!

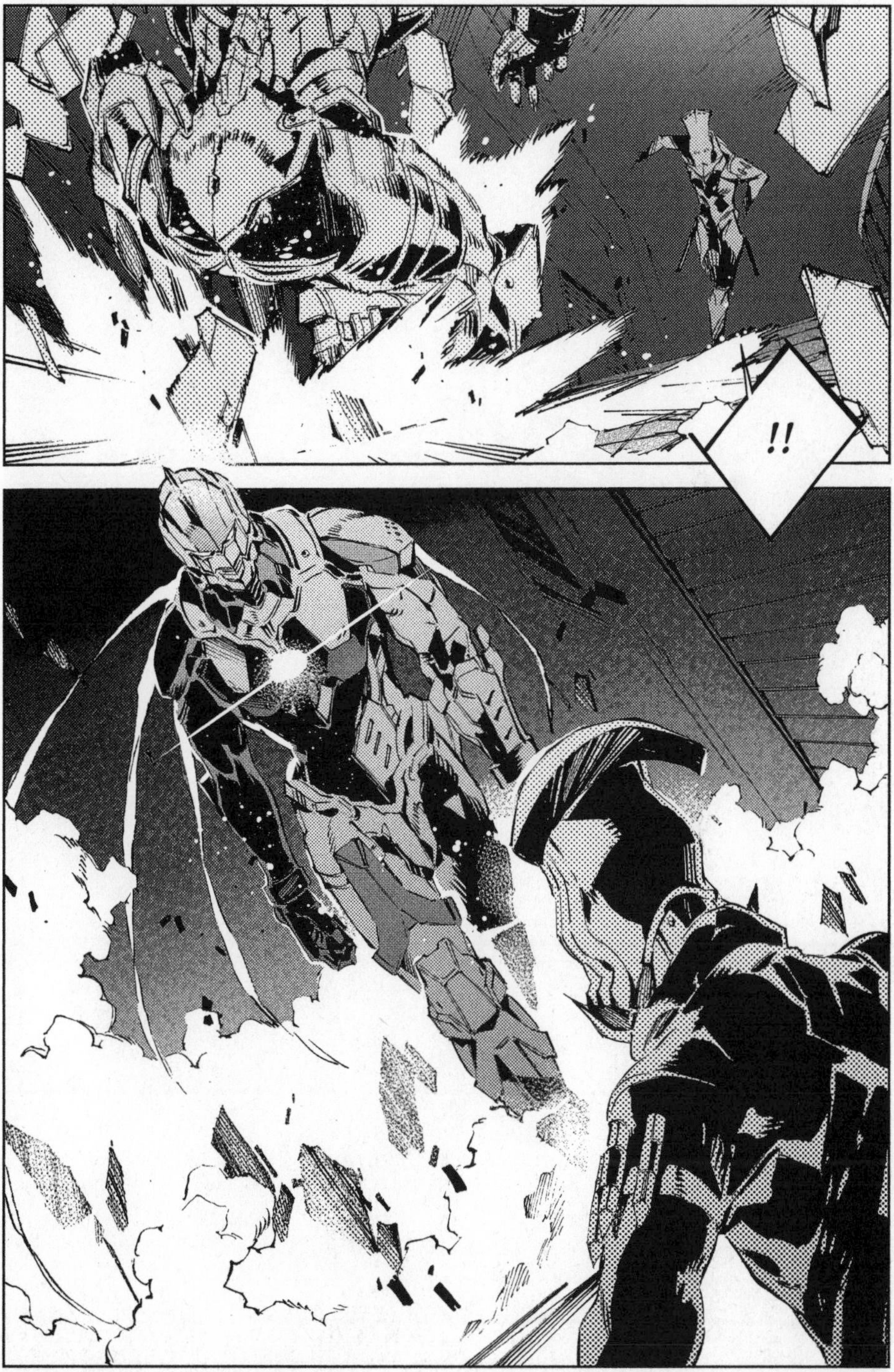
!!

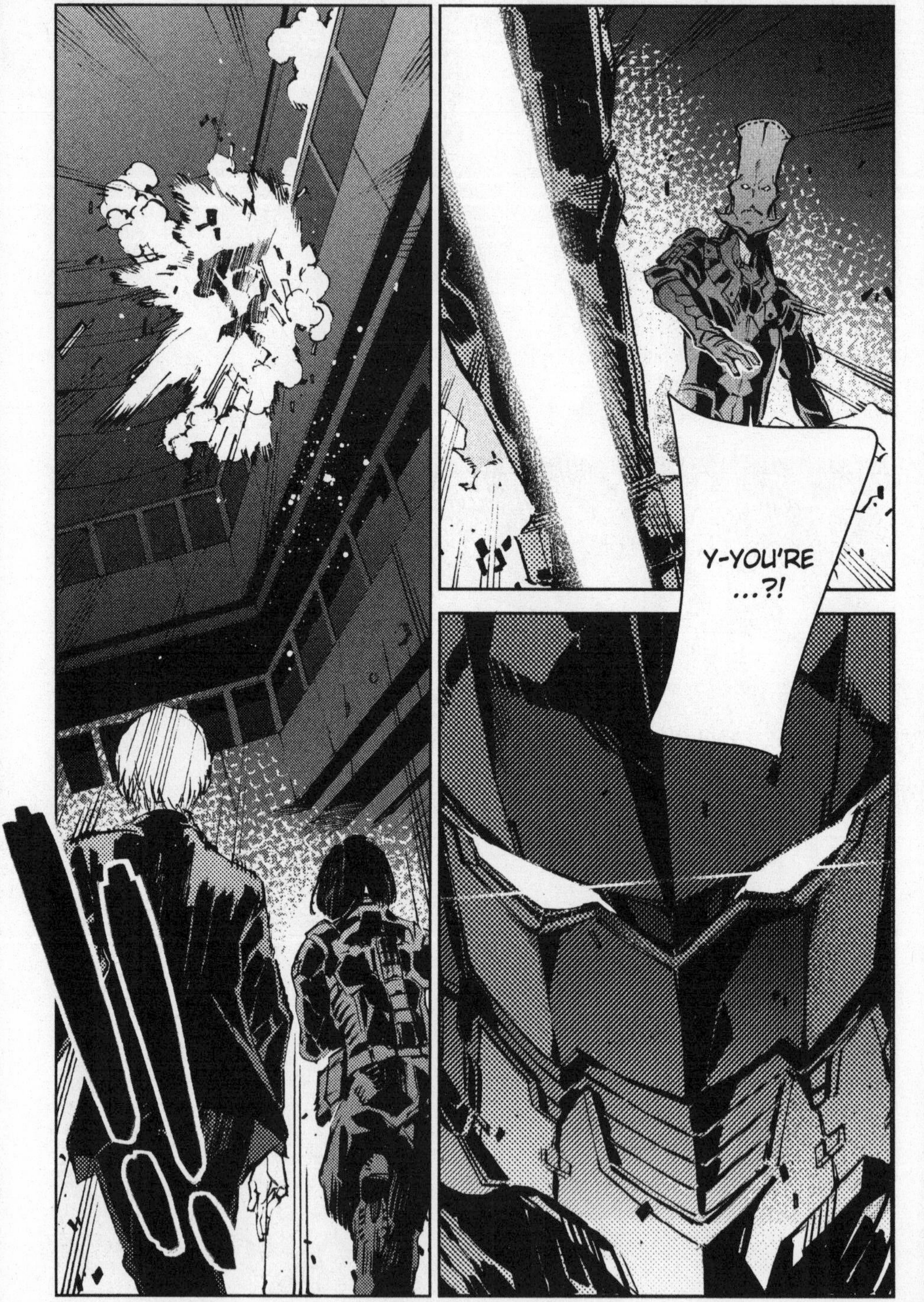
Y-YOU'RE ...?!

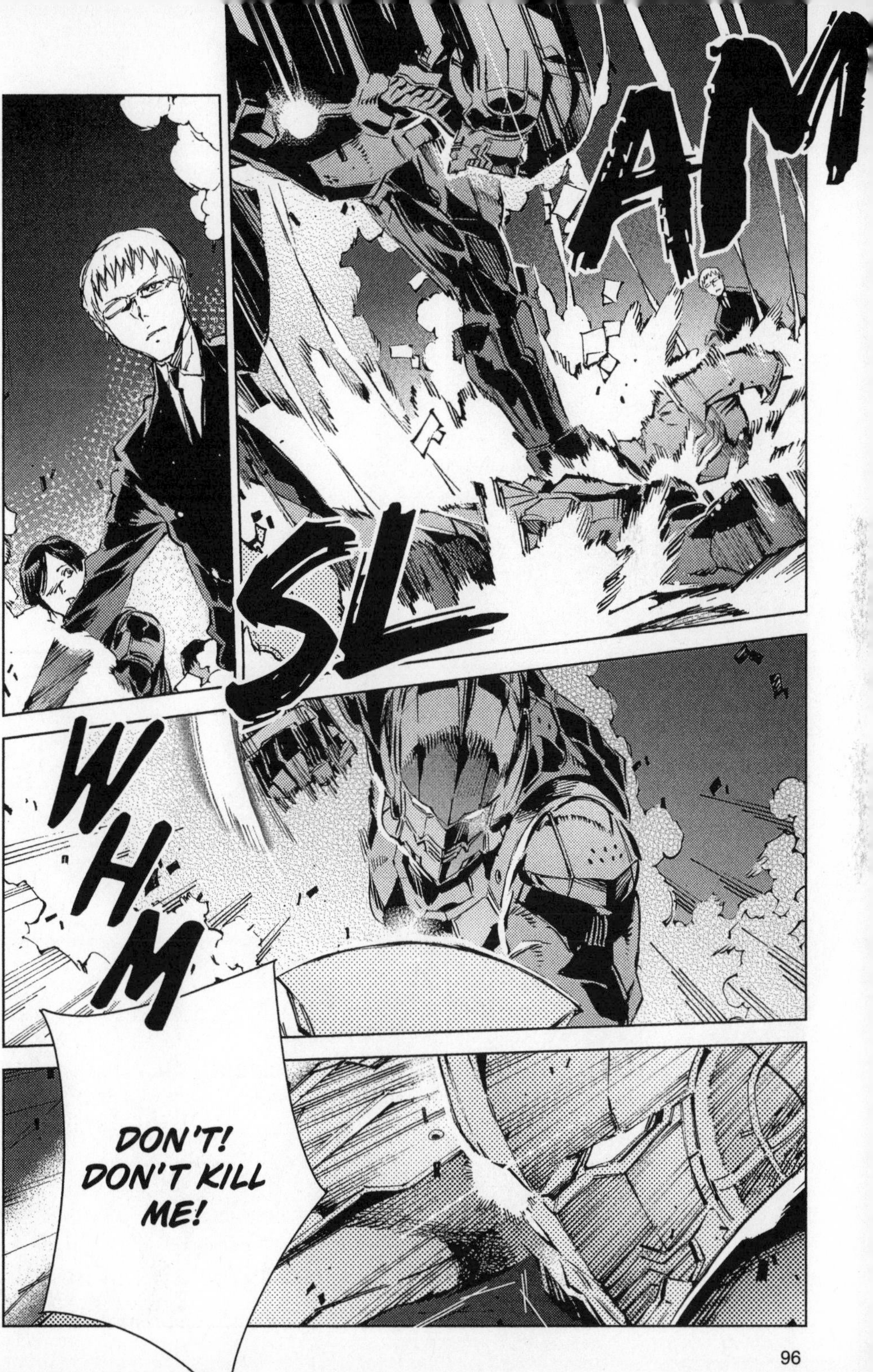
SLAM
WHM
DON'T! DON'T KILL ME!

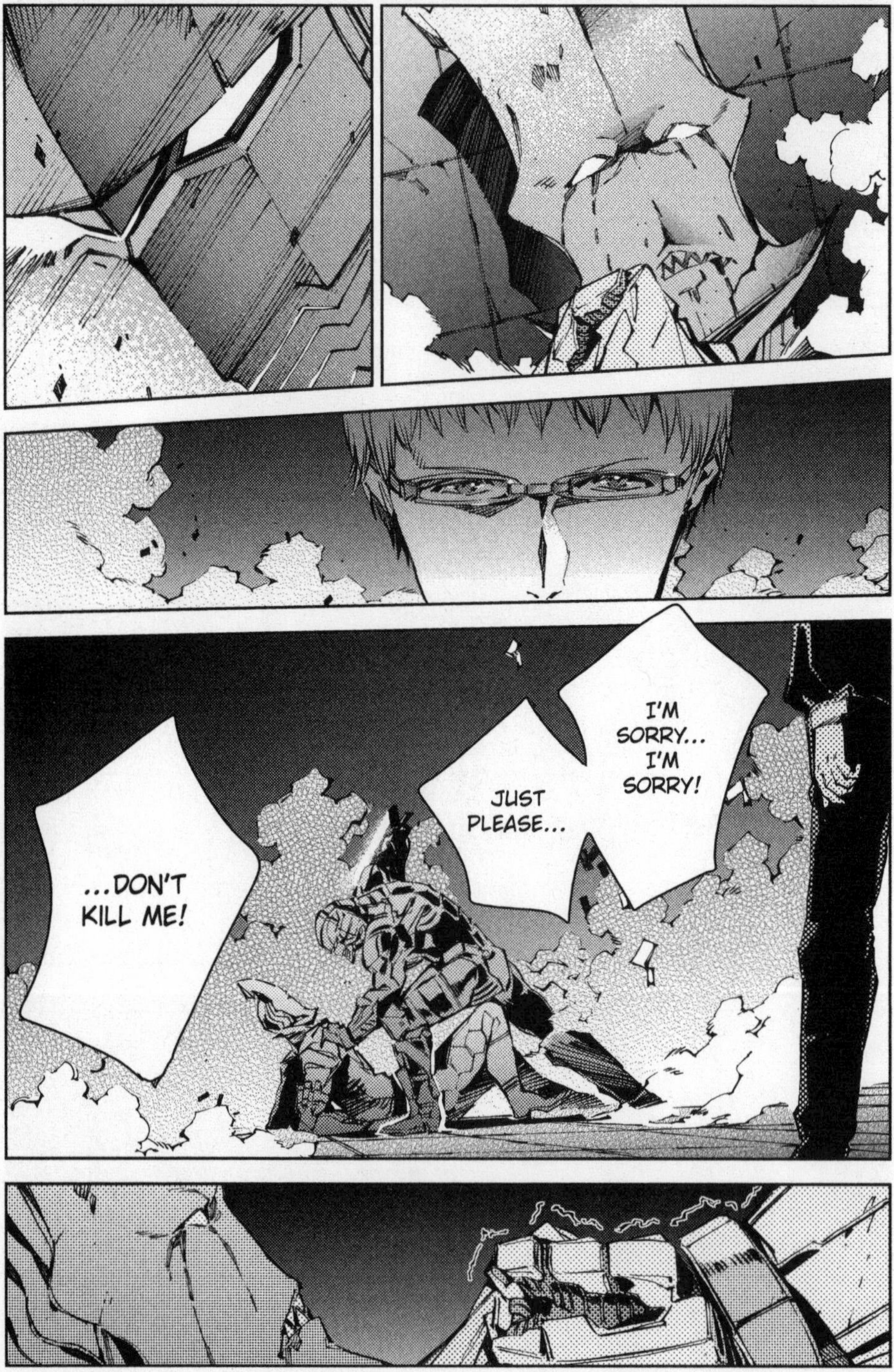
I'M SORRY... I'M SORRY!
JUST PLEASE...
...DON'T KILL ME!

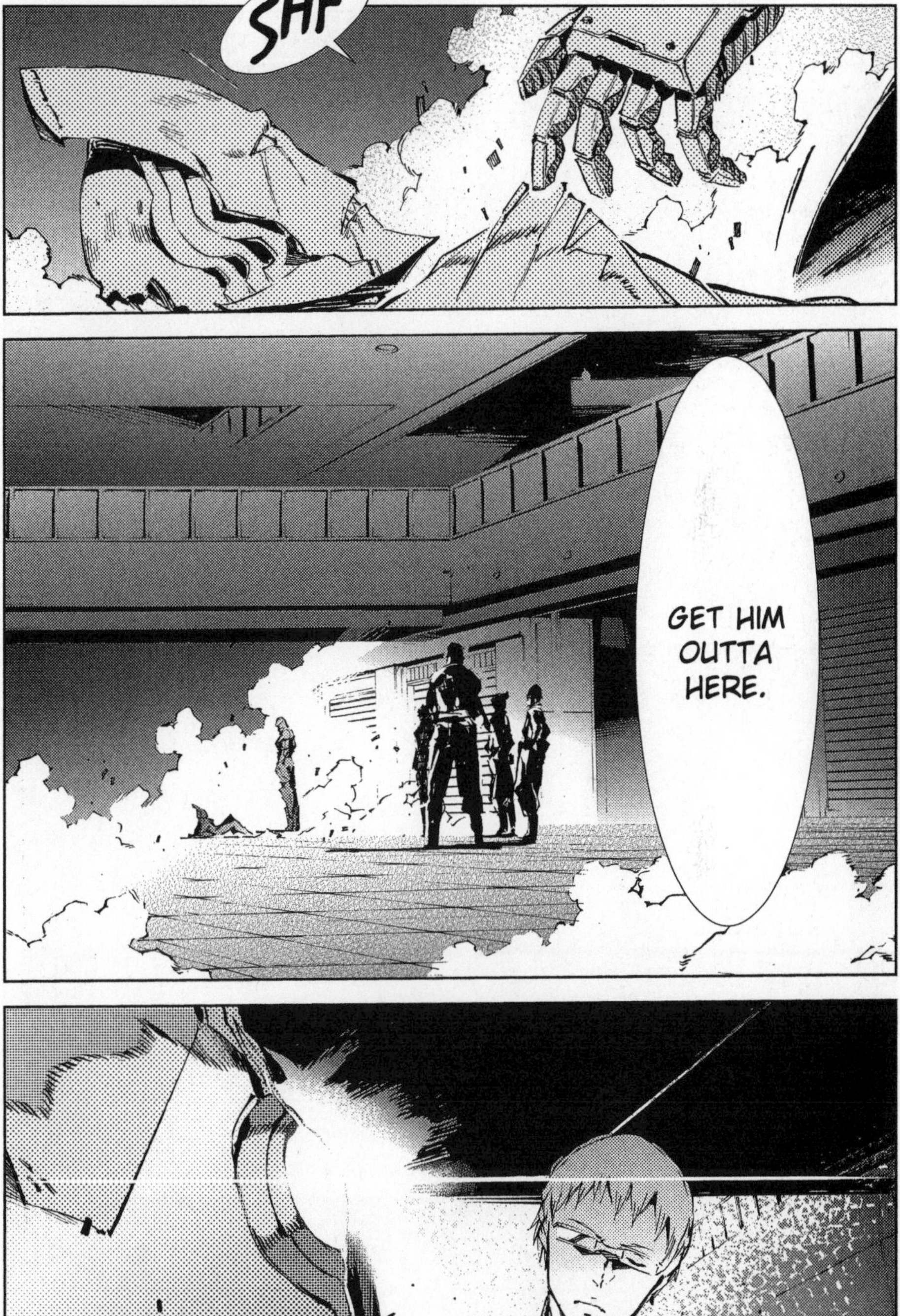
SHF
GET HIM OUTTA HERE.

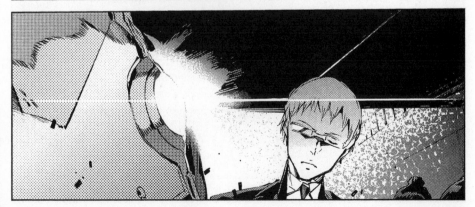

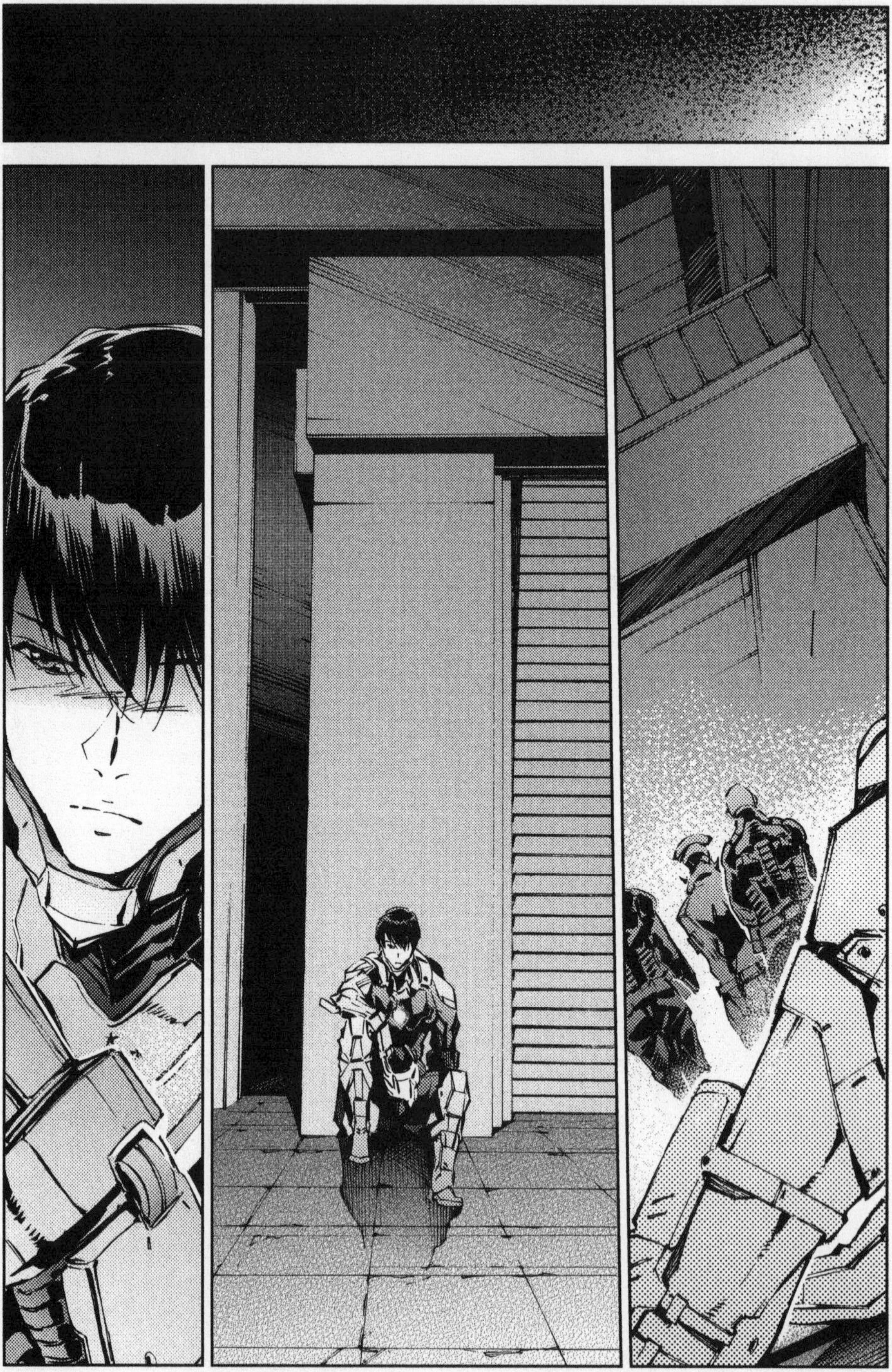

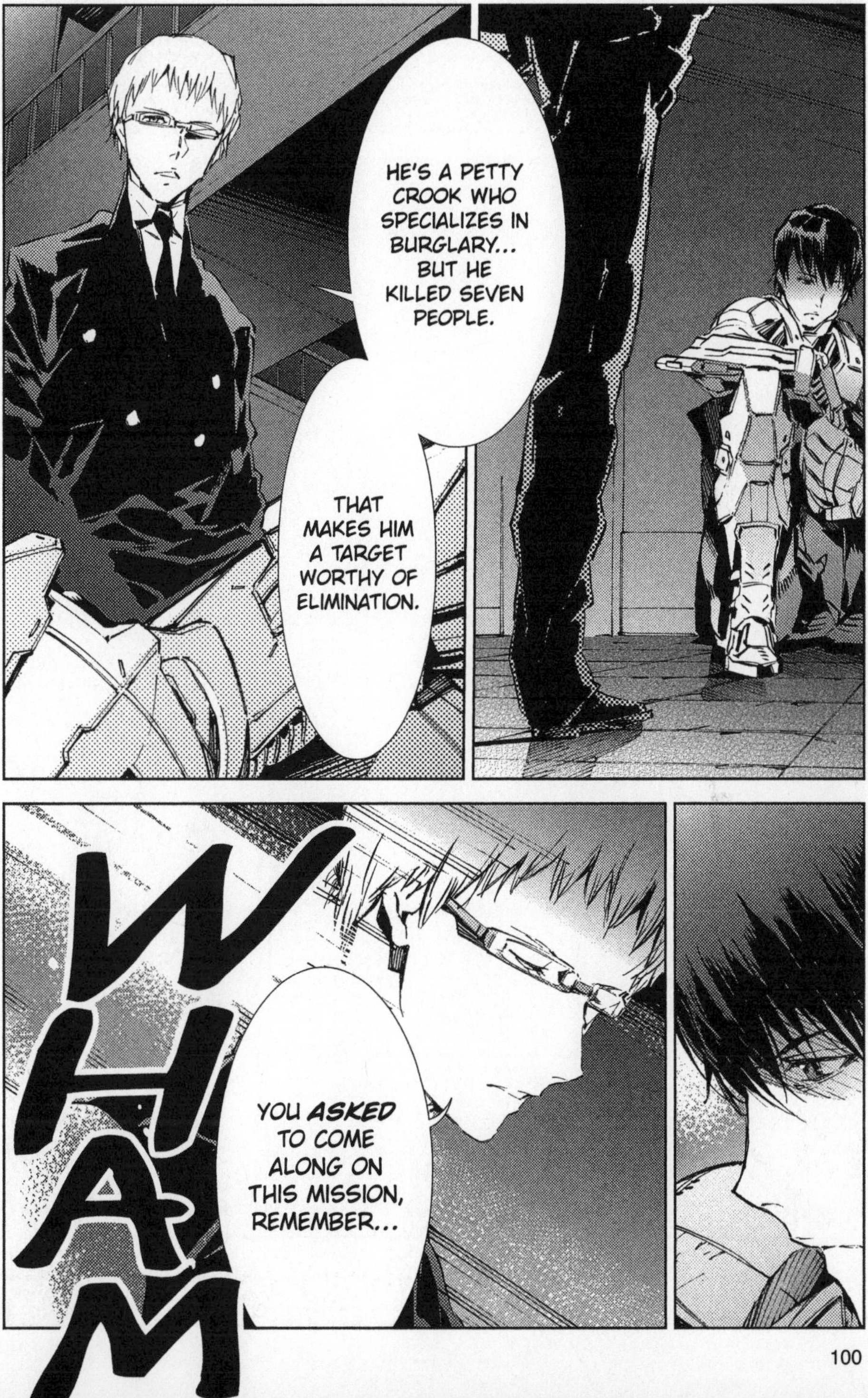
HE'S A PETTY CROOK WHO SPECIALIZES IN BURGLARY... BUT HE KILLED SEVEN PEOPLE.
THAT MAKES HIM A TARGET WORTHY OF ELIMINATION.
YOU **ASKED** TO COME ALONG ON THIS MISSION, REMEMBER...
WHAM

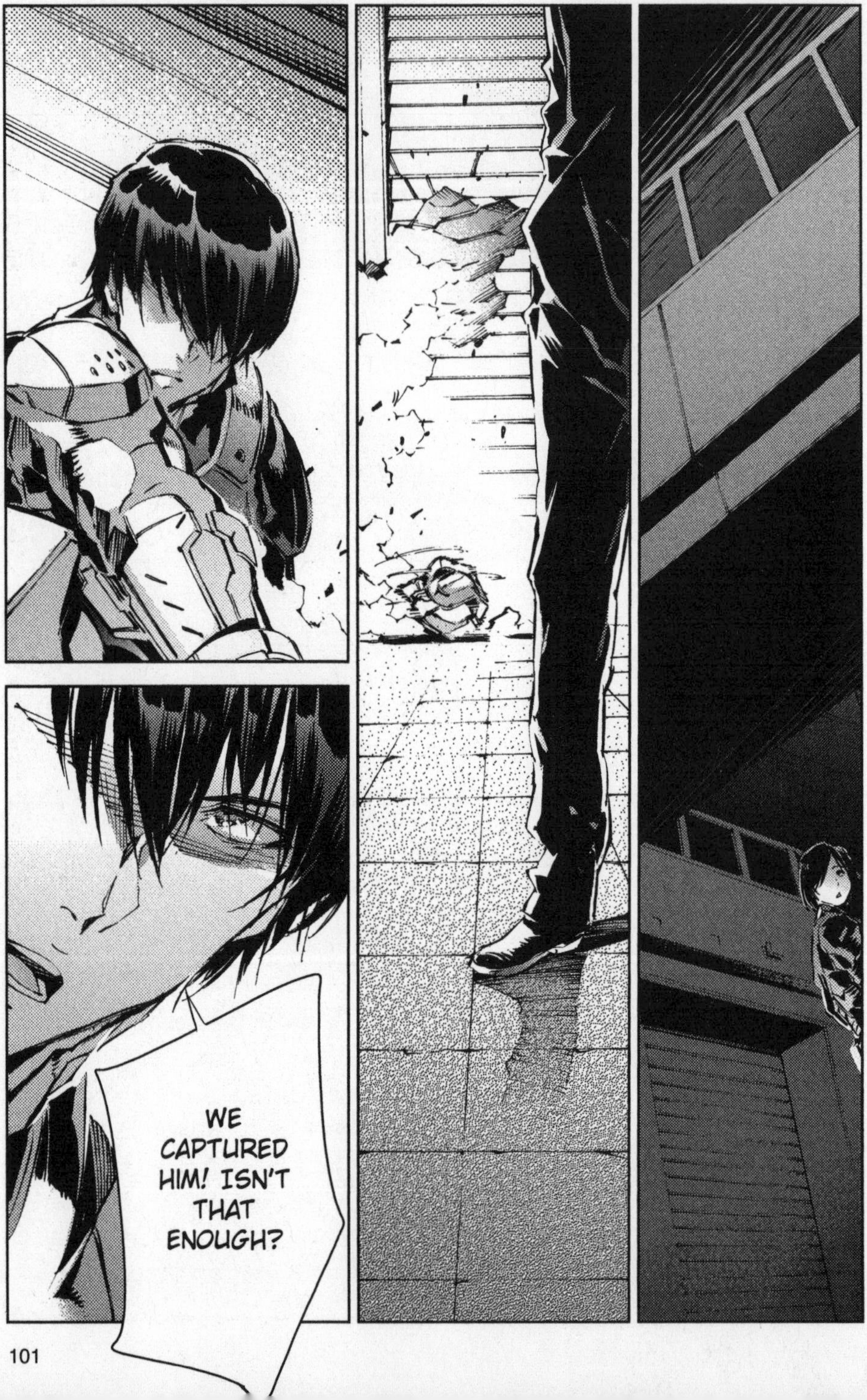
WE CAPTURED HIM! ISN'T THAT ENOUGH?

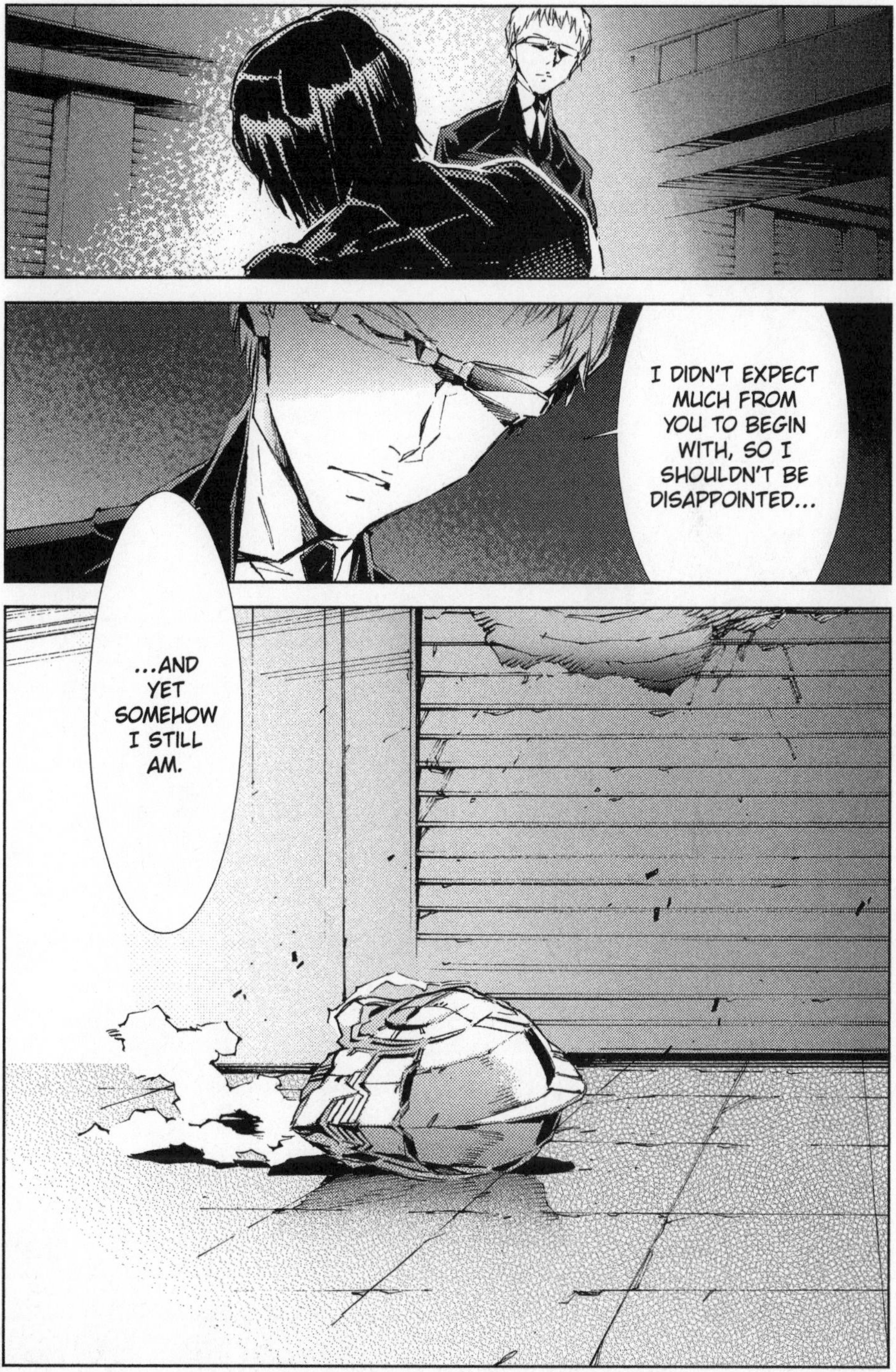
I DIDN'T EXPECT MUCH FROM YOU TO BEGIN WITH, SO I SHOULDN'T BE DISAPPOINTED...
...AND YET SOMEHOW I STILL AM.

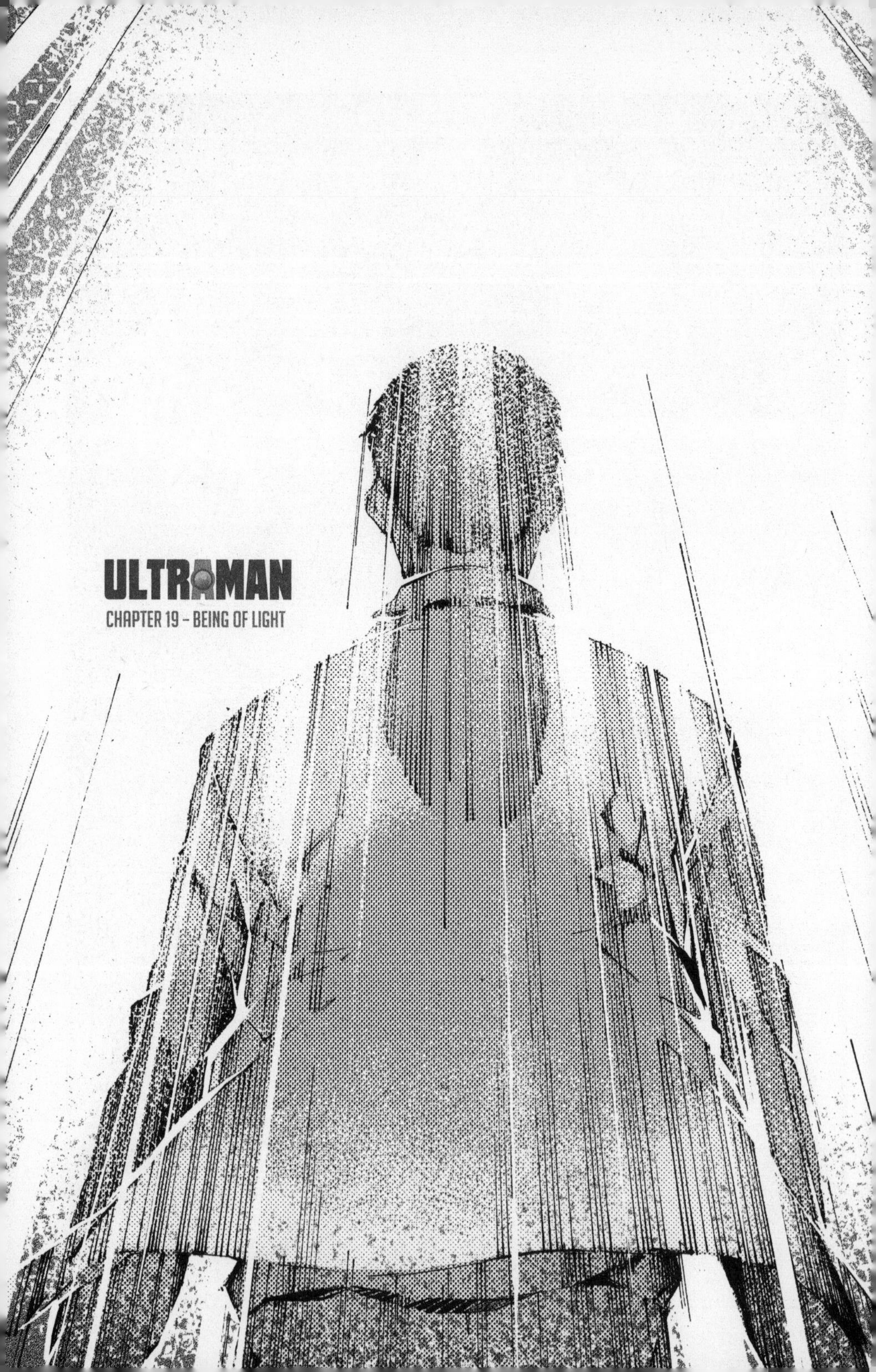
ULTRAMAN
CHAPTER 19 – BEING OF LIGHT

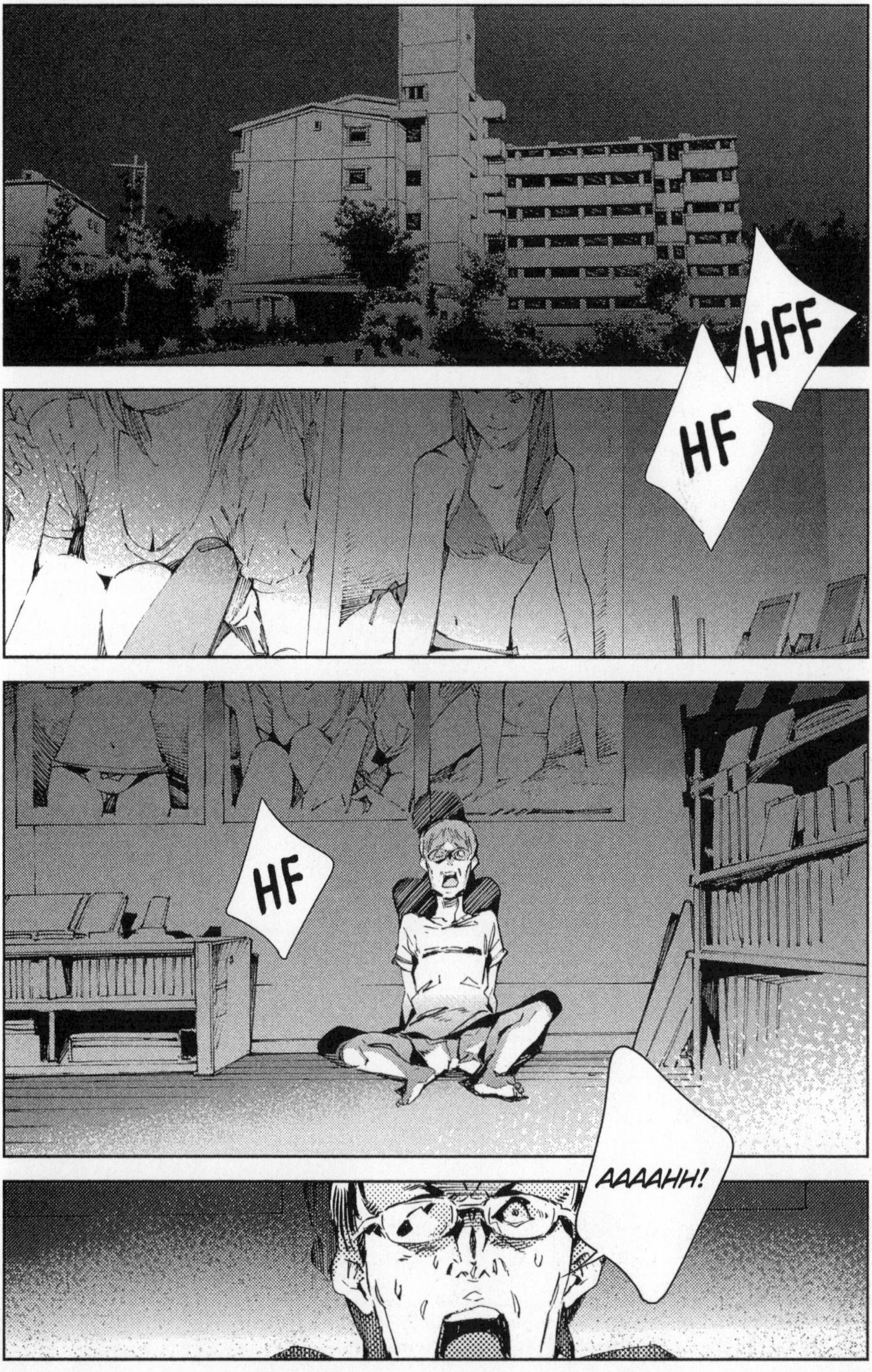
HFF
HF
HF
AAAAHH!

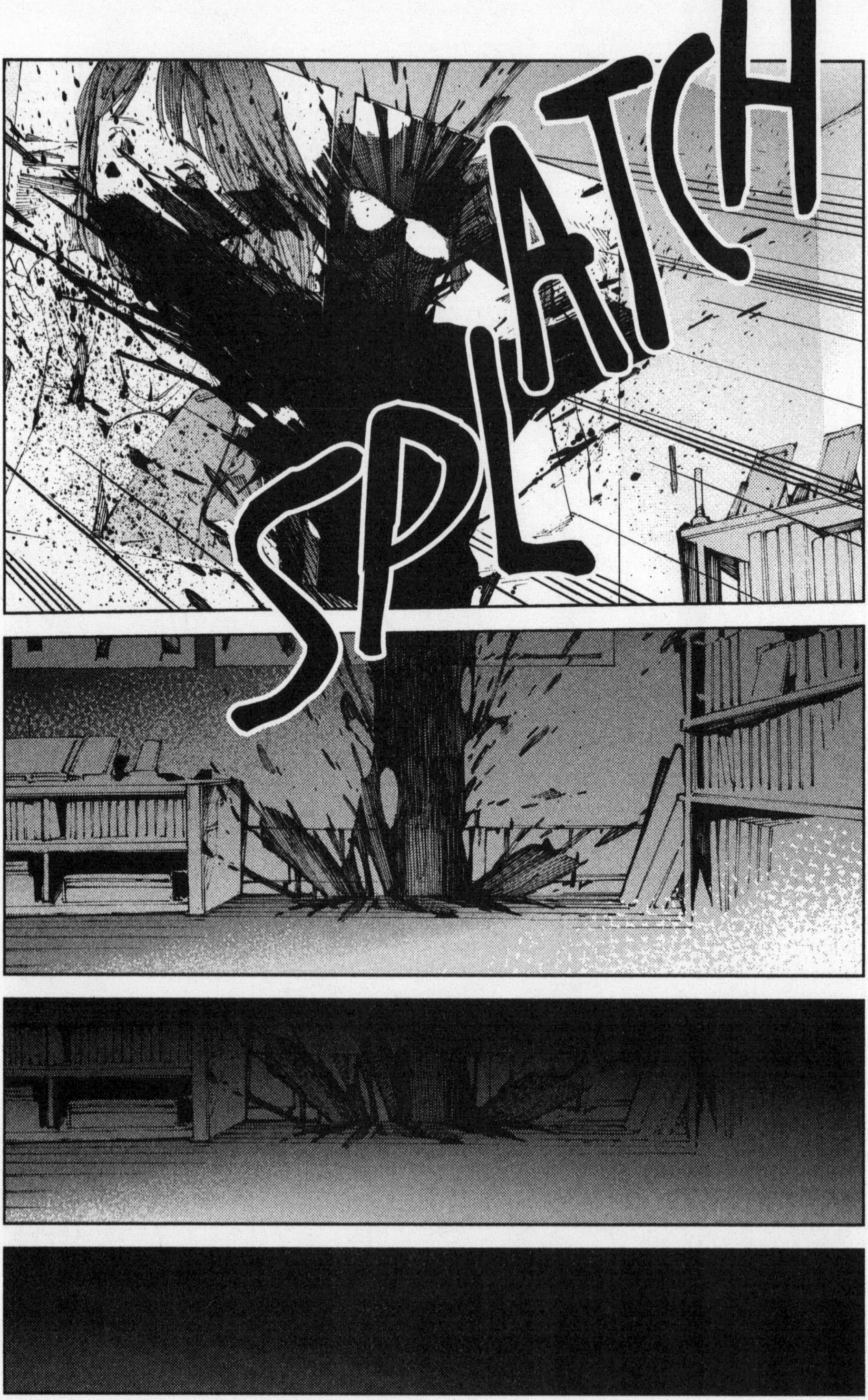
SPLATCH

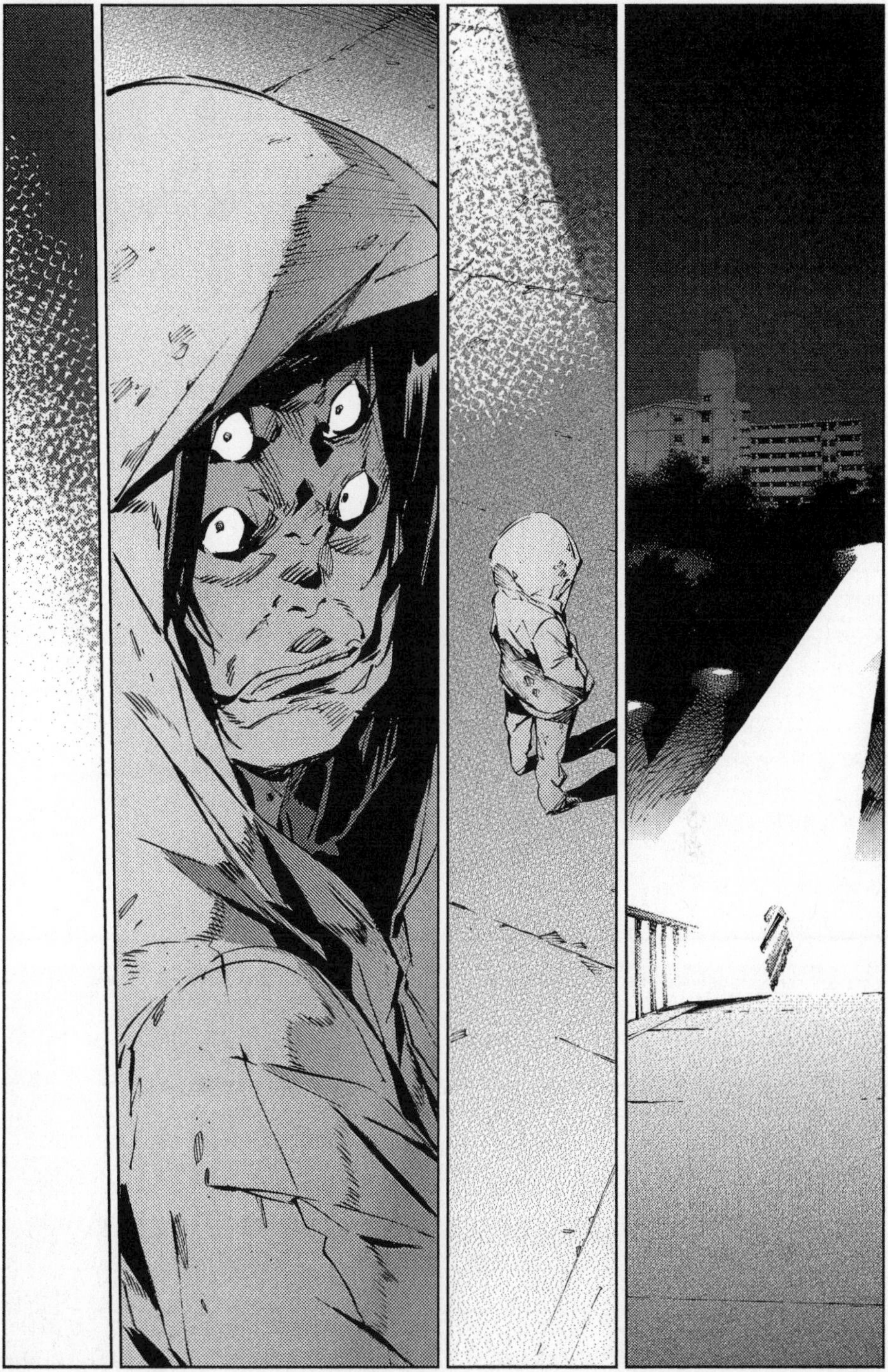

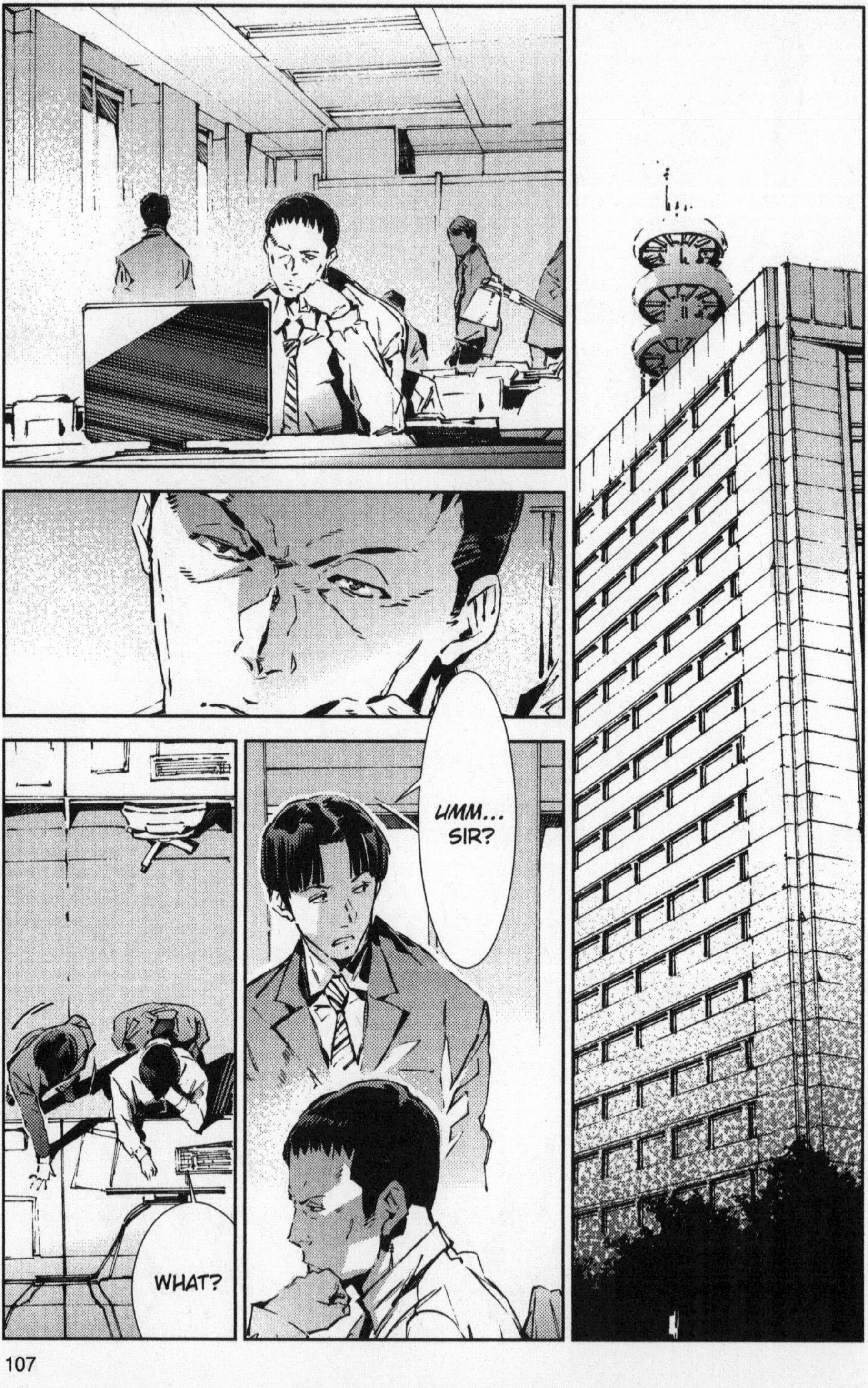
UMM... SIR?
WHAT?

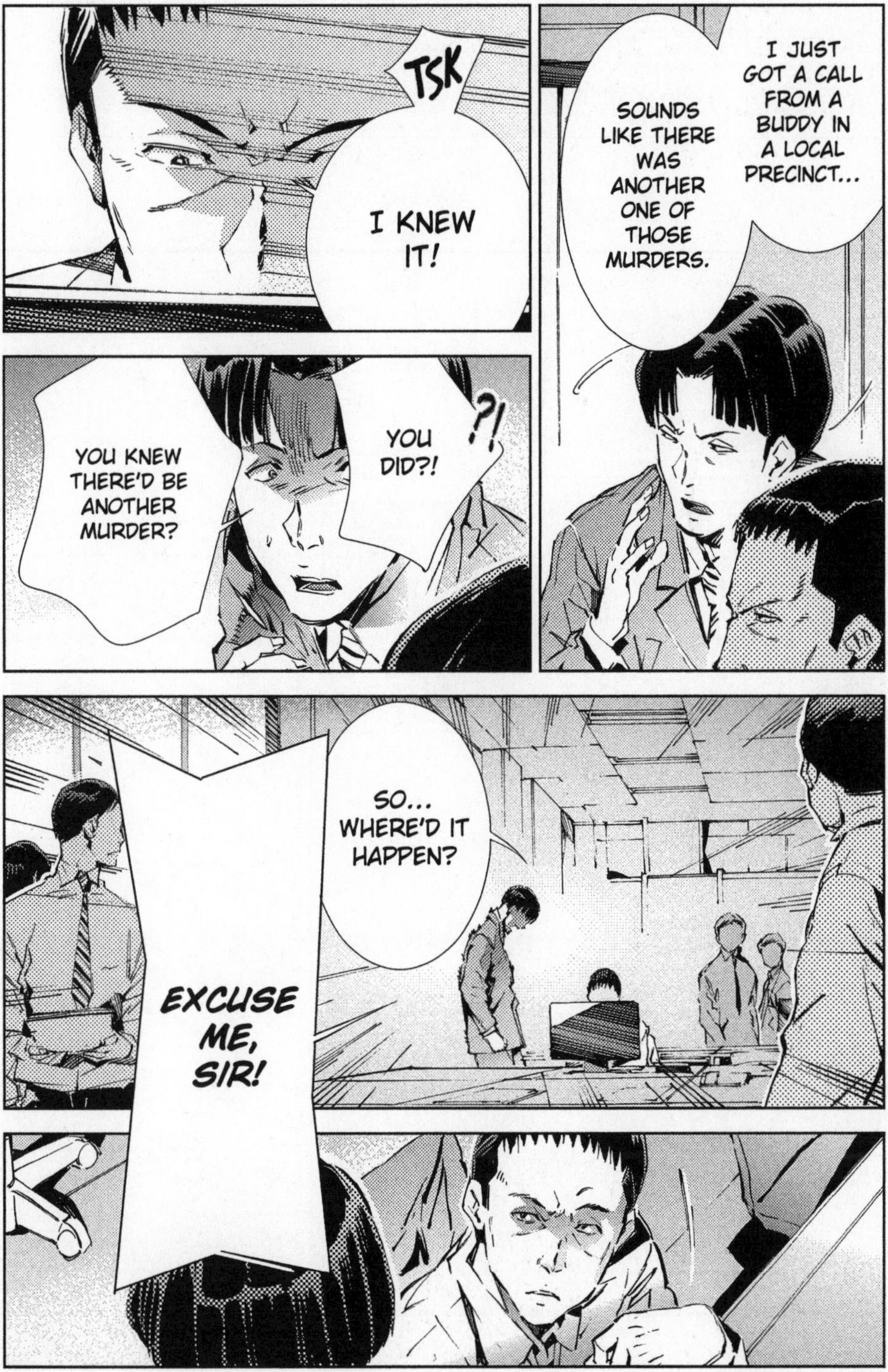
I JUST GOT A CALL FROM A BUDDY IN A LOCAL PRECINCT...
SOUNDS LIKE THERE WAS ANOTHER ONE OF THOSE MURDERS.
TSK
I KNEW IT!
?!
YOU DID?!
YOU KNEW THERE'D BE ANOTHER MURDER?
SO... WHERE'D IT HAPPEN?
EXCUSE ME, SIR!

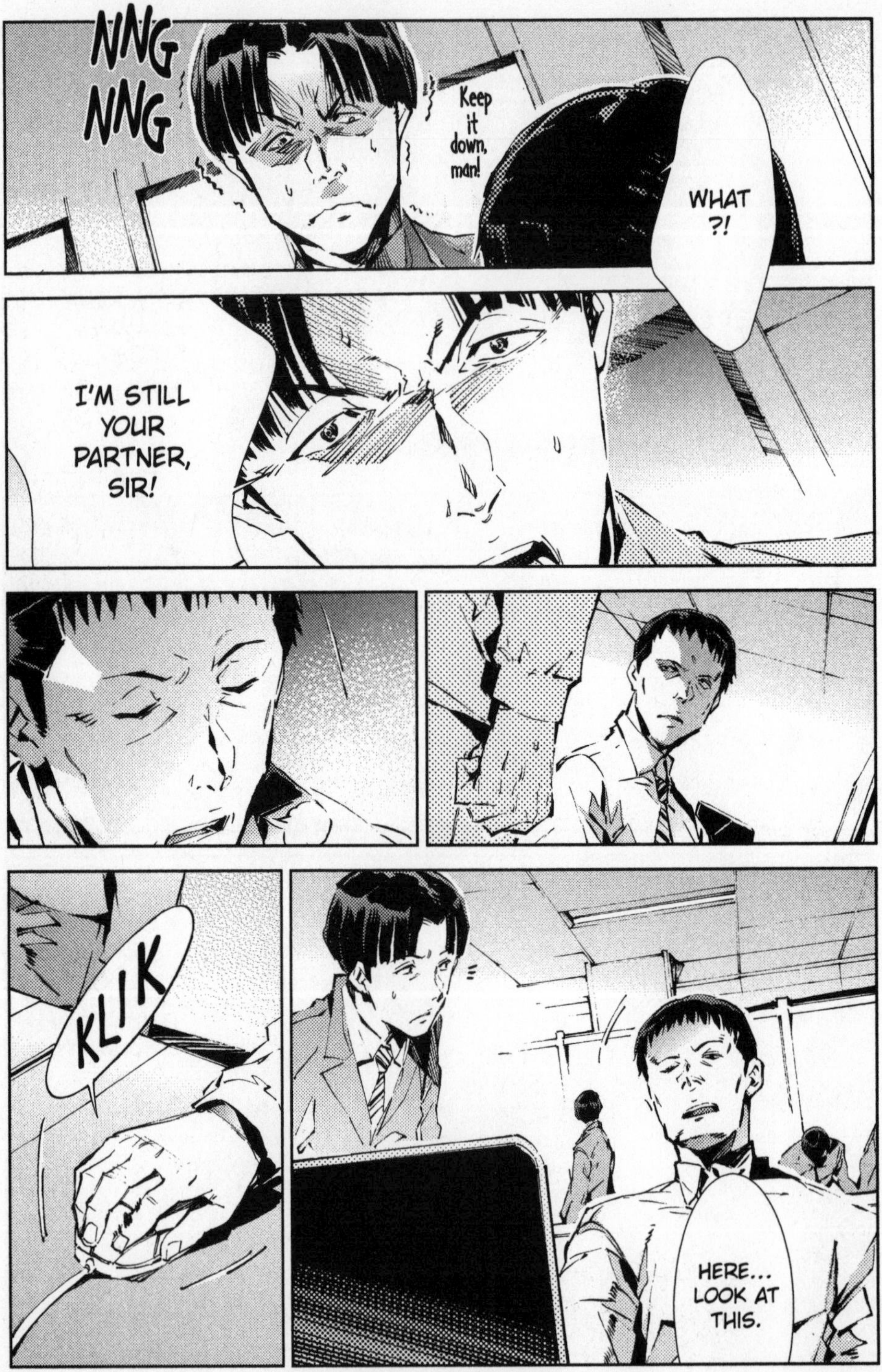
WHAT ?!
Keep it down, man!
NNG NNG
I'M STILL YOUR PARTNER, SIR!
HERE... LOOK AT THIS.
KLIK

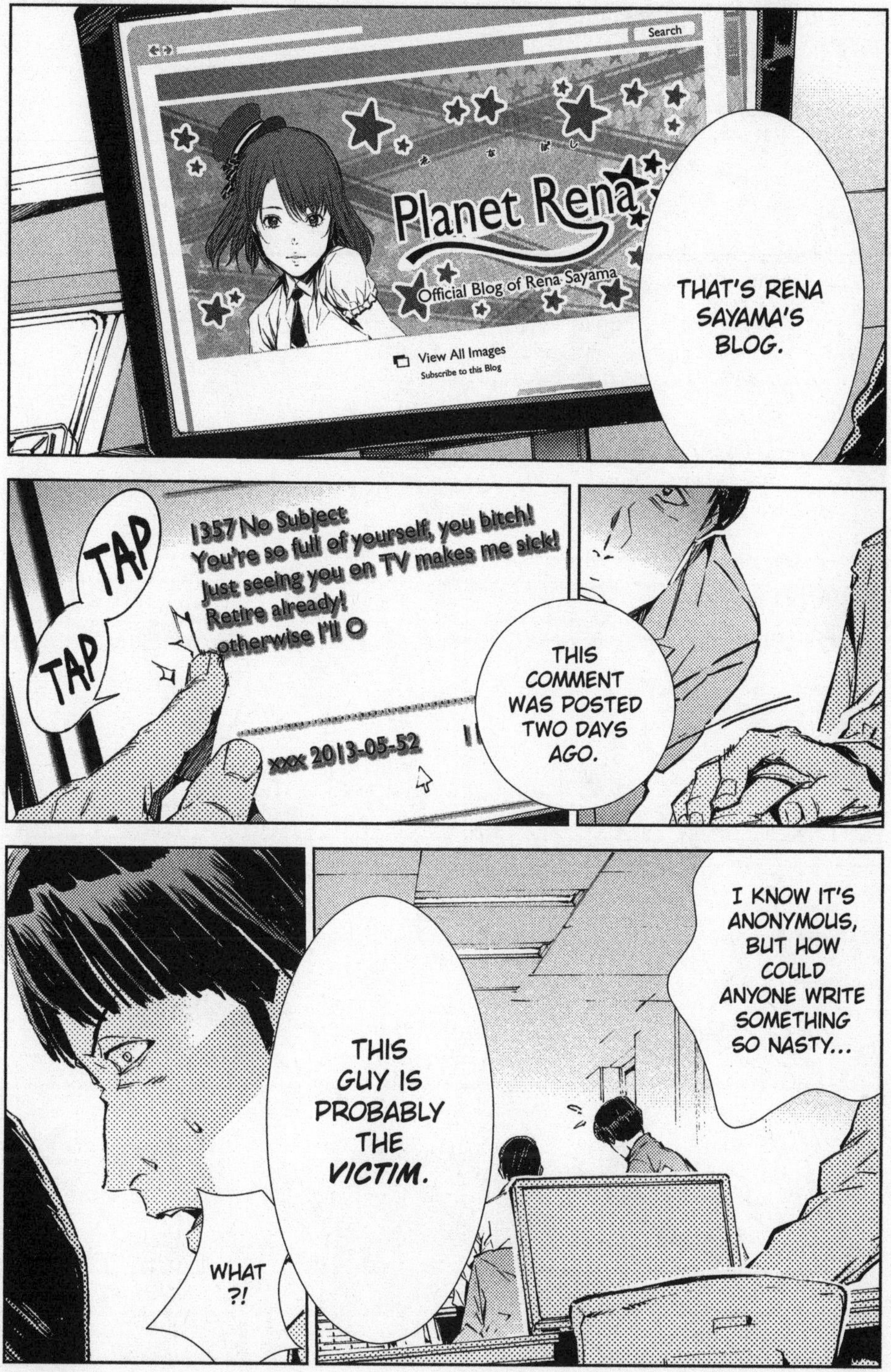
Search
Planet Rena
Official Blog of Rena Sayama
View All Images
Subscribe to this Blog
THAT'S RENA SAYAMA'S BLOG.
THIS COMMENT WAS POSTED TWO DAYS AGO.
1357 No Subject
You're so full of yourself, you bitch!
Just seeing you on TV makes me sick!
Retire already!
otherwise I'll O
xxx 2013-05-52
TAP
TAP
I KNOW IT'S ANONYMOUS, BUT HOW COULD ANYONE WRITE SOMETHING SO NASTY...
THIS GUY IS PROBABLY THE *VICTIM.*
WHAT ?!

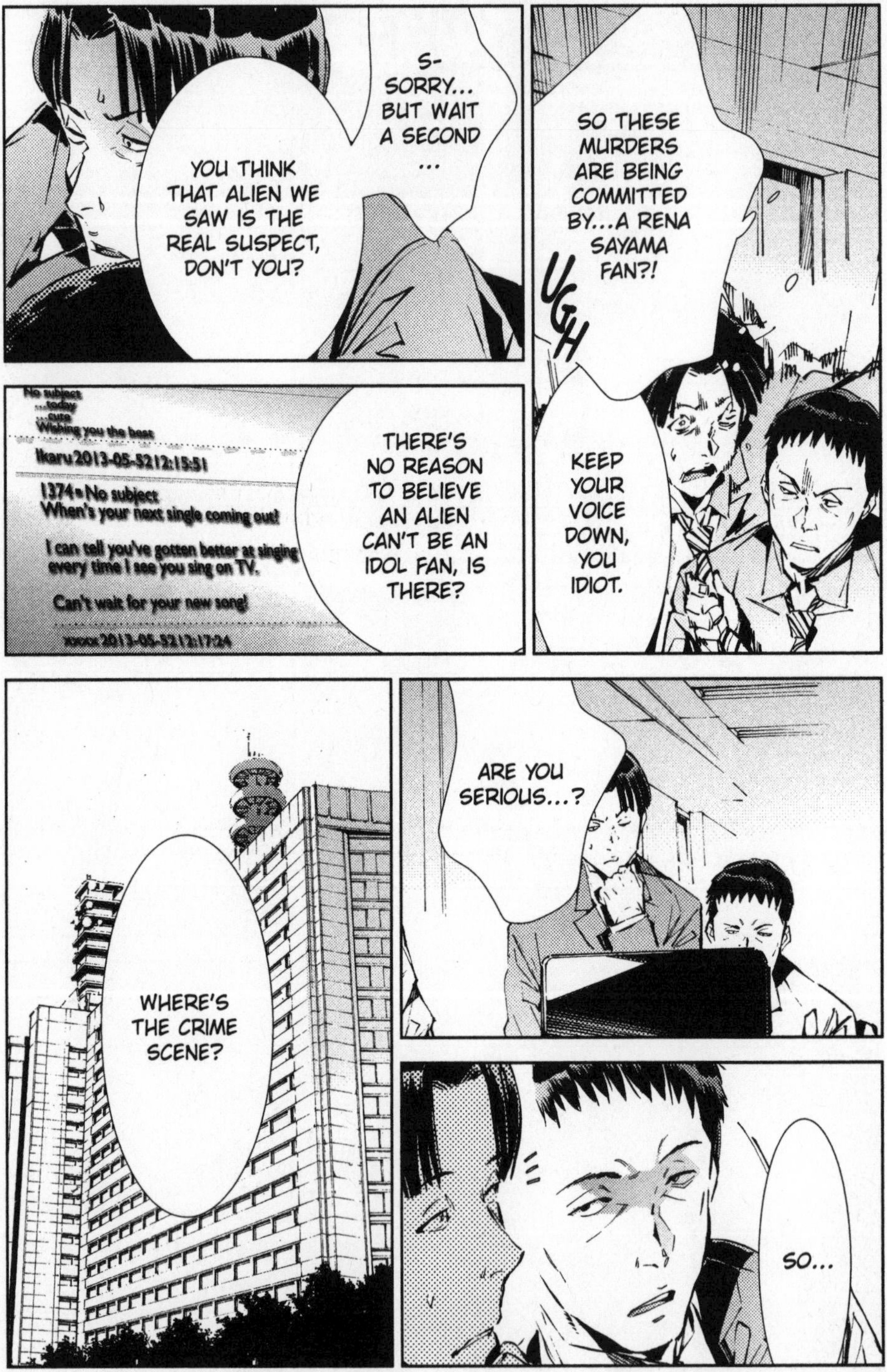
SO THESE MURDERS ARE BEING COMMITTED BY...A RENA SAYAMA FAN?!
UGH
KEEP YOUR VOICE DOWN, YOU IDIOT.
S-SORRY... BUT WAIT A SECOND...
YOU THINK THAT ALIEN WE SAW IS THE REAL SUSPECT, DON'T YOU?
Ikaru 2013-05-52 12:15:51
1374 • No subject
When's your next single coming out!
I can tell you've gotten better at singing every time I see you sing on TV.
Can't wait for your new song!
xxxx 2013-05-52 12:17:24
THERE'S NO REASON TO BELIEVE AN ALIEN CAN'T BE AN IDOL FAN, IS THERE?
ARE YOU SERIOUS...?
SO...
WHERE'S THE CRIME SCENE?

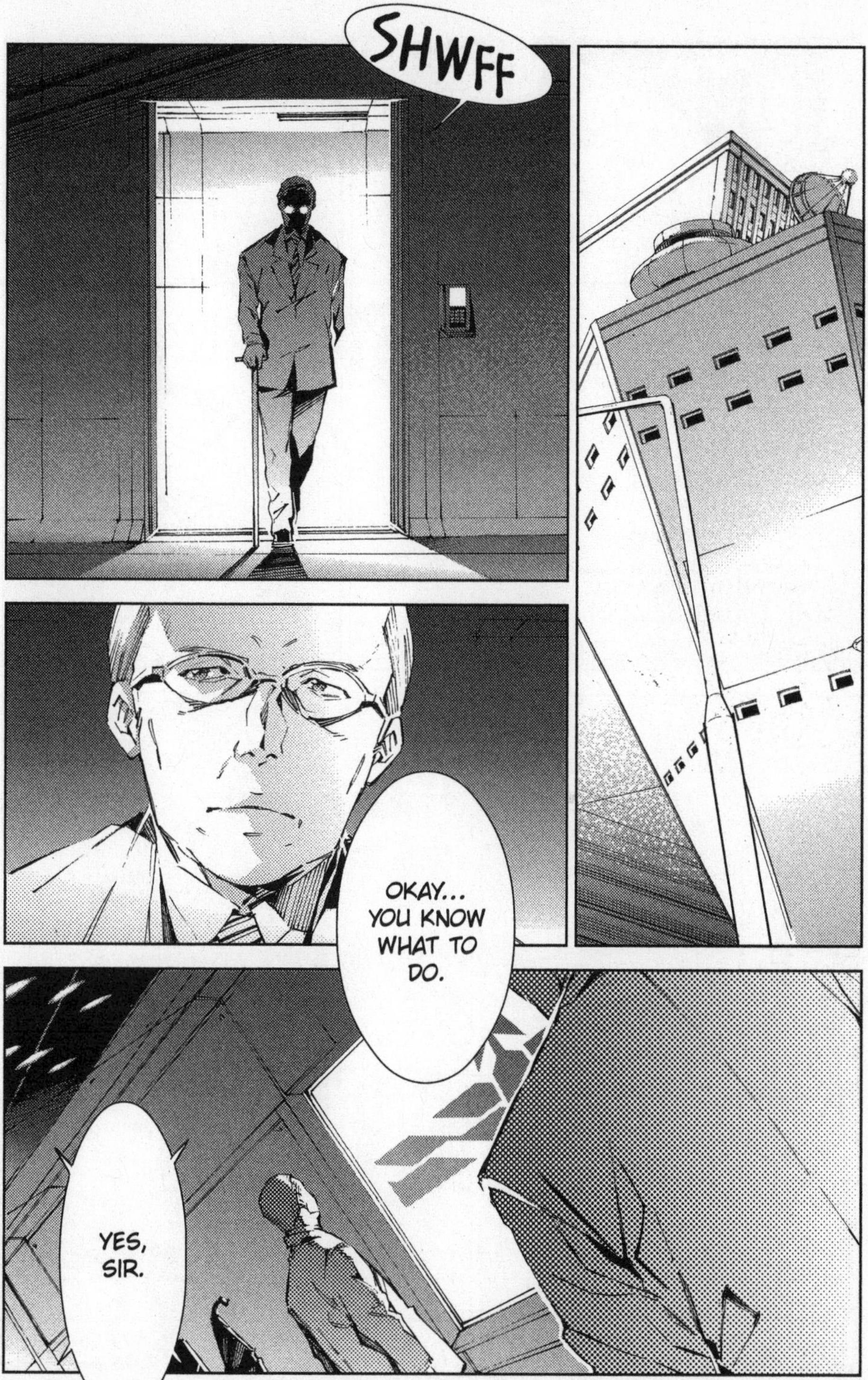
SHWFF
OKAY... YOU KNOW WHAT TO DO.
YES, SIR.

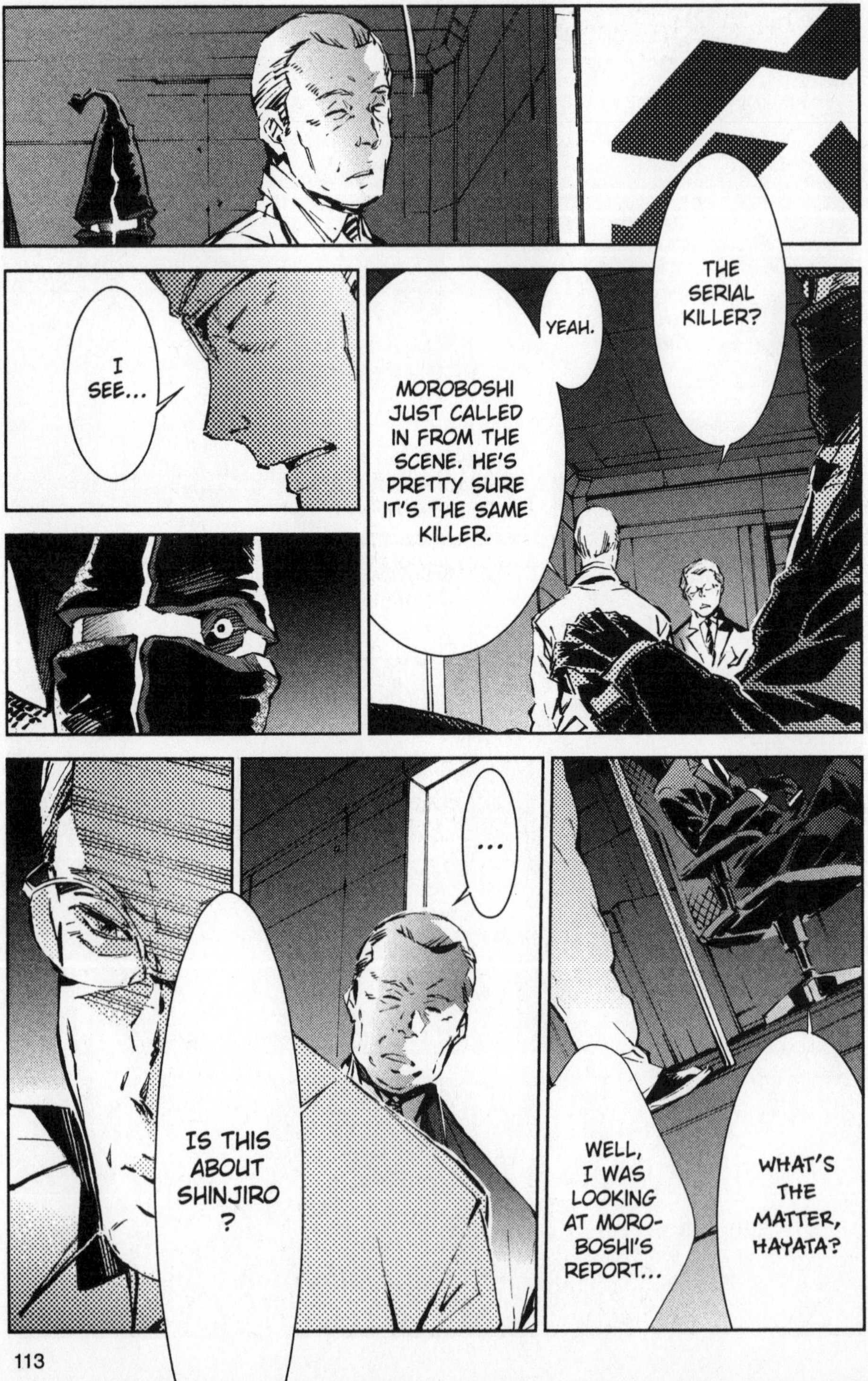
THE SERIAL KILLER?
YEAH.
MOROBOSHI JUST CALLED IN FROM THE SCENE. HE'S PRETTY SURE IT'S THE SAME KILLER.
I SEE...
WHAT'S THE MATTER, HAYATA?
WELL, I WAS LOOKING AT MORO-BOSHI'S REPORT...
...
IS THIS ABOUT SHINJIRO?

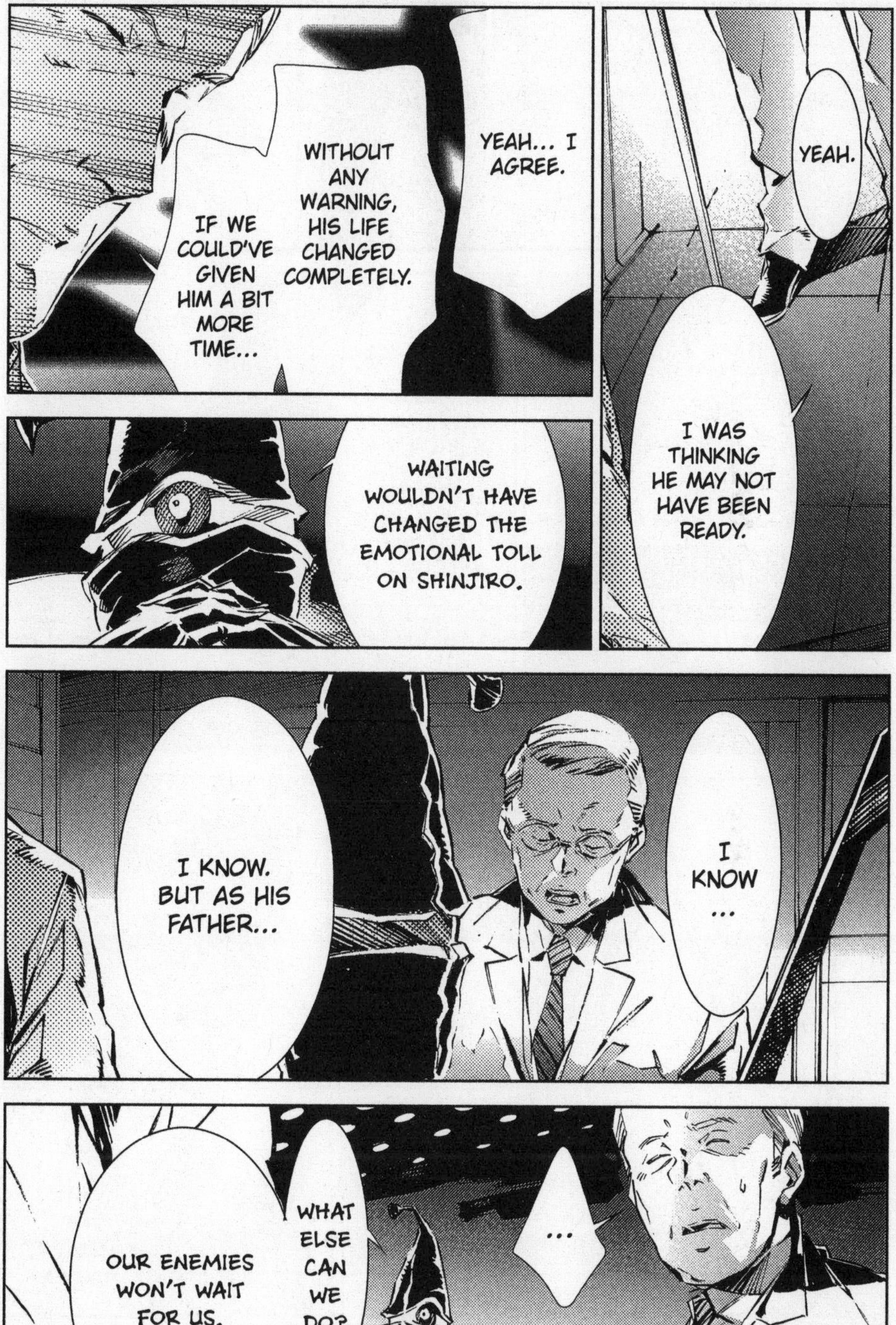
YEAH.
I WAS THINKING HE MAY NOT HAVE BEEN READY.
YEAH... I AGREE.
WITHOUT ANY WARNING, HIS LIFE CHANGED COMPLETELY.
IF WE COULD'VE GIVEN HIM A BIT MORE TIME...
WAITING WOULDN'T HAVE CHANGED THE EMOTIONAL TOLL ON SHINJIRO.
I KNOW ...
I KNOW. BUT AS HIS FATHER...
...
WHAT ELSE CAN WE DO?
OUR ENEMIES WON'T WAIT FOR US.

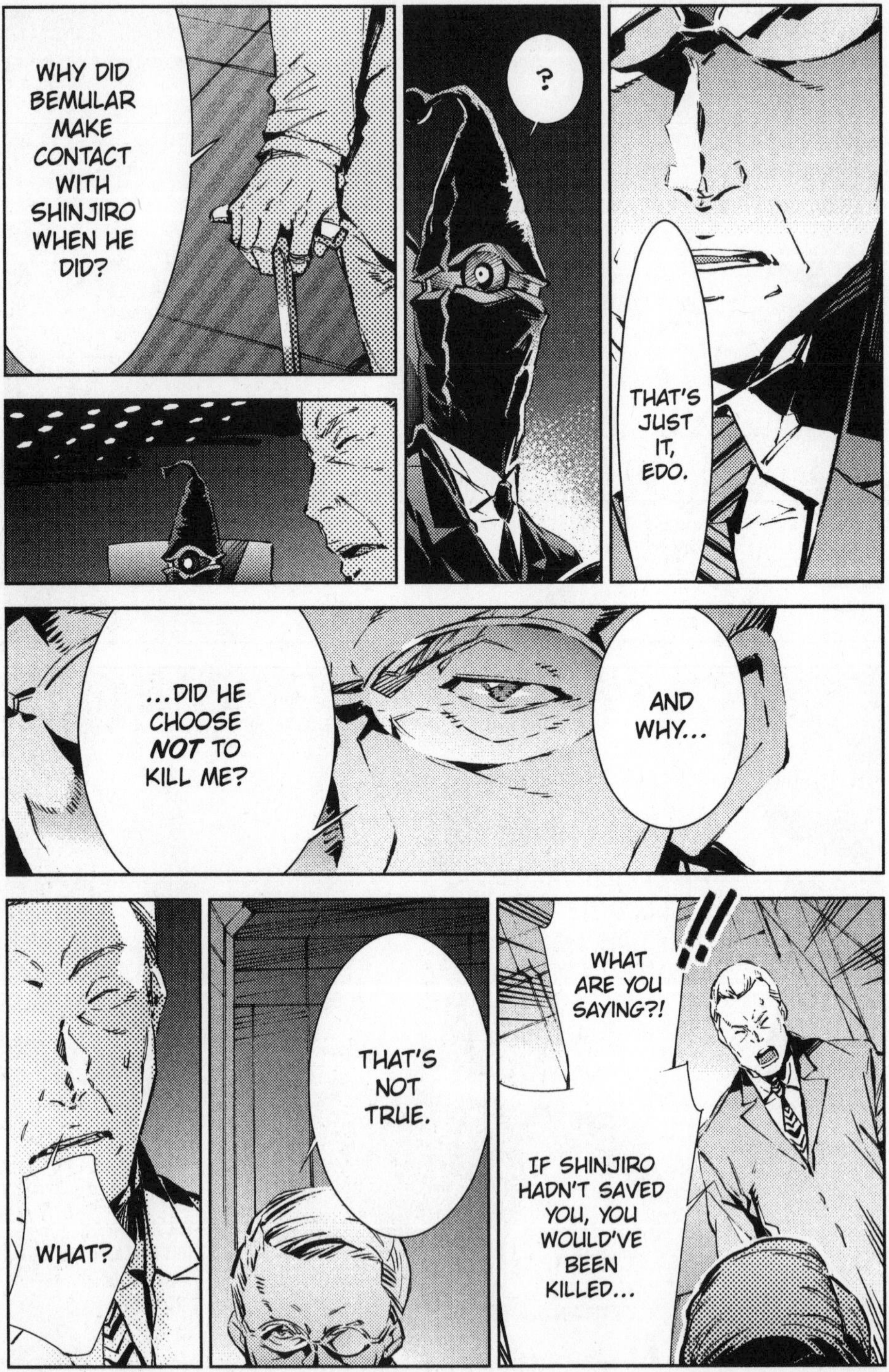
THAT'S JUST IT, EDO.
?
WHY DID BEMULAR MAKE CONTACT WITH SHINJIRO WHEN HE DID?
AND WHY...
...DID HE CHOOSE ***NOT*** TO KILL ME?
!!
WHAT ARE YOU SAYING?!
IF SHINJIRO HADN'T SAVED YOU, YOU WOULD'VE BEEN KILLED...
THAT'S NOT TRUE.
WHAT?

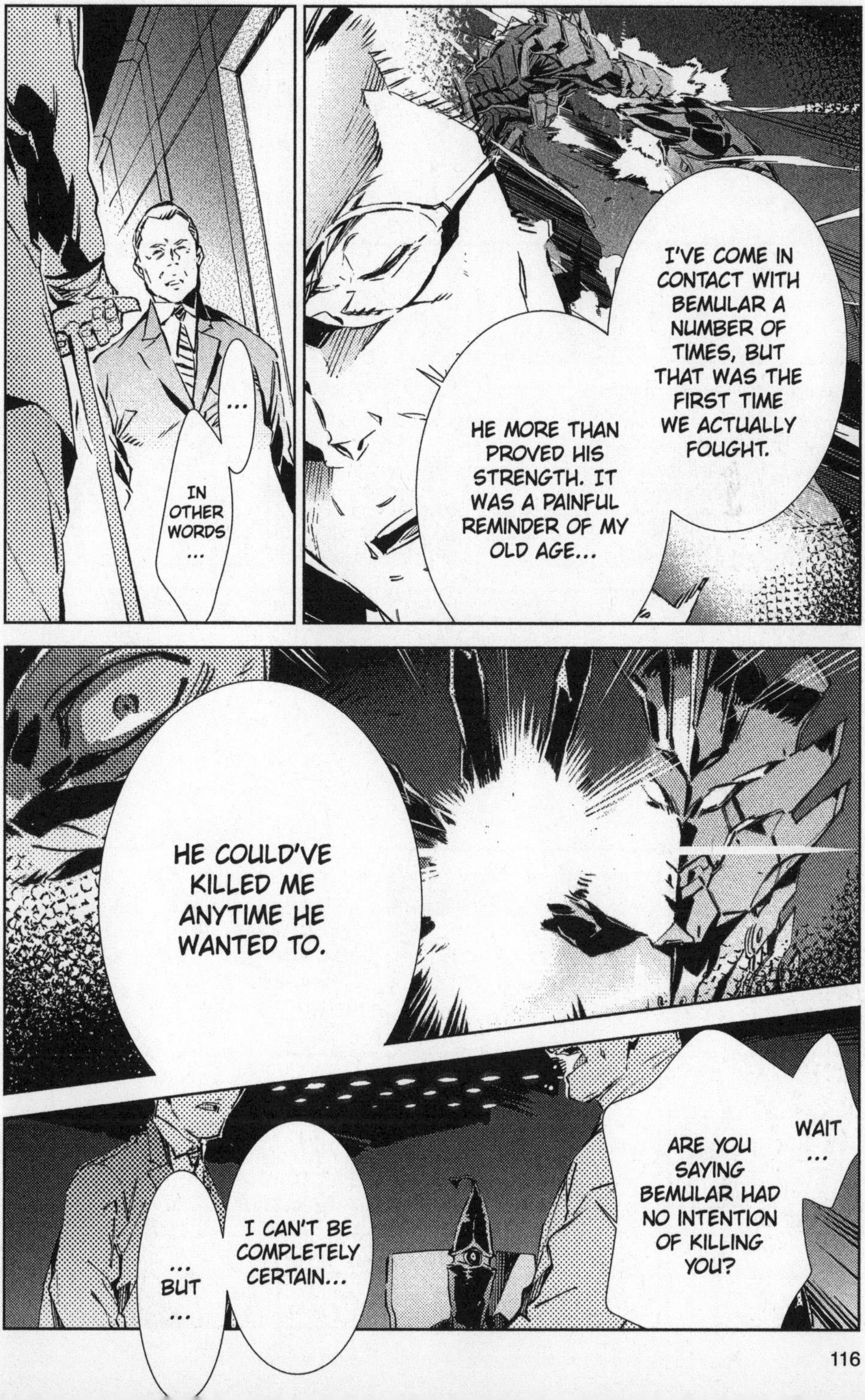
I'VE COME IN CONTACT WITH BEMULAR A NUMBER OF TIMES, BUT THAT WAS THE FIRST TIME WE ACTUALLY FOUGHT.
HE MORE THAN PROVED HIS STRENGTH. IT WAS A PAINFUL REMINDER OF MY OLD AGE...
...
IN OTHER WORDS ...
HE COULD'VE KILLED ME ANYTIME HE WANTED TO.
WAIT ...
ARE YOU SAYING BEMULAR HAD NO INTENTION OF KILLING YOU?
I CAN'T BE COMPLETELY CERTAIN...
... BUT ...

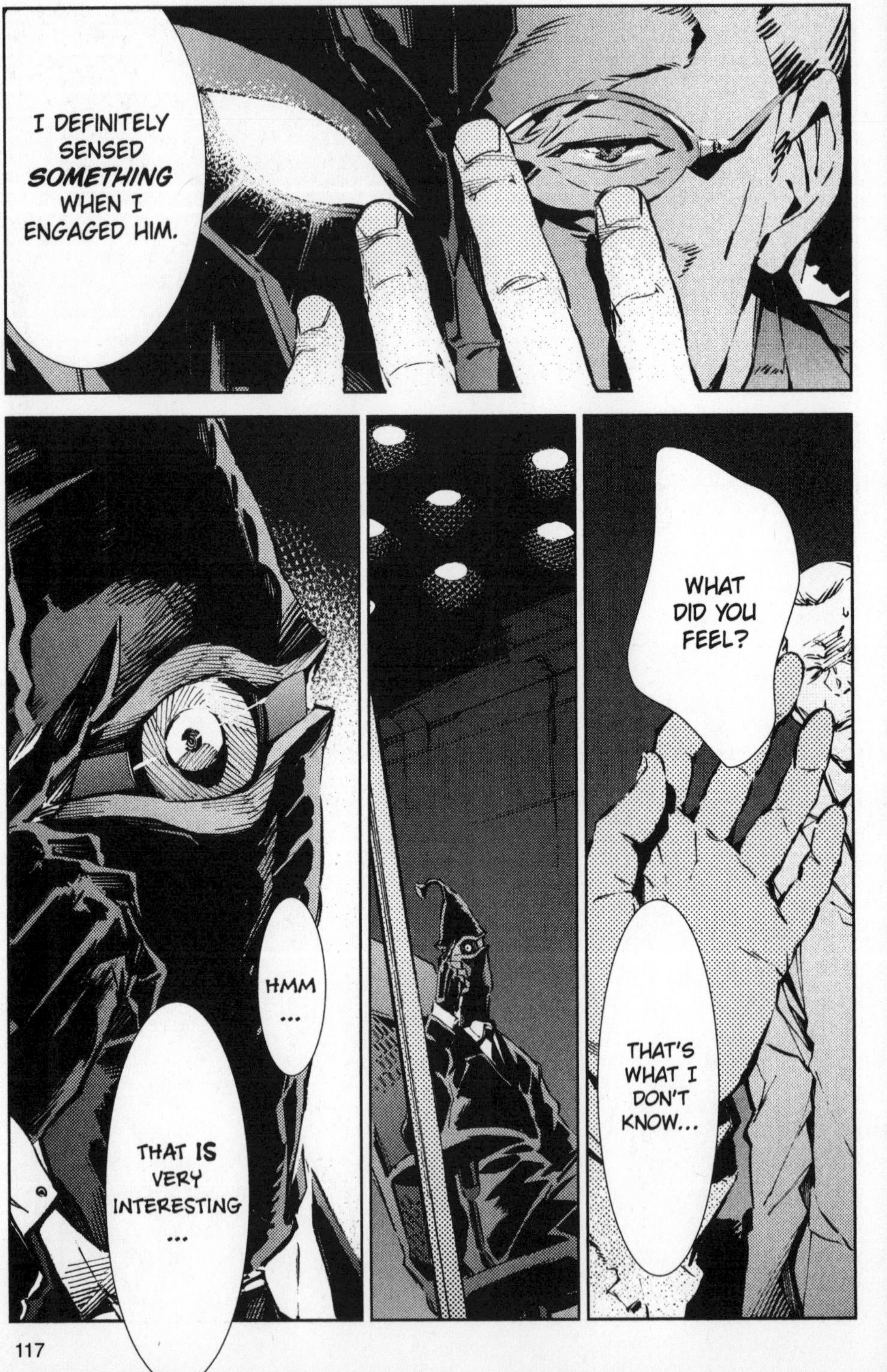
I DEFINITELY SENSED SOMETHING WHEN I ENGAGED HIM.
WHAT DID YOU FEEL?
THAT'S WHAT I DON'T KNOW...
HMM...
THAT IS VERY INTERESTING...

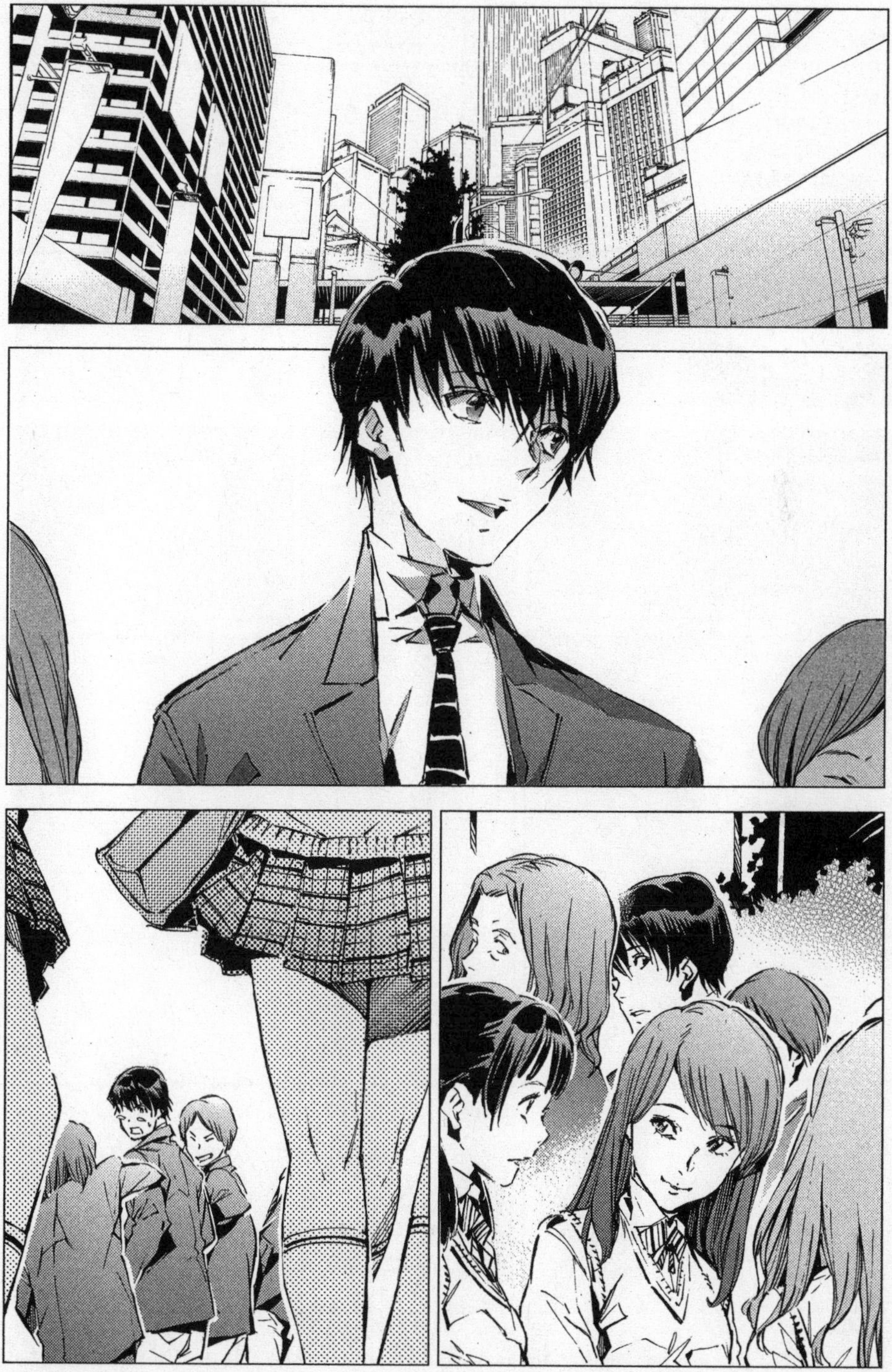

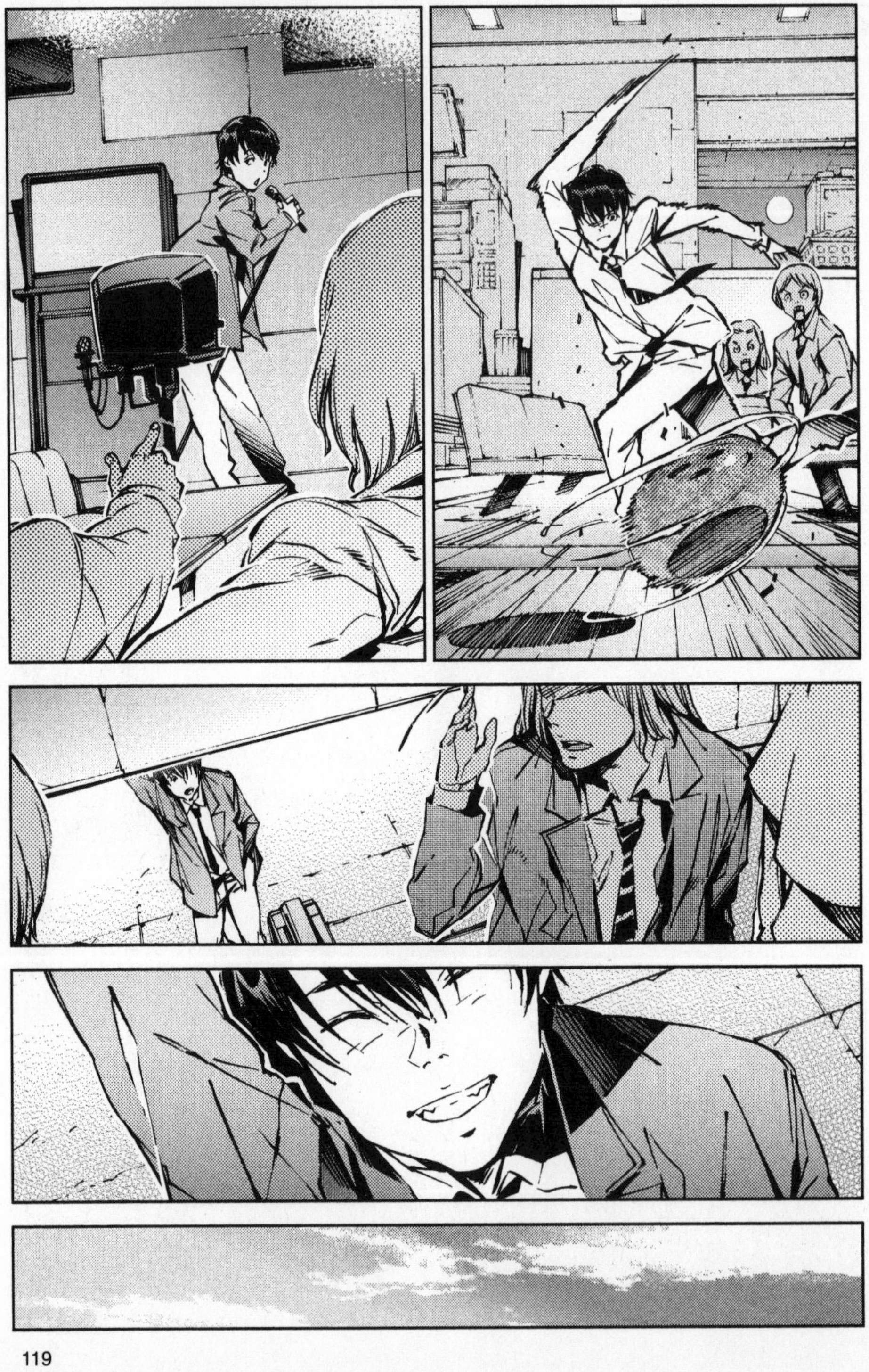

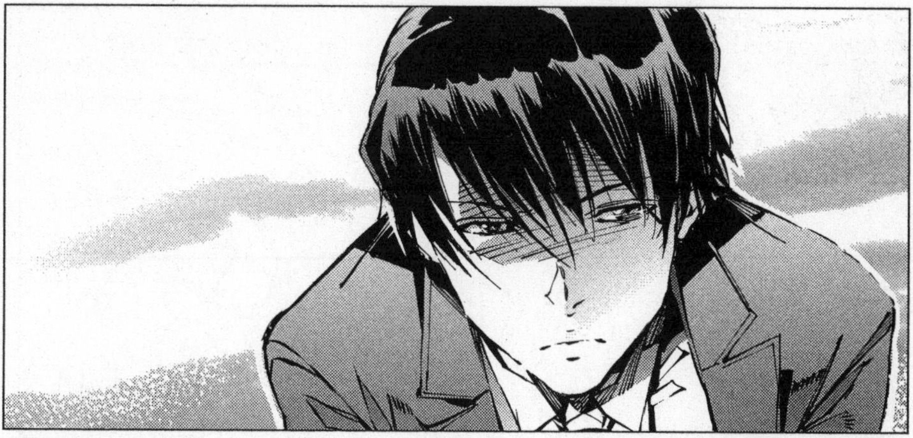

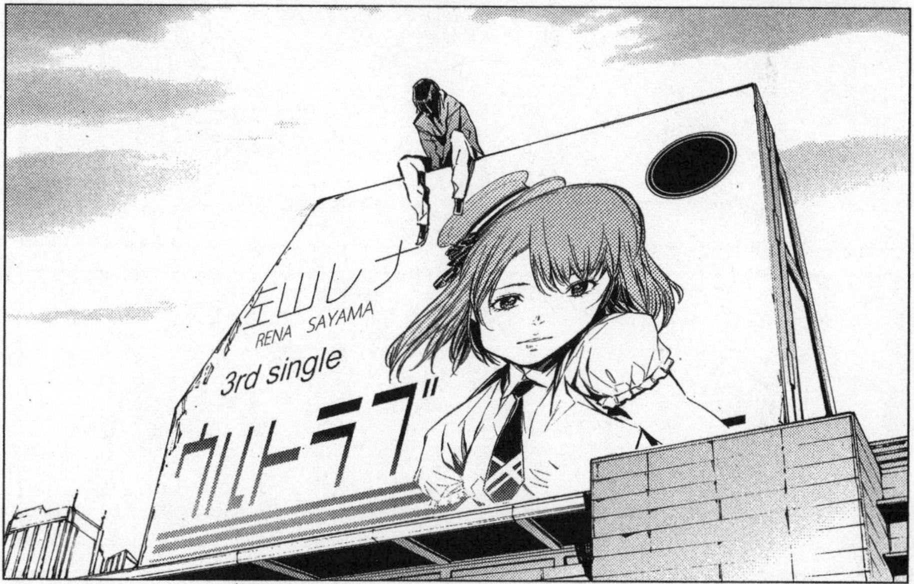
佐山レナ
RENA SAYAMA
3rd single
ウルトラブ
*Ultra Love

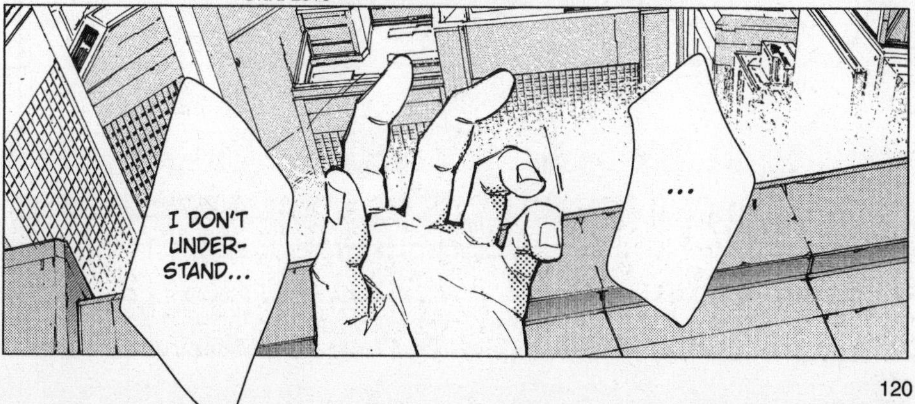
...
I DON'T UNDER-STAND...

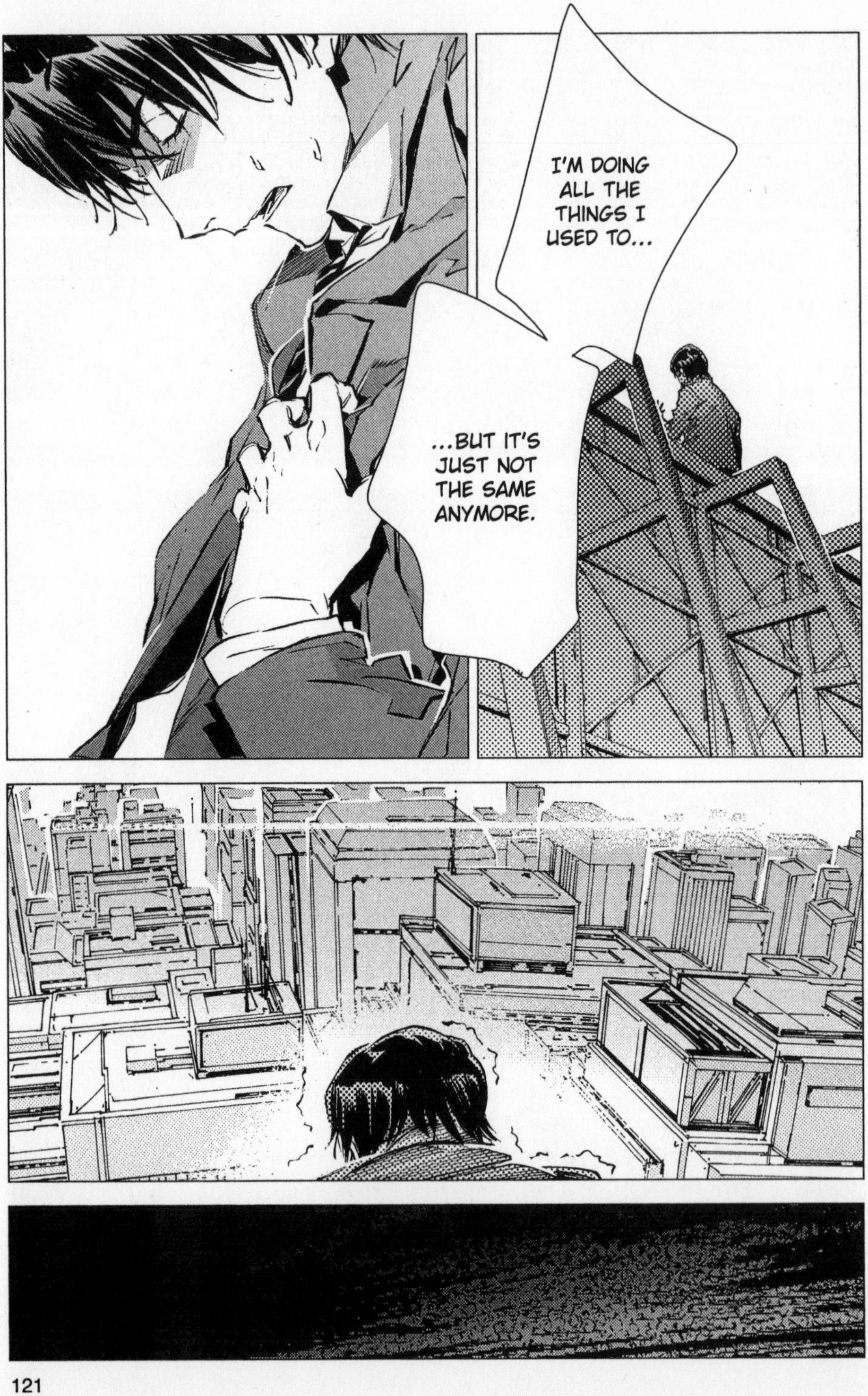
I'M DOING ALL THE THINGS I USED TO...
...BUT IT'S JUST NOT THE SAME ANYMORE.

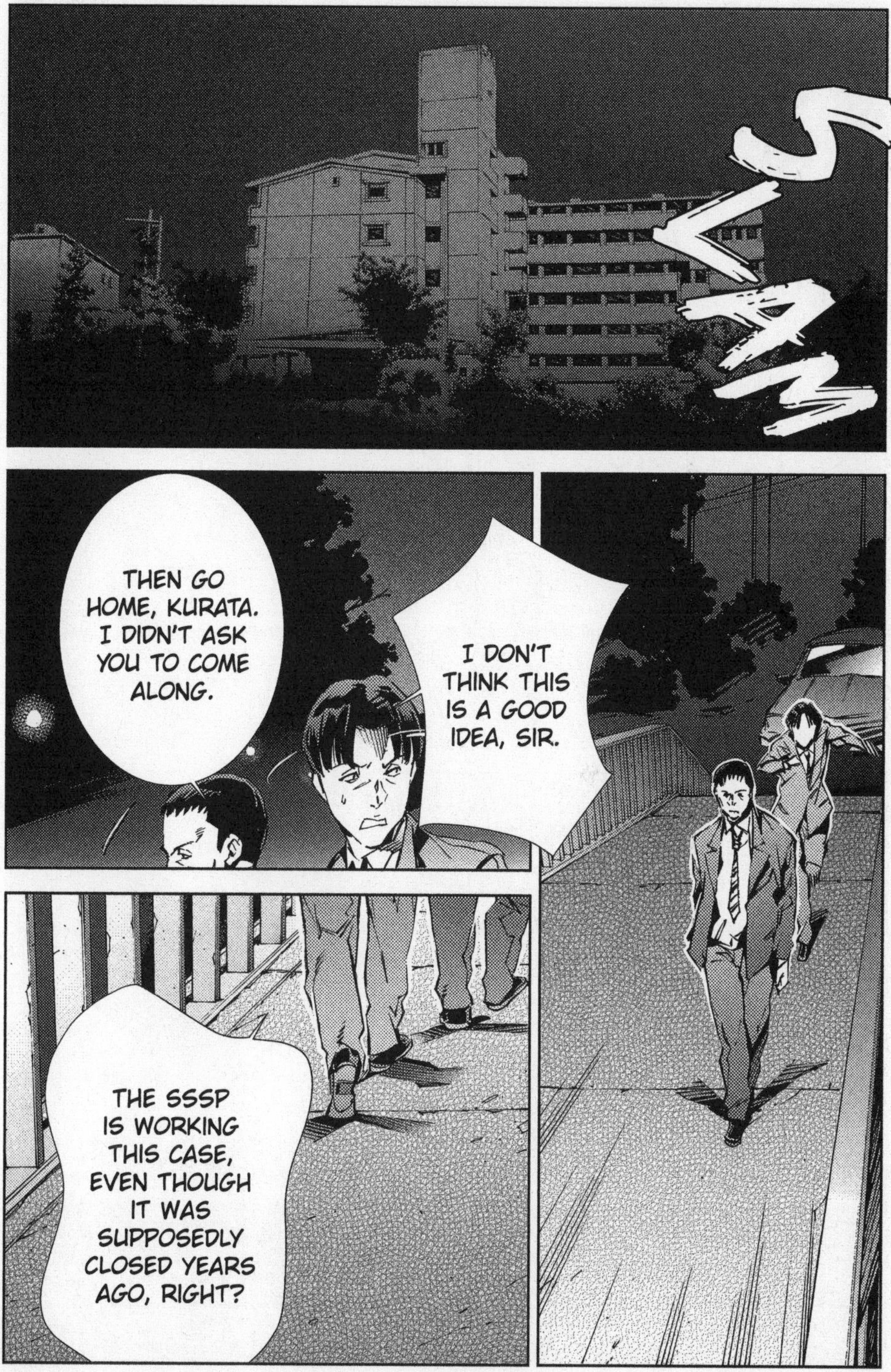
SLAM
I DON'T THINK THIS IS A GOOD IDEA, SIR.
THEN GO HOME, KURATA. I DIDN'T ASK YOU TO COME ALONG.
THE SSSP IS WORKING THIS CASE, EVEN THOUGH IT WAS SUPPOSEDLY CLOSED YEARS AGO, RIGHT?

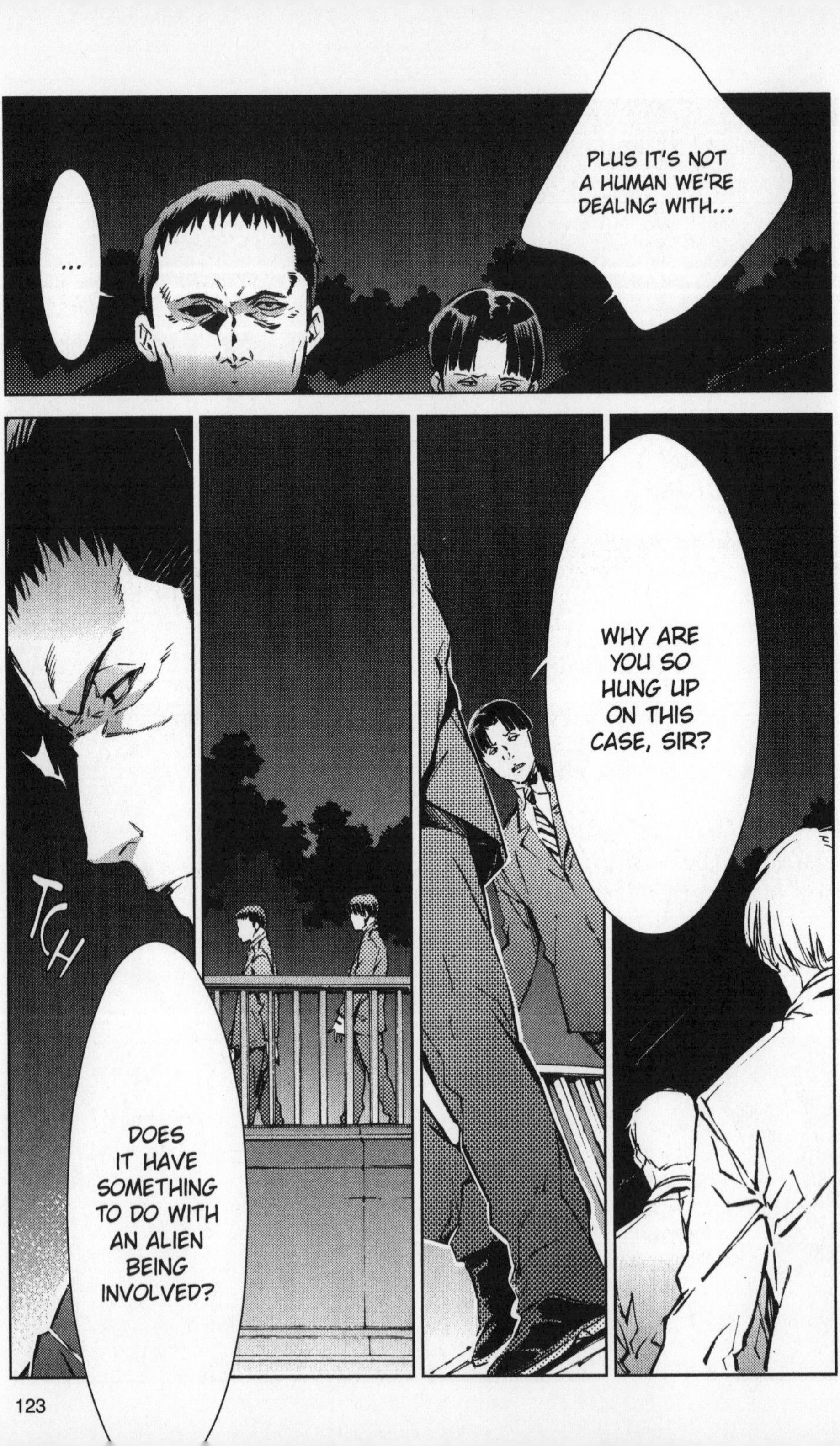
PLUS IT'S NOT A HUMAN WE'RE DEALING WITH...
...
WHY ARE YOU SO HUNG UP ON THIS CASE, SIR?
TCH
DOES IT HAVE SOMETHING TO DO WITH AN ALIEN BEING INVOLVED?

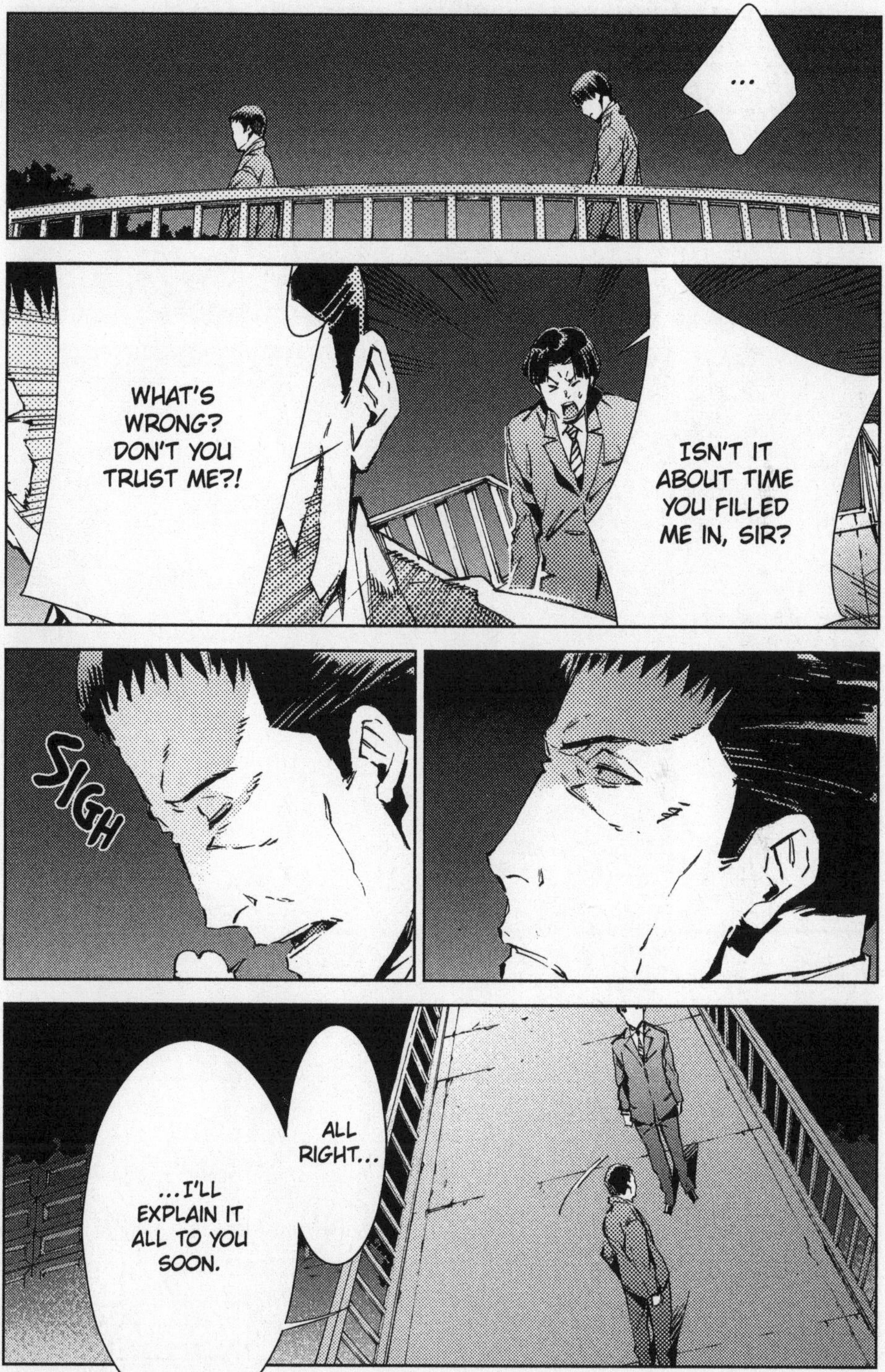
...
ISN'T IT ABOUT TIME YOU FILLED ME IN, SIR?
WHAT'S WRONG? DON'T YOU TRUST ME?!
SIGH
ALL RIGHT...
...I'LL EXPLAIN IT ALL TO YOU SOON.

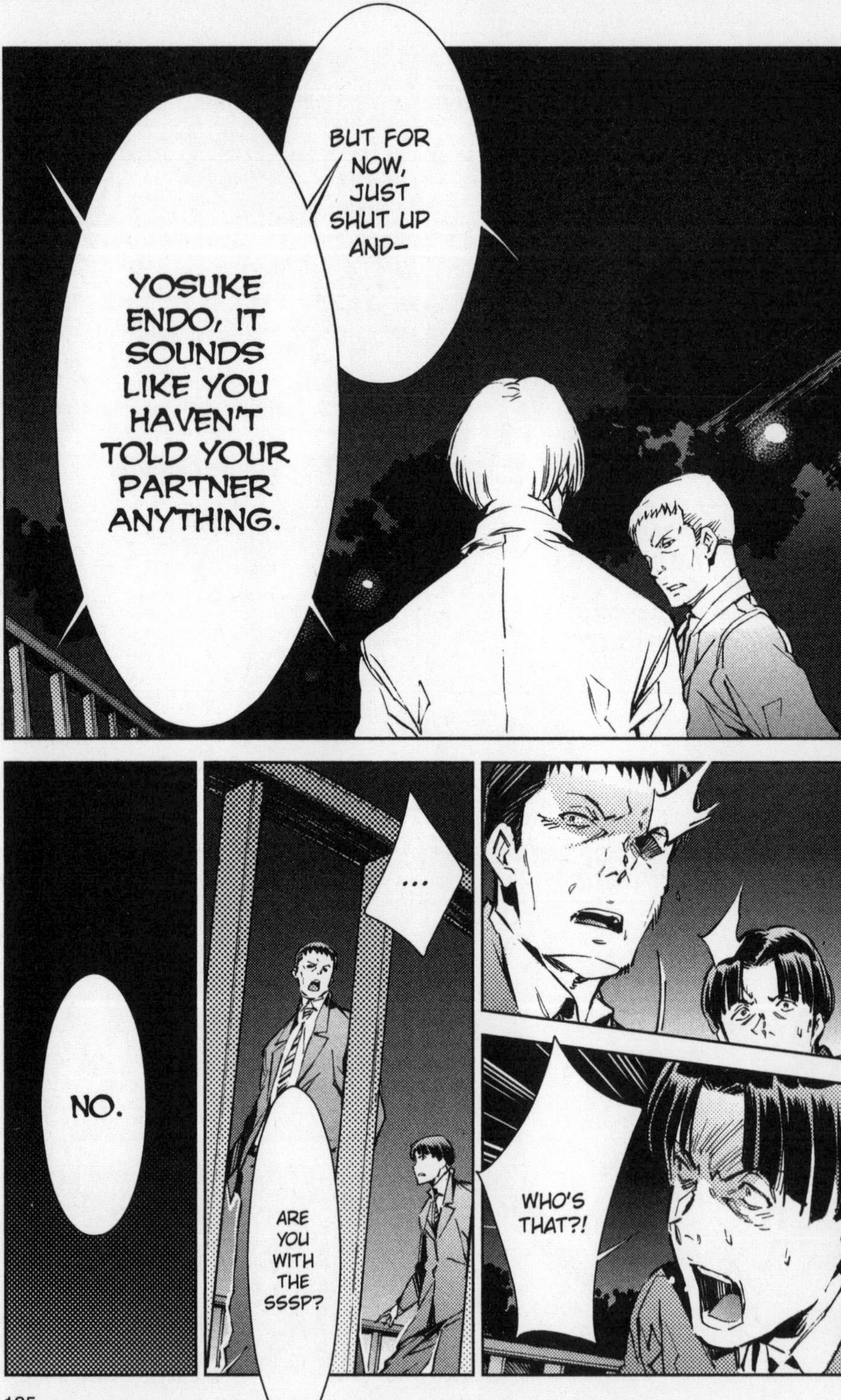
BUT FOR NOW, JUST SHUT UP AND—
YOSUKE ENDO, IT SOUNDS LIKE YOU HAVEN'T TOLD YOUR PARTNER ANYTHING.
WHO'S THAT?!
...
ARE YOU WITH THE SSSP?
NO.

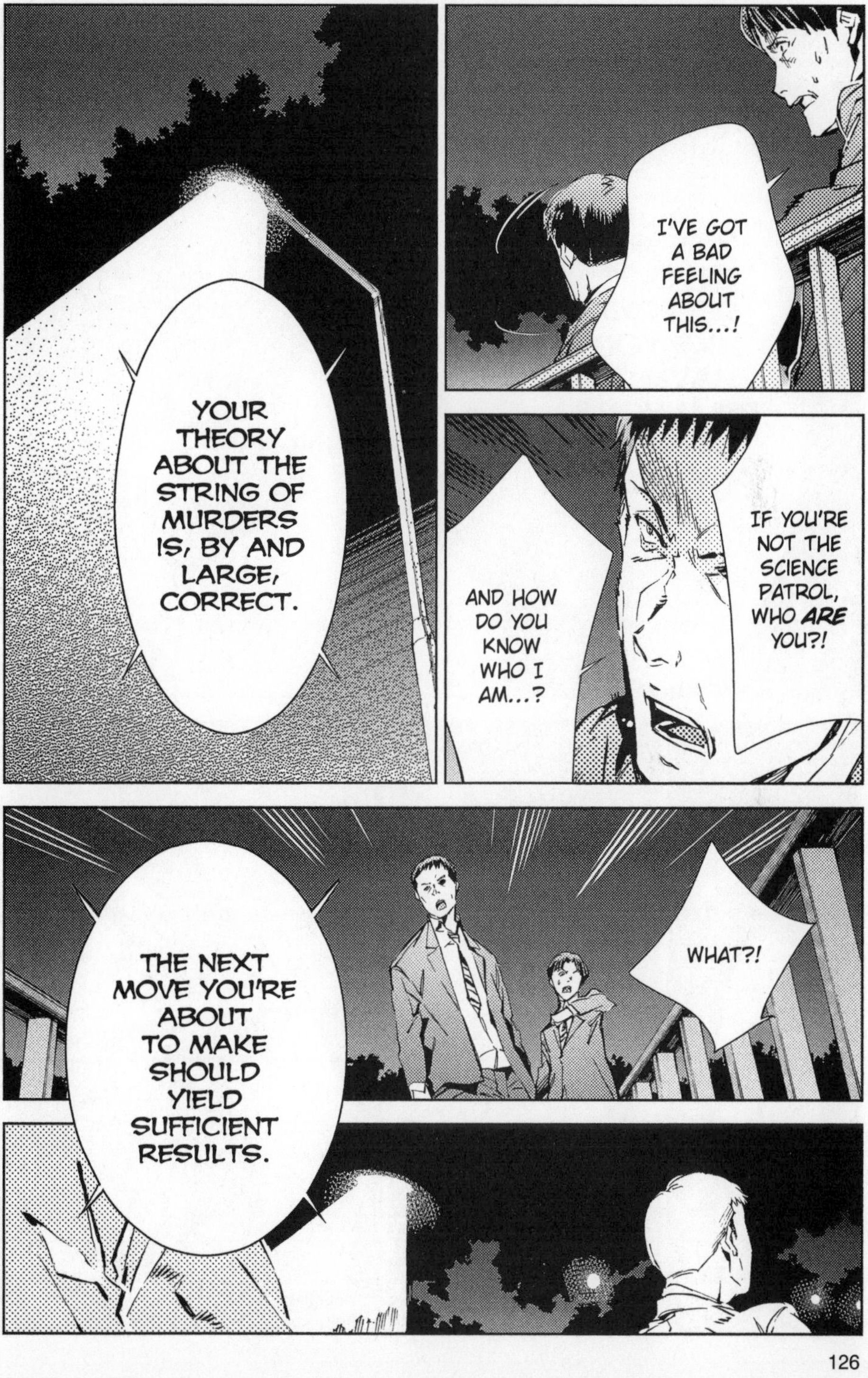
I'VE GOT A BAD FEELING ABOUT THIS...!
IF YOU'RE NOT THE SCIENCE PATROL, WHO *ARE* YOU?!
AND HOW DO YOU KNOW WHO I AM...?
YOUR THEORY ABOUT THE STRING OF MURDERS IS, BY AND LARGE, CORRECT.
WHAT?!
THE NEXT MOVE YOU'RE ABOUT TO MAKE SHOULD YIELD SUFFICIENT RESULTS.

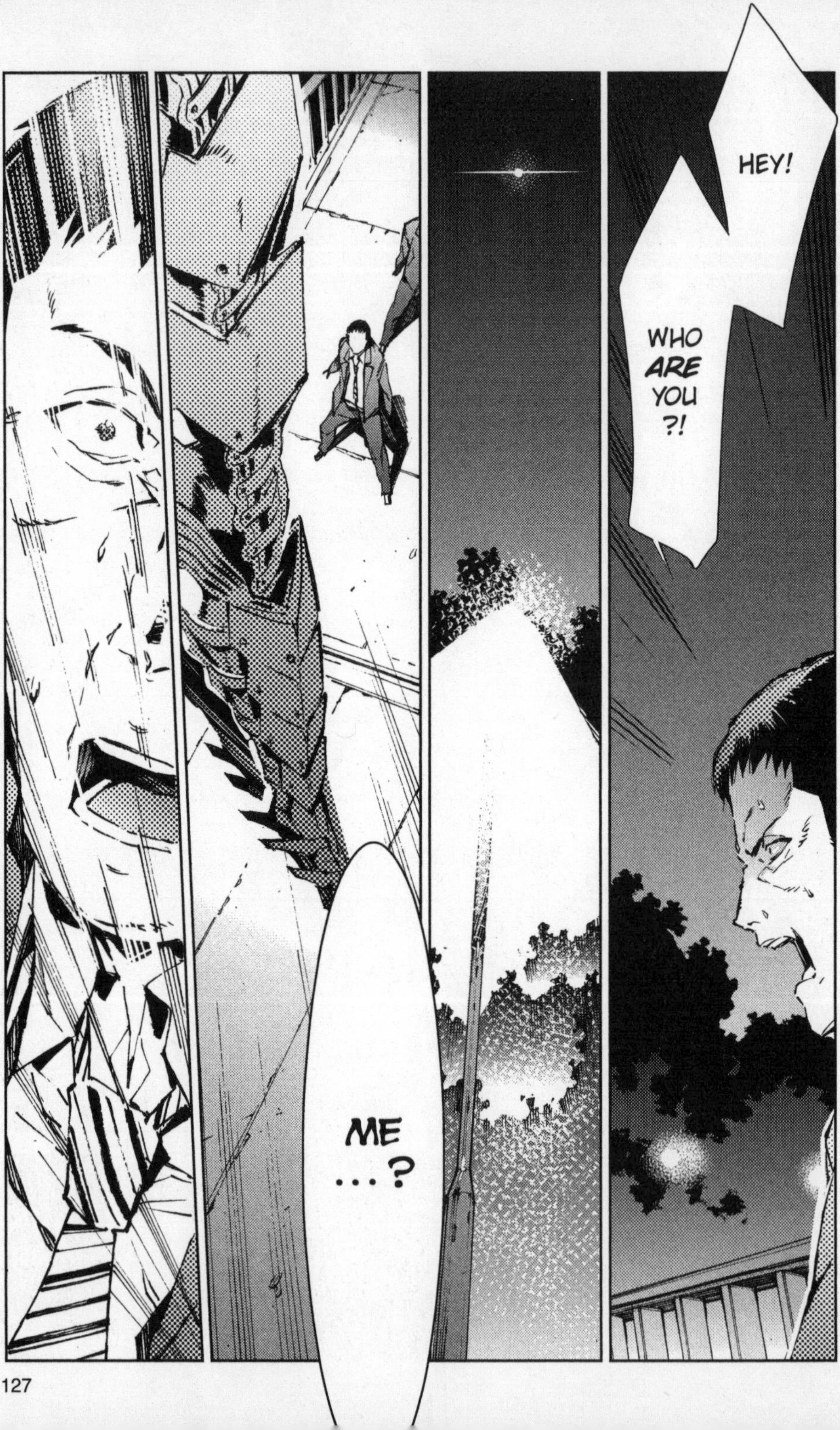
HEY!
WHO ARE YOU ?!
ME ...?

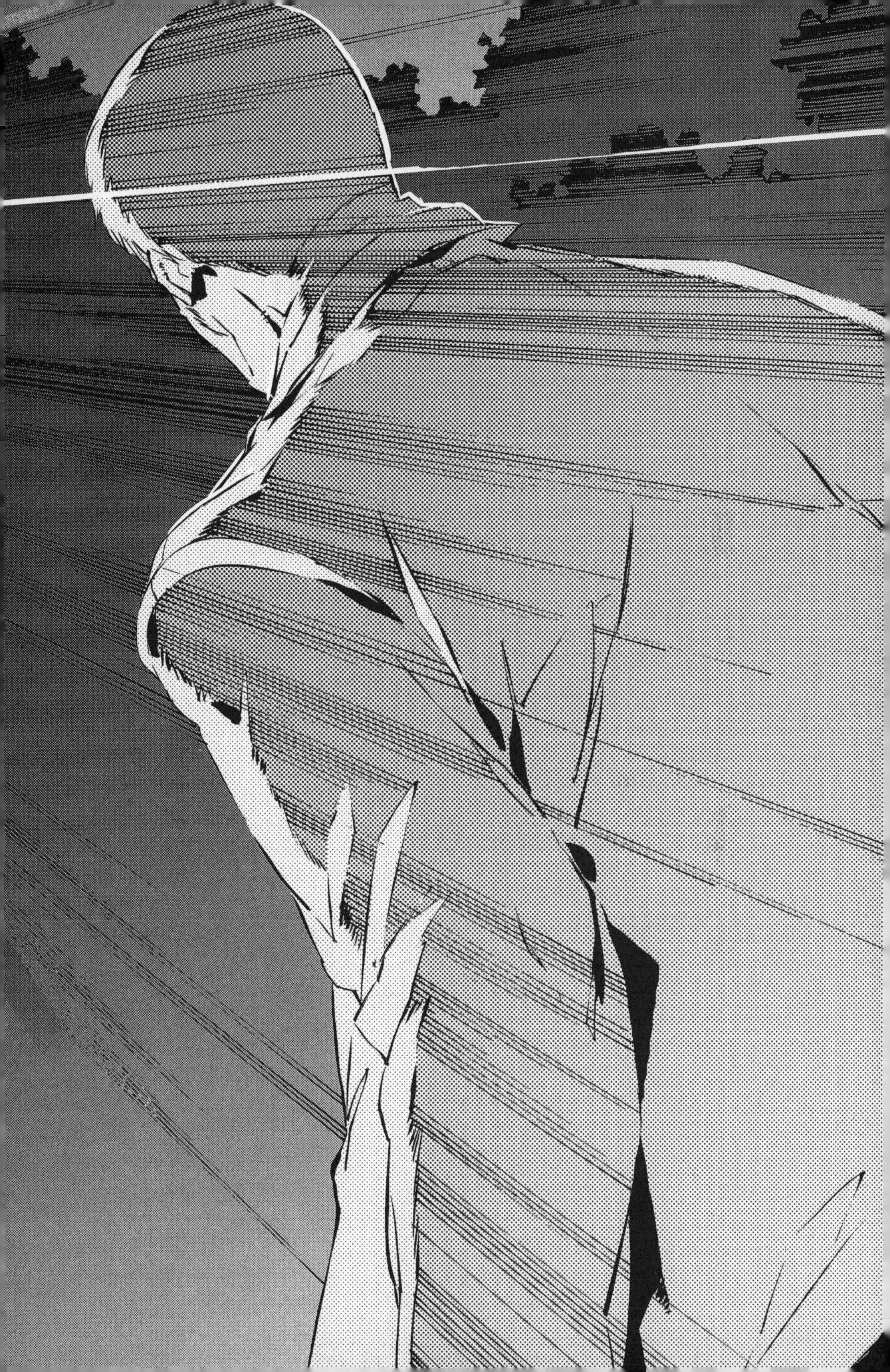

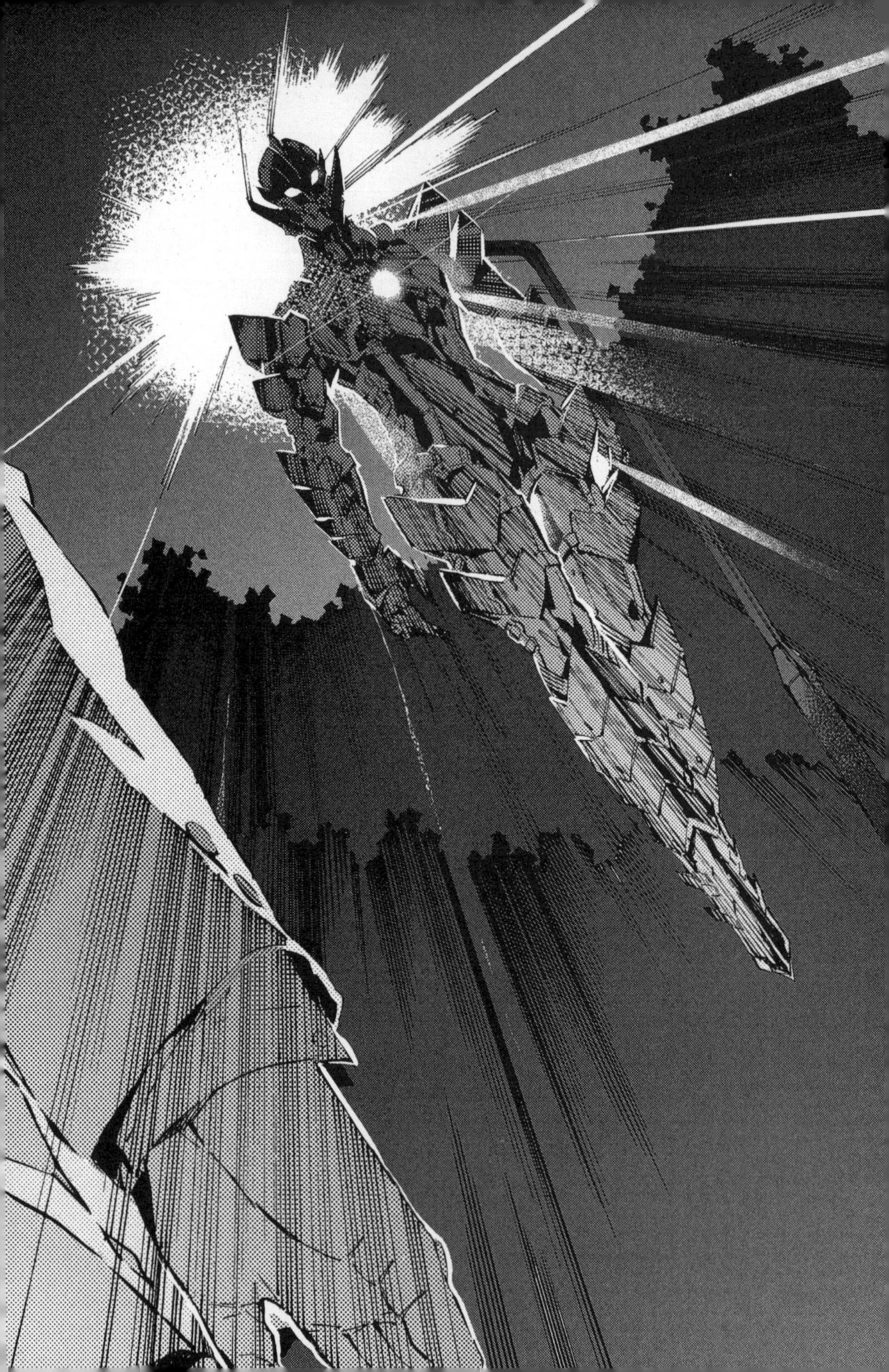

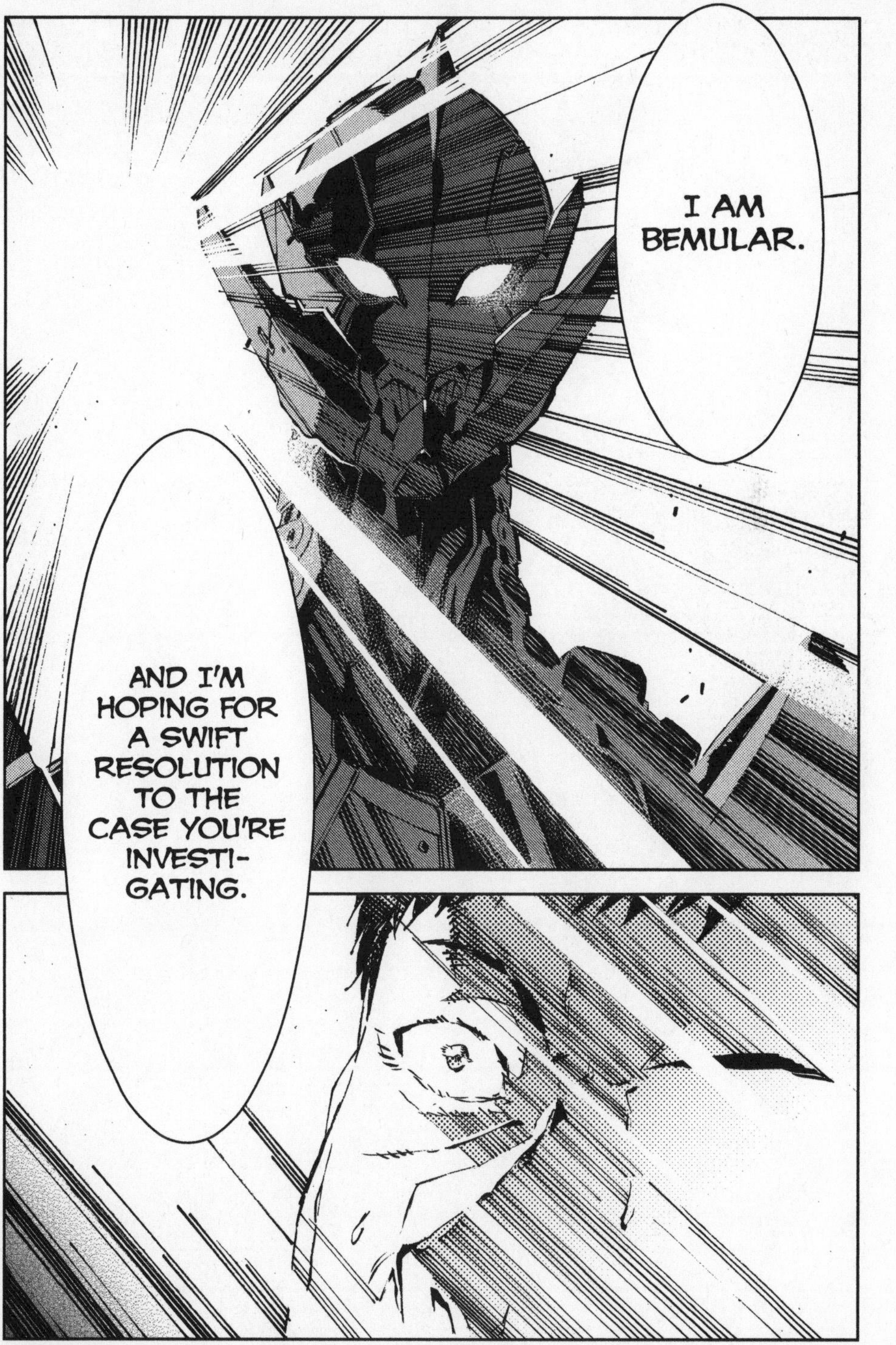
I AM BEMULAR.
AND I'M HOPING FOR A SWIFT RESOLUTION TO THE CASE YOU'RE INVESTI- GATING.

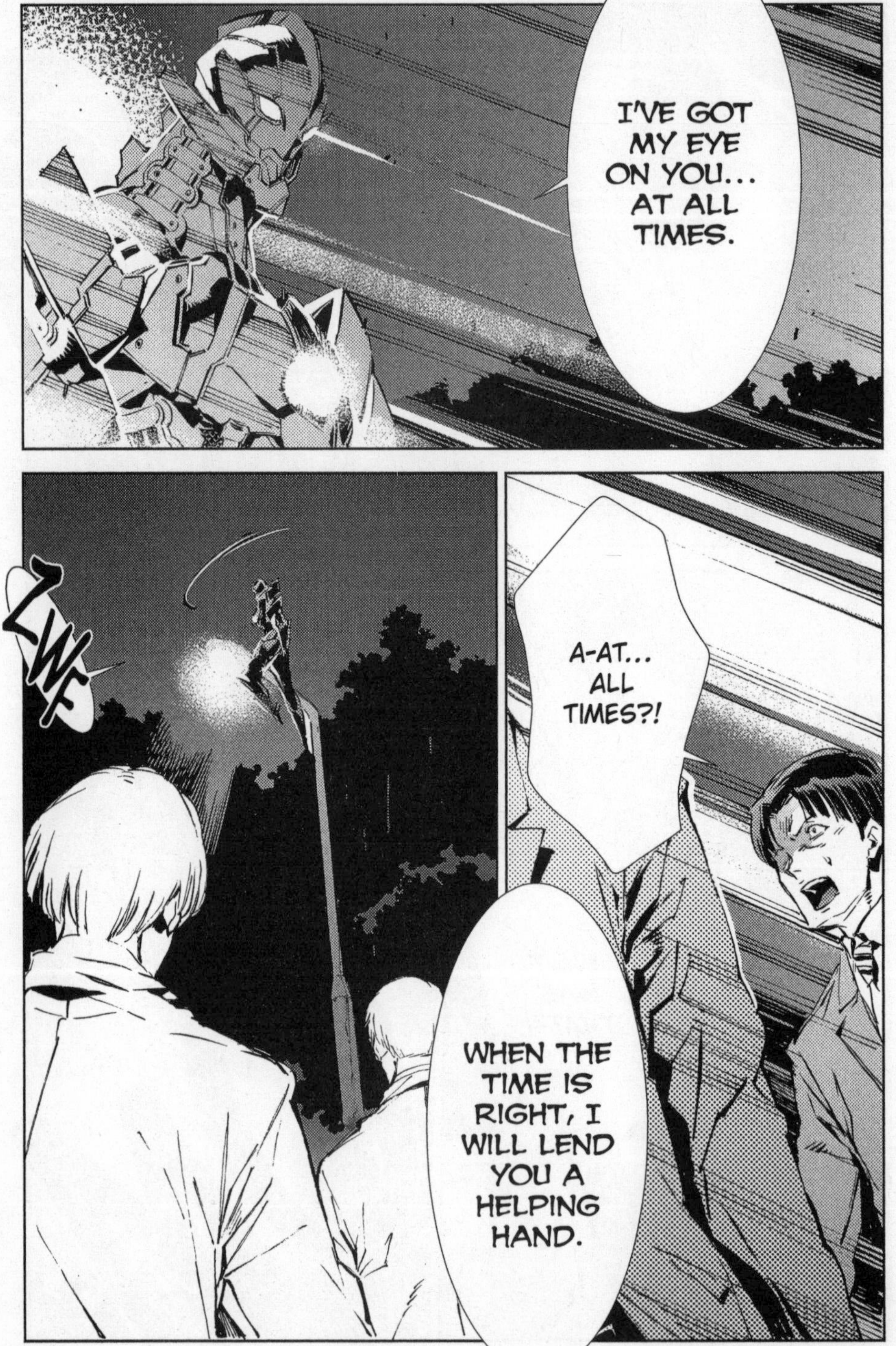
I'VE GOT MY EYE ON YOU... AT ALL TIMES.
A-AT... ALL TIMES?!
WHEN THE TIME IS RIGHT, I WILL LEND YOU A HELPING HAND.
ZWF

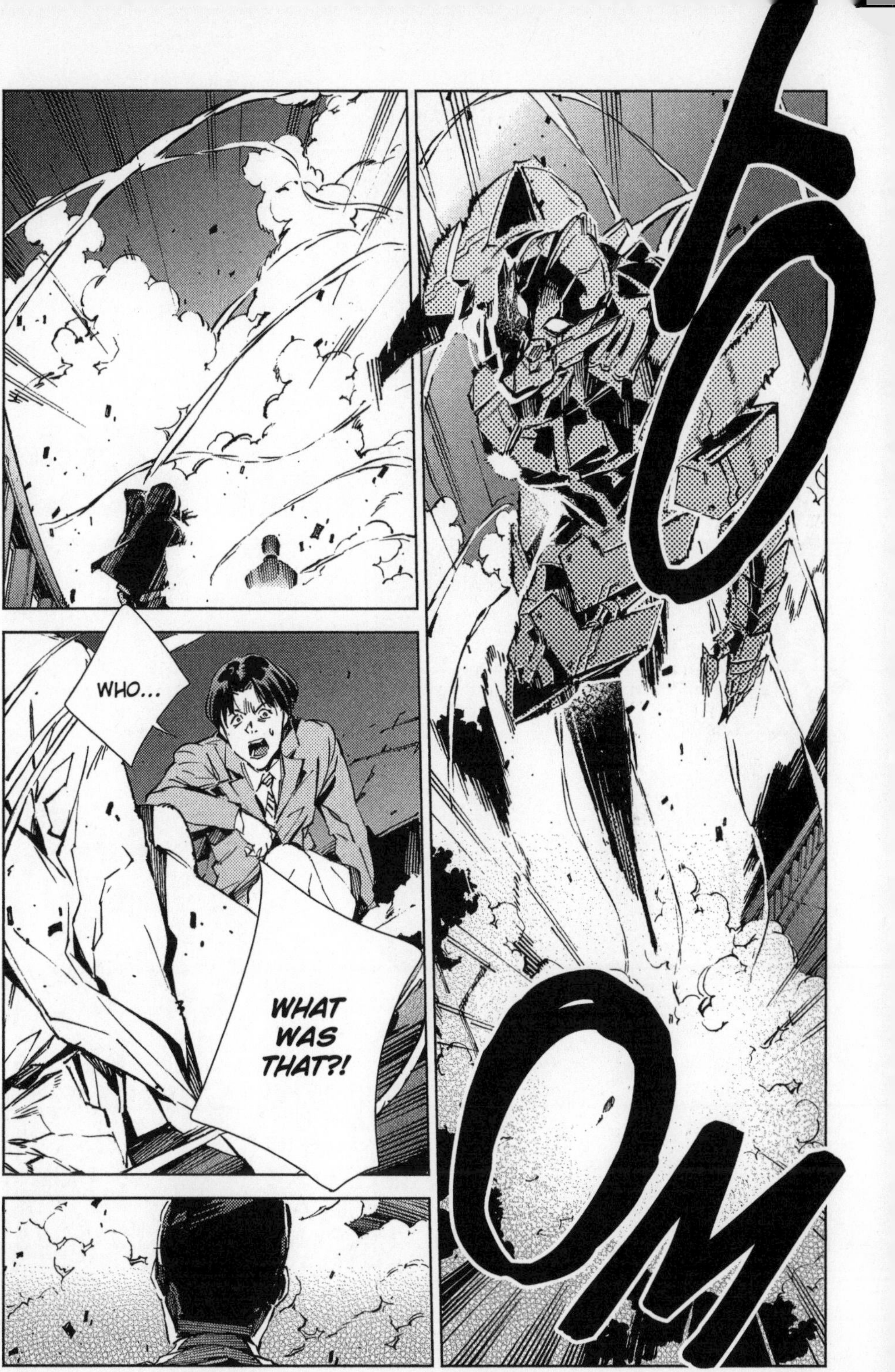
DOOM
WHO...
WHAT WAS THAT?!

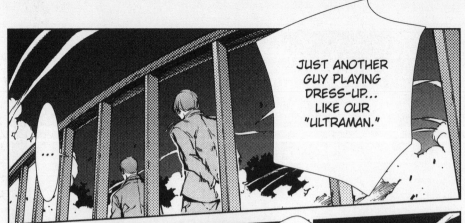

JUST ANOTHER GUY PLAYING DRESS-UP... LIKE OUR "ULTRAMAN."

...

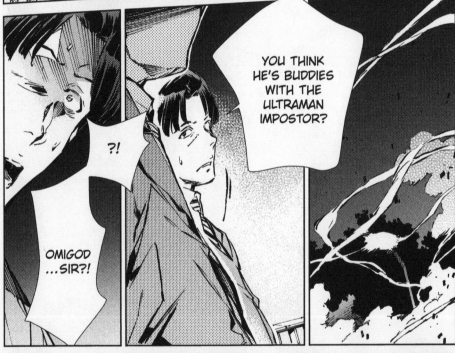

YOU THINK HE'S BUDDIES WITH THE ULTRAMAN IMPOSTOR?

?!

OMIGOD ...SIR?!

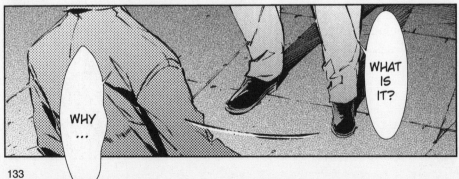

WHY...

WHAT IS IT?

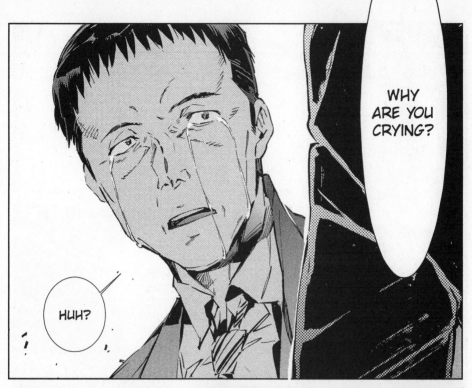

WHY ARE YOU CRYING?

HUH?

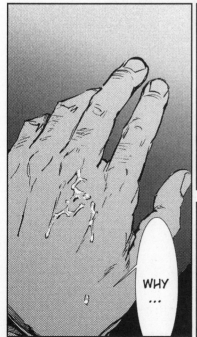

WHY ...

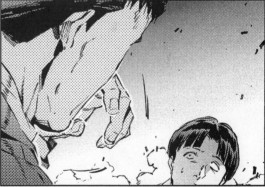

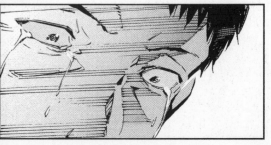

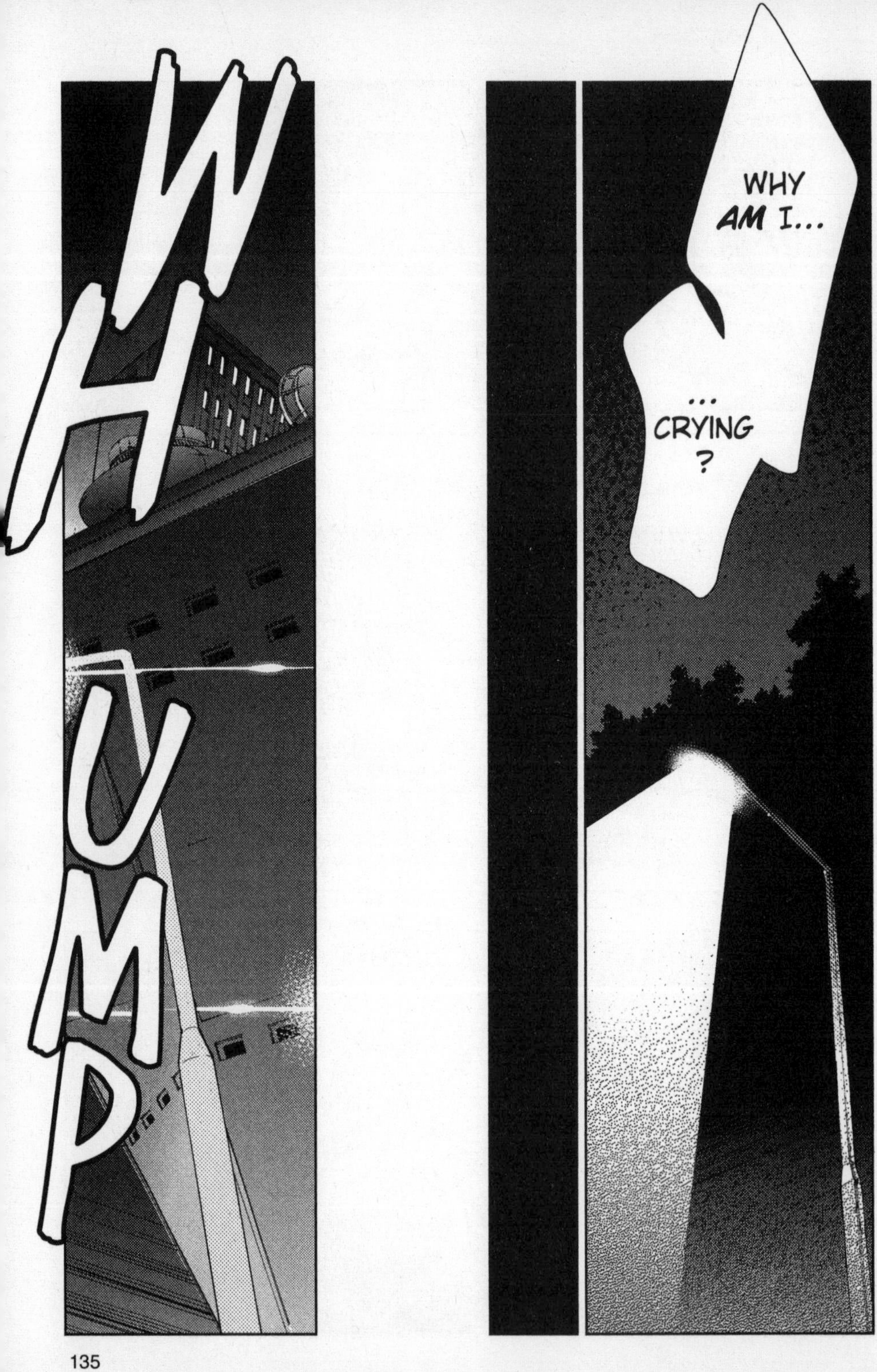
WHY AM I...
...CRYING?
WHUMP

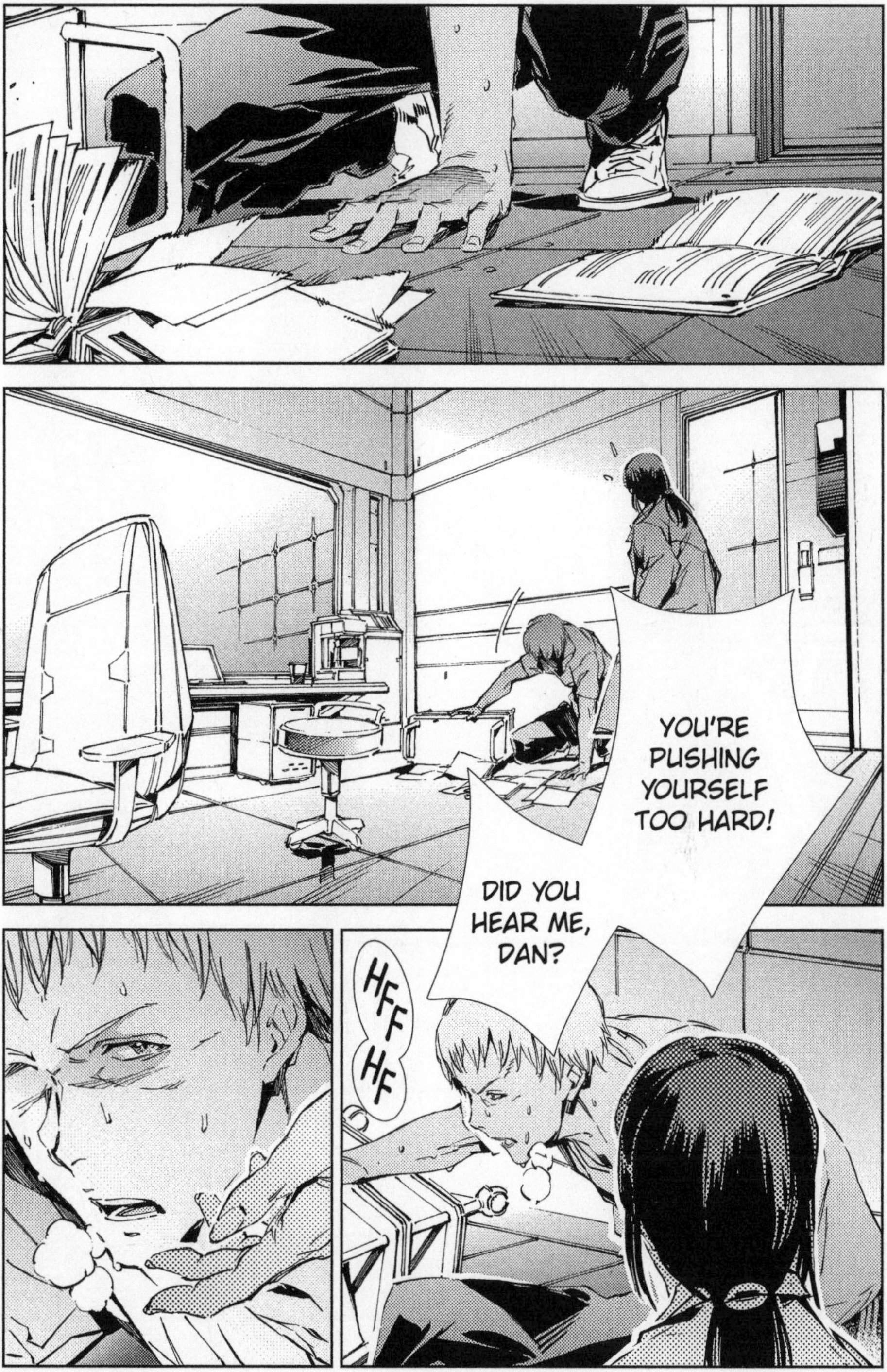
YOU'RE PUSHING YOURSELF TOO HARD!
DID YOU HEAR ME, DAN?
HFF HF

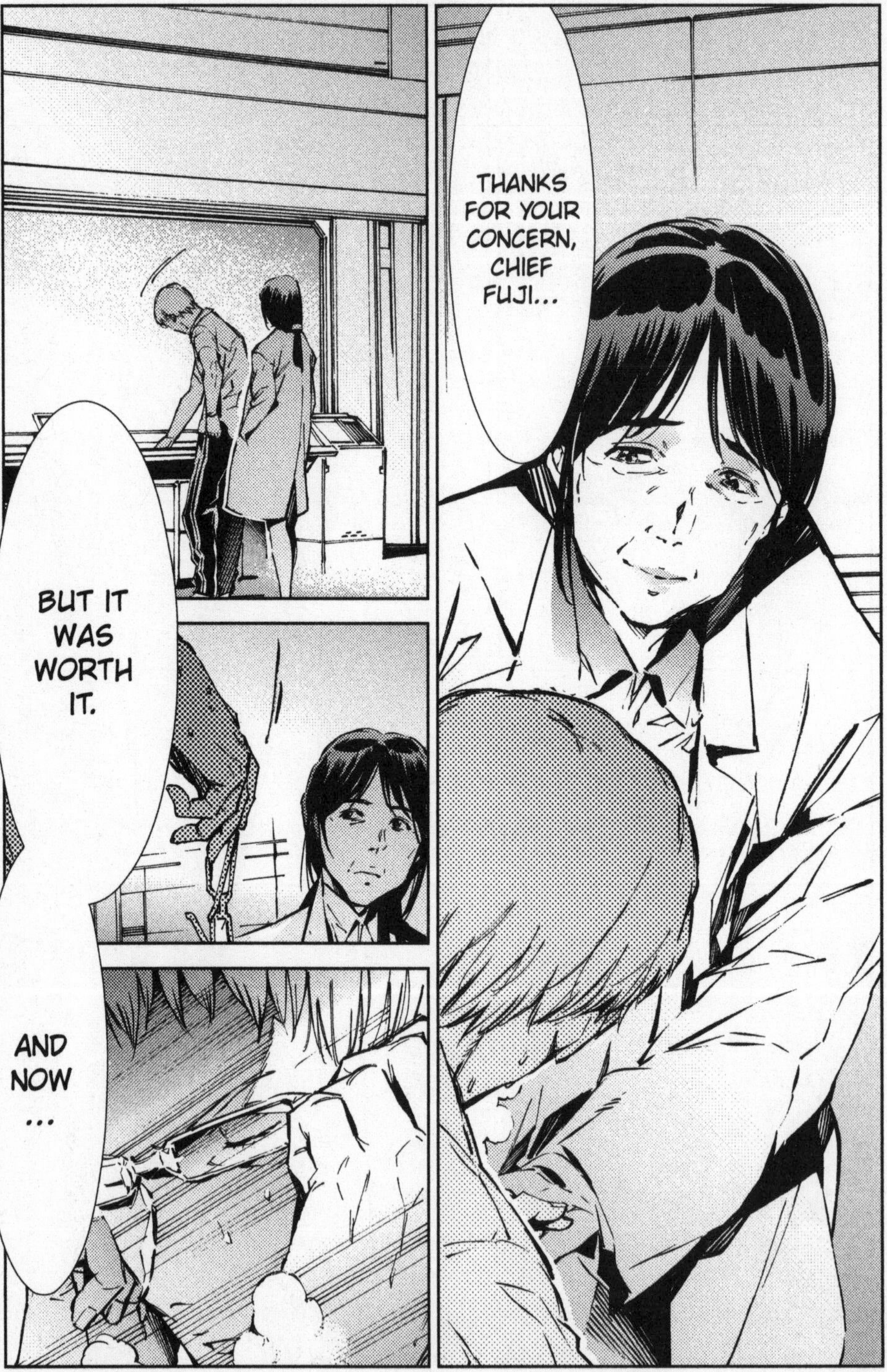
THANKS FOR YOUR CONCERN, CHIEF FUJI...
BUT IT WAS WORTH IT.
AND NOW ...

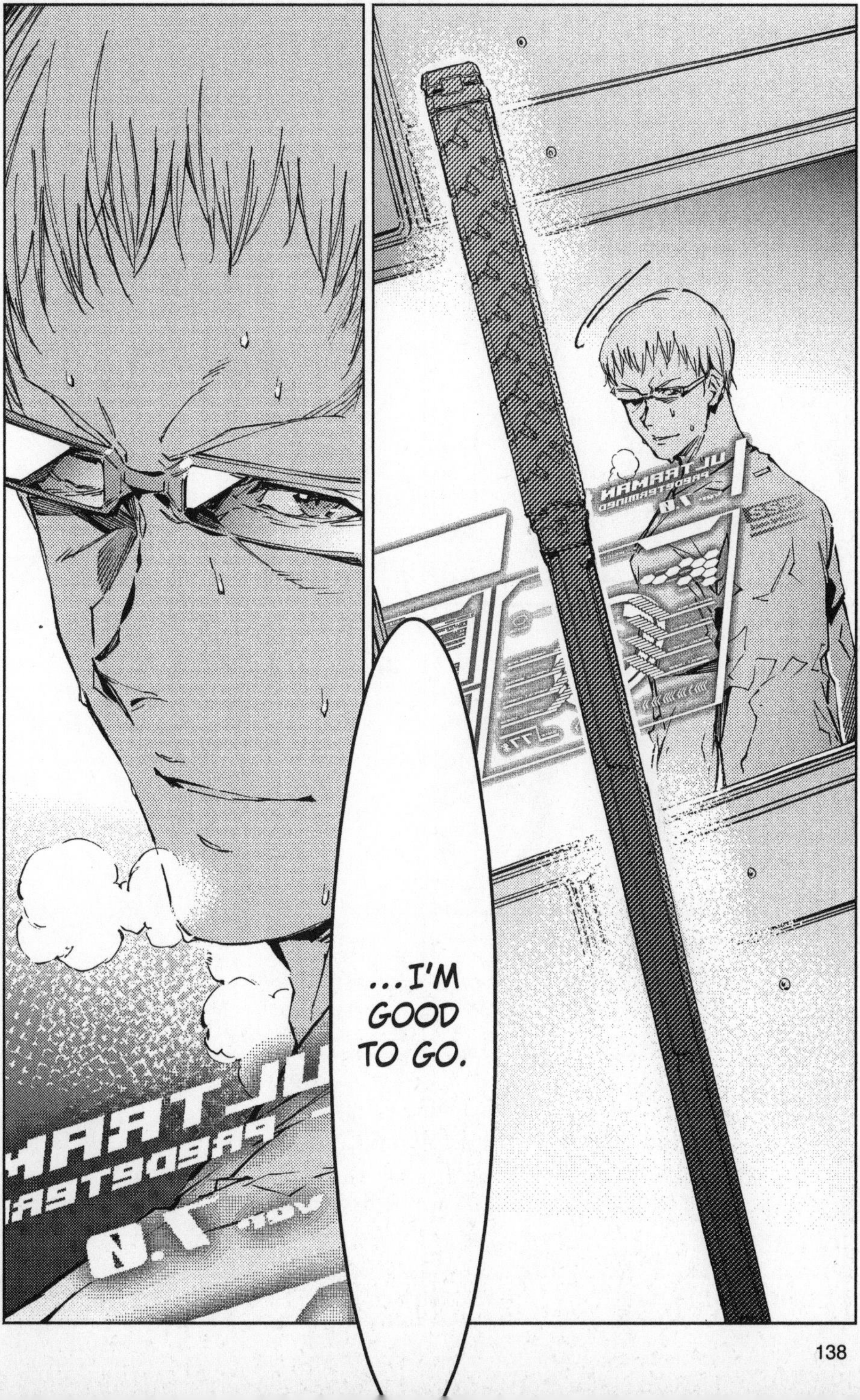
...I'M GOOD TO GO.

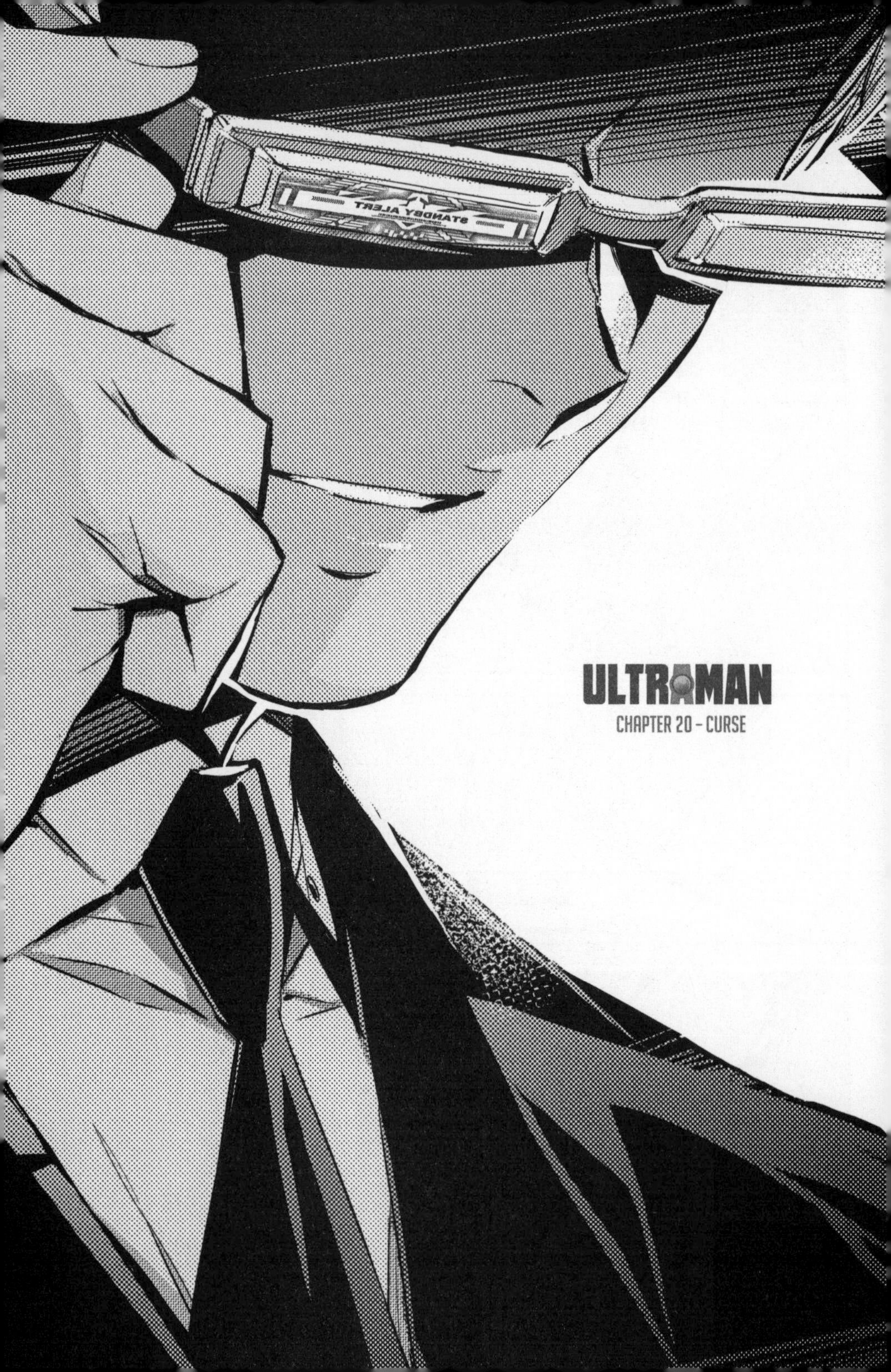
ULTRAMAN
CHAPTER 20 - CURSE

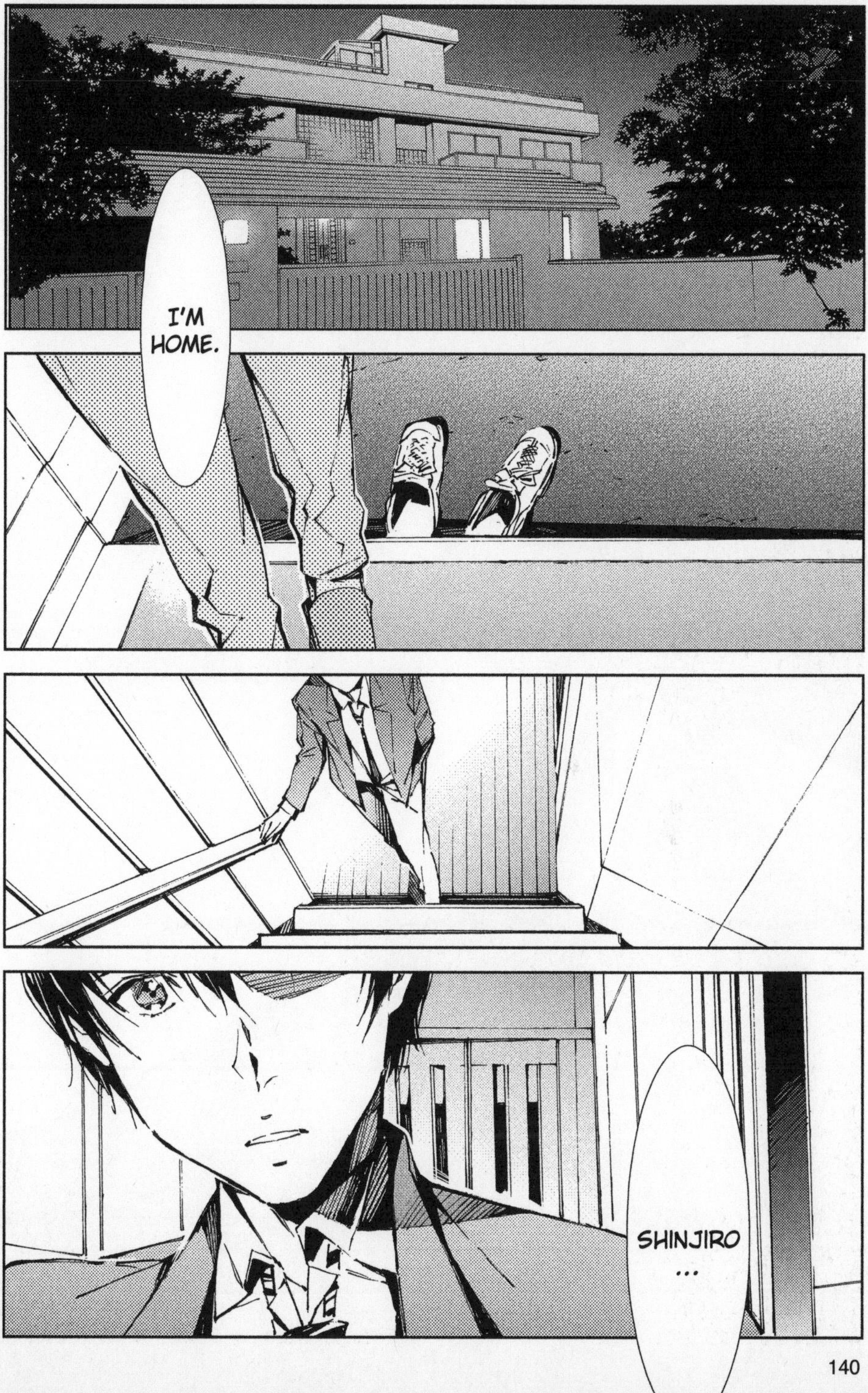
I'M HOME.
SHINJIRO ...

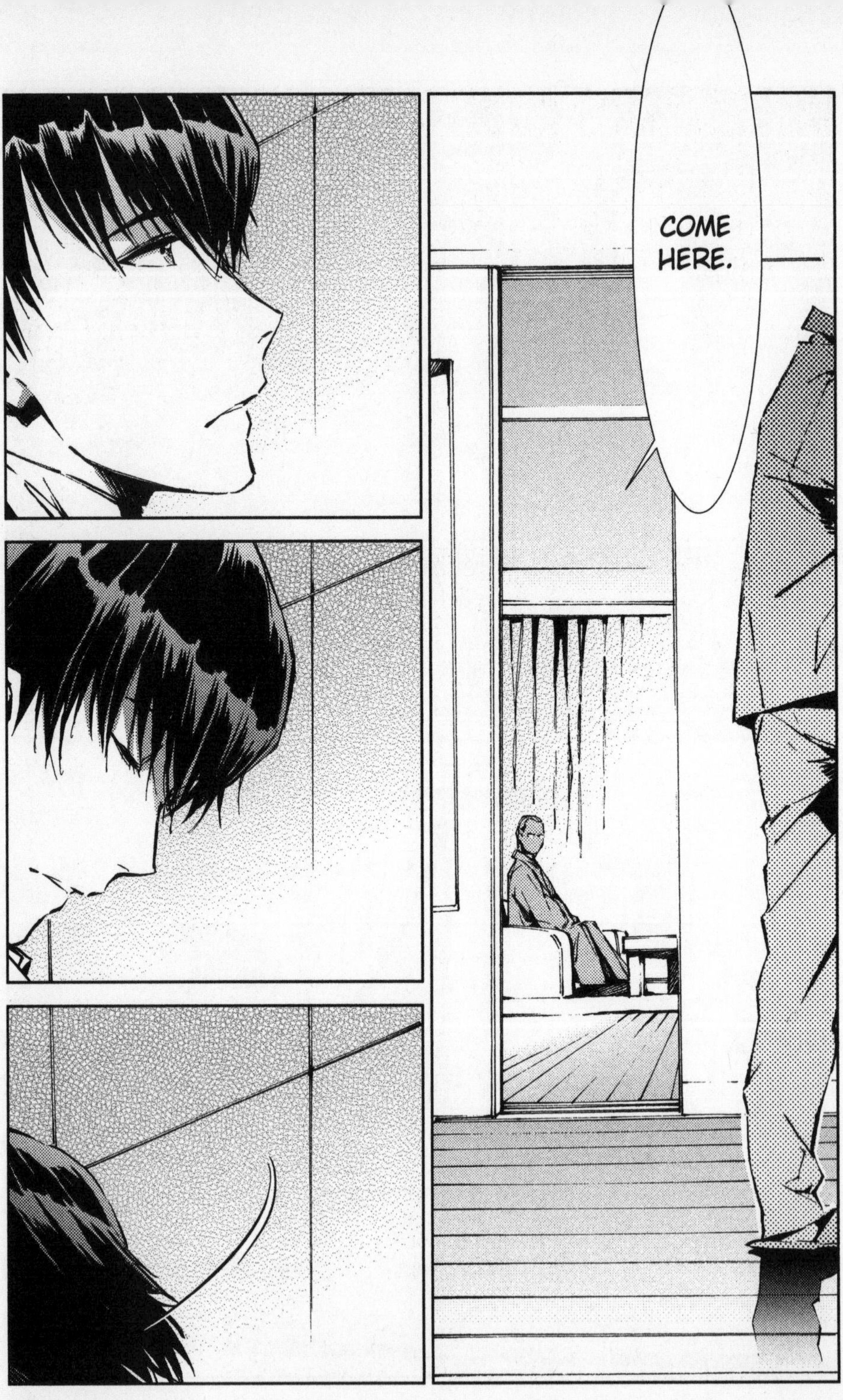
COME HERE.

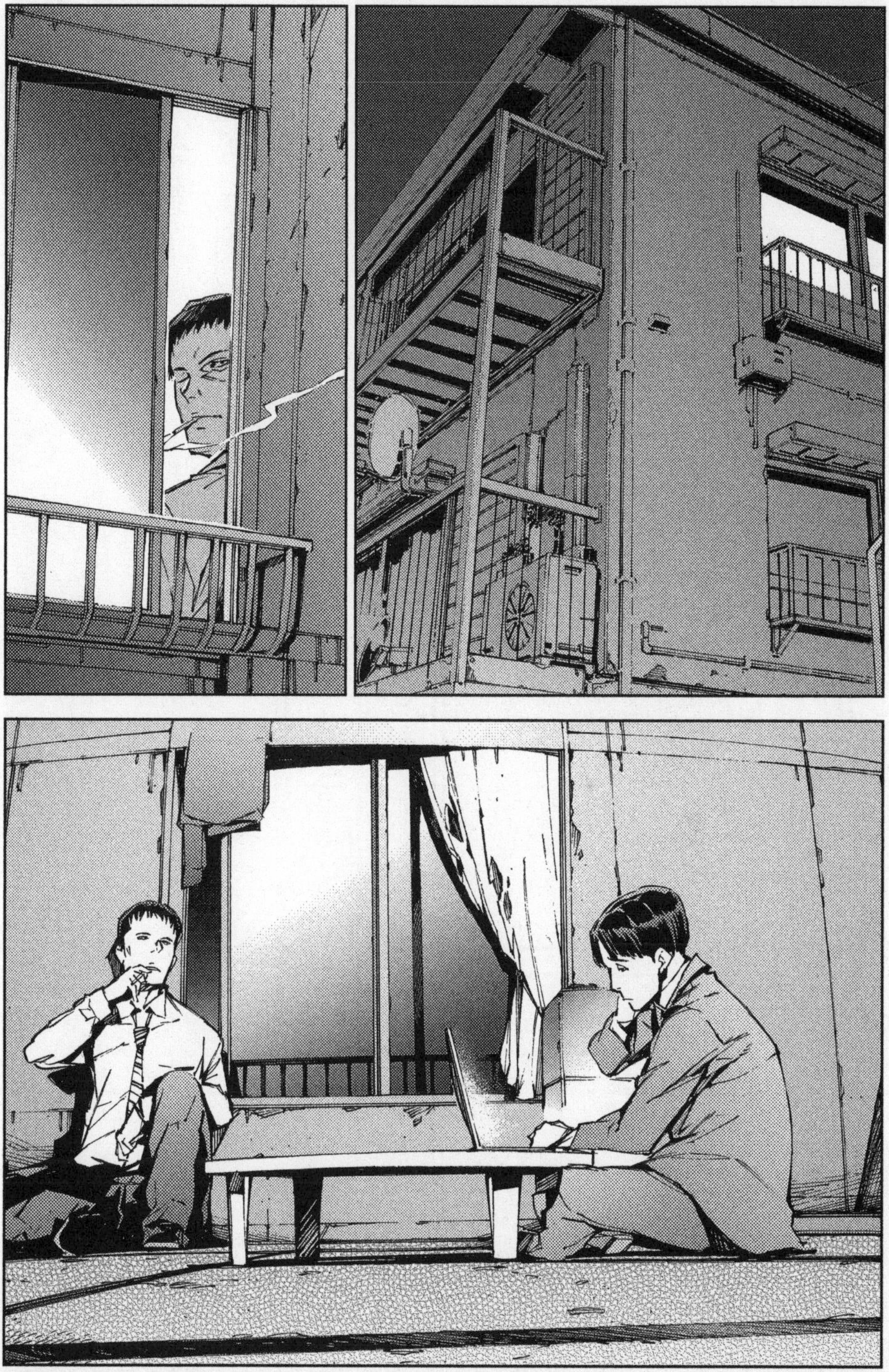

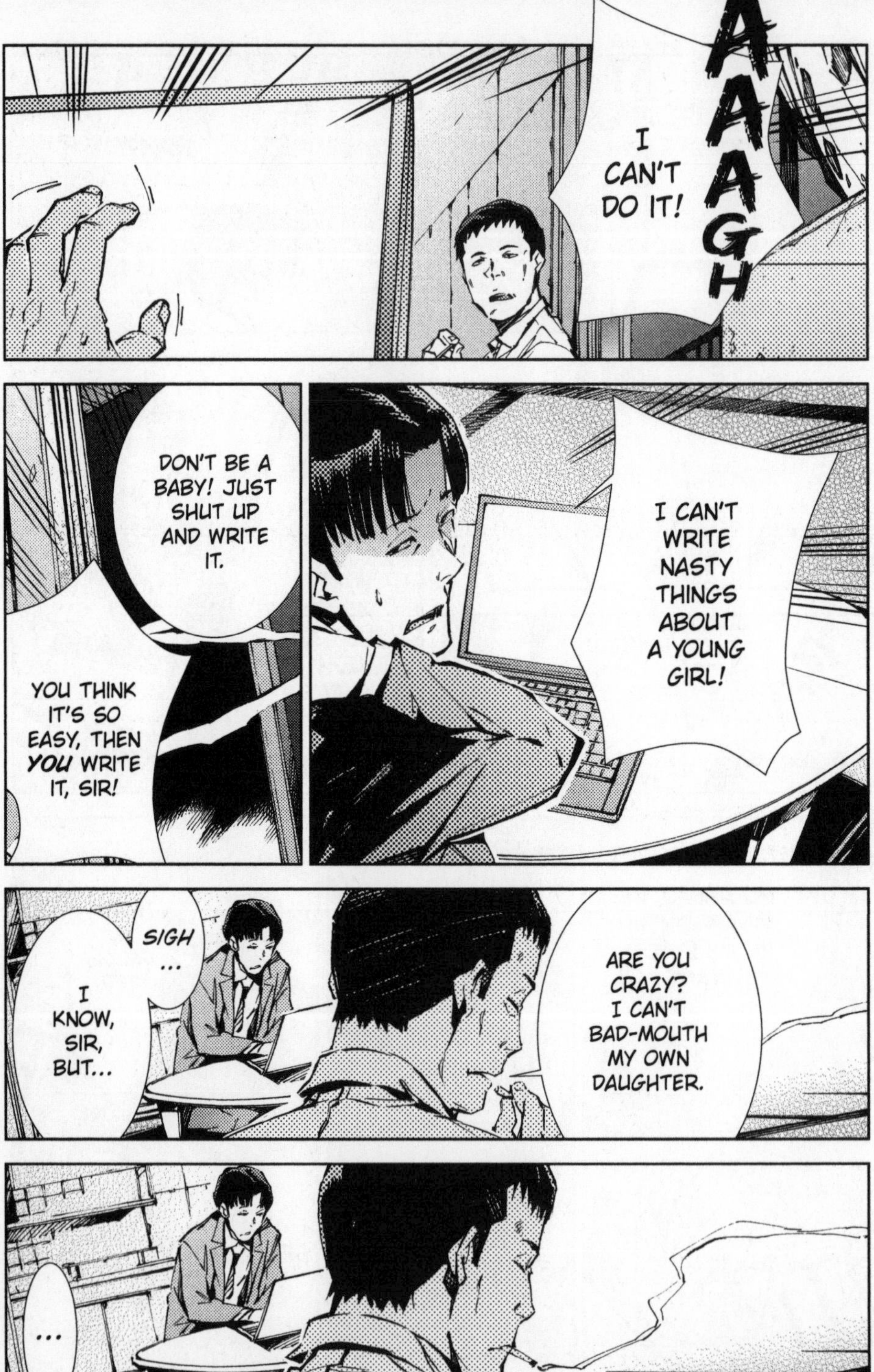
AAAGH
I CAN'T DO IT!
I CAN'T WRITE NASTY THINGS ABOUT A YOUNG GIRL!
DON'T BE A BABY! JUST SHUT UP AND WRITE IT.
YOU THINK IT'S SO EASY, THEN *YOU* WRITE IT, SIR!
ARE YOU CRAZY? I CAN'T BAD-MOUTH MY OWN DAUGHTER.
SIGH...
I KNOW, SIR, BUT...
...

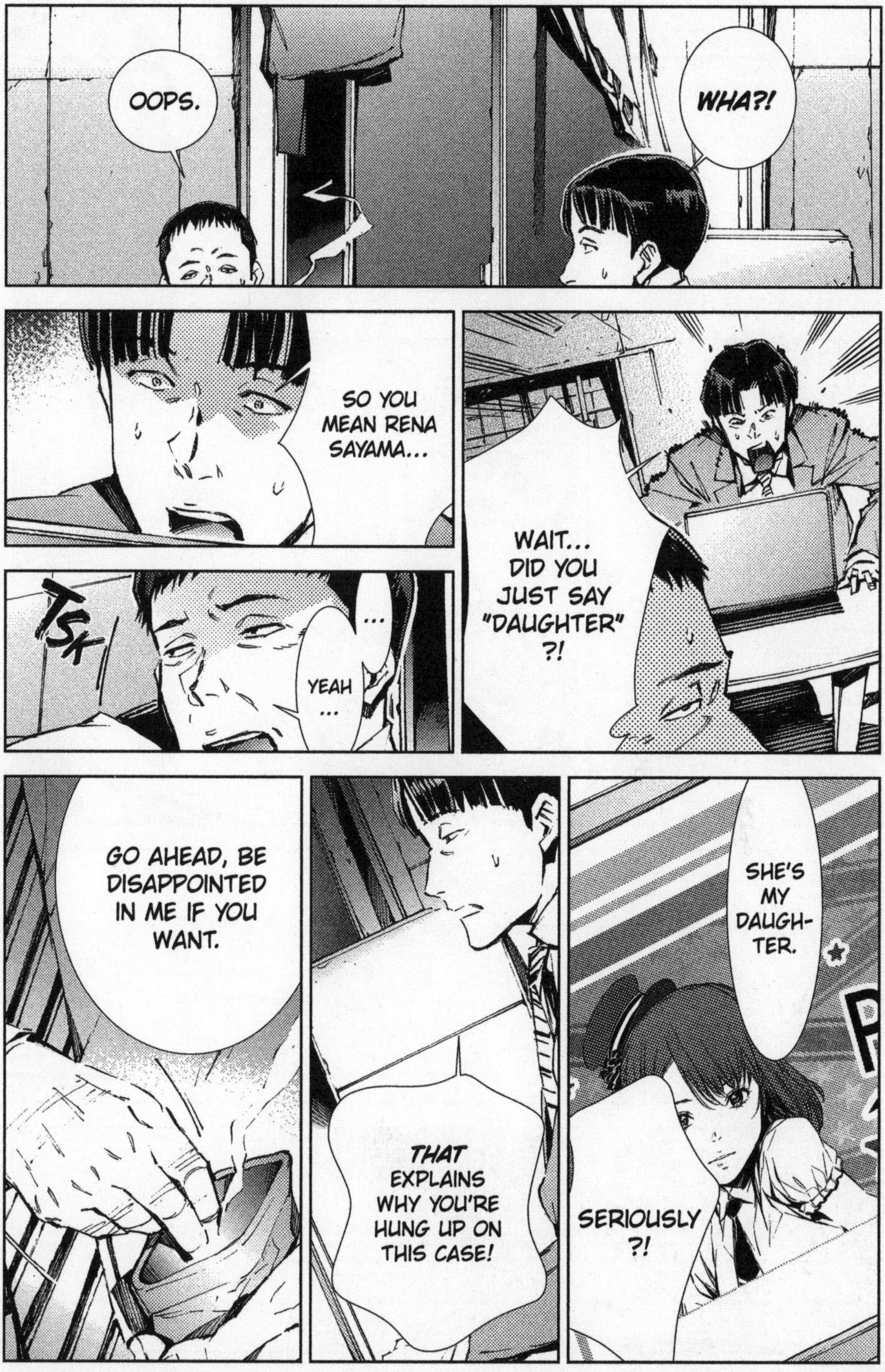
OOPS.
WHA?!
WAIT... DID YOU JUST SAY "DAUGHTER"?!
SO YOU MEAN RENA SAYAMA...
TSK
...
YEAH...
SHE'S MY DAUGHTER.
SERIOUSLY?!
THAT EXPLAINS WHY YOU'RE HUNG UP ON THIS CASE!
GO AHEAD, BE DISAPPOINTED IN ME IF YOU WANT.

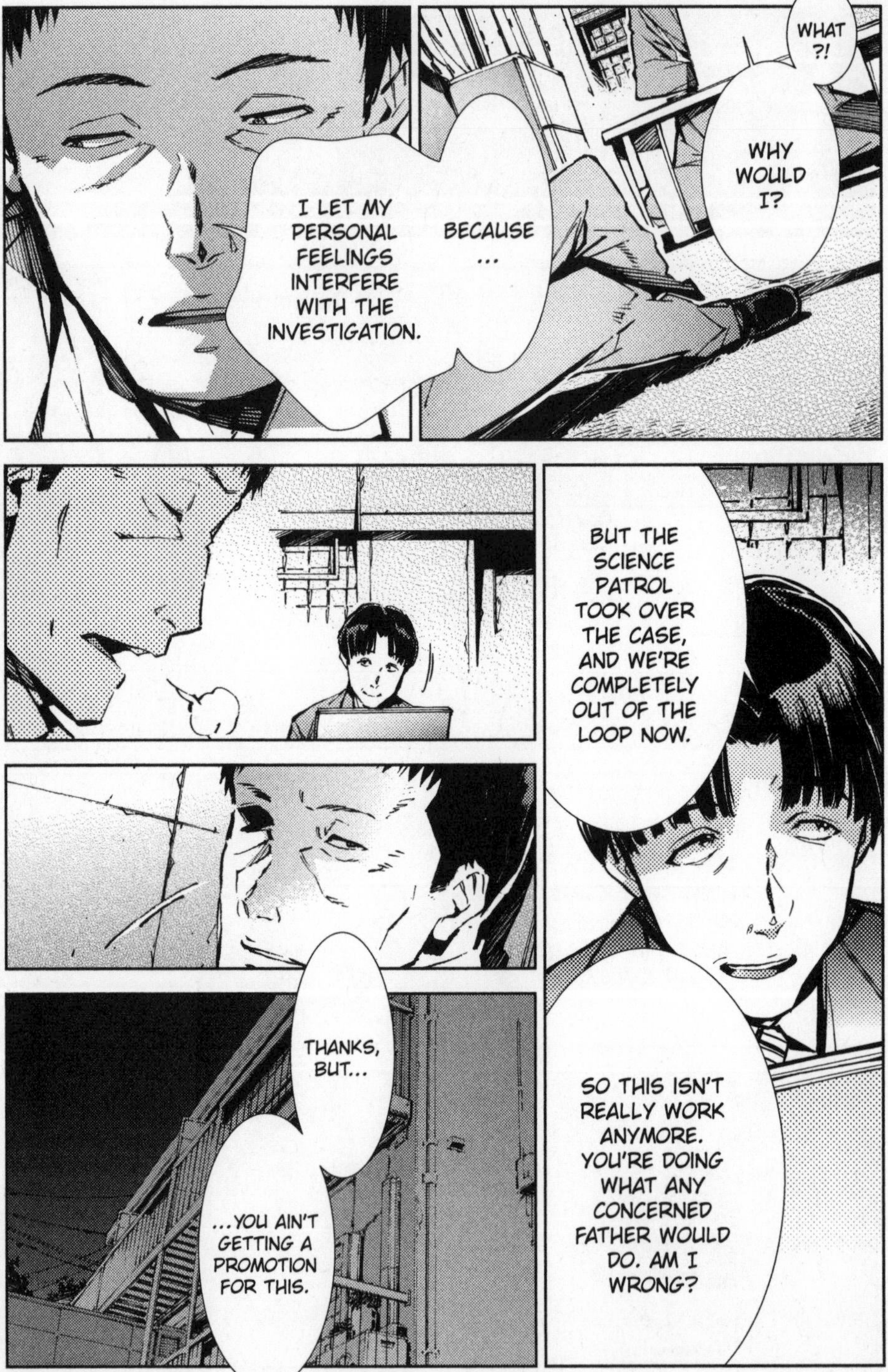
WHAT?!
WHY WOULD I?
BECAUSE...
I LET MY PERSONAL FEELINGS INTERFERE WITH THE INVESTIGATION.
BUT THE SCIENCE PATROL TOOK OVER THE CASE, AND WE'RE COMPLETELY OUT OF THE LOOP NOW.
SO THIS ISN'T REALLY WORK ANYMORE. YOU'RE DOING WHAT ANY CONCERNED FATHER WOULD DO. AM I WRONG?
THANKS, BUT...
...YOU AIN'T GETTING A PROMOTION FOR THIS.

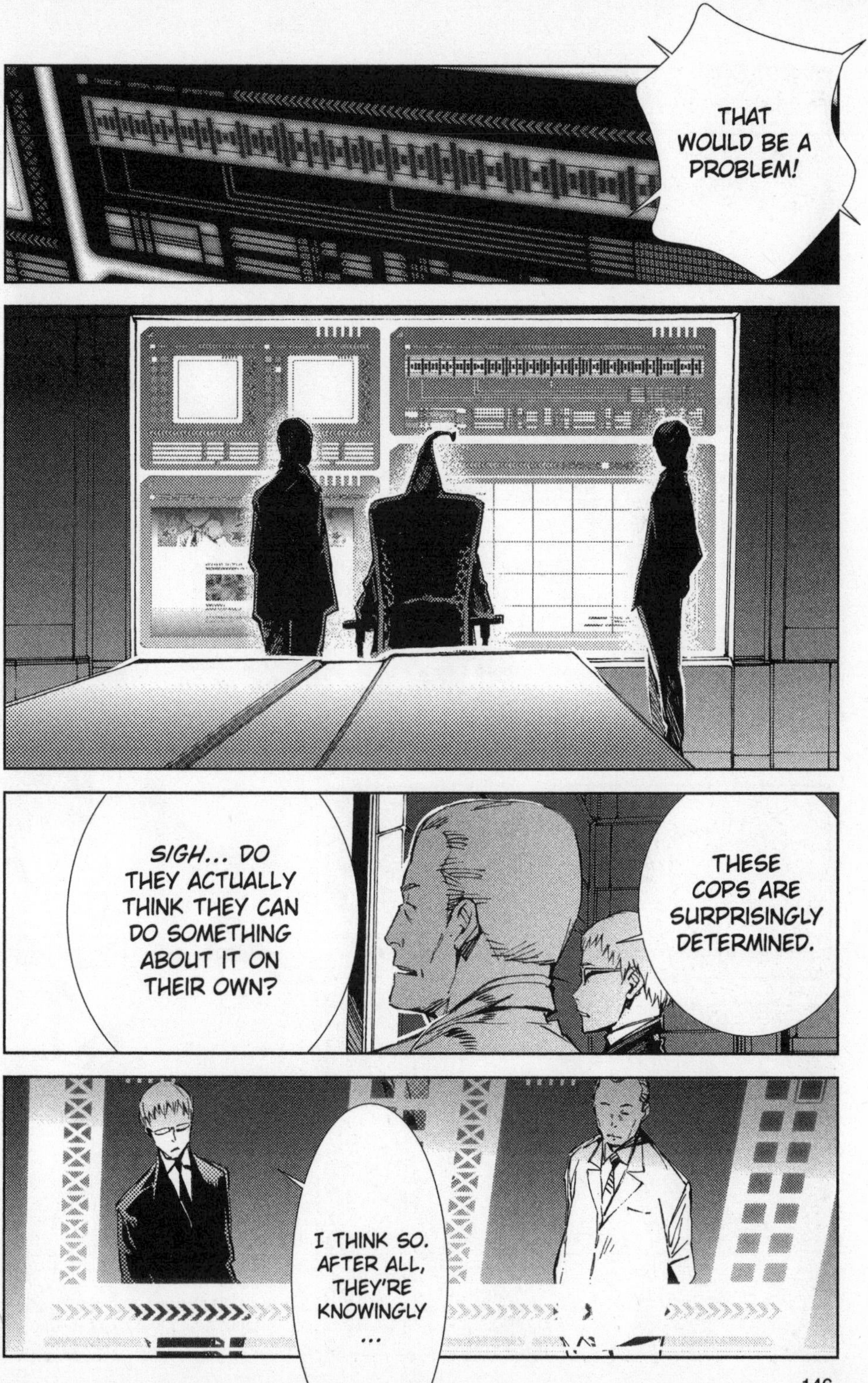
THAT WOULD BE A PROBLEM!
THESE COPS ARE SURPRISINGLY DETERMINED.
SIGH... DO THEY ACTUALLY THINK THEY CAN DO SOMETHING ABOUT IT ON THEIR OWN?
I THINK SO. AFTER ALL, THEY'RE KNOWINGLY ...

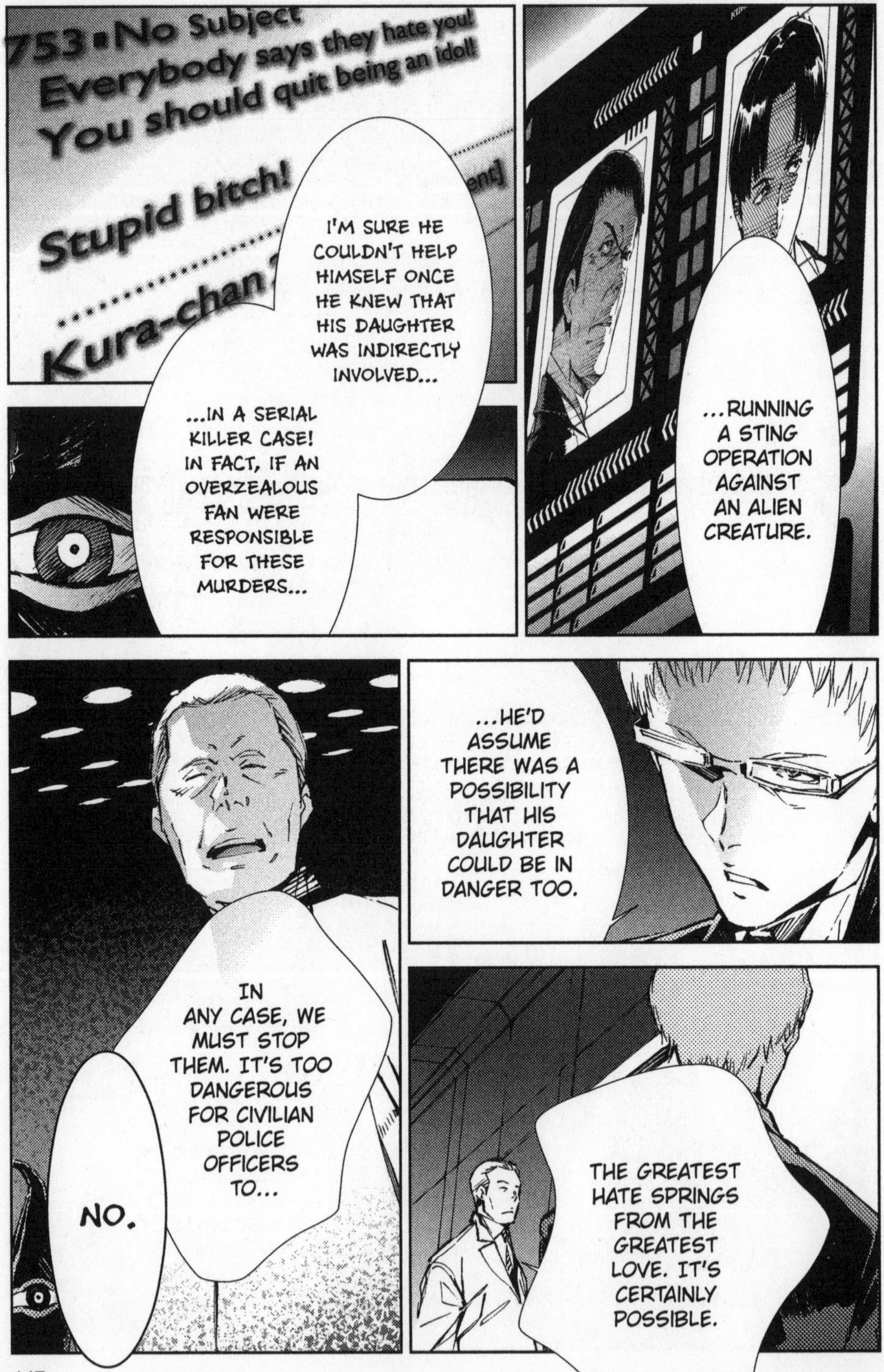
...RUNNING A STING OPERATION AGAINST AN ALIEN CREATURE.
753 ■ No Subject
Everybody says they hate you!
You should quit being an idol!
Stupid bitch!
Kura-chan
I'M SURE HE COULDN'T HELP HIMSELF ONCE HE KNEW THAT HIS DAUGHTER WAS INDIRECTLY INVOLVED...
...IN A SERIAL KILLER CASE! IN FACT, IF AN OVERZEALOUS FAN WERE RESPONSIBLE FOR THESE MURDERS...
...HE'D ASSUME THERE WAS A POSSIBILITY THAT HIS DAUGHTER COULD BE IN DANGER TOO.
THE GREATEST HATE SPRINGS FROM THE GREATEST LOVE. IT'S CERTAINLY POSSIBLE.
IN ANY CASE, WE MUST STOP THEM. IT'S TOO DANGEROUS FOR CIVILIAN POLICE OFFICERS TO...
NO.

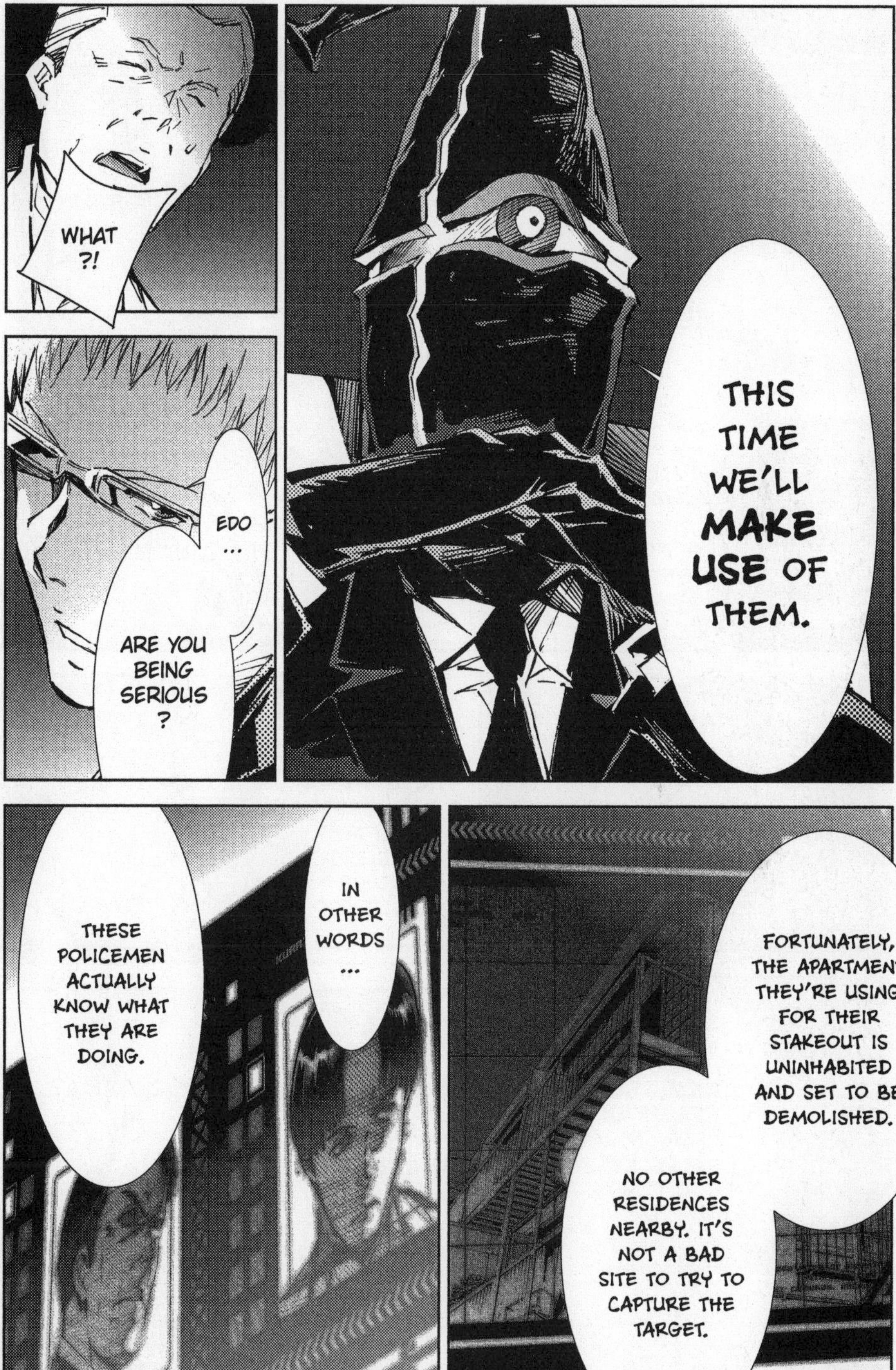
THIS TIME WE'LL MAKE USE OF THEM.
WHAT ?!
EDO ...
ARE YOU BEING SERIOUS ?
FORTUNATELY, THE APARTMENT THEY'RE USING FOR THEIR STAKEOUT IS UNINHABITED AND SET TO BE DEMOLISHED.
NO OTHER RESIDENCES NEARBY. IT'S NOT A BAD SITE TO TRY TO CAPTURE THE TARGET.
IN OTHER WORDS ...
THESE POLICEMEN ACTUALLY KNOW WHAT THEY ARE DOING.

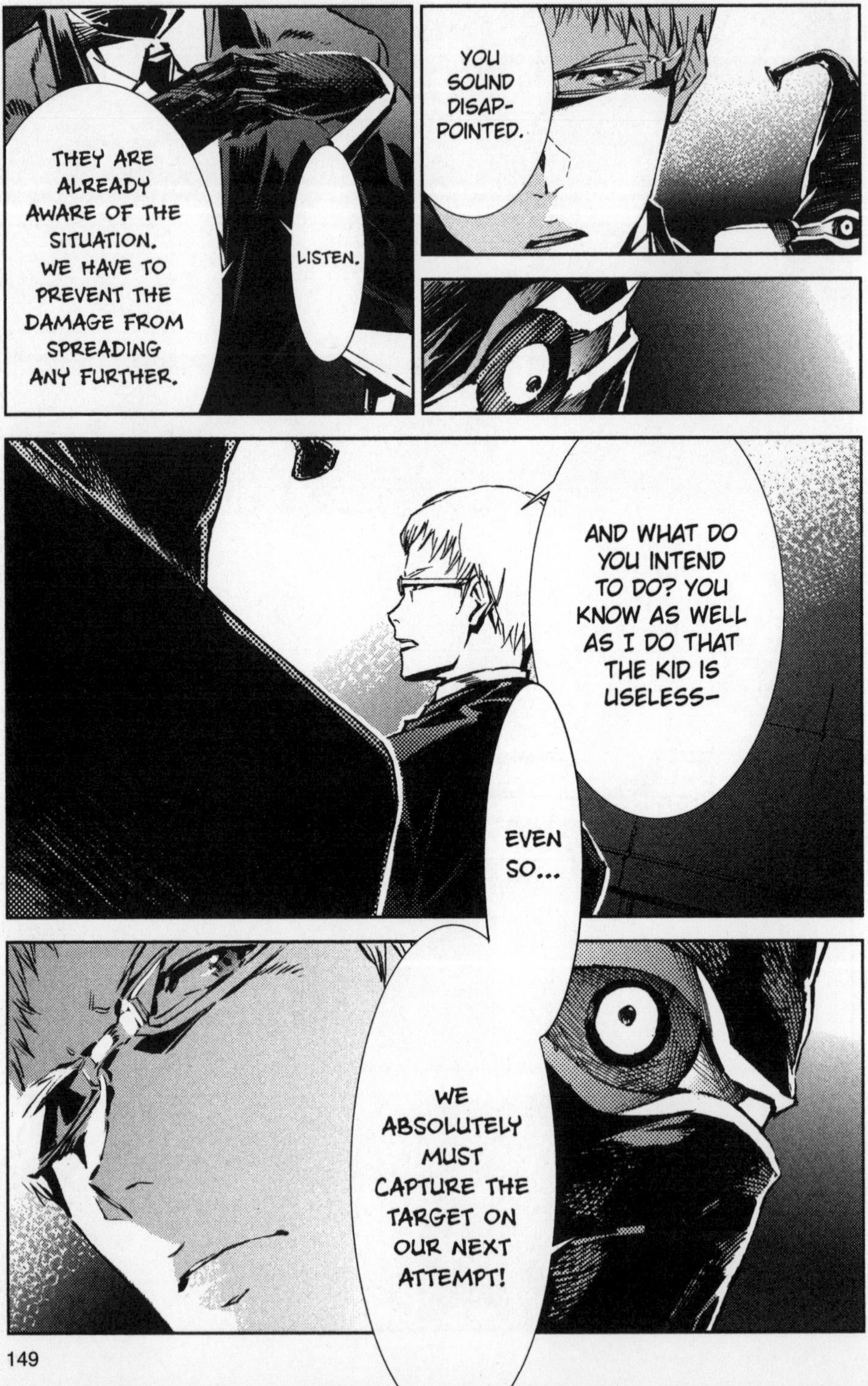
YOU SOUND DISAPPOINTED.
LISTEN.
THEY ARE ALREADY AWARE OF THE SITUATION. WE HAVE TO PREVENT THE DAMAGE FROM SPREADING ANY FURTHER.
AND WHAT DO YOU INTEND TO DO? YOU KNOW AS WELL AS I DO THAT THE KID IS USELESS-
EVEN SO...
WE ABSOLUTELY MUST CAPTURE THE TARGET ON OUR NEXT ATTEMPT!

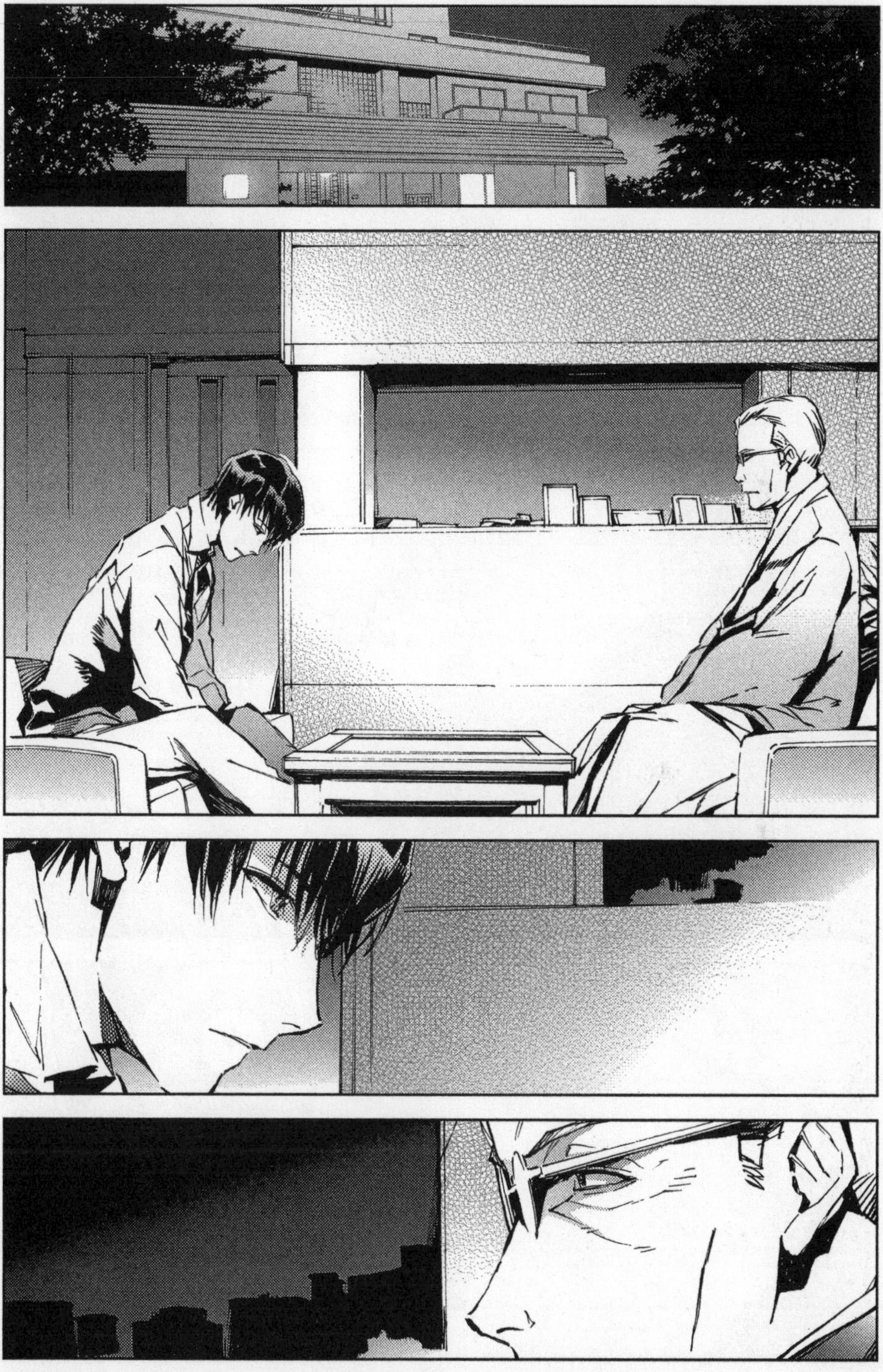

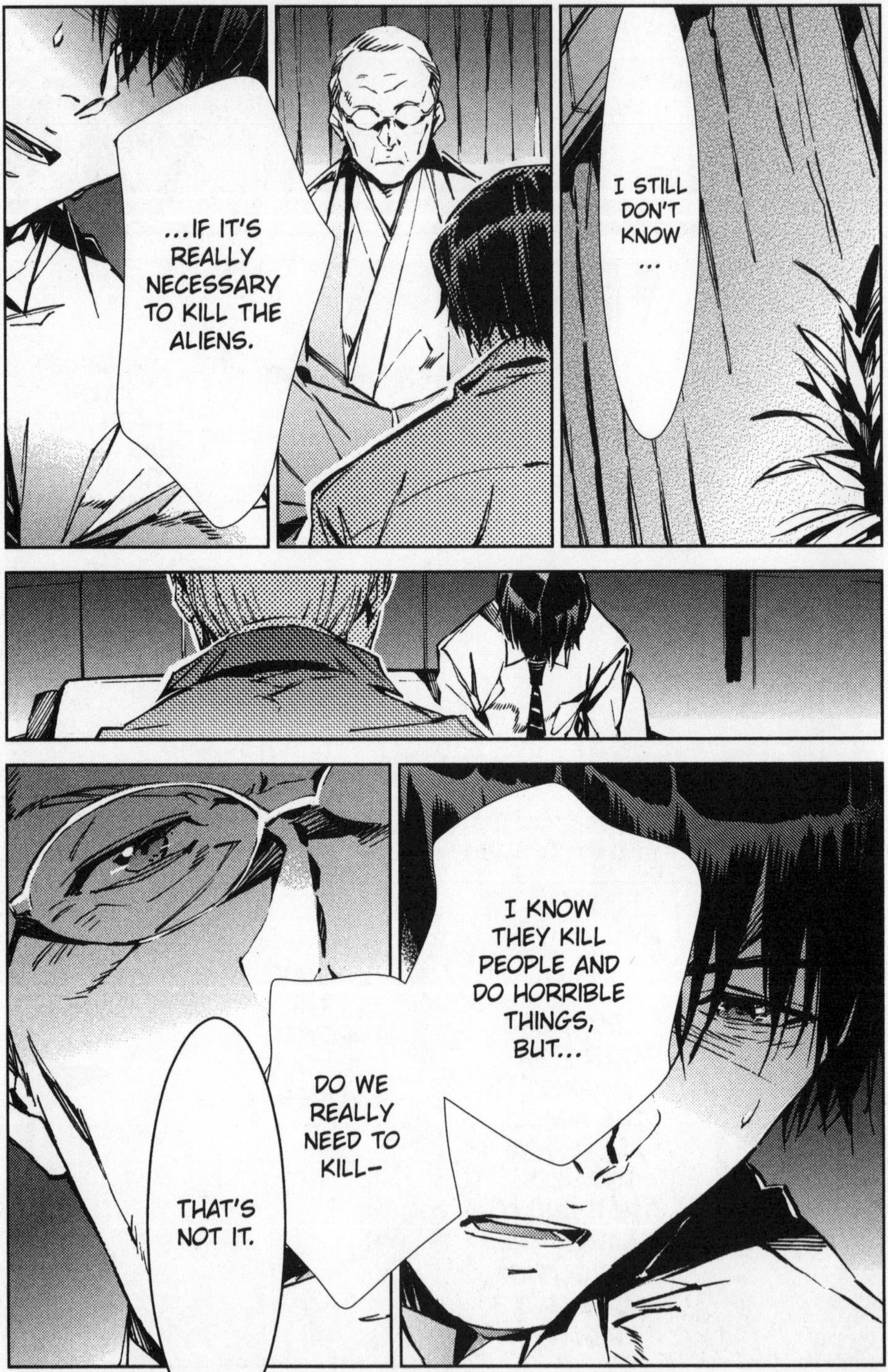
I STILL DON'T KNOW ...
...IF IT'S REALLY NECESSARY TO KILL THE ALIENS.
I KNOW THEY KILL PEOPLE AND DO HORRIBLE THINGS, BUT...
DO WE REALLY NEED TO KILL-
THAT'S NOT IT.

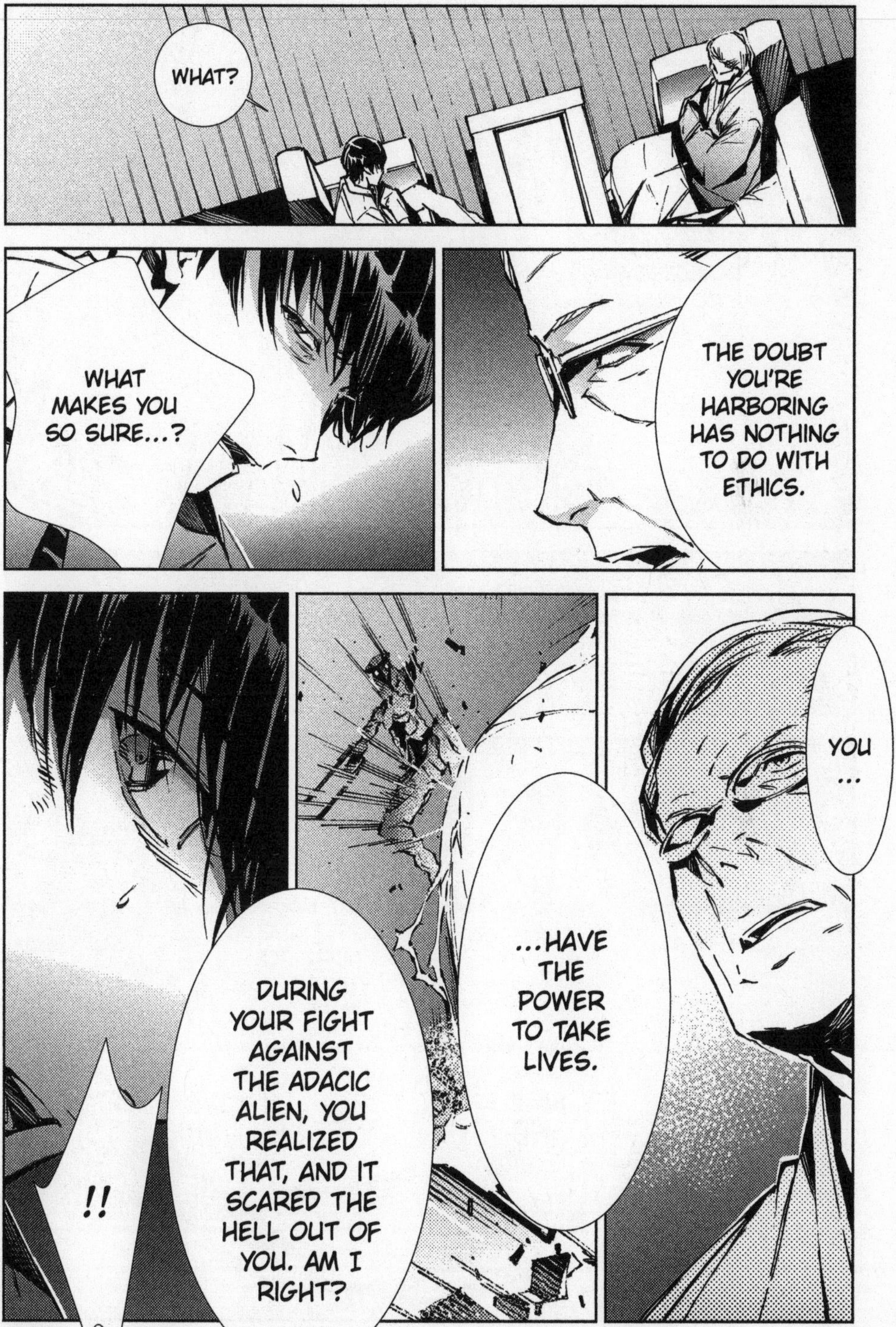
WHAT?
THE DOUBT YOU'RE HARBORING HAS NOTHING TO DO WITH ETHICS.
WHAT MAKES YOU SO SURE...?
YOU ...
...HAVE THE POWER TO TAKE LIVES.
DURING YOUR FIGHT AGAINST THE ADACIC ALIEN, YOU REALIZED THAT, AND IT SCARED THE HELL OUT OF YOU. AM I RIGHT?
!!

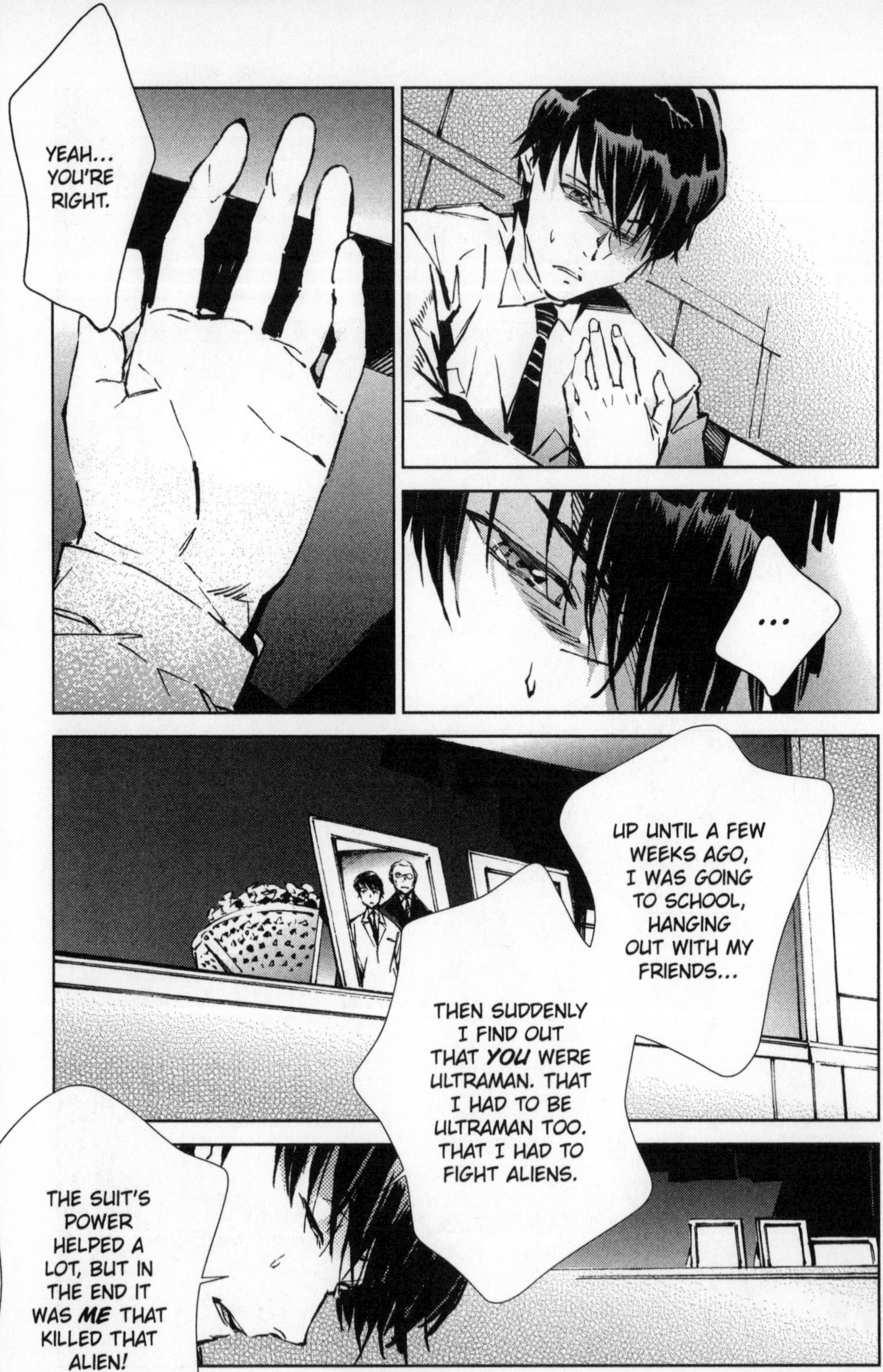
...
YEAH... YOU'RE RIGHT.
UP UNTIL A FEW WEEKS AGO, I WAS GOING TO SCHOOL, HANGING OUT WITH MY FRIENDS...
THEN SUDDENLY I FIND OUT THAT *YOU* WERE ULTRAMAN. THAT I HAD TO BE ULTRAMAN TOO. THAT I HAD TO FIGHT ALIENS.
THE SUIT'S POWER HELPED A LOT, BUT IN THE END IT WAS *ME* THAT KILLED THAT ALIEN!

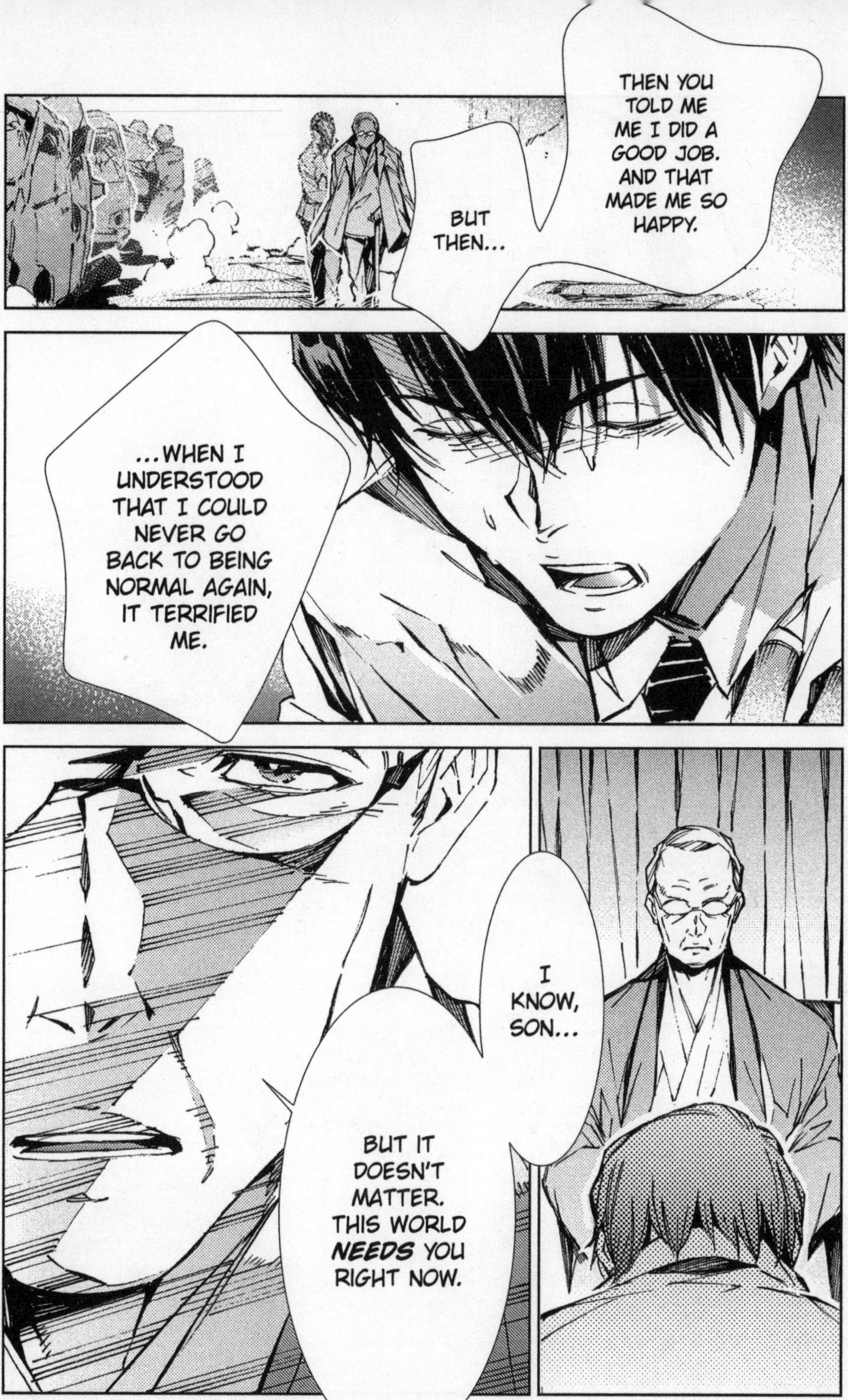
THEN YOU TOLD ME ME I DID A GOOD JOB. AND THAT MADE ME SO HAPPY.
BUT THEN...
...WHEN I UNDERSTOOD THAT I COULD NEVER GO BACK TO BEING NORMAL AGAIN, IT TERRIFIED ME.
I KNOW, SON...
BUT IT DOESN'T MATTER. THIS WORLD ***NEEDS*** YOU RIGHT NOW.

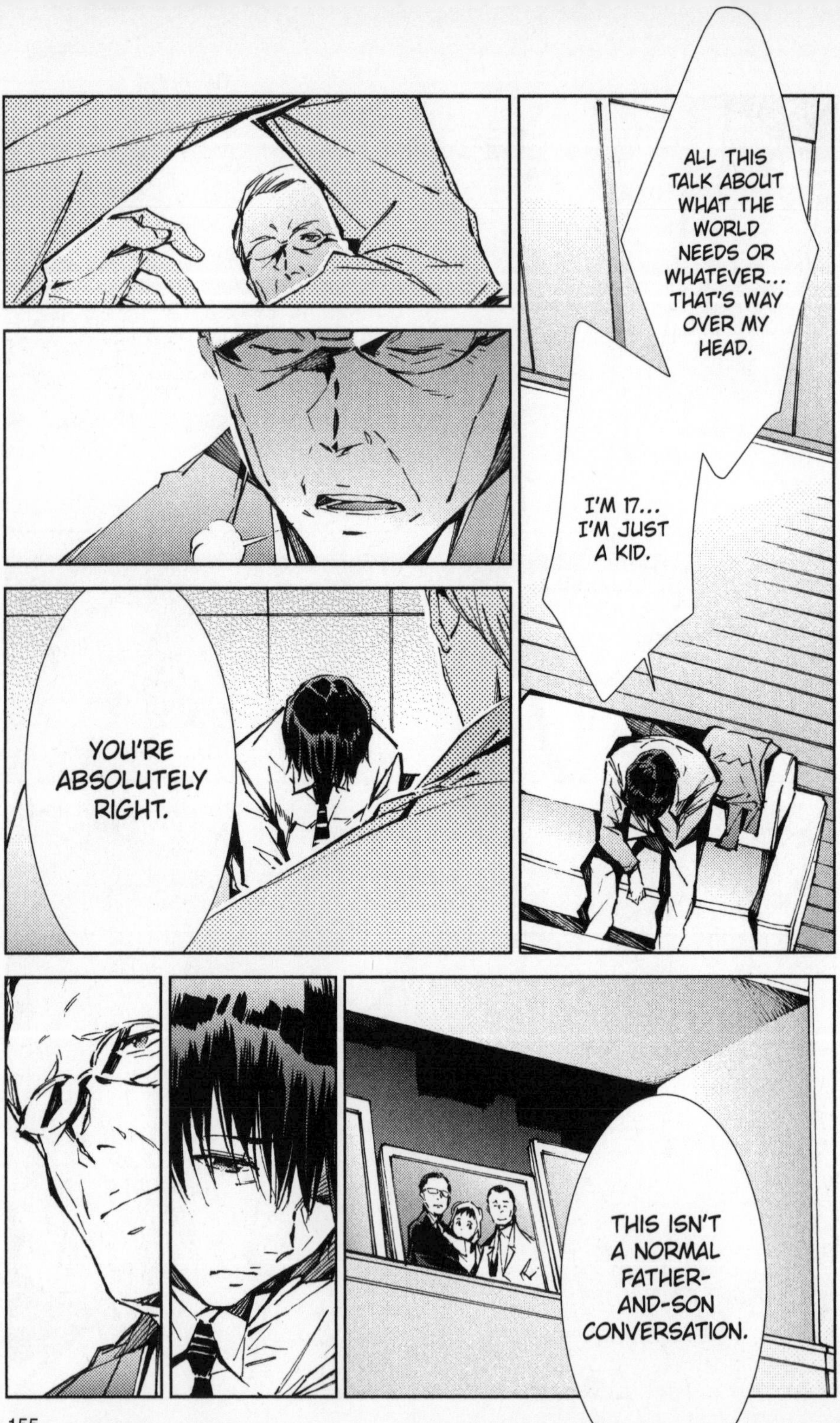
ALL THIS TALK ABOUT WHAT THE WORLD NEEDS OR WHATEVER... THAT'S WAY OVER MY HEAD.
I'M 17... I'M JUST A KID.
YOU'RE ABSOLUTELY RIGHT.
THIS ISN'T A NORMAL FATHER-AND-SON CONVERSATION.

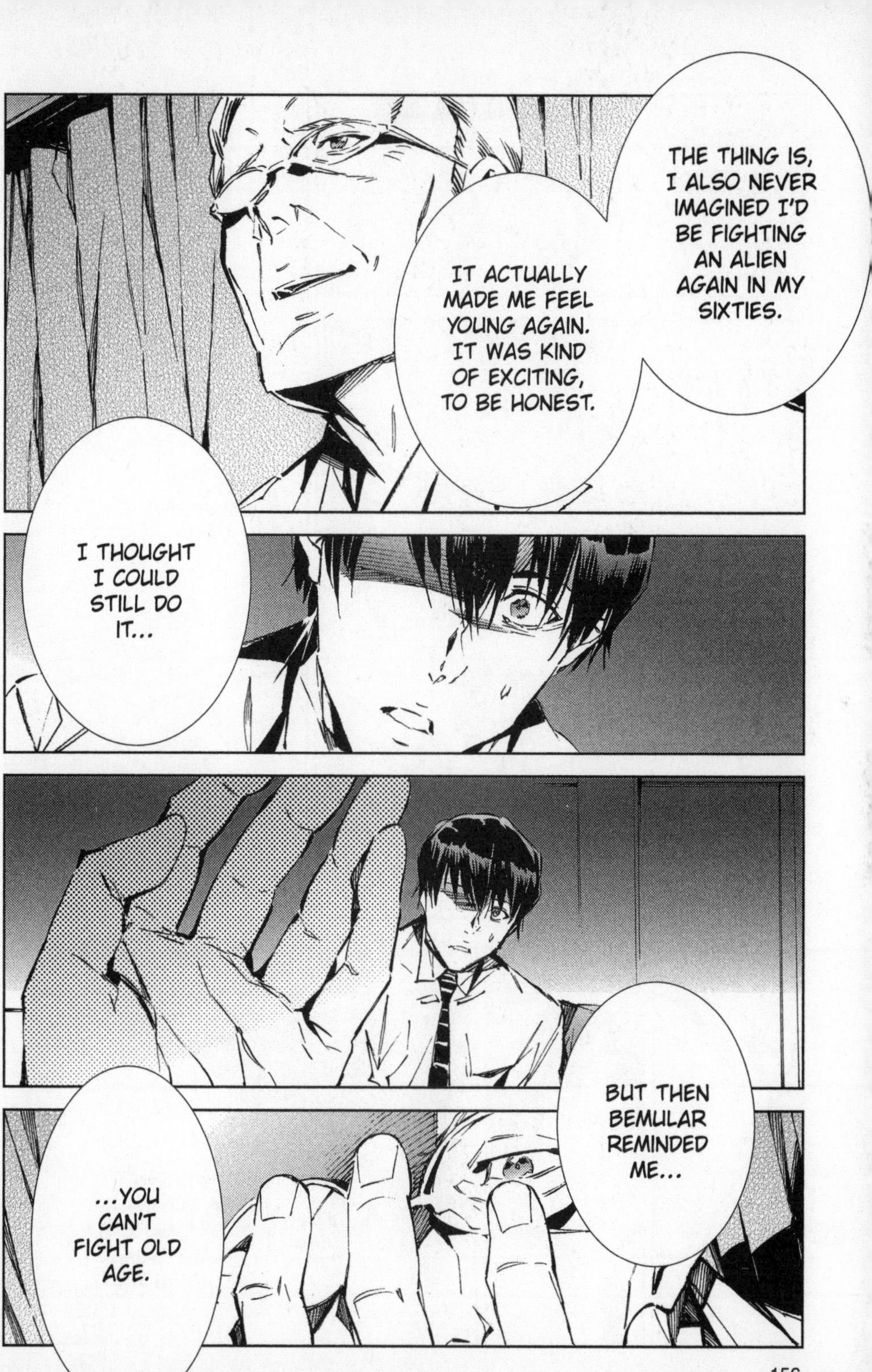
THE THING IS, I ALSO NEVER IMAGINED I'D BE FIGHTING AN ALIEN AGAIN IN MY SIXTIES.
IT ACTUALLY MADE ME FEEL YOUNG AGAIN. IT WAS KIND OF EXCITING, TO BE HONEST.
I THOUGHT I COULD STILL DO IT...
BUT THEN BEMULAR REMINDED ME...
...YOU CAN'T FIGHT OLD AGE.

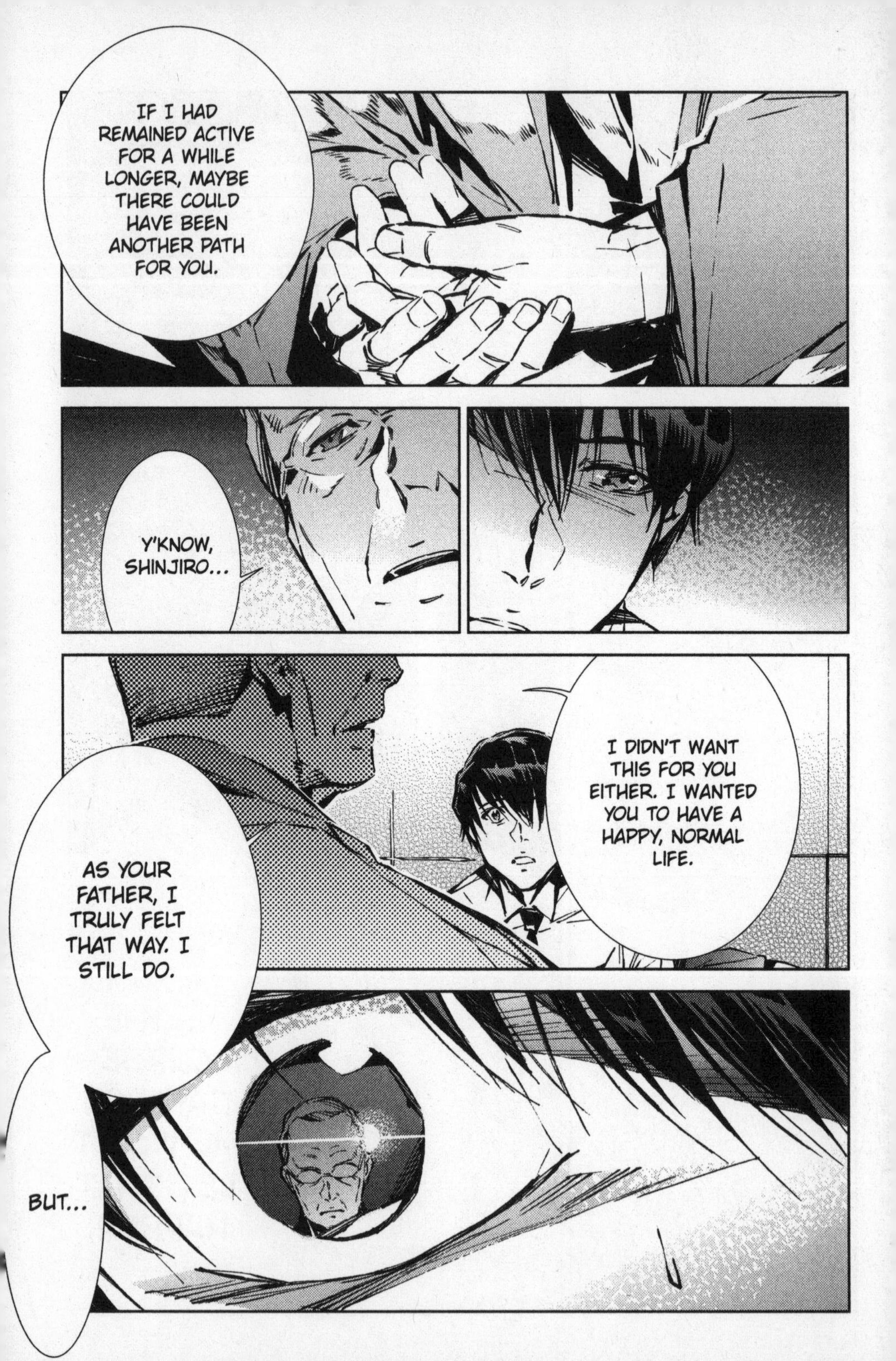
IF I HAD REMAINED ACTIVE FOR A WHILE LONGER, MAYBE THERE COULD HAVE BEEN ANOTHER PATH FOR YOU.
Y'KNOW, SHINJIRO...
I DIDN'T WANT THIS FOR YOU EITHER. I WANTED YOU TO HAVE A HAPPY, NORMAL LIFE.
AS YOUR FATHER, I TRULY FELT THAT WAY. I STILL DO.
BUT...

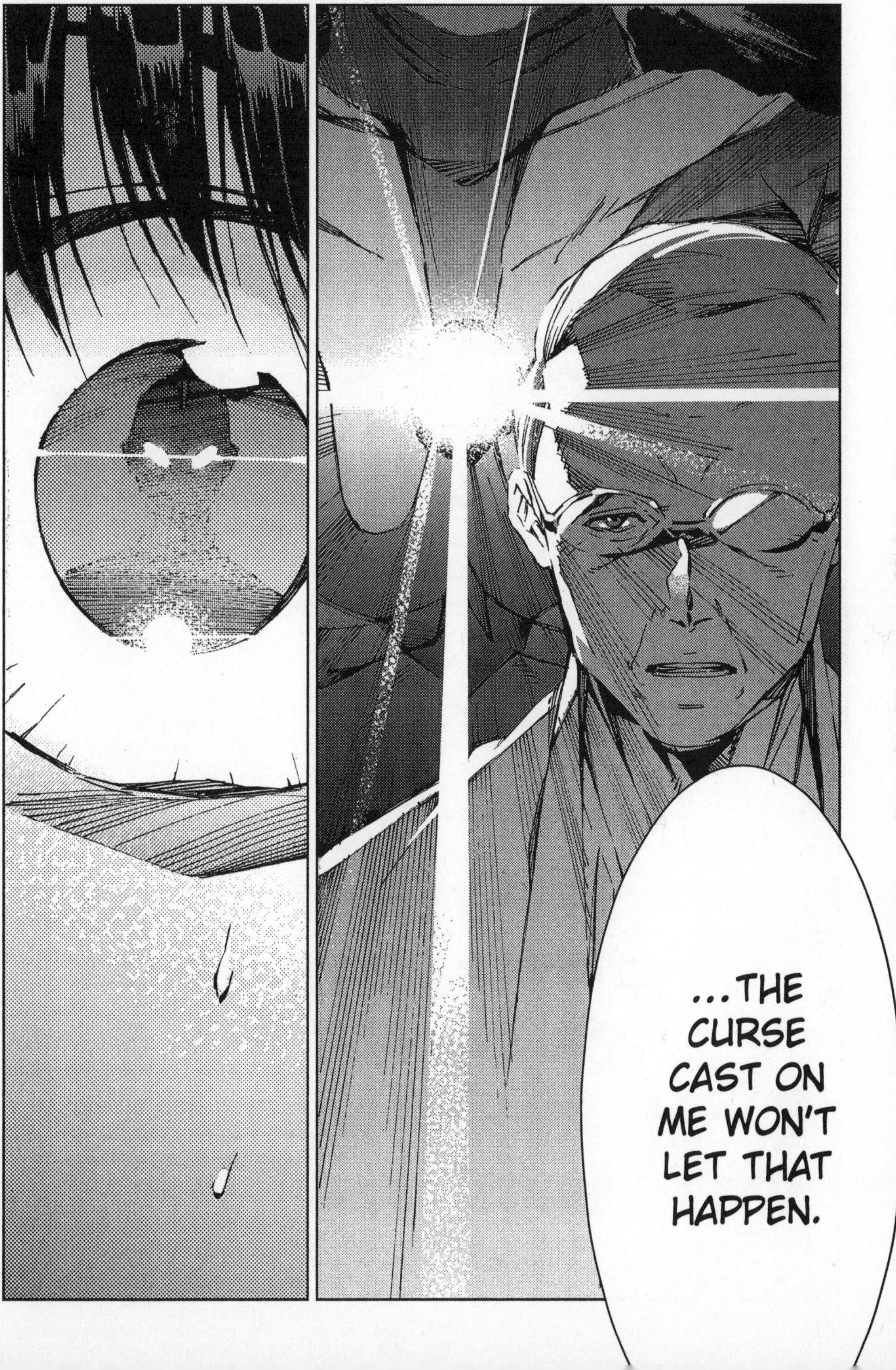
...THE CURSE CAST ON ME WON'T LET THAT HAPPEN.

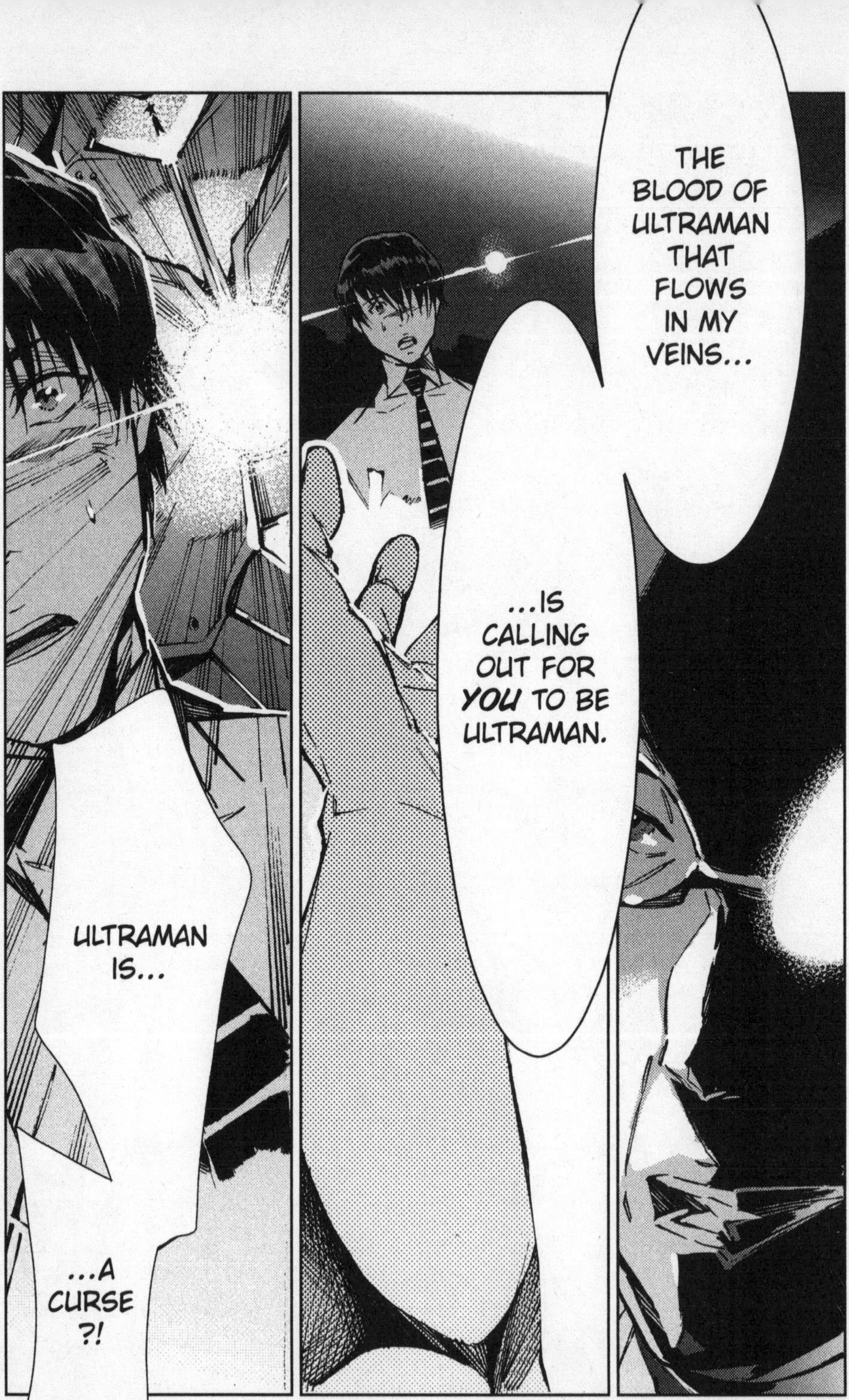
THE BLOOD OF ULTRAMAN THAT FLOWS IN MY VEINS...
...IS CALLING OUT FOR *YOU* TO BE ULTRAMAN.
ULTRAMAN IS...
...A CURSE ?!

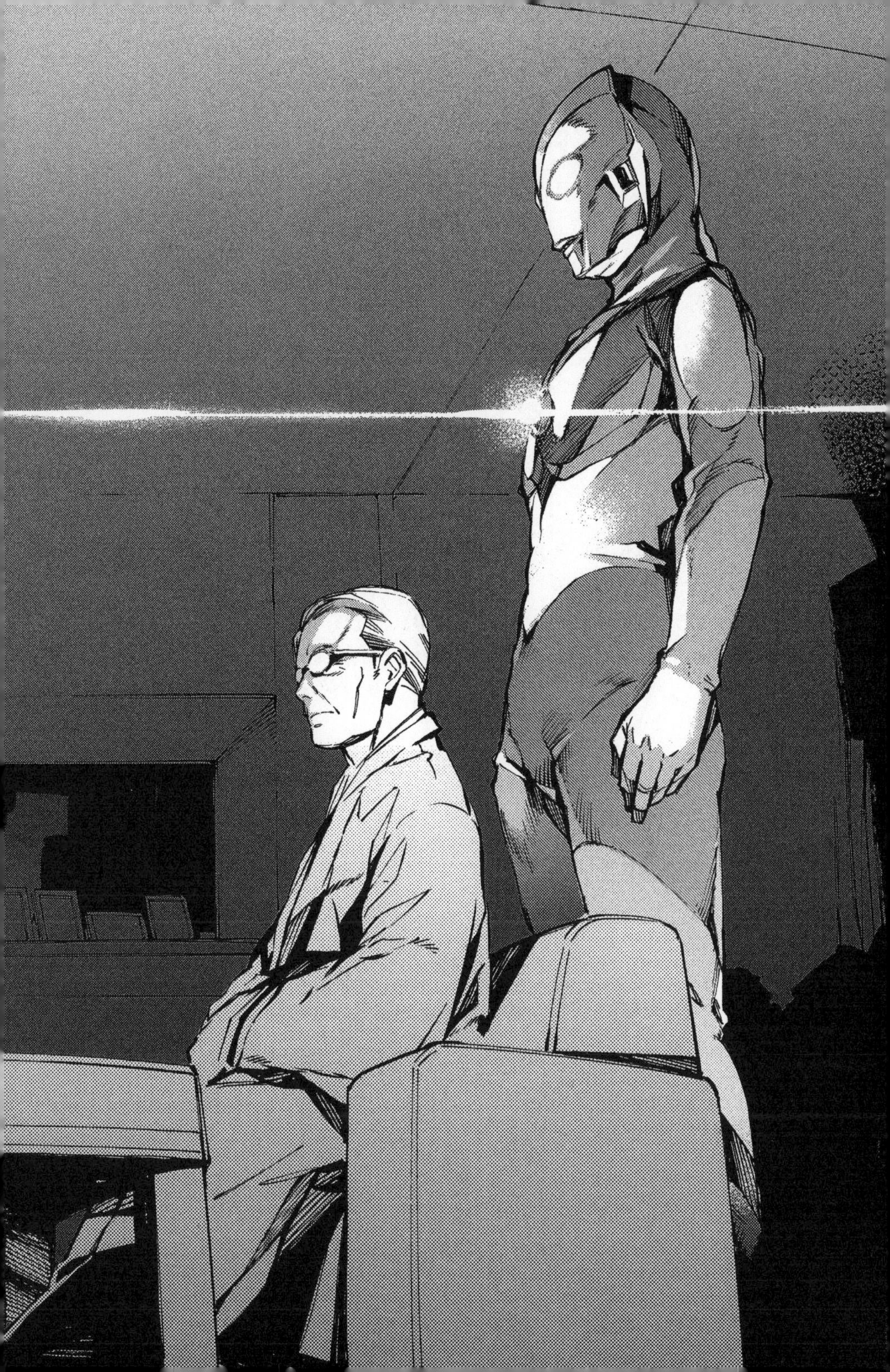

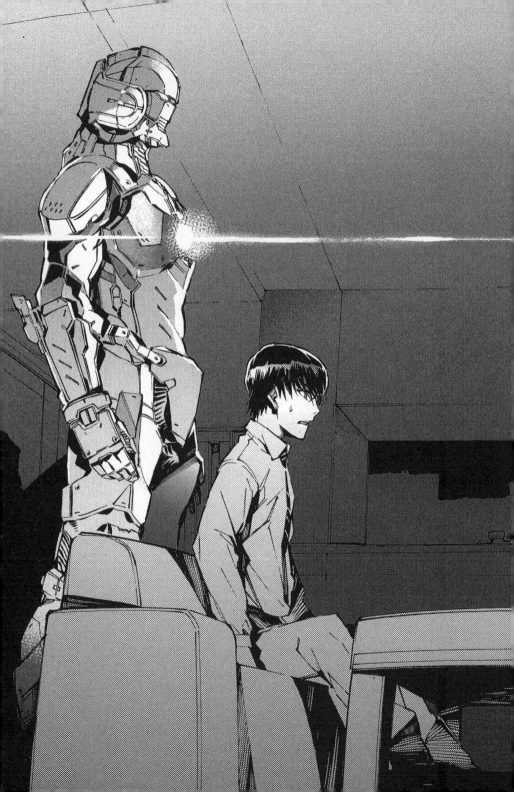

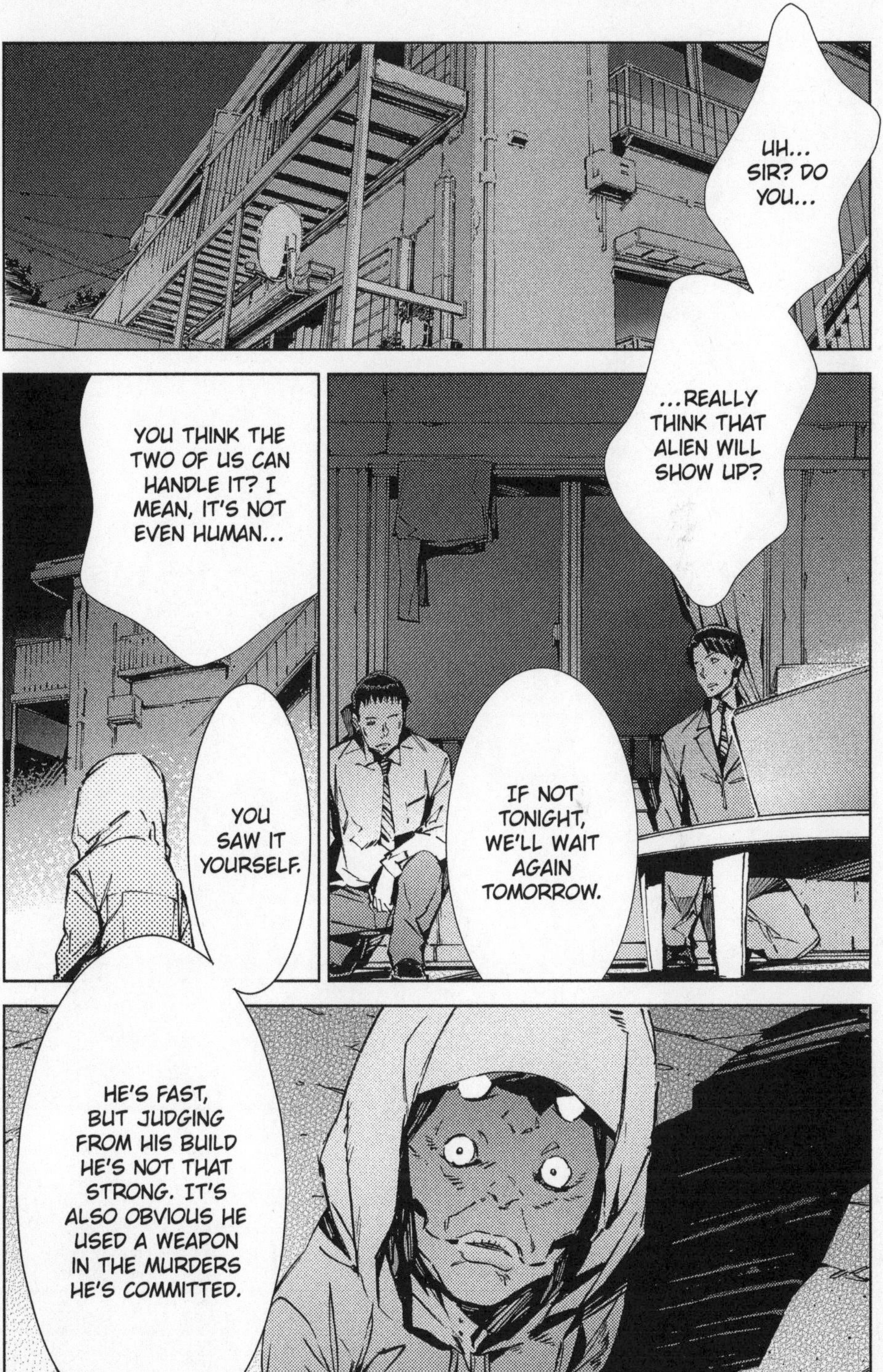
UH... SIR? DO YOU...
...REALLY THINK THAT ALIEN WILL SHOW UP?
IF NOT TONIGHT, WE'LL WAIT AGAIN TOMORROW.
YOU THINK THE TWO OF US CAN HANDLE IT? I MEAN, IT'S NOT EVEN HUMAN...
YOU SAW IT YOURSELF.
HE'S FAST, BUT JUDGING FROM HIS BUILD HE'S NOT THAT STRONG. IT'S ALSO OBVIOUS HE USED A WEAPON IN THE MURDERS HE'S COMMITTED.

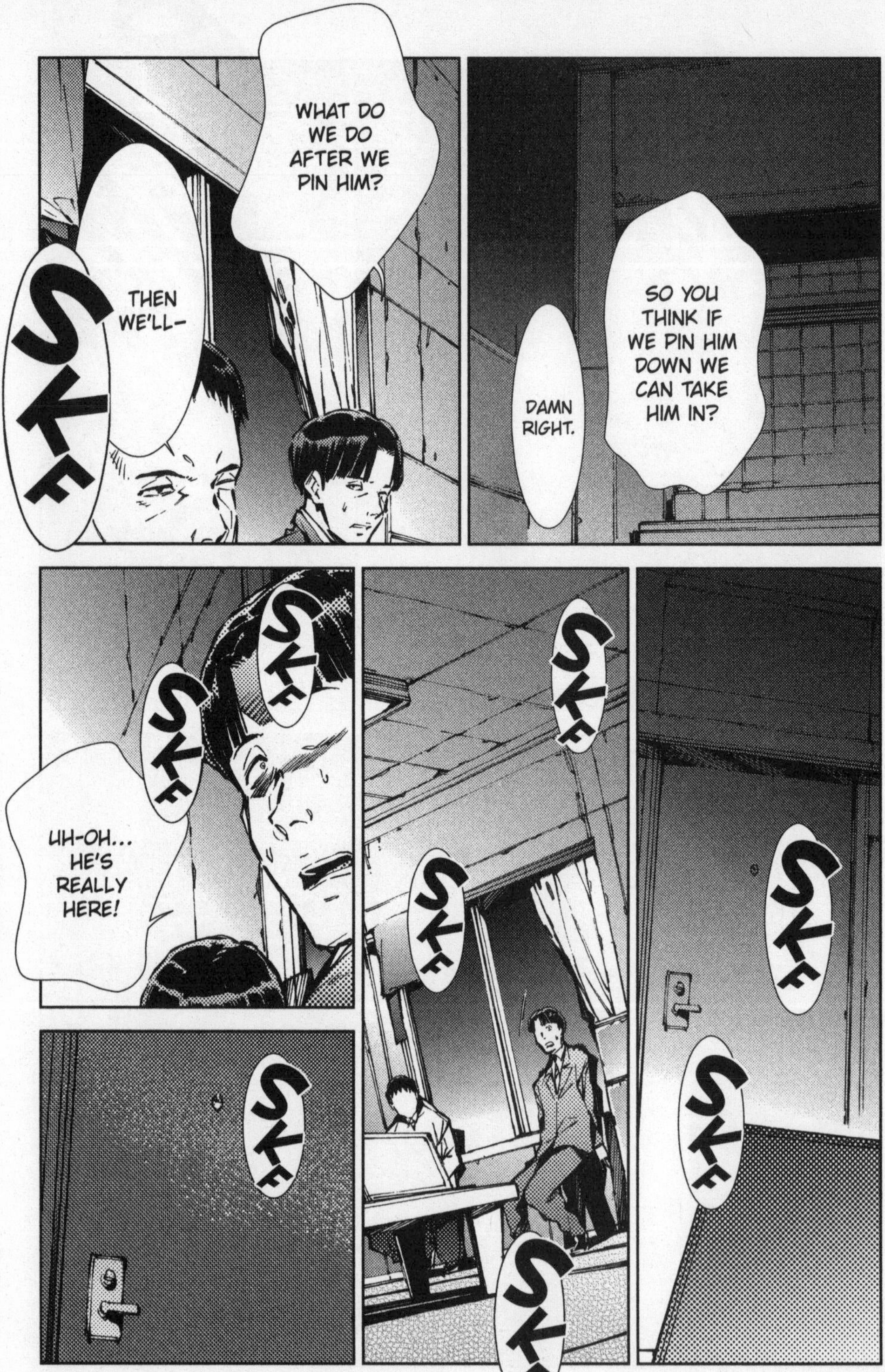
SO YOU THINK IF WE PIN HIM DOWN WE CAN TAKE HIM IN?
DAMN RIGHT.
WHAT DO WE DO AFTER WE PIN HIM?
THEN WE'LL-
SKF
SKF
SKF
SKF
SKF
SKF
SKF
SKF
UH-OH... HE'S REALLY HERE!
SKF

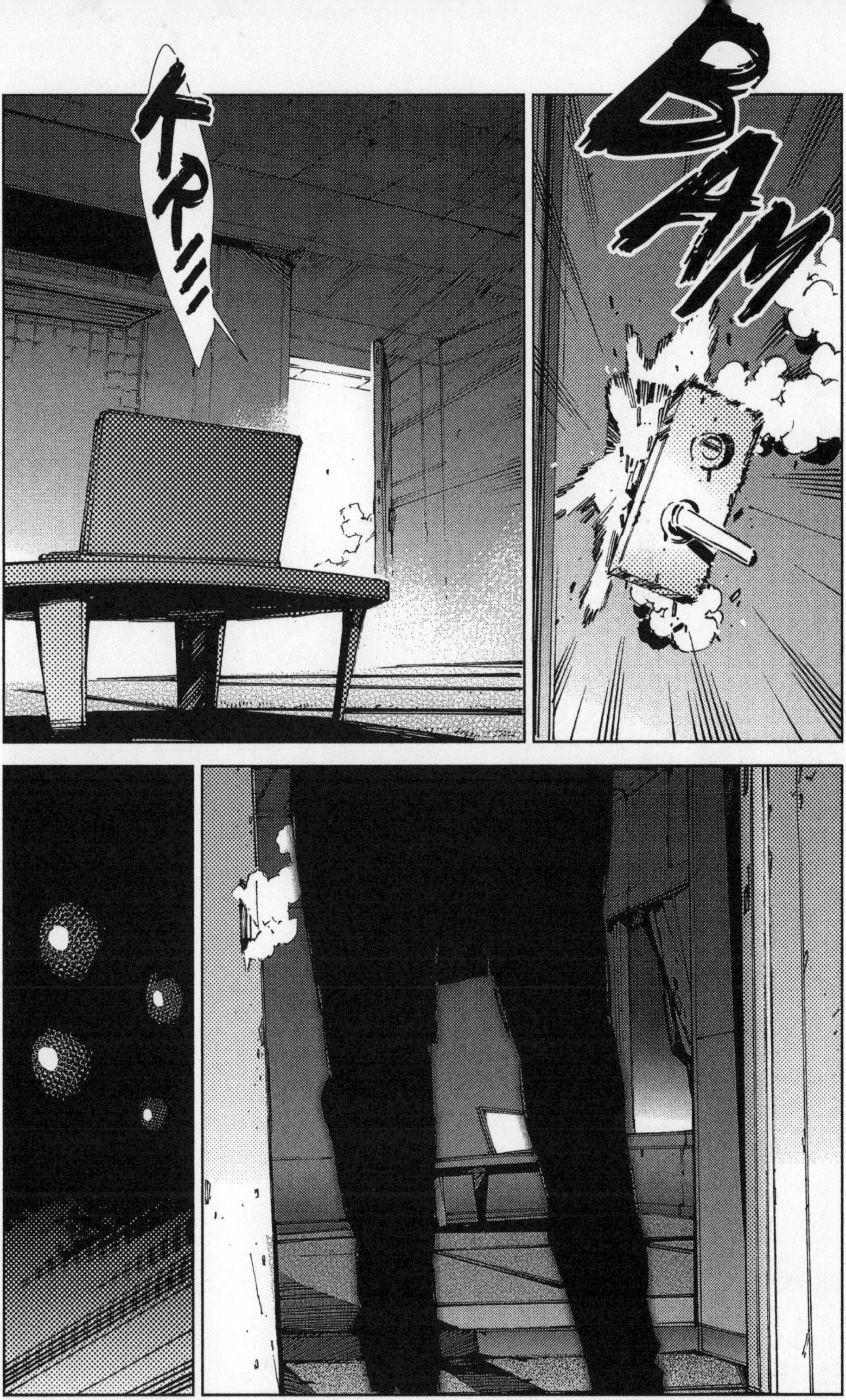
BAM
KR

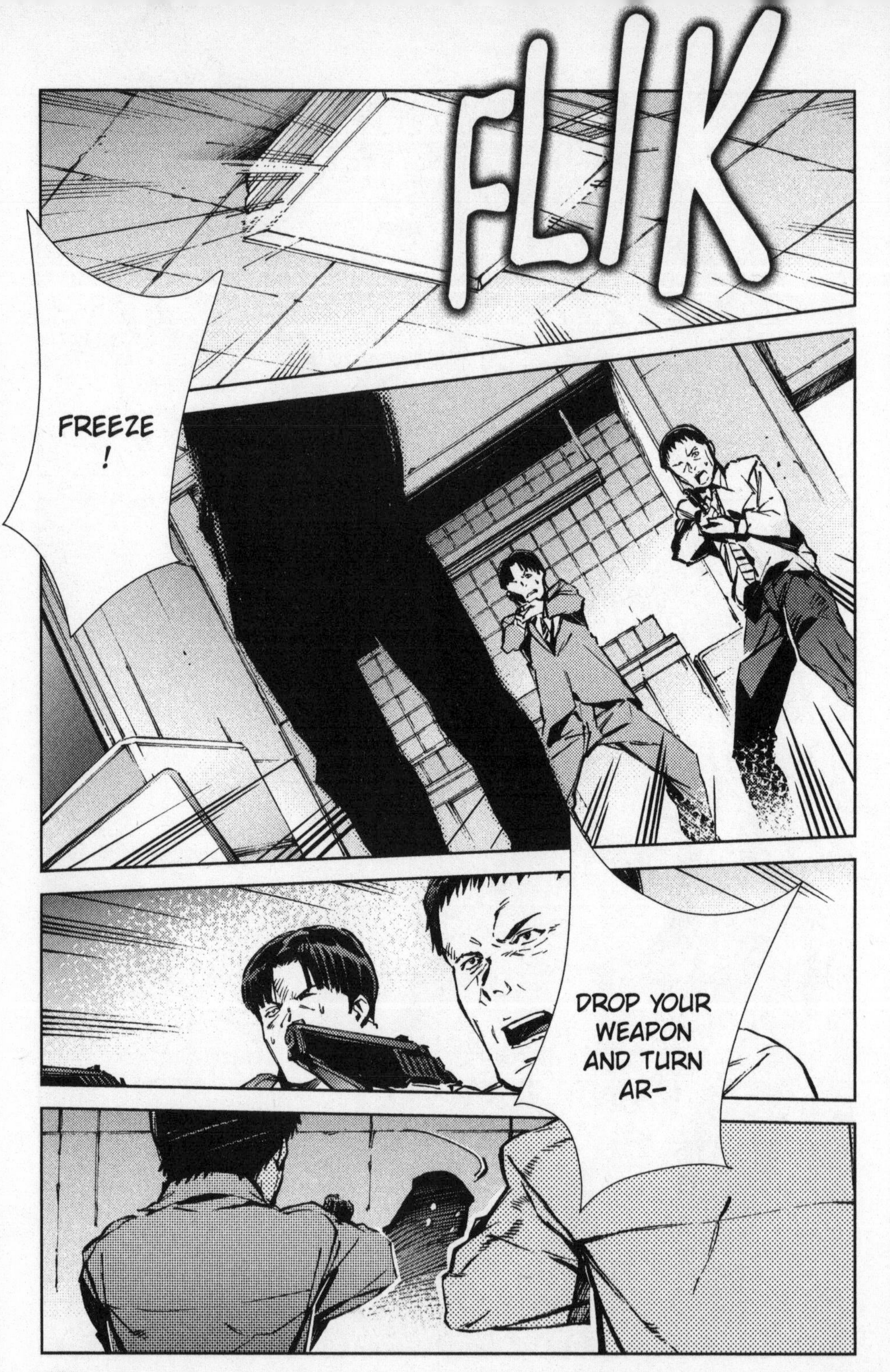
FLIK
FREEZE !
DROP YOUR WEAPON AND TURN AR-

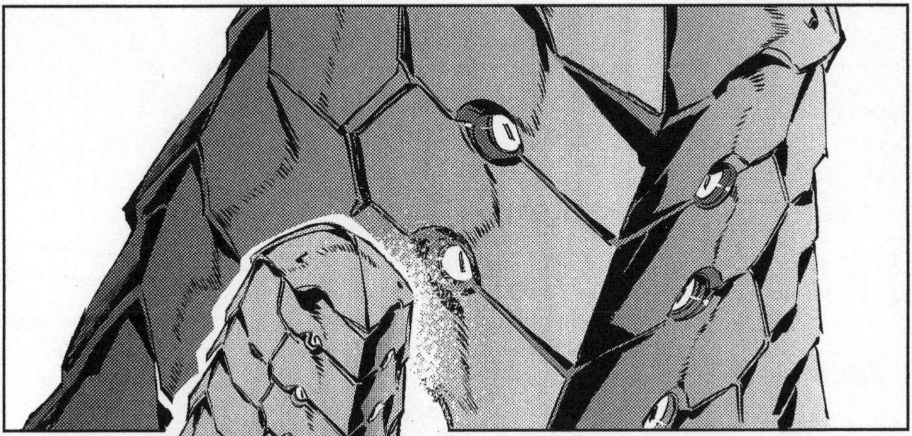
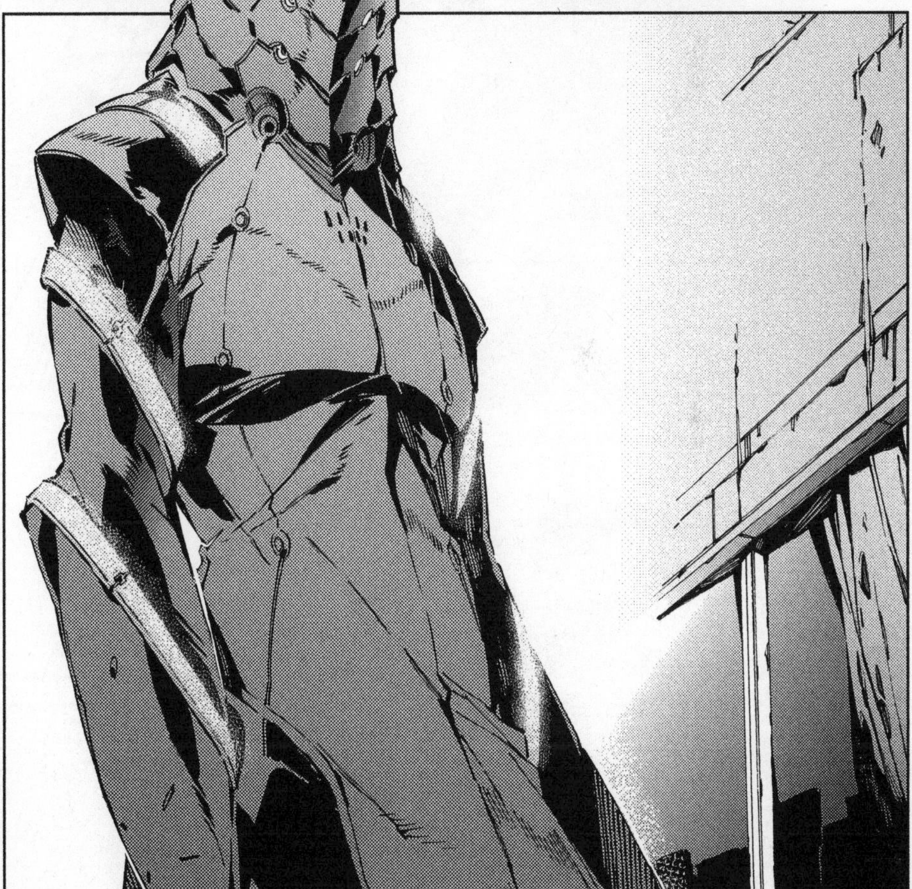

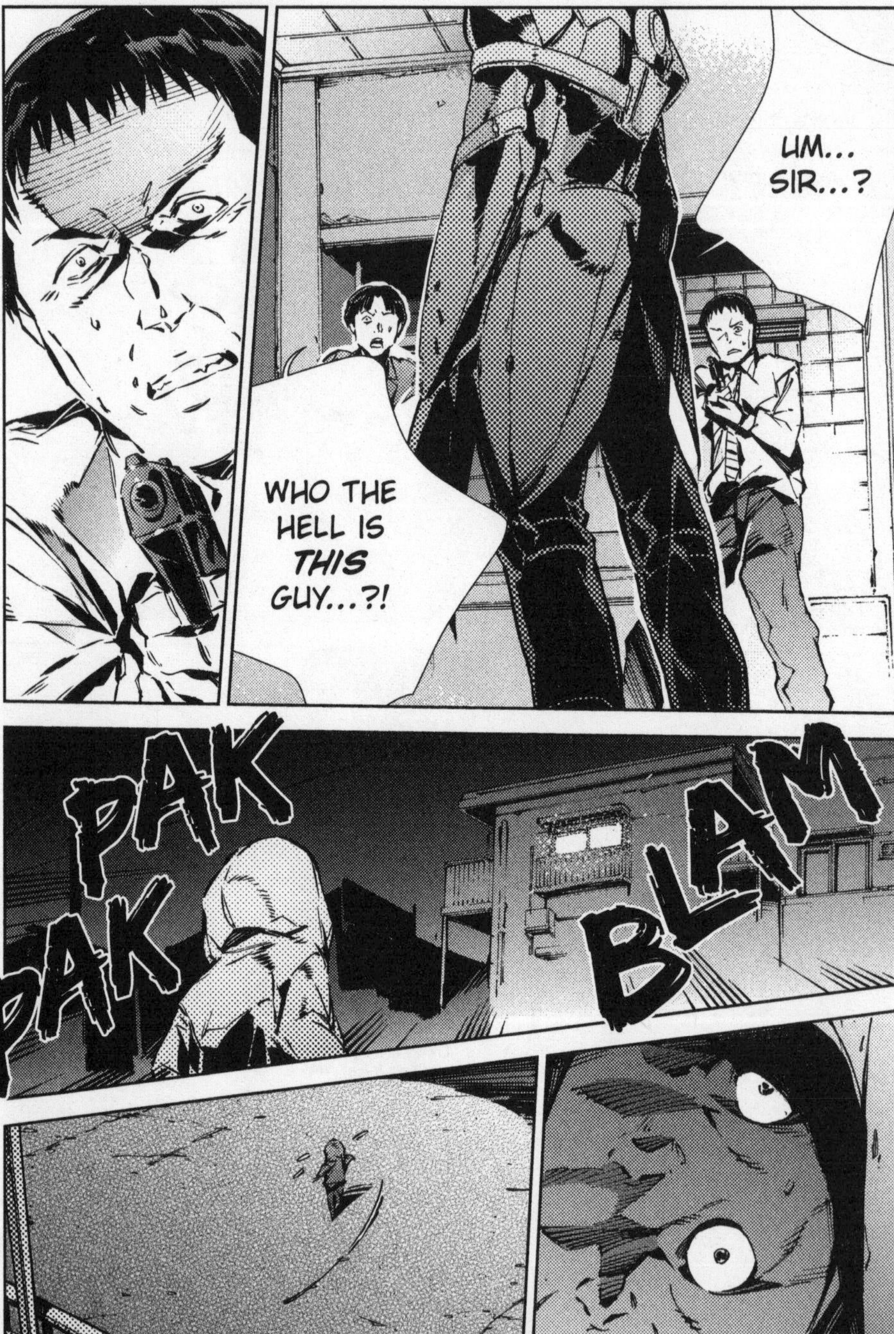
UM... SIR...?
WHO THE HELL IS THIS GUY...?!
BLAM
PAK PAK

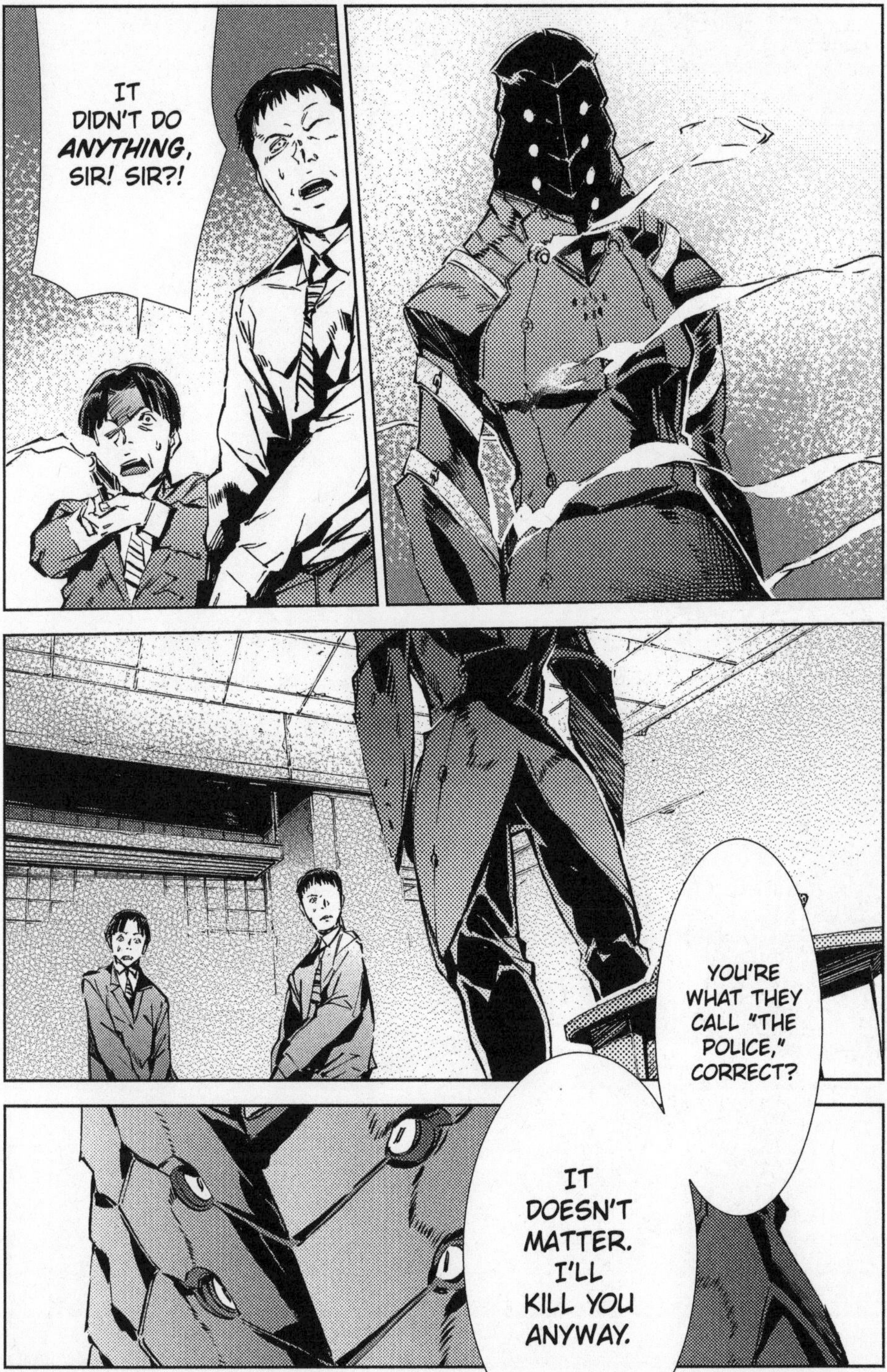
IT DIDN'T DO ***ANYTHING***, SIR! SIR?!
YOU'RE WHAT THEY CALL "THE POLICE," CORRECT?
IT DOESN'T MATTER. I'LL KILL YOU ANYWAY.

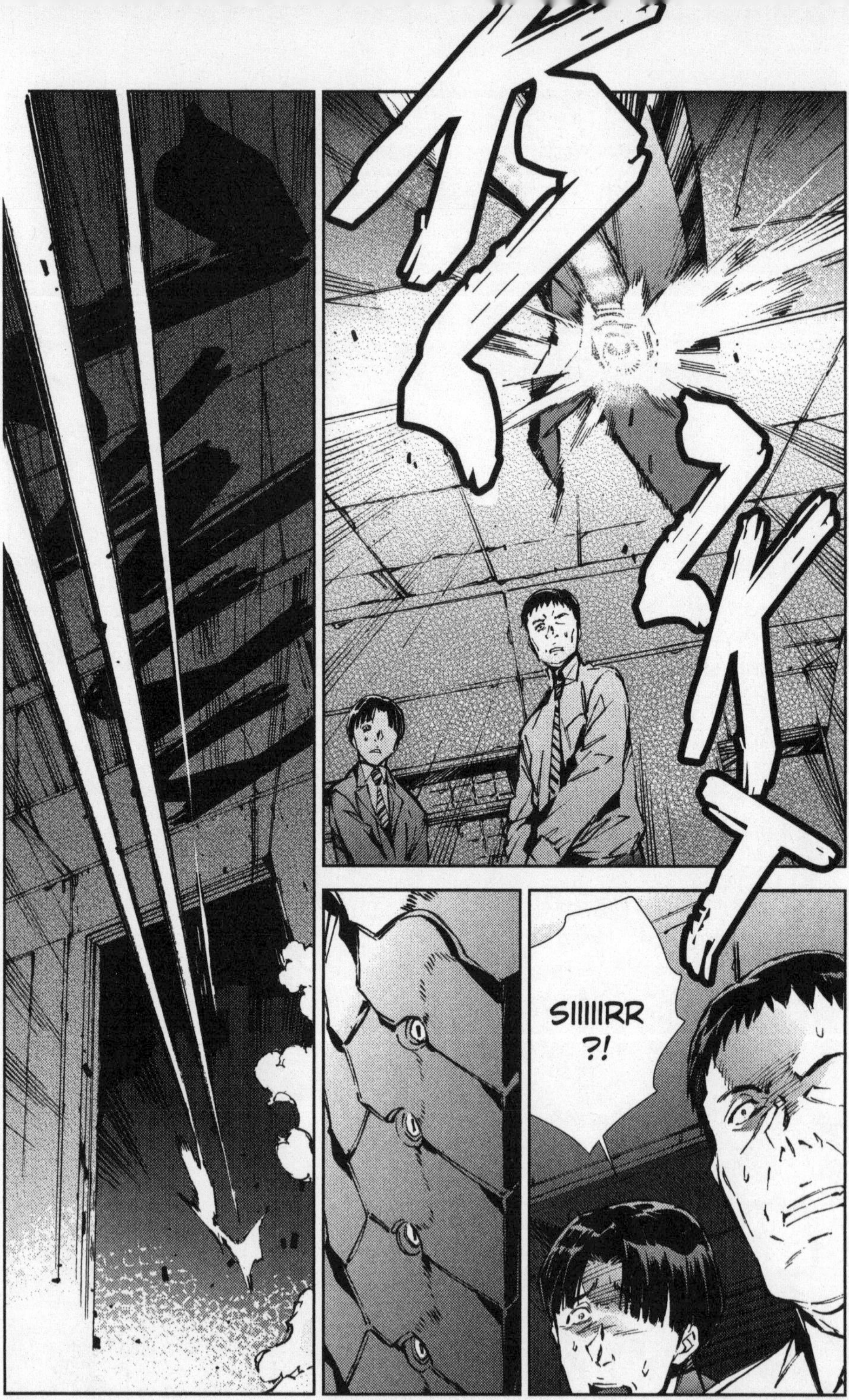
SIIIIIRR
?!

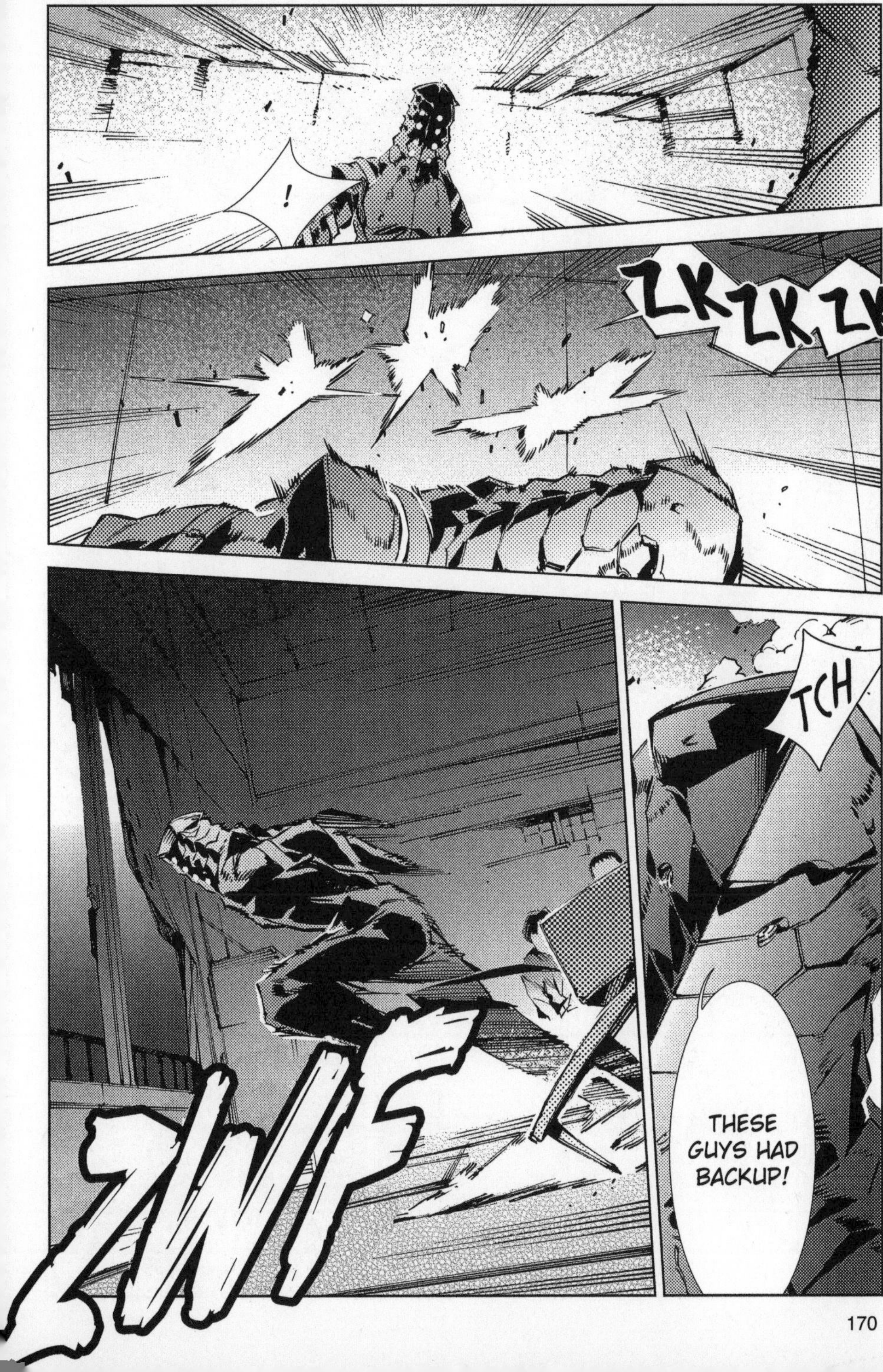
!
ZK ZK ZK
TCH
THESE GUYS HAD BACKUP!
ZNF

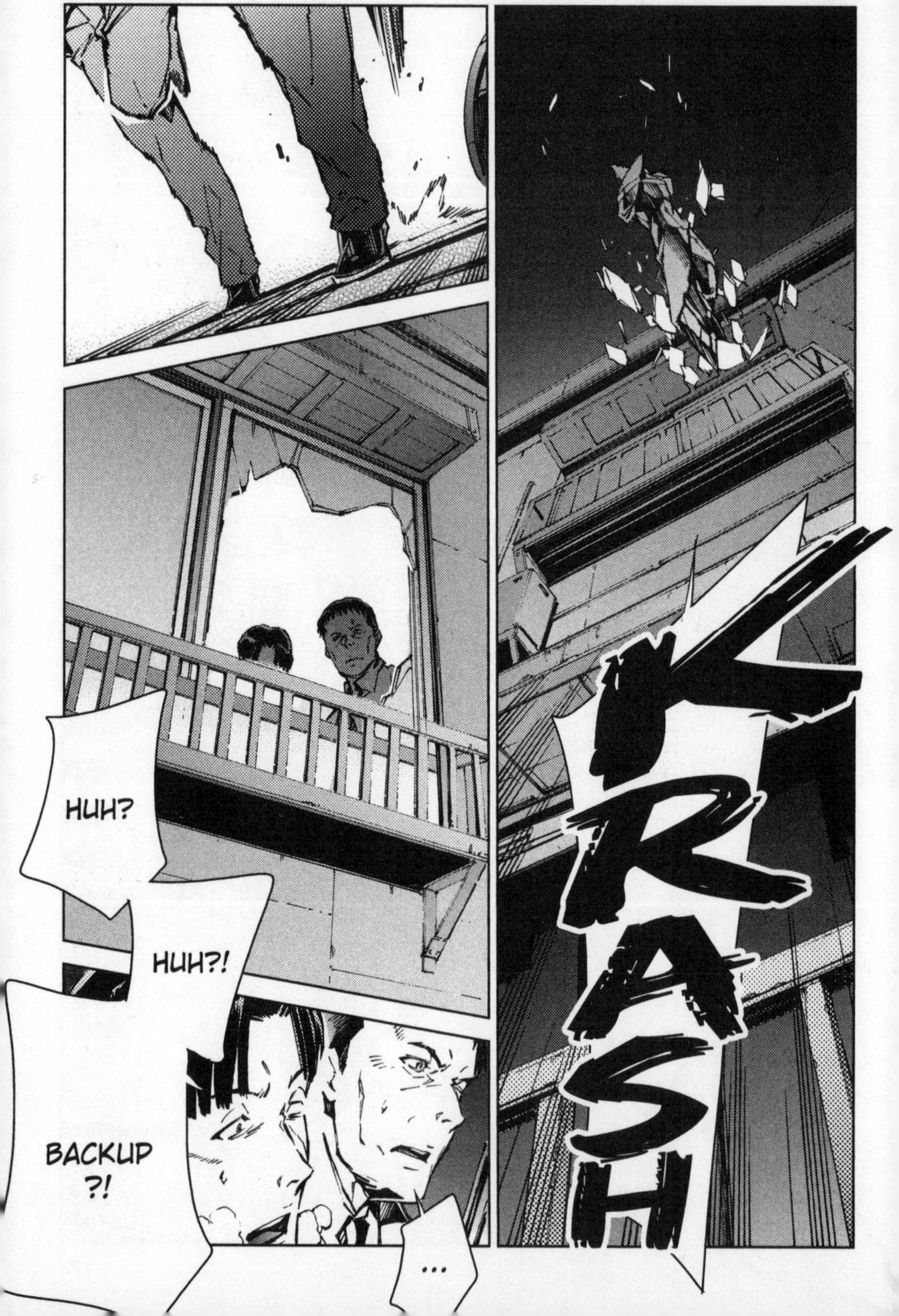
KRASH
HUH?
HUH?!
BACKUP ?!
...

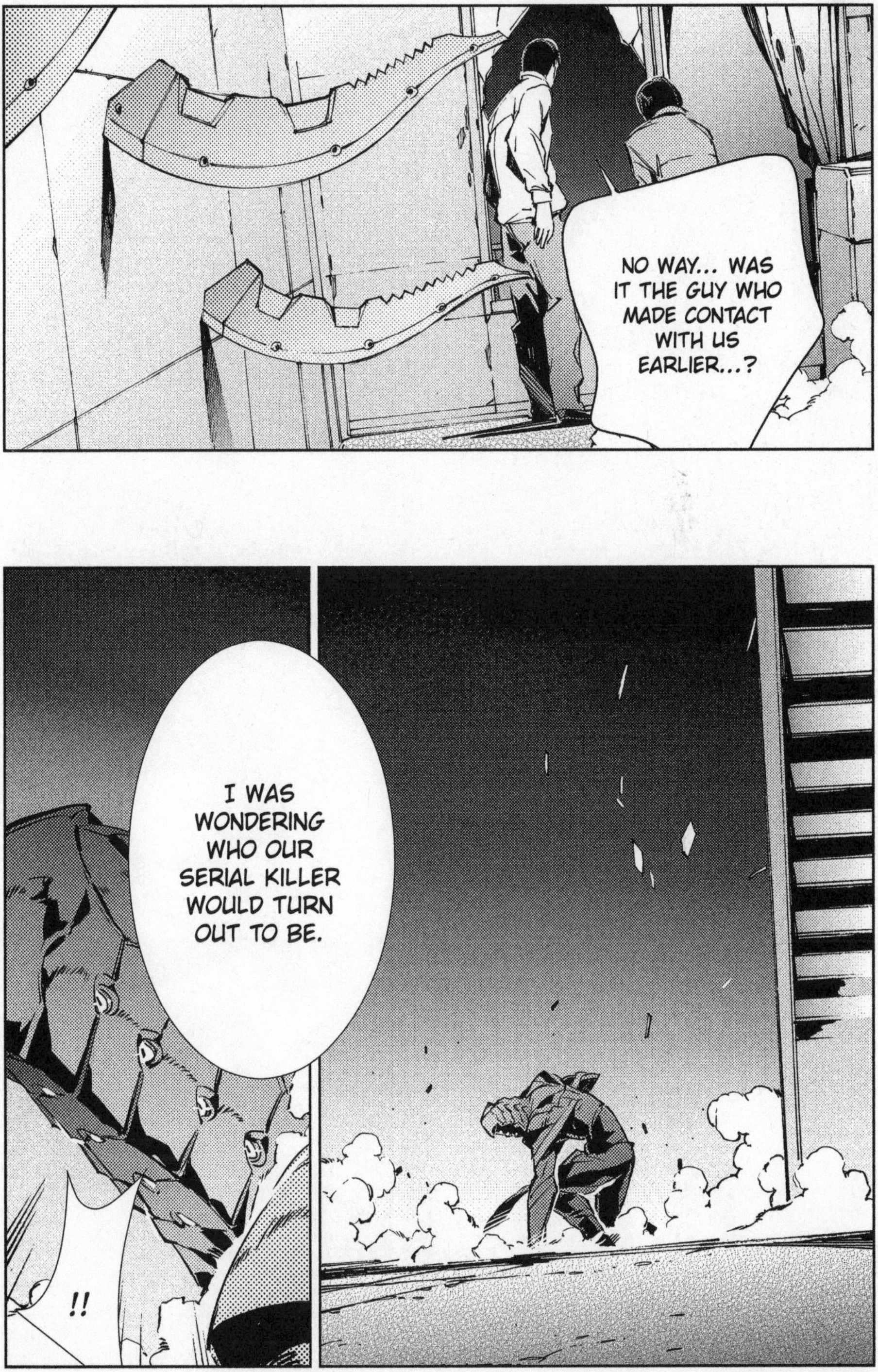
NO WAY... WAS IT THE GUY WHO MADE CONTACT WITH US EARLIER...?
I WAS WONDERING WHO OUR SERIAL KILLER WOULD TURN OUT TO BE.
!!

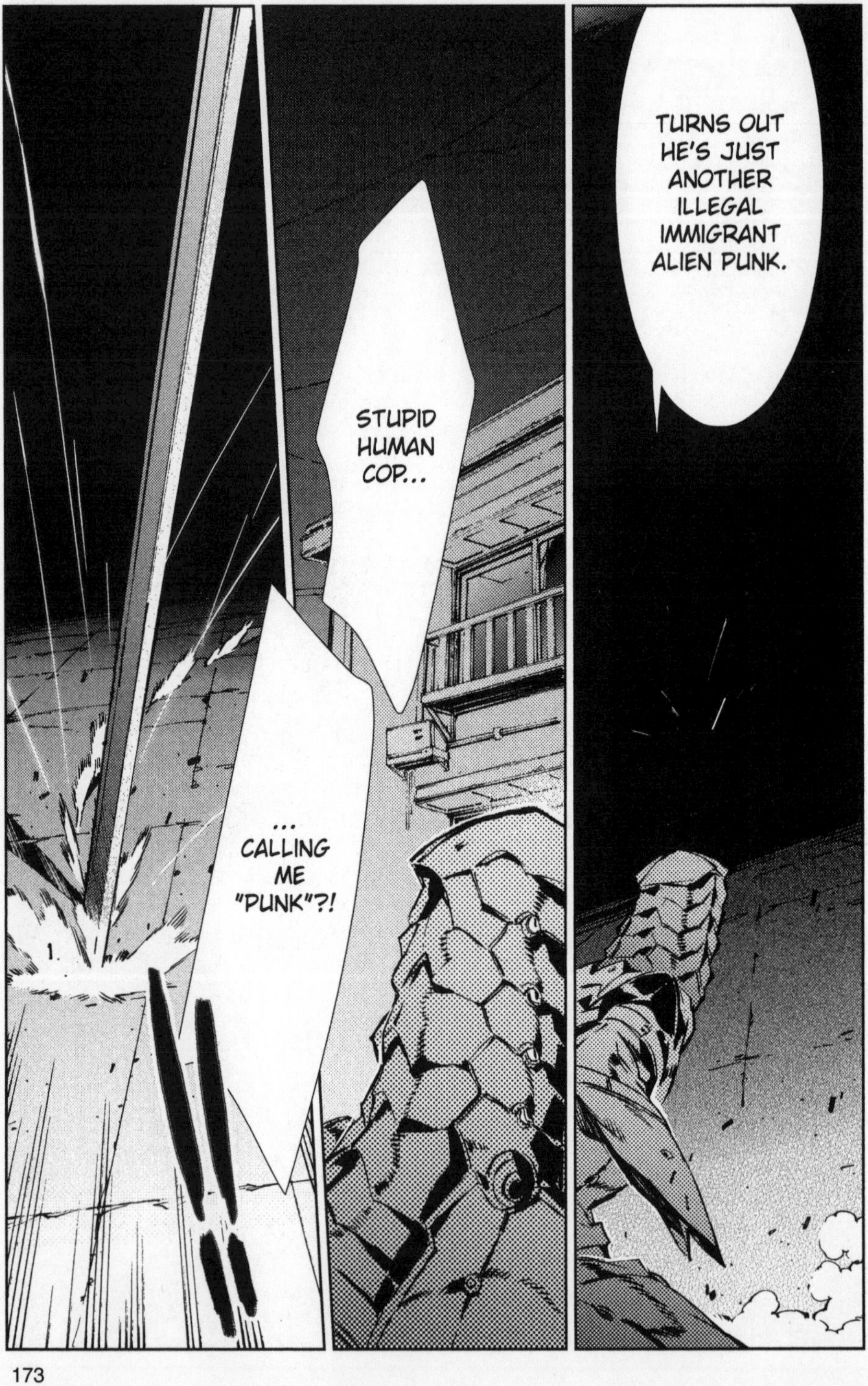
TURNS OUT HE'S JUST ANOTHER ILLEGAL IMMIGRANT ALIEN PUNK.
STUPID HUMAN COP...
... CALLING ME "PUNK"?!

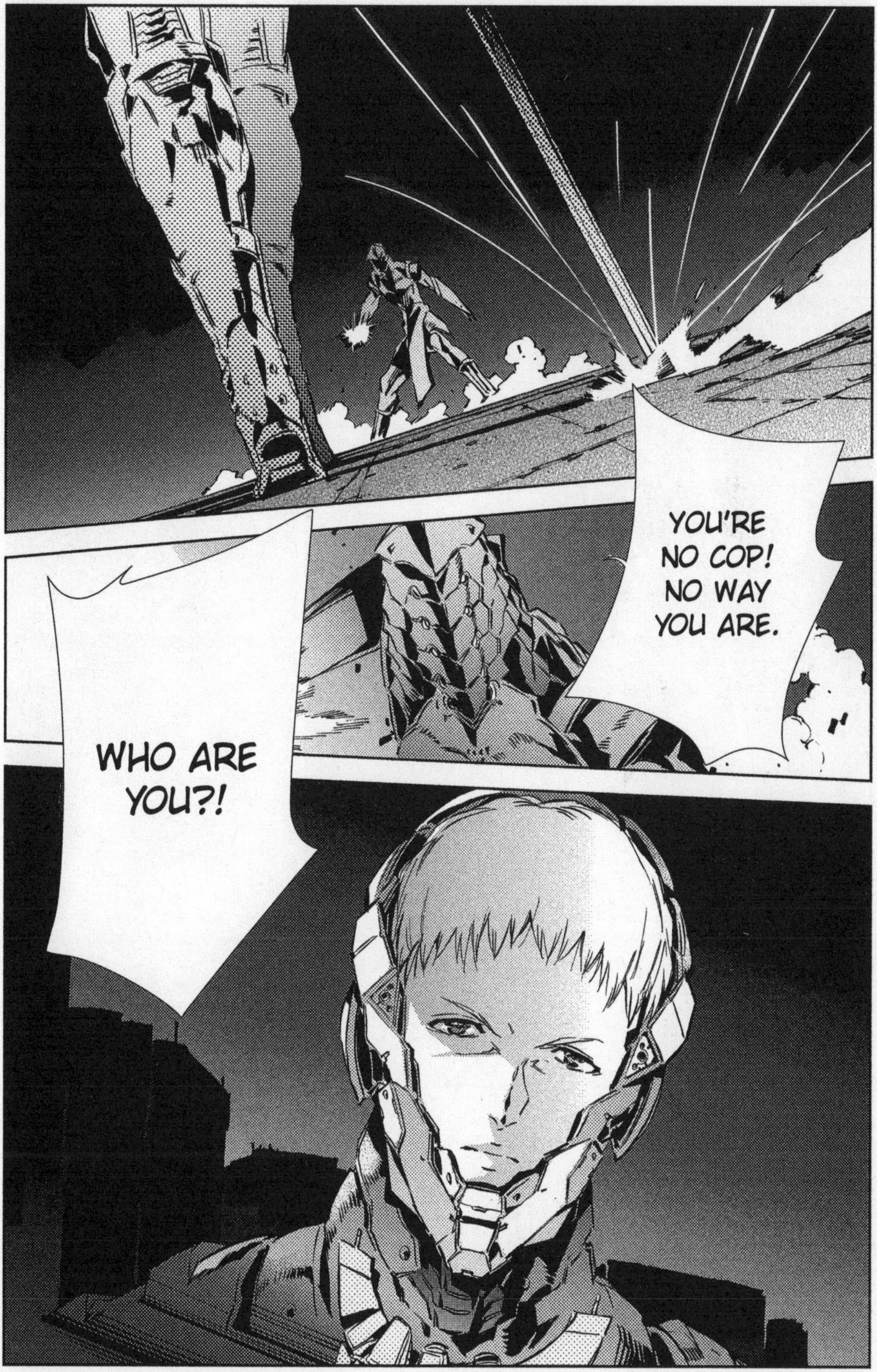
YOU'RE NO COP! NO WAY YOU ARE.
WHO ARE YOU?!

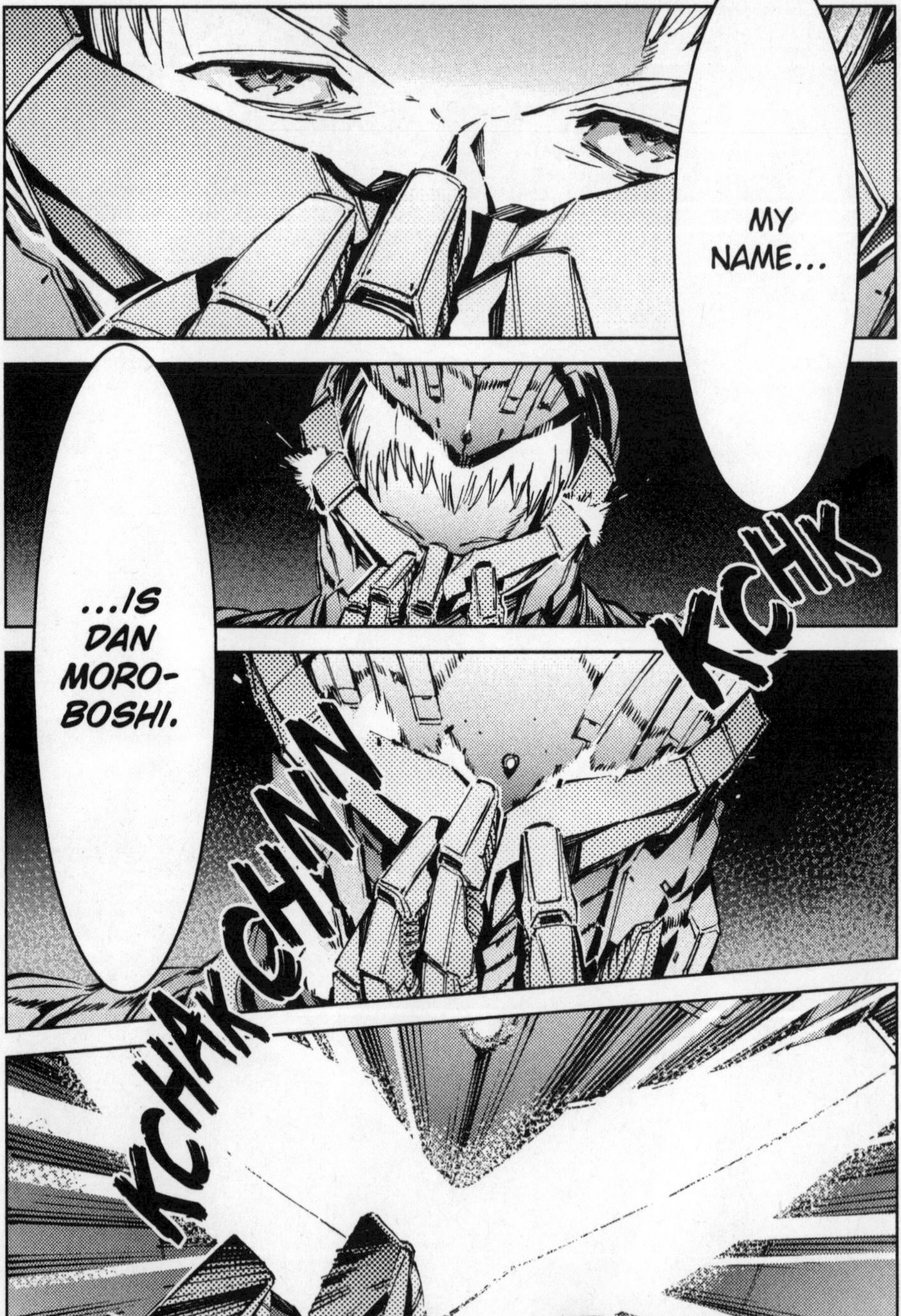
MY NAME...
...IS DAN MORO-BOSHI.
KCHK
KCHAKCHNN

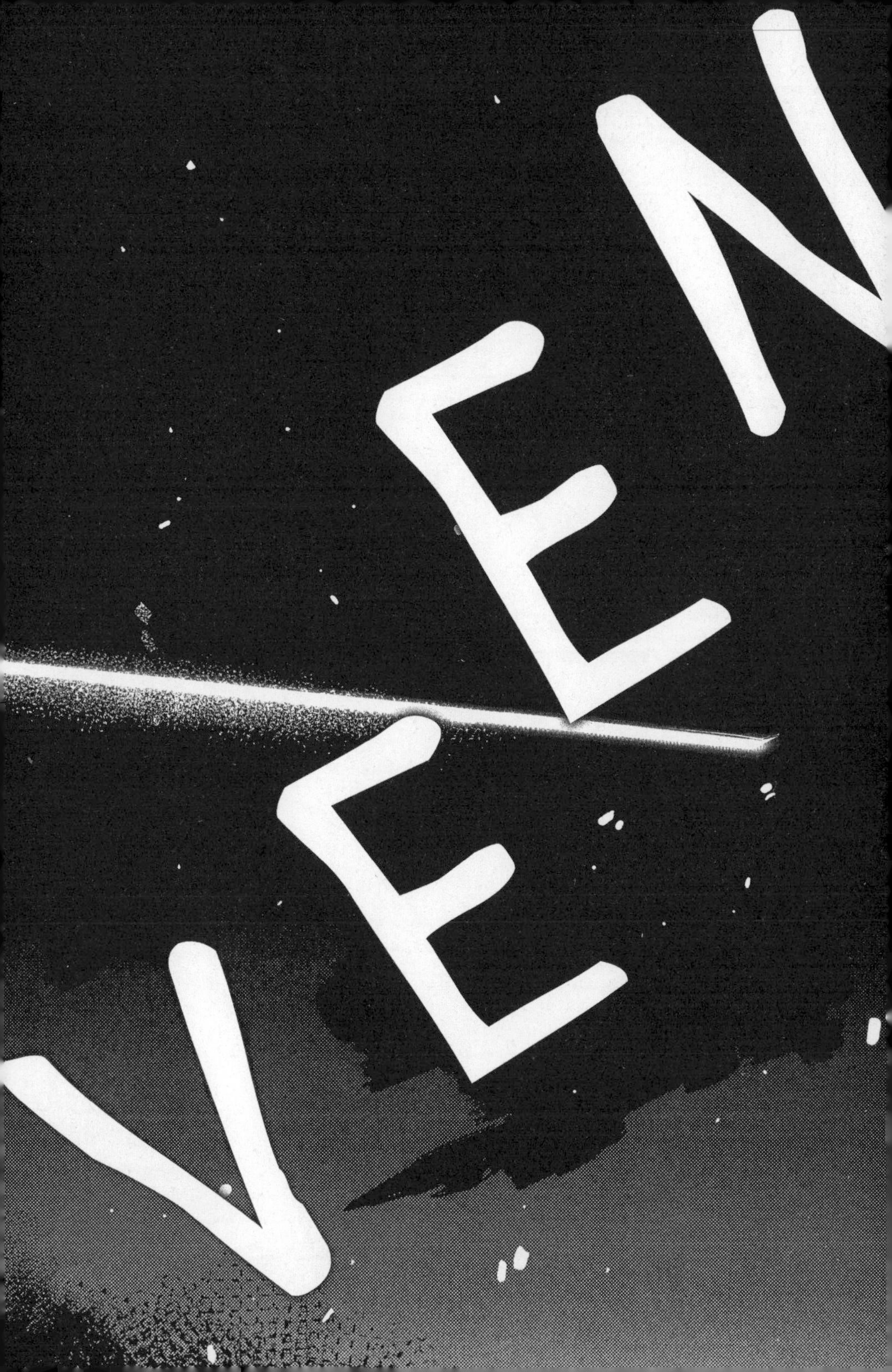

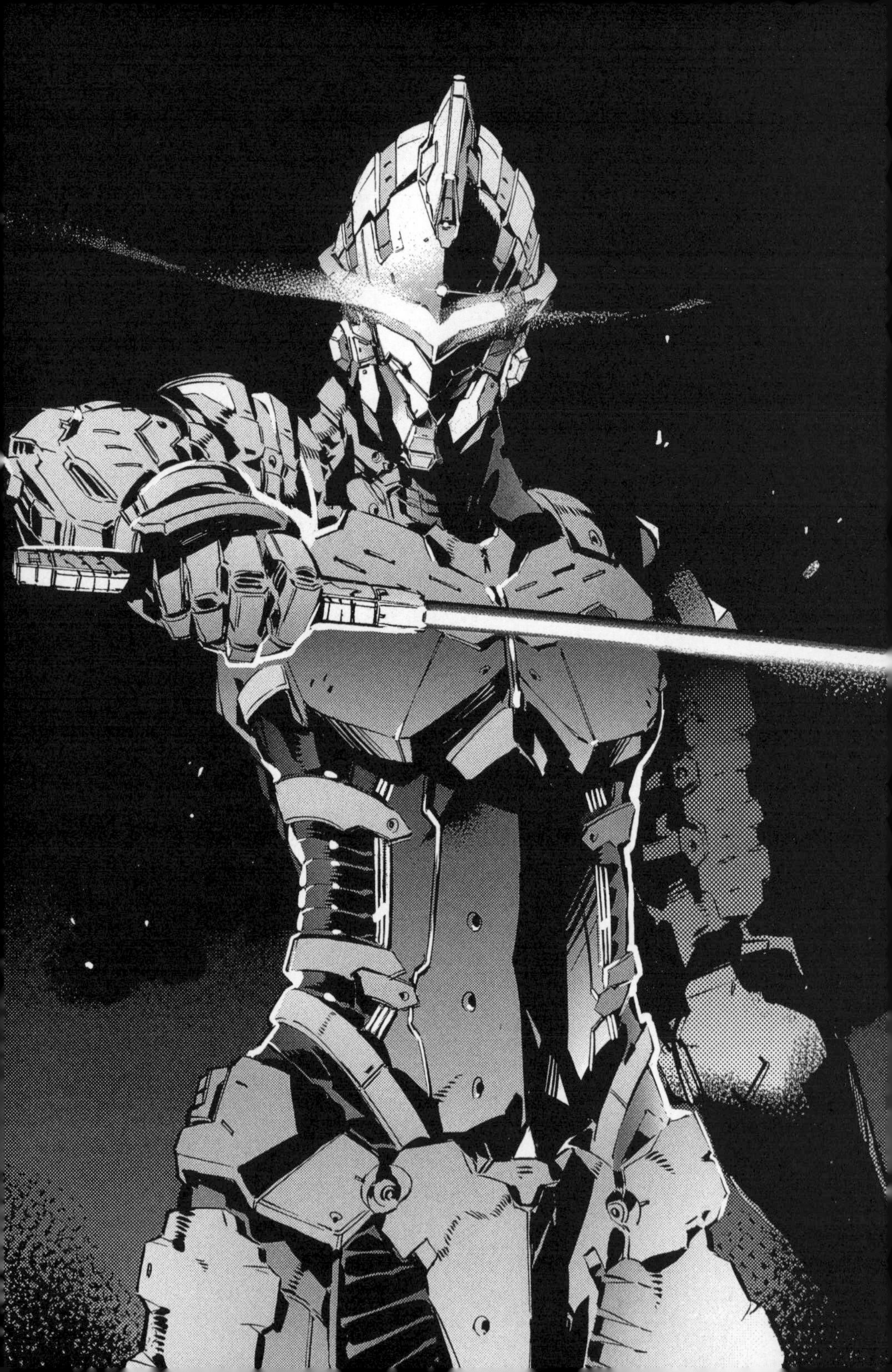

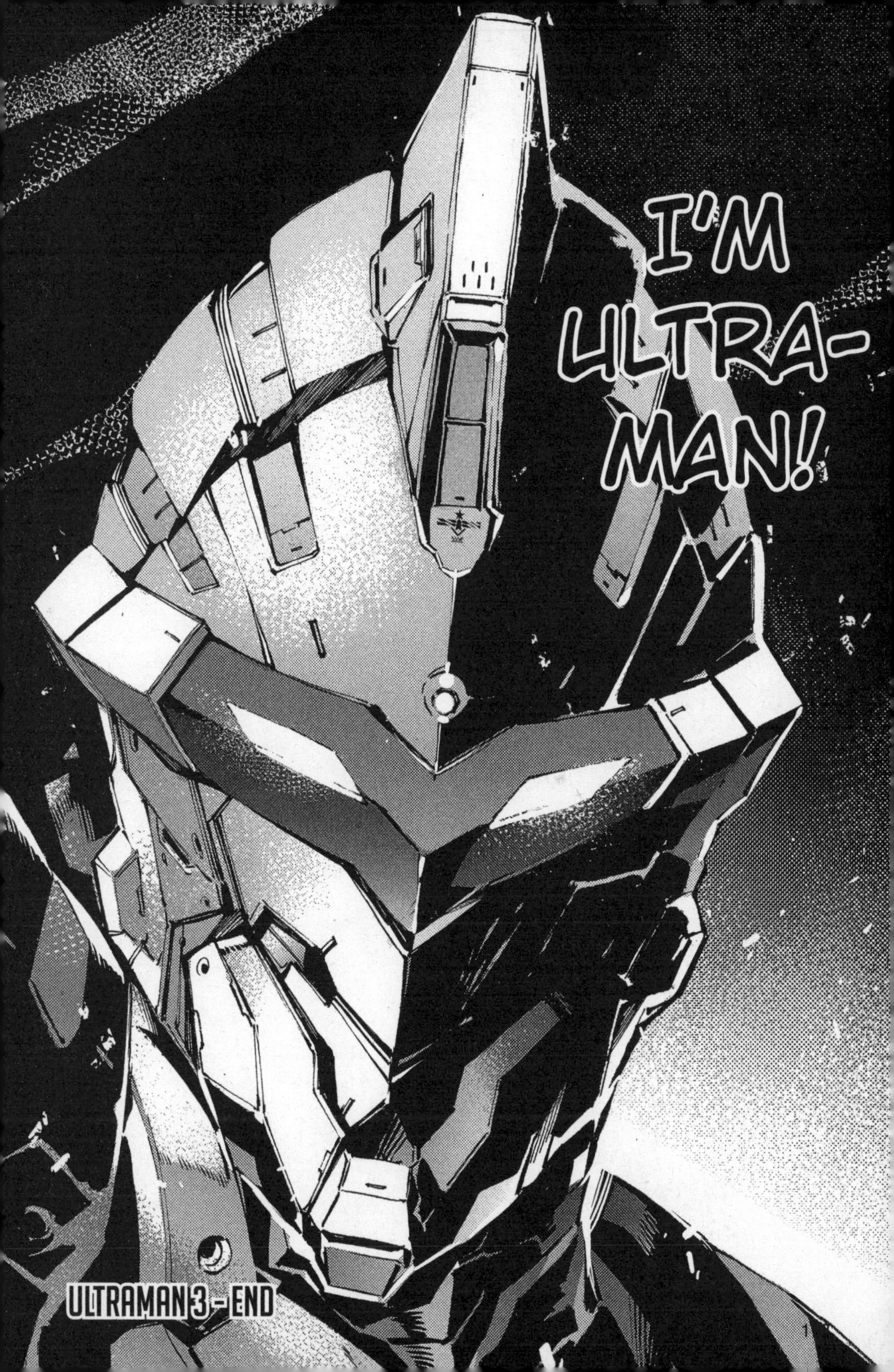
I'M ULTRA-MAN!
ULTRAMAN 3 - END

THIS IS THE BEGINNING OF A NEW AGE.

FRONT

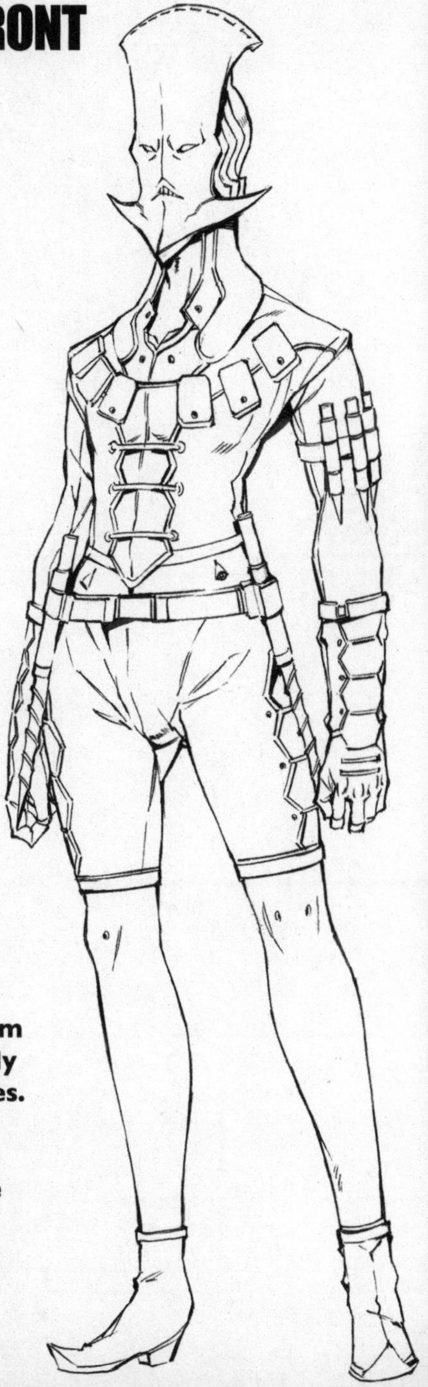

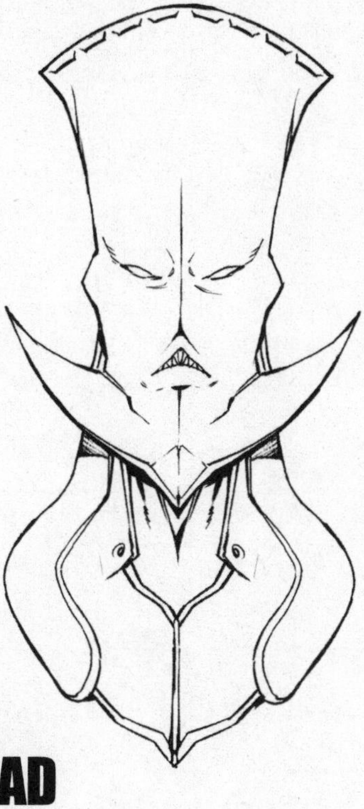

HEAD

The Kadder alien race is permitted to emigrate to Earth by the Star Cluster Council. However, they are a race of hunters by nature, and a number of them have turned to crime. They are currently categorized as a highly dangerous species.

Kadder ordinarily use spears as their weapon of choice for hunting, but those taken into custody by the SSSP were instead carrying steel stakes with spiral tips.

ALIEN BRIS

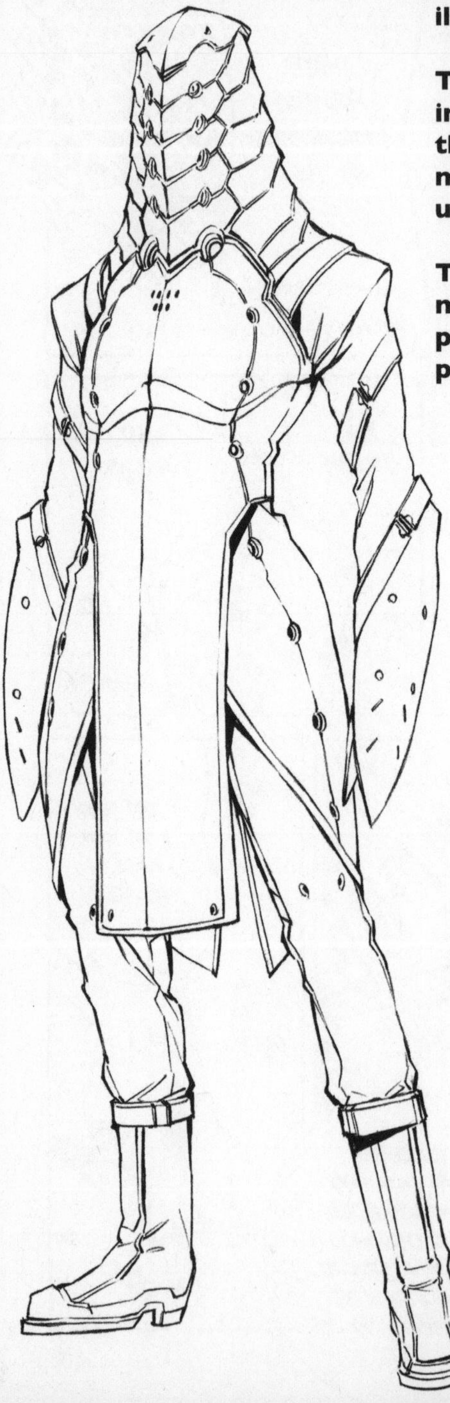

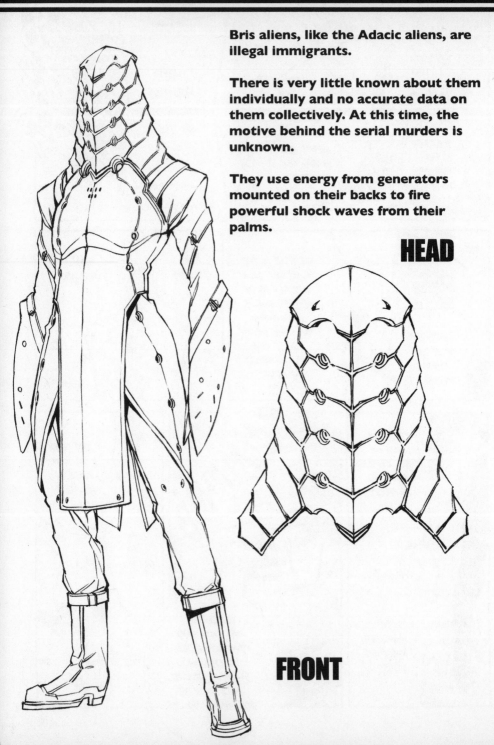

Bris aliens, like the Adacic aliens, are illegal immigrants.

There is very little known about them individually and no accurate data on them collectively. At this time, the motive behind the serial murders is unknown.

They use energy from generators mounted on their backs to fire powerful shock waves from their palms.

HEAD

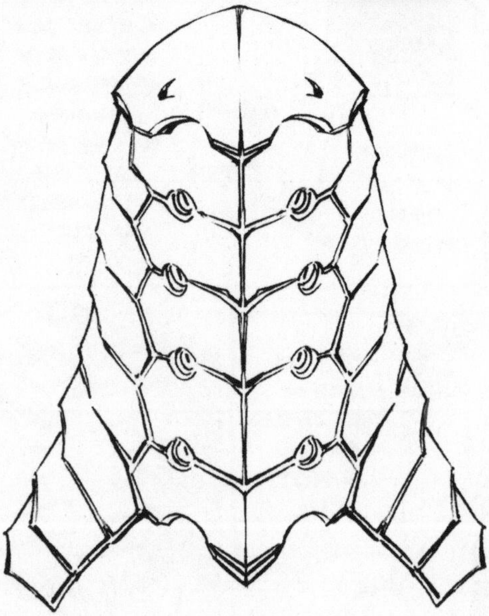

FRONT

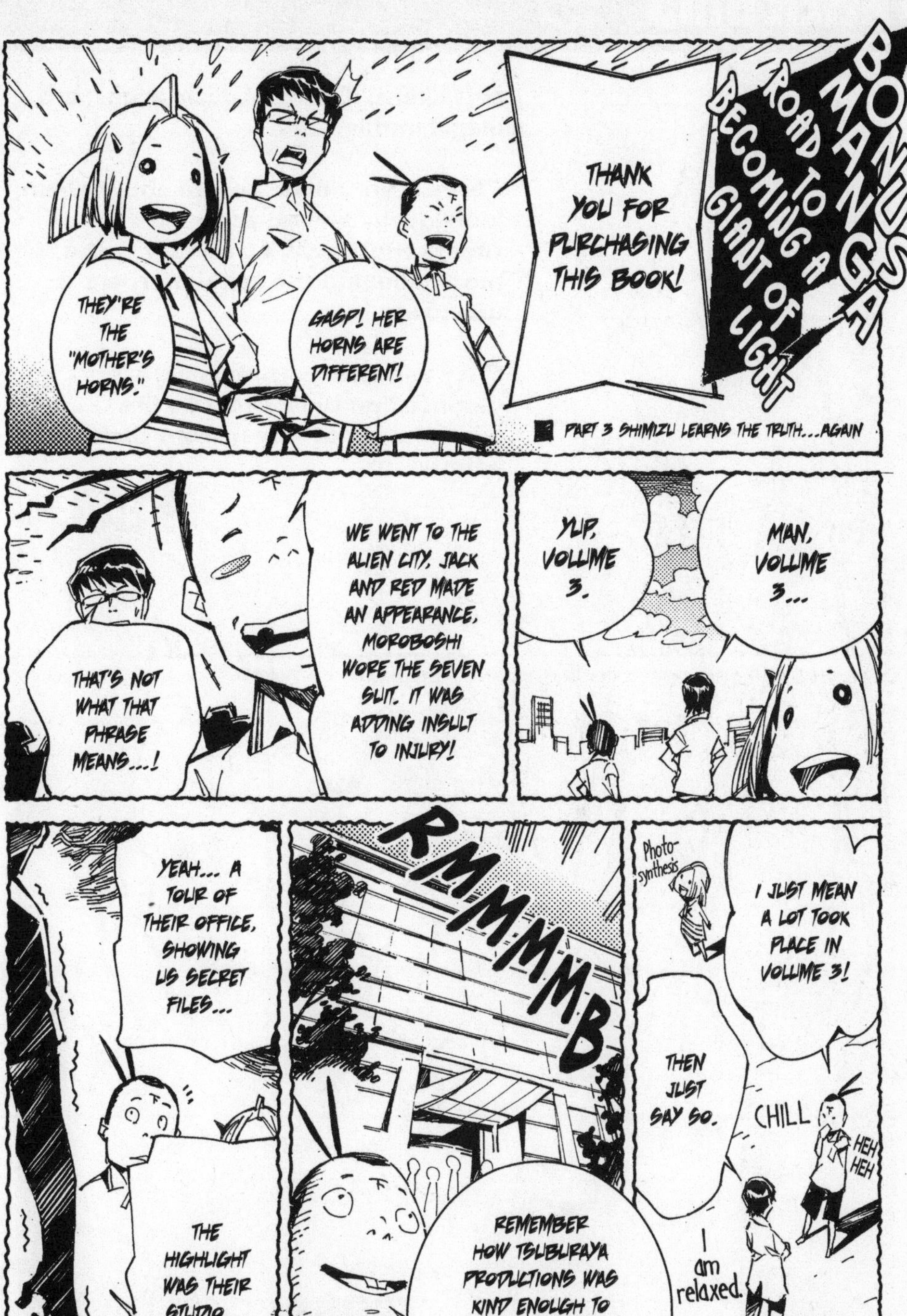
BONUS MANGA
ROAD TO BECOMING A GIANT OF LIGHT
THANK YOU FOR PURCHASING THIS BOOK!
GASP! HER HORNS ARE DIFFERENT!
THEY'RE THE "MOTHER'S HORNS."
PART 3 SHIMIZU LEARNS THE TRUTH...AGAIN
MAN, VOLUME 3...
YUP, VOLUME 3.
WE WENT TO THE ALIEN CITY, JACK AND RED MADE AN APPEARANCE, MOROBOSHI WORE THE SEVEN SUIT. IT WAS ADDING INSULT TO INJURY!
THAT'S NOT WHAT THAT PHRASE MEANS...!
I JUST MEAN A LOT TOOK PLACE IN VOLUME 3!
Photo-synthesis
THEN JUST SAY SO.
CHILL
HEH HEH
I am relaxed.
RMMMMB
REMEMBER HOW TSUBURAYA PRODUCTIONS WAS KIND ENOUGH TO SHOW US AROUND WHILE WE WERE WORKING ON VOLUME 3?
YEAH... A TOUR OF THEIR OFFICE, SHOWING US SECRET FILES...
THE HIGHLIGHT WAS THEIR STUDIO...

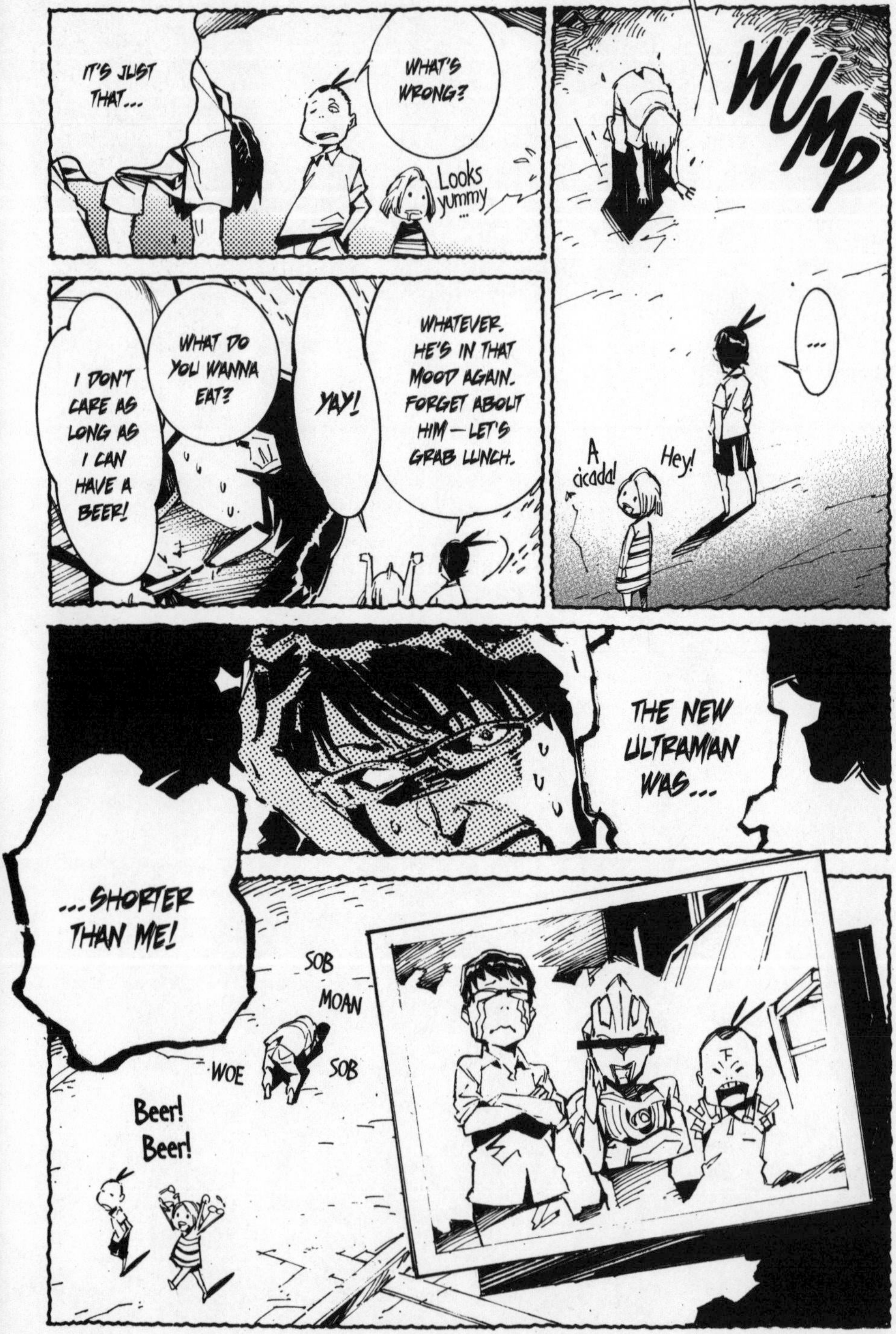
WUMP
...
Hey!
A cicada!
WHAT'S WRONG?
Looks yummy...
IT'S JUST THAT...
WHATEVER. HE'S IN THAT MOOD AGAIN. FORGET ABOUT HIM—LET'S GRAB LUNCH.
YAY!
WHAT DO YOU WANNA EAT?
I DON'T CARE AS LONG AS I CAN HAVE A BEER!
THE NEW ULTRAMAN WAS...
...SHORTER THAN ME!
SOB
MOAN
SOB
WOE
Beer! Beer!

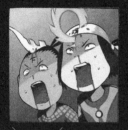

EIICHI SHIMIZU × TOMOHIRO SHIMOGUCHI

Finally! We made it to volume 3!

We'd like to thank everyone from Tsuburaya Productions for being so trustful and accepting of our stories. I must say that from the beginning they've given us a lot of leeway, but especially with the chapters included in this volume.

And to all of you who picked up this volume,
we'd like to express our utmost gratitude.

ULTRAMAN

VOLUME 3
VIZ SIGNATURE EDITION

STORY/ART BY **EIICHI SHIMIZU** AND **TOMOHIRO SHIMOGUCHI**

©2013 Eiichi Shimizu and Tomohiro Shimoguchi / TSUBURAYA PROD.
Originally published by HERO'S INC.

TRANSLATION **JOE YAMAZAKI**
ENGLISH ADAPTATION **STAN!**
TOUCH-UP ART & LETTERING **EVAN WALDINGER**
DESIGN **FAWN LAU, BRIANNA DEPUE**
EDITOR **MIKE MONTESA**

Printed in the U.S.A.

Published by VIZ Media, LLC
P.O. Box 77010
San Francisco, CA 94107

10 9 8 7 6 5 4 3 2 1
First printing, February 2016

VIZ SIGNATURE

www.viz.com

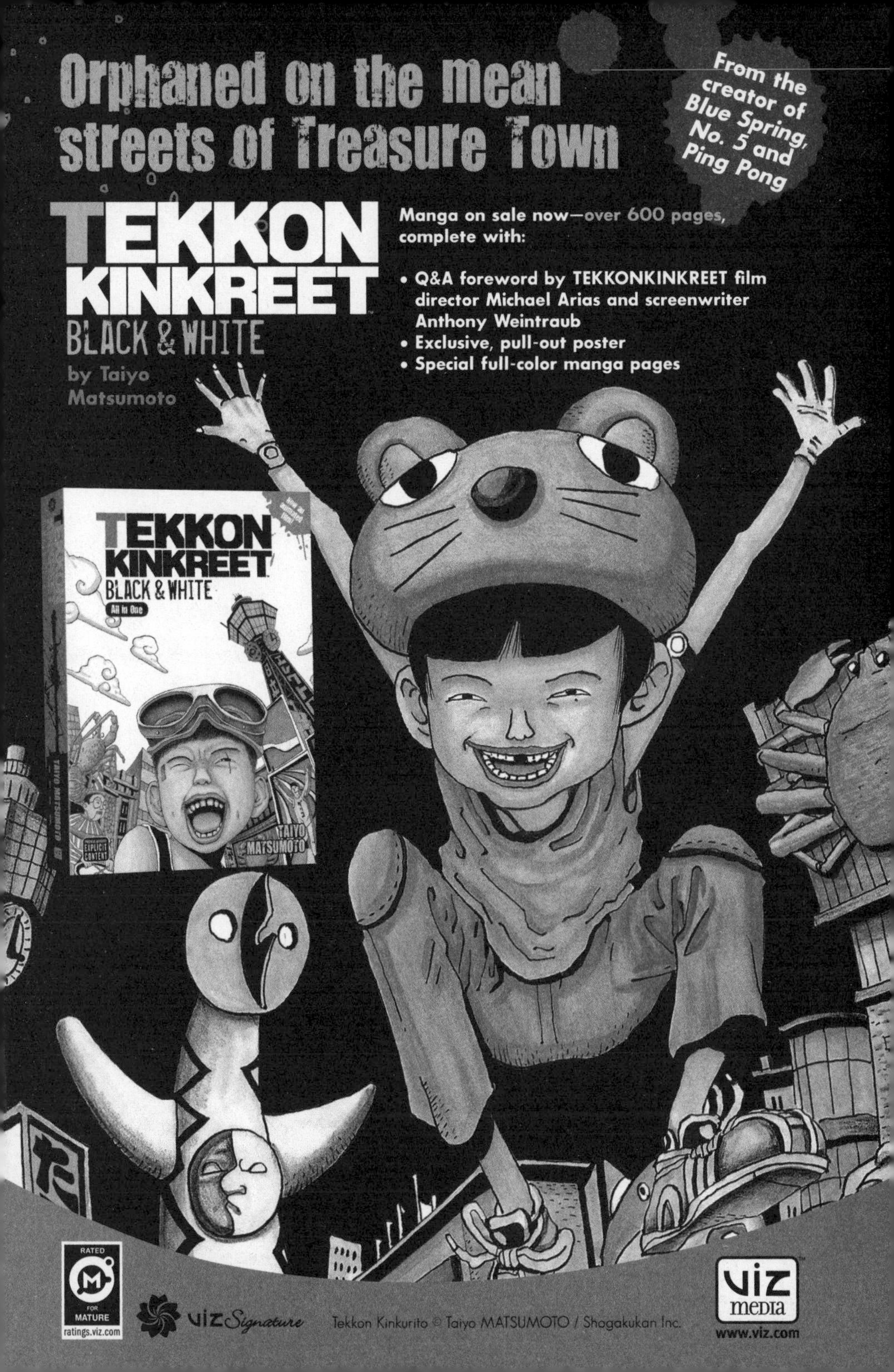
Orphaned on the mean streets of Treasure Town
From the creator of Blue Spring, No. 5 and Ping Pong
TEKKON KINKREET BLACK & WHITE
by Taiyo Matsumoto
Manga on sale now—over 600 pages, complete with:
• Q&A foreword by TEKKONKINKREET film director Michael Arias and screenwriter Anthony Weintraub
• Exclusive, pull-out poster
• Special full-color manga pages
TEKKON KINKREET BLACK & WHITE
All in One
TAIYO MATSUMOTO
EXPLICIT CONTENT
RATED M FOR MATURE
ratings.viz.com
VIZ Signature
Tekkon Kinkurito © Taiyo MATSUMOTO / Shogakukan Inc.
VIZ media
www.viz.com

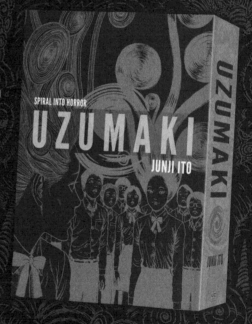

HEY! YOU'RE READING IN THE WRONG DIRECTION!

This is the END of the graphic novel

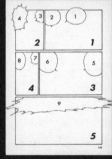

Follow the action this way.

To properly enjoy this VIZ graphic novel, please turn it around and begin reading from RIGHT TO LEFT. Unlike English, Japanese is read right to left, so Japanese comics are read in reverse order from the way English comics are typically read.

This book has been printed in the original Japanese format in order to preserve the orientation of the original artwork.

HAVE FUN WITH IT!